JUSTIN MAROZZI was born in 1970 and read History at Gonville & Caius College, Cambridge. A former *Financial Times* foreign correspondent, he writes regularly for the *FT*, *Sunday Telegraph*, *The Times* and *Spectator*, where he was a contributing editor until disappearing to Central Asia to research this book. He has also written for the *Economist* and broadcast for the BBC World Service and Radio Four. His first book, *South from Barbary*, was an account of a 1,200-mile journey by camel along the old slave routes of the Libyan Sahara. He is married and lives in Norfolk and London.

From the reviews of *Tamerlane*:

'[An] impressive biography of the warrior king . . . thrilling if grisly reading'

MICHAEL PRODGER, *Sunday Telegraph* Books of the Year

'A gripping tale . . . This is not just a biography; it is also a travel book. Mr Marozzi has traced in person much of Temur's relentless campaign trail, and he elegiacally shows us how far Samarkand and Bukhara, once the most glorious cities in Asia, have descended'

Economist

'Excellent . . . Marozzi provides a superbly rounded and vivid portrait of one of history's most fascinating personalities'

ANDREW ROBERTS, *Evening Standard*

'As well researched in libraries as with boots on the ground in some of the world's more impenetrable places, this is a fine study of a neglected but linchpin historical figure'   *Daily Mail*

'Justin Marozzi has a good story to tell and he tells it very well'

Times Literary Supplement

'Marozzi creates a convincing portrait of a complex man living in an unsettled world ... he has brought the mighty warrior in from the cold and allowed him to stalk these pages with bloody magnificence'   *Sunday Times*

'Justin Marozzi's assured biography ... is a real education ... he brilliantly conveys how everything goes in cycles, both in nature and in human affairs'   NICHOLAS SHAKESPEARE, *Daily Telegraph*

'Outstanding ... Justin Marozzi is the most brilliant of the new generation of travelwriter-historians'
           JOHN ADAMSON, *Sunday Telegraph* Books of the Year

'Robust, enthusiastic and richly detailed ... full of fascinating, if often gruesome, anecdotes. Marozzi's travels bring Tamerlane and his violent reign to life'   *Literary Review*

'An engaging mixture of history, travelogue and contemporary reportage ... well written and skilfully put together ... Mr Marozzi is a romantic with an observant eye, and he has chosen his subject well'   JONATHAN SUMPTION, *Sunday Telegraph*

'Temur's story is indeed sensational ... this book is captivating, a delightful and fortunate conjunction between the world of Temur then and that world transformed today, between history and journalism'   ALLAN MASSIE, *Spectator*

'A fascinating read that's as much travelogue as history' *Wallpaper*

'Illuminating'   *Financial Times*

By the same author

South From Barbary

TAMERLANE

Sword of Islam,
Conqueror of the World

JUSTIN MAROZZI

HARPER PERENNIAL
London, New York, Toronto and Sydney

Harper Perennial
An imprint of HarperCollins*Publishers*
77–85 Fulham Palace Road
Hammersmith, London W6 8JB

www.harperperennial.co.uk

This edition published by Harper Perennial 2005

5

First published by HarperCollins*Publishers* 2004

Copyright © Justin Marozzi 2004

A catalogue record for this book
is available from the British Library

ISBN 0 00 711612 8

Set in Linotype Minion by
Rowland Phototypesetting Ltd,
Bury St Edmunds, Suffolk

Printed and bound in Great Britain by
Clays Limited, St Ives plc

*This book is dedicated to my mother
and to the memory of my father*

Contents

Illustrations

All photographs © Justin Marozzi unless otherwise indicated.

Temur's birthplace in Khoja Ilgar, near Shakhrisabz, south of Samarkand.

Temur stares down Victory Park, Shakhrisabz.

Shakhrisabz market. 'The water melons there are as large as a horse's head,' wrote Ruy Gonzalez de Clavijo, 'the very best and biggest that may be found in the whole world.'

Balkh, northern Afghanistan, where Temur was enthroned in 1370.

The National chose *Tamburlaine the Great* to open the Olivier Theatre in 1976. *(National Theatre Archives)*

Antony Sher as a bloody Tamburlaine in the RSC's 1993 production. *(Henrietta Butler/ArenaPAL)*

The Registan, Samarkand. *(Bruno Morandi/AGE/Powerstock)*

The Ulugh Beg Madrassah, Samarkand, a tribute to Temur's grandson.

Inside the magnificent Tillya Kari Madrassah, Samarkand. *(Zefa/J.F. Raga)*

Azure blue domes in Shah-i-Zinda, Samarkand's city of the dead.

A sun-baked dome in Shah-i-Zinda, Samarkand.

Detail from a blue ribbed dome, Samarkand.

Detail from a minaret, Samarkand.

Newlyweds pay their respects to Temur in Samarkand.

Temur's forces attacking a fort. An illustration from the *Zafarnama*. *(Bridgeman Art Library/British Library, London OR1359 f.298v)*

Bukhara, Temur's second city, the 'Dome of Islam'. *(Keren Su/Corbis)*

Kalon Mosque, Bukhara.

Herat citadel. Temur stormed the city in 1379, his first conquest in the west.

The sacking of Isfahan in 1387, scene of one of Temur's worst atrocities. From the sixteenth-century *Timurnama* of Abdullah Hatifi. *(Persian literary text by Persian School (16th century), Bridgeman Art Library/British Library Add22703 f.52v)*

The Shrine of Shah Rukn-e-Alam in Multan, City of the Saints, in the Pakistani Punjab. Temur destroyed the city in 1398.

Babur's tomb, Kabul.

The captured Ottoman Sultan Bayazid I is brought before Temur after his defeat at the Battle of Ankara in 1402. From a sixteenth-century edition of the *Zafarnama*. *(Bridgeman Art Library/British Library OR1359 f.413a)*

Babur, Temur's great-great-great-grandson, founder of the Mughal dynasty of India. *(Watercolour on paper by Bishn Das (fl.1613–19). Bridgeman Art Library/British Library)*

Temur's grandson Ulugh Beg.

State propaganda Uzbekistan-style.

Temur, role model for Uzbeks.

Temur's burial place, the Gur Amir Mausoleum in Samarkand.

Statue of Temur in Amir Temur Square, Tashkent.

Temur through the ages: portraits from seventeenth-century Germany *(Bridgeman Art Library)*, eighteenth-century France *(Hand-coloured engraving by Pierre Duflos/Bridgeman Art Library)* and nineteenth-century India *(Lithograph, 1826 © Bettmann/CORBIS)*.

Soviet archaeologist Mikhail Gerasimov examines Temur's skull, exhumed on 22 June 1941. *(Reproduced with permission of* The Odyssey Guide to Uzebkistan*)*

Temur's tomb inside the Gur Amir.

Maps

Temur's Family Tree

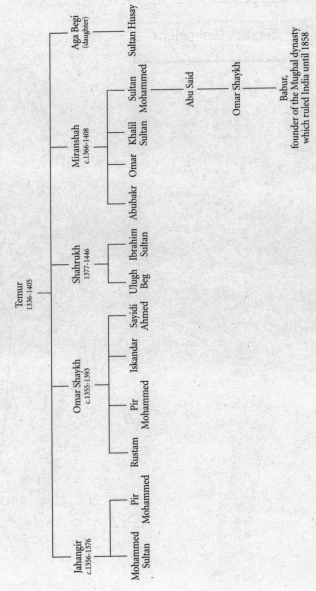

Temur
1336–1405

Jahangir
c.1356–1376

Omar Shaykh
c.1355–1393

Shahrukh
1377–1446

Miranshah
c.1366–1408

Aga Begi
(daughter)

Mohammed Sultan

Pir Mohammed

Rustam

Pir Mohammed

Iskandar

Sayidi Ahmed

Ulugh Beg

Ibrahim Sultan

Abubakr

Omar

Khalil Sultan

Sultan Mohammed

Sultan Husay

Abu Said

Omar Shaykh

Babur,
founder of the Mughal dynasty
which ruled India until 1858

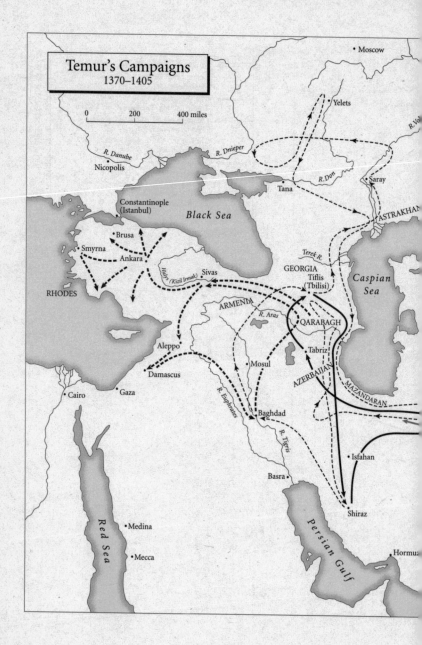

Temur's Campaigns
1370–1405

0   200   400 miles

Moscow

Yelets

R. Danube

Nicopolis

R. Dnieper

R. Don

Tana

Saray

ASTRAKHAN

R. Volga

Constantinople
(Istanbul)

Black Sea

Brusa

Smyrna

Ankara

RHODES

Halys (Kizil Irmak)

Sivas

Terek R.

GEORGIA

Tiflis
(Tbilisi)

Caspian
Sea

ARMENIA

R. Aras

QARABAGH

Tabriz

AZERBAIJAN

MAZANDARAN

Aleppo

Mosul

Damascus

Gaza

Cairo

R. Euphrates

Baghdad

R. Tigris

Basra

Isfahan

Shiraz

Red
Sea

Medina

Mecca

Persian Gulf

Hormuz

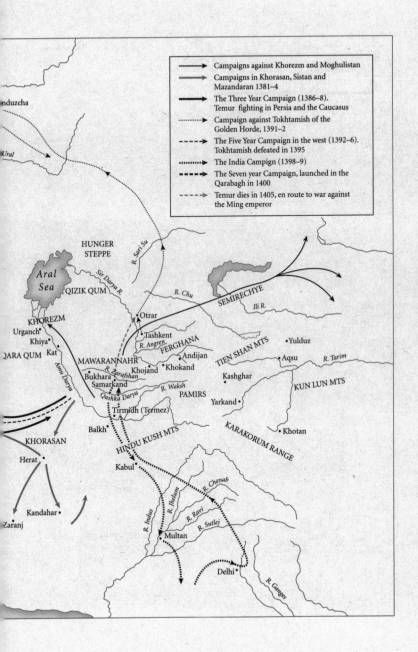

Campaigns against Khorezm and Moghulistan

Campaigns in Khorasan, Sistan and Mazandaran 1381–4

The Three Year Campaign (1386–8). Temur fighting in Persia and the Caucasus

Campaign against Tokhtamish of the Golden Horde, 1391–2

The Five Year Campaign in the west (1392–6). Tokhtamish defeated in 1395

The India Campign (1398–9)

The Seven year Campaign, launched in the Qarabagh in 1400

Temur dies in 1405, en route to war against the Ming emperor

nduzcha

Ural

HUNGER STEPPE

R. Sari Su

Aral Sea

Sir Darya R.

QIZIK QUM

R. Chu

SEMIRECHYE

Ili R.

KHOREZM

Otrar

Urganch

Khiya

QARA QUM

Kat

Tashkent

R. Angren

FERGHANA

Yulduz

MAWARANNAHR

R. Zarafshan

Khojand

Andijan

Khokand

TIEN SHAN MTS

Aqsu

R. Tarim

Bukhara

Samarkand

Qashka Darya

R. Waksh

PAMIRS

Kashghar

KUN LUN MTS

Tirmidh (Termez)

Yarkand

Amu Darya

Balkh

HINDU KUSH MTS

KARAKORUM RANGE

Khotan

KHORASAN

Kabul

Herat

R. Indus

R. Jhelum

R. Chenab

Kandahar

R. Ravi

Zaranj

Multan

R. Sutlej

Delhi

R. Ganges

Acknowledgements

I owe thanks to many people who have helped with this book in many ways.

My friend Vic Hutchinson, though she did not know it at the time, got me started by giving me Jason Elliot's *An Unexpected Light: Travels in Afghanistan*. A tantalising line about Tamerlane set me on my path.

Travels in Central Asia would have been less fruitful and interesting without the assistance of a number of people. Though they represent one of the world's more unpleasant regimes, Alisher Faizullaev, Uzbek Ambassador to the Court of St James's, and his colleague Mardon Yakubov both provided useful introductions.

In Uzbekistan, I was fortunate enough to meet Eric Walberg, who was a generous guide to all things Uzbek. He repeatedly pointed me in the right direction, smoothed my path across the country, and remained a tireless source of information. This acknowledgement is a meagre reward for his uncomplaining assistance and good-hearted friendship. I would also like to thank my translator Farkhad for his patience as we pursued the trail of Tamerlane across desert, steppe and mountain. Another translator, Sabit, was invaluable in making sense of a rare and important manuscript.

In Tashkent, I am grateful to the Temurid historians Professor

Omonullo Boriyev and Turgun Faiziev at the Institute of Oriental Studies; Dr Asom Urinboyev; Nozim Khabibullaev, Director of the Amir Temur Museum; Murad Gulamov, the Librarian at the Tellya Sheikh Mosque; the archivist Gulsara Ostonova; and Misrob Turdiev, Dean of International Relations and Diplomacy at Tashkent State University.

In Samarkand, the poet and historian Akbar Piruzi was my guide to many of the city's astounding Temurid monuments. Thanks to the historian Fazlidin Fakhridinov and Ahmed Rustamov, the imam of the Khoja Abdi Darun Mosque, who shared his thoughts on the state of Islam in Central Asia.

Noila Kasijanova was an indispensable guide to Bukhara, as was another Noila, Director of the Department for the Protection of Bukhara's Mosques and Monuments. Omar Rashidov, Dean of the History Faculty at Bukhara State University, his colleague Professor Farkhad Kasimov, and Bakhodir Ergashev, the Deputy Mayor, all shed light on Tamerlane and his second city, the Dome of Islam. Abdul Gafur Razzaq, imam of the Kalon Mosque, whose minaret was the only monument left standing by Genghis Khan when he razed the city to the ground in 1912, was a fascinating source on Bukhara's Sufi heritage.

For a searingly unforgettable visit to Muynak, victim of the Aral Sea environmental catastrophe, I would like to thank Murod, who had the sense and good fortune subsequently to emigrate to the United States. At the other end of the country, Dr Kulmamat Avliyokulov, member of the Amir Temur Fund and a historian at Termez University, provided details of the Indian campaign of 1398–99.

In Pakistan, Rahimullah Yusufzai, the BBC's correspondent in Peshawar, was a one-man encyclopaedia on Afghanistan and the Taliban. Dr Nazir Gardezi, a historian at Peshawar University, was informative and perceptive in equal measure.

Acknowledgements

Ahmed Rashid, the *Daily Telegraph*'s Central Asia correspondent and author of several excellent books on the region, was illuminating in Lahore, as was Mohammed Iqbal Chawla, Professor of History at Punjab University. In Multan, City of the Saints, which Tamerlane flattened in 1398, Mirza Beg was a stalwart companion. In Islamabad, thank you to my hosts Zahra and Nadir for their exemplary hospitality, and also to Professor Ahmad Dani, the doyen of Pakistani historians.

During a month in benighted Taliban-controlled Afghanistan, several friends and contacts were brave enough to help me at great risk to themselves. Some will remain unnamed. My old companion Arif, in particular, went far beyond the call of duty. Peter Jouvenal, the news cameraman *par excellence*, Robin Barnwell and Abdul Sattar were cheering and knowledgeable travelling companions. One of the sadder and more ridiculous moments came when Walid, my putative translator from Peshawar, was sent packing by the Taliban Foreign Ministry in Kabul (shame on you, Faiz Ahmad Faiz). His crime? His beard was too short. Thanks to Issa Khan, his hirsute replacement, Amir Shah of Associated Press, and Shukur, our long-suffering driver. Maulavi Qudratullah Jamal, the Taliban Minister of Culture, was a revelation. Maulavi Hafiz Faizlil Rubbi, Taliban Head of Foreign Affairs in Mazar-i-Sharif, was reassuringly protective when things got hairy. In Kandahar, Maulavi Wakil Ahmed Mutawakil, the Taliban Foreign Minister last seen helping American forces with their enquiries, was a stimulating interviewee who traced parallels between Tamerlane and Osama bin Laden.

In Herat, I benefited from long conversations with Maulavi Said Mohammed Omar Shahid, President of Herat University, and Maulana Khudad, President of the Council of Mullahs, and in Kabul with the historians Professor Abdul Baqi at Kabul University and Mirza Gul Yawar. Returning to Kabul in the summer of 2004, I was helped around the city by Yama and Dil Mohammed. Ratish Nanda, conservation architect with the Aga Khan Trust for Culture, was a thoughtful guide to Babur's Gardens, then undergoing an impressive and desperately needed restoration.

Khatuna Chkheidze shared her considerable expertise with me in Georgia, where the conqueror, known as 'Temur the Evil', is viewed with horror and loathing. She was a marvellous guide to the capital of Tbilisi, which he ravaged on half a dozen occasions. Thanks also to Tedo Japaridze, the President's National Security Adviser, and David Katsitadze, Chair of the Eastern History Department of Tbilisi State University.

The splendid Shane Winser, Director of the Royal Geographical Society's Expedition Advisory Centre, rode to the rescue again with her comprehensive database of Central Asian hands, including John Pilkington, who kindly introduced me to Dr Anvar Shakirov at Samarkand State University.

At HarperCollins thanks to Michael Fishwick for his rigorous editing, and to Robert Lacey, Kate Hyde, Caroline Hotblack, Rachel Nicholson and cartographer John Gilkes for their tremendous input. My agent Georgina Capel never flagged. I am grateful, as ever, for her terrific support.

I am indebted to Beatrice Forbes Manz, Associate Professor of History at Tufts University and one of the foremost Temurid scholars, both for her reading suggestions and for her insightful comments on the manuscript. Her study *The Rise and Rule of Tamerlane* was an essential guide to a complex subject, as was Hilda Hookham's *Tamburlaine the Conqueror*. Harold Lamb's *Tamerlane the Earth Shaker*, though more dated, gave a sense of the sheer fury of the Tatar conqueror in action. John Woods, Director of the Center of Middle Eastern Studies at Chicago University and Professor of Iranian and Central Asian History and of Near Eastern Languages and Civilizations, provided an instructive reading list.

Roger Katz at Hatchard's directed me to Peter Hall's production of *Tamburlaine the Great*, which opened the Olivier Theatre at the National in 1976, and the Royal Shakespeare Company's ground-breaking production in 1993. The RSC supplied the reviews of Antony Sher's blood-soaked performance.

Thank you to the staff of the British Library, in particular those in the Rare Books and Music Room, my second home in recent years, and to Murad Esenov, Director of the Centre for Central Asia and Caucasus Studies and editor of the *Central Asia and Caucasus Journal* in Sweden.

A number of editors provided moral and financial support. My sincere thanks to Michael Prodger and Miriam Gross at the *Sunday Telegraph*, Mark Amory at the *Spectator*, Jan Dalley at the *Financial Times*, David Sexton at the *Evening Standard* and Nancy Sladek at the *Literary Review* for their encouragement during this project. Thanks also to Jill James, Gill Plimmer and Rahul Jacob, successive travel editors of the *FT*, and Cath Urquhart, travel editor of *The Times*, for allowing me to return to the Muslim world at a time when it was not at the top of everyone's list of holiday destinations.

Friends and colleagues were kind enough to help me during my research. Andrew Roberts alerted me to Anthony Powell's reference to Tamburlaine. Calum Macleod, co-author of the first-rate guidebook *Uzbekistan: The Golden Road to Samarkand*, provided the illustration of Soviet archaeologist Mikhail Gerasimov admiring Tamerlane's skull. Thanks to John Adamson at Peterhouse, Cambridge; Christina Lamb; Matthew Leeming; Bijan Omrani; David Stern, the *FT*'s Central Asia correspondent; Masoud Golsorkhi, editor of *TANK* magazine John Murphy; and the incomparable Tom Sutherland at the Travellers Club. The Writers in Prison section of International PEN provided a great deal of information on the abysmal human rights situation in Uzbekistan.

Writers need to eat. I pay tribute to the excessively generous hospitality of my uncle and aunt, Nick and Susan Ward, my neighbours in Norfolk who feasted me handsomely in all seasons, not least during the long winters when I laid waste to their cellar.

I would like to thank Clementine, aged nine, who has had to put up with her stepfather disappearing regularly to various countries ending in 'stan', and who has become a juvenile expert on Central Asia. Last of all, I must sing the praises of my wife Julia, whose life has been consumed by the Scourge of God for longer than either of us expected, and who has read and edited the manuscript more times than she would care to remember. I am thankful for her understanding about my absences, for her patience, encouragement, humour and love.

My parents have always been inspiring, devoted and loving champions. I had hoped my father would live to see this book published. That was not possible, but *Tamerlane: Sword of Islam, Conqueror of the World* is dedicated to my mother and to his memory.

A Note on Spelling and Terminology

A couple of years ago, Frances Wood observed in *The Silk Road*: 'I think this is the most complicated book I have ever written when it comes to spelling place names.' I know the feeling. Central Asia is a minefield. And it is not just place names.

The world's most famous Mongol conqueror is a case in point. Take your pick from Genghis Khan, Chinghiz Khan, Chingiz Khan, or even Chinggis Khan. The lands he bequeathed his son became the Juchid empire. Others call it Jochid. Still others prefer Djöčid.

Scholars invariably favour the more obscure spellings, but I have tried to use terms familiar to the general reader. Central Asian names are complicated enough, it seems to me, without making things more difficult.

Tamerlane was in fact Temur (or Timur). The longer name by which we in the West know him was a corruption of Temur the Lame. He was a Chaghatay (or Čaghatay if you like your diacritic symbols), or a Turkicised Mongol, or a Turk; but I have followed a long line of Europeans who describe him as a Tatar.

Consistency in these matters is as elusive as peace and tranquillity were to Temur. As T.E. Lawrence so emphatically expressed it in *Seven Pillars of Wisdom* after a plea for clarity from his editor: 'There are some "scientific systems" of transliteration, helpful to people who know enough Arabic not to need helping, but a wash-out for the world. I spell my names anyhow, to show what rot the systems are.' In a less brazen way I have followed his example.

1

Beginnings on the Steppe

1336–1370

'Tamerlane, the "Lord of the Conjunctions", was the greatest Asiatic conqueror known in history. The son of a petty chieftain, he was not only the bravest of the brave, but also profoundly sagacious, generous, experienced, and persevering; and the combination of these qualities made him an unsurpassed leader of men and a very god of war adored by all ranks ... The object of Tamerlane was glory, and, as in the case of all conquerors ancient or modern, his career was attended by terrible bloodshed. He sometimes ordered massacres by way of retribution or from policy, but there were few that had their origin in pure savagery.'

LIEUT. COL. P.M. SYKES, *A History of Persia*

At around 10 o'clock on the morning of 28 July 1402, from a patch of raised ground high above the valley, the elderly emperor surveyed his army. It was a vast body of men, spreading over the Chibukabad plain, north-east of Ankara, like a dark and terrible stain. Through the glinting sunlight the ordered lines of mounted archers stretched before him until they were lost in the shimmering blaze, each man waiting for the signal to join battle. There were two hundred thousand

1

professional soldiers drawn from the farthest reaches of his empire, from Armenia to Afghanistan, Samarkand to Siberia. Their confidence was high, their discipline forged in the fire of many battles. They had never known defeat.

For the past thirty years these men and their sons and fathers had thundered through Asia. Through deserts, steppes and mountains the storm had raged, unleashing desolation on a fearful scale. One by one, the great cities of the East had fallen. Antioch and Aleppo, Balkh and Baghdad, Damascus and Delhi, Herat, Kabul, Shiraz and Isfahan had been left in flaming ruins. All had crumpled before the irresistible Tatar hordes. They had killed, raped, plundered and burnt their way through the continent, marking each triumph with their dreadful trophies. On every battlefield they left soaring towers and bloody pyramids built from the skulls of their decapitated victims, deadly warnings to anyone who dared oppose them.

Now, as the soldiers stared up at the distant silhouette of a man on horseback, framed against the heavens, they steeled themselves for another victory. Truly their emperor had earned his magnificent titles. Lord of the Fortunate Conjunction (of the Planets, a reference to the auspicious position of the stars at his birth); Conqueror of the World; Emperor of the Age; Unconquered Lord of the Seven Climes. But one name suited him above all others: Temur, Scourge of God.

On his vantage point beneath the smouldering midsummer sky, the emperor felt no disquiet. Moments away from the most important battle of his life, he felt nothing but the unshakeable faith in his destiny that had served him so well. Dismounting from his stallion, he knelt to offer up his customary prayers to the creator of the universe, humbly prostrating himself on the scorched earth, dedicating his victories to Allah and asking Him to continue bestowing divine favour on His servant. Then, with all the saddle-stiffness of his sixty-six years he rose to his feet and looked out over the field of battle, where the future of his dynasty lay with his beloved sons and grandsons.

The left wing was commanded by his son Prince Shahrukh and grandson Khalil Sultan. Its advance guard was under another grandson, Sultan Husayn. Temur's third son Prince Miranshah led the right wing, his own son Abubakr at the head of the vanguard. But it was the main body of the army, a glittering kaleidoscope of men under the command of his grandson and heir Prince Mohammed Sultan, on which the emperor's clouded eyes may have lingered longest. From the midst of these men rose Temur's crimson standard, a horse-tail surmounted by a golden crescent. Newly arrived from the imperial capital of Samarkand, unlike their battle-weary brothers in arms, these troops were splendidly attired, each detachment resplendent in its own colour. There were soldiers carrying crimson ensigns with crimson shields and saddles. Others were clad from head to toe in yellow, violet or white, with matching lances, quivers, cuirasses and clubs. In front of them stood a line of thirty exquisitely equipped purveyors of destruction, war elephants seized after the sacking of Delhi in 1398. On their backs, guarded behind wooden castles, stood bodies of archers and flame-throwers.

The Tatar army was, wrote the fifteenth-century Syrian chronicler Ibn Arabshah, a devastating sight. 'Wild beasts seemed collected and scattered over the earth and stars dispersed, when his army flowed hither and thither, and mountains to walk, when it moved, and tombs to be overturned, when it marched, and the earth seemed shaken by violent movement.'

Staring at them across the sweltering plain were the ranks of Temur's mightiest enemy. The Ottoman Sultan Bayazid I, the self-styled Sword Arm of Islam, had put a similar number of troops into the field. There were twenty thousand Serbian cavalry in full armour, mounted Sipahis, irregular cavalry and infantry from the provinces of Asia Minor. Bayazid himself commanded the centre at the head of five thousand Janissaries – the makings of a regular infantry – supported by three of his sons, the princes Musa, Isa and Mustapha. The right wing was led by the sultan's Christian brother-in-law, Lazarovic of Serbia, the left by another of his sons, Prince Sulayman Chelebi. These men, victors of the last Crusade at Nicopolis in 1396, where they had snuffed out the flame of European chivalry, were thirsty, exhausted and dispirited after a series of forced marches. Even before battle commenced their morale had been shattered by Temur's brilliant tactical manoeuvrings. Only a week earlier they had occupied the higher ground on which their adversary's army now stood. Feigning flight, the Tatar had outmanoeuvred them, diverted and poisoned their water supply, doubled back, plundered their undefended camp and taken their position.

All was still on both sides. A ripple stirred through Temur's lines of cavalry as the horses sensed a charge. Then, slicing through the silence, came the heavy rumble of the great kettle-drums, joined by cymbals and trumpets, the signal for battle. Now the valley echoed to the thundering of horses' hooves, the swoosh of arrows and the clash of metal upon metal. From the first blows struck the fighting was ferocious. Charging across the plain came the formidable Serbian cavalry, bright globules of armour amid the choking wreaths of dust stirred up by their mounts. Under pressure, the Tatar left flank retreated, defending itself with volley after volley of arrows and flames of naphtha. On the right wing Abubakr's forces, advancing against Prince Chelebi's left wing under cover of a cloud of arrows, fought like lions and finally broke through their enemy's ranks. Bayazid's Tatar cavalry chose this moment to switch sides, turning suddenly against Chelebi's Macedonians and Turks from the rear. It was a decisive moment which broke the Ottoman attack. Temur, a master of cunning, had engineered the defection of the Tatars in the months before the battle by playing on their sense of tribal loyalty and holding out the prospect of richer plunder. Seeing both the disarray of his own forces who were being overwhelmed by the Tatars, and the confusion of the Ottoman right wing, in desperate retreat from the mounted cavalry of Temur's grandson Sultan Husayn, Chelebi judged the battle lost and fled the field with the remainder of his men.

Temur watched history unfurl itself before him on the valley floor. He was interrupted by the rushing blur of a gorgeously armoured man on horseback. Throwing himself off his mount, Temur's favourite grandson Mohammed Sultan went down on one knee and begged his grandfather for permission to enter the battle. It was the right time to press home the advantage, he insisted. The emperor listened gravely to the young's man arguments and nodded his agreement with pride. Mohammed Sultan was a fearsome warrior and a worthy heir.

The elite Samarkand division, together with a body of the emperor's guards, charged the Serbian cavalry, who, observing with horror Chelebi's departure from the field, buckled under the attack and followed him in retreat towards Brusa. It was a bitter blow for Bayazid, whose infantry were now the only forces left intact. Worse was to follow. The Tatar centre now moved forward to settle the affair with eighty regiments and the dreaded elephants. They held the ground. The Ottoman infantry was routed; anyone left standing was slaughtered on the spot or captured.

Sultan Bayazid, the man whose name struck fear in the hearts of Europe's kings and princes, stood on the brink of catastrophe. Most of his army had fled. Only the Janissaries and his reserves held on. Still he would not surrender, and the fighting continued furiously until nightfall, Bayazid's forces defending their sultan valiantly.

'Yet they were like a man who sweeps away dust with a comb or drains the sea with a sieve or weighs mountains with a scruple,' wrote Arabshah. 'And out of the clouds of thick dust they poured out upon those mountains and the fields filled with those lions continuous storms of bloody darts and showers of black arrows and the tracker

of Destiny and hunter of Fate set dogs upon cattle and they ceased
not to be overthrown and overthrow and to be smitten by the sentence
of the sharp arrow with effective decree, until they became like hedge-
hogs, and the zeal of battle lasted between those hordes from sunrise
to evening, when the hosts of iron gained the victory and there was
read against the men of Rum the chapter of "Victory".* Then their
arms being exhausted and the front line and reserves alike decimated,
even the most distant of the enemy advanced upon them at will and
strangers crushed them with swords and spears and filled pools with
their blood and marshes with their limbs and Ibn Othman [Bayazid]
was taken and bound with fetters like a bird in a cage.'

The battle of Ankara, and the career of Sultan Bayazid, had ended.
Temur had achieved his most outstanding victory. 'From the Irtish
and Volga to the Persian Gulf and from the Ganges to Damascus and
the Archipelago, Asia was in the hands of Timour,' wrote Edward
Gibbon. 'His armies were invincible, his ambition was boundless,
and his zeal might aspire to conquer and convert the Christian kingdoms of the West, which already trembled at his name.' Now he stood
at the gates of Europe; its feeble, divided and penurious kings –
Henry IV of England, Charles VI of France, Henry III of Castile –
trembled indeed at the ease with which this unknown warlord had
trounced their most feared enemy, rushing off sycophantic letters of
congratulation and professions of goodwill to 'the most victorious
and serene Prince Themur' in the hope of forestalling invasion. All
feared his advance.

In the Tatar camp there were no such fears. Temur's men, from

---

* A reference to Book 48 of the Koran, Al Fath (Victory): 'We have given
you a glorious victory, so that God may forgive you your past and future
sins, and perfect His goodness to you; that He may guide you to a straight
path and bestow on you His mighty help ... God has promised you rich
booty, and has given you this with all promptness. He has stayed your
enemies' hands, so that He may make your victory a sign to true believers
and guide you along a straight path.'

the highest amirs to the most lowly soldier, wondered what the emperor would do next. Perhaps he would lead the hordes farther west into Christendom to mete out more destruction against the infidel and store up greater credit with the beneficent Allah. Perhaps he would look east to another, more powerful infidel, the Ming emperor of China. Such decisions could wait.

For now it was enough for the emperor and his forces to luxuriate in their greatest triumph. Soldiers sifted through the carnage on the blood-soaked battlefield, hacking heads from corpses to build the customary towers of skulls. Ottoman weapons were collected, horses rounded up and anything else of use stripped from the dead. Other, more agreeable, pursuits awaited. There was feasting to be had, dancing girls to admire and, most delicious of all, Bayazid's harem to despoil.

Who was this exotic Oriental warlord who had annihilated one of the world's most powerful sovereigns and now stared so ominously across the Bosporus? To answer that question, to understand how in 1402 Temur literally catapulted into European consciousness, first by routing Bayazid, then by launching the severed heads of the Knights Hospitallers of Smyrna* as missiles against their terrified brethren, we must travel back six momentous decades and 1,800 miles to the east, to a small town in southern Uzbekistan called Kesh.

It was near here on 9 April 1336, according to the chronicles, that a boy was born to Taraghay, a minor noble of the Barlas clan.† These

---

* Founded in the eleventh century as the Knights of the Hospital of St John at Jerusalem, the military religious order in Smyrna was, by 1402, the last Christian stronghold in Asia Minor.

† Academics tend to dispute Temur's actual birthday. Beatrice Forbes Manz, for example, author of a scholarly study of Temur, says this date was 'clearly invented. He was probably at least five years older than the date suggests.'

were Tatars, a Turkic people of Mongol origin, descendants of Genghis Khan's hordes who had stormed through Asia in the thirteenth century.* 'The birthplace of this deceiver was a village of a lord named Ilgar in the territory of Kesh – may Allah remove him from the garden of Paradise!' wrote Arabshah. The child was given the name Temur, meaning iron, which later gave rise to the Persian version, Temur-i-lang, Temur the Lame, after a crippling injury suffered in his youth. From there it was only a slight corruption to Tamburlaine and Tamerlane, the names by which he is more generally known in the West.†

According to legend, the omens at his birth were inauspicious. 'It is ... said that when he came forth from his mother's womb his palms were found to be filled with blood; and this was understood to mean that blood would be shed by his hand,' wrote Arabshah. (It

---

* The Tatars were originally a powerful horde which held sway in north-east Mongolia as early as the fifth century. As with many of the other ethnic groups drawn from the melting-pot of Central Asia, a region which for thousands of years has been a crossroads for great movements of populations, the term is neither exact nor exclusive. The word itself may have originated from the name of an early chieftain, Tatur.

   In the thirteenth century, Genghis Khan's westward rampages with his Mongols brought about a cross-fertilisation of cultures and peoples throughout the continent. Despite the fact that he had already virtually eliminated the Tatars as a tribe, these Turkicised Mongols became known as Tatars. Europeans, however, used the term indiscriminately for all nomadic peoples and, because they regarded these rough barbarians with fear and loathing, spelt it Tartar, from Tartarus, the darkest hell of Greek mythology. Today, the words Mongol and Tatar are often used interchangeably.

† 'To speak of him as Tamerlane is indeed a matter of insult, being a name inimical to him,' noted Ruy Gonzalez de Clavijo, the Spanish envoy sent to Temur's court by Henry III of Castile in 1402. Such diplomatic niceties are still scrupulously observed among Uzbeks, as the author discovered 598 years later during an interview with Tashkent's ambassador to the Court of St James's. 'We are very proud of Amir Temur. We do not call him Tamerlane,' he told me with only the lightest and most diplomatic of reproaches.

is worth explaining at the outset the ill-will Arabshah bore towards Temur.* As a boy of eight or nine, the Syrian had been captured by the Tatar forces who sacked Damascus in 1401. Carried off to Samarkand as a prisoner with his mother and brothers, he learnt Persian, Turkish and Mongolian, studying under distinguished scholars and travelling widely. Later, in a curious twist of fate, he became confidential secretary to the Ottoman Sultan Mohammed I, son of Bayazid, the man whose dazzling military career had been extinguished by Temur. He returned to Damascus in 1421, but never forgot the terrible scenes of rape and pillage enacted by Temur's hordes. They culminated in the razing of the great Umayyad Mosque, 'matchless and unequalled' throughout the lands of Islam, according to the fourteenth-century Moroccan traveller Ibn Battutah.†)

Shakhrisabz lay in the heart of what was known in Arabic as Mawarannahr, 'What is Beyond the River'. On a modern atlas Mawarannahr extends across the cotton basket of the former Soviet Union, encompassing the independent Central Asian republics of Uzbekistan, Kazakhstan, Turkmenistan, Tajikistan and Kyrgyzstan, running into north-west Xinjiang in China. The territory was also known as Transoxiana, whose centre was a three-hundred-mile-wide corridor of land sandwiched between the two greatest rivers of Central Asia,

---

* The chapter headings of Arabshah's *Life of Temur the Great Amir* make this animosity abundantly clear: 'This Bastard Begins to Lay Waste Azerbaijan and the Kingdoms of Irak'; 'How that Proud Tyrant was Broken & Borne to the House of Destruction, where he had his Constant Seat in the Lowest Pit of Hell'. Elsewhere, Temur is described variously as 'Satan', 'demon', 'viper', 'villain', 'despot', 'deceiver' and 'wicked fool'. Any praise for Temur from this quarter is therefore not to be taken lightly.

† Ibn Battutah earned the soubriquet 'Traveller of Islam' after a twenty-nine-year, seventy-five-thousand-mile odyssey around the world. He journeyed indefatigably by camel, mule and horse, on junks, dhows and rafts, from the Volga to Tanzania, from China to Morocco. Variously a judge, ambassador and hermit, he was also pre-eminently a travel writer, the stories of his epic wanderings recounted in the monumental *The Precious Gift of Lookers into the Marvels of Cities and Wonders of Travel*.

the Amu Darya and Sir Darya. Better known by their more evocative classical names, the Oxus and the Jaxartes, these were two of the four medieval rivers of paradise, slivers of fertility rushing through an otherwise barren landscape. At 1,800 miles, the Amu Darya is the region's longest, sweeping west in a gentle arc from the Pamir mountains before checking north-west towards the southern tip of the Aral Sea. The Sir Darya, 1,400 miles long, flows west from the snow-covered Tien Shan mountains before it, too, diverts north-west, almost watering the rapidly shrinking Aral Sea on its northern shores.

On the banks of these hallowed waterways and their tributaries rose the noble cities of antiquity, whose names echoed with the distant memories of Alexander the Great and the Mongol warlord Genghis Khan:* Bukhara, Samarkand, Tirmidh (Termez), Balkh, Urganch and Khiva. Beyond the rivers the deadly sands of the desert erupted, fizzing across the landscape on hot, dry winds. West of the Amu Darya stretched the spirit-shattering wilderness of the Qara Qum (Black Sands) desert. East of the Sir Darya, the equally inhospitable Hunger Steppe unfurled, a vast, unforgiving flatness melting into the horizon. Even between the two rivers, the pockets of civilisation were under siege from the timeless forces of nature as the lush farming land gave way to the burning Qizik Qum (Red Sands) desert of the north. In the summer, the heat was stupefying and the skins of those who toiled in the fields blistered and turned to leather. In winter, snows gusted down without mercy on a lifeless land and the men, women and children who had made their home here, nomads and settled alike, retreated behind lined *gers* (felt tents) and mudbrick walls, wrapping themselves tightly in furs and woollen blankets against winds strong enough to blow a man out of his saddle. Only

---

* The title of Khan was the most popular designation for a sovereign in medieval Asia. Initially it referred to kings and princes, but it was debased over the centuries to include local rulers and even chiefs.

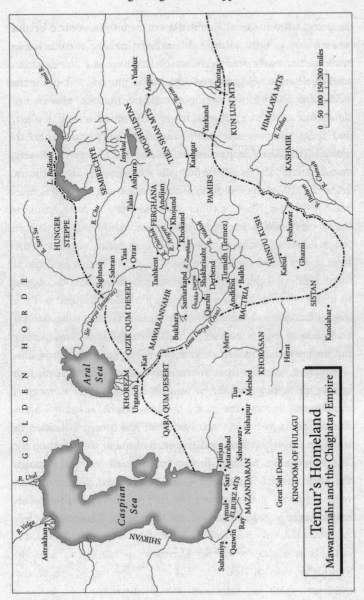

Temur's Homeland
Mawarannahr and the Chaghatay Empire

in spring, when the rivers tumbled down from the mountain heights, when blossoms burst forth in the orchards and the markets heaved with apples, mulberries, pears, peaches, plums and pomegranates, melons, apricots, quinces and figs, when mutton and horsemeat hissed and crackled over open fires and huge bumpers of wine were downed in tribal banquets, did the country at last rejoice in plenty.

The Mongol conquests, which historians like to say 'turned the world upside down', began in 1206. Having subdued and unified the warlike tribes of Mongolia under his command, a Mongol leader called Temuchin, somewhere in his late thirties, was crowned Genghis Khan – Oceanic Khan or Ruler of the Universe – on the banks of the Onon river. The seat of his empire was Karakorum. Though the tribes subsumed under his command were many, henceforth they were known simply as the Mongols. Once created, this vast fighting force, which probably numbered at least a hundred thousand, needed to be kept occupied. If it was not, the likelihood was that it would quickly fracture into the traditional pattern of feuding tribal factions, undermining its new master's authority. Genghis looked south across his borders and decided to strike the Chin empire of northern China.

His army, noted for its exceptional horsemanship and superb archery, swept across Asia like a tsunami, flattening every enemy it encountered. In 1209, the Turkic Uyghurs in what is today Xinjiang offered their submission. Two years later, the Mongols invaded the northern Chinese empire and Peking, its capital, was taken in 1215. The Qara-Khitay, nomads who controlled lands from their base in the Altaic steppes of northern China, surrendered three years later, so that by 1218 the frontiers of Genghis's nascent empire rubbed against those of Sultan Mohammed, the Muslim Khorezmshah who ruled over most of Persia and Mawarannahr with his capital in Samarkand. It is debatable whether Genghis was looking to fight this formidable ruler at this time, but after a caravan of 450 Muslim merchants from his territories was butchered in cold blood in

Mohammed's border city of Otrar on suspicion of being spies, and after reparations were refused, war was the only course open to him.

In 1219 the Mongols swarmed into Central Asia. Otrar was put under siege and captured. Genghis's sons Ogedey and Chaghatay seized its governor and executed him by pouring molten gold down his throat. It was the first sign of the terrifyingly vicious campaign to come. Mohammed fled in terror, closely pursued to an island on the Caspian Sea where he soon died. The prosperous city of Bukhara fell, followed quickly by Samarkand, whose defensive force of 110,000 troops and twenty war elephants proved no match for the Mongols. The Islamic state felt the full force of Genghis's fury. This was a man who revelled in war and bloodshed, who believed, as he told his generals, that 'Man's greatest good fortune is to chase and defeat his enemy, seize all his possessions, leave his married women weeping and wailing, ride his gelding, use the bodies of his women as nightshirts and supports, gazing upon and kissing their rosy breasts, sucking their lips which are as sweet as the berries of the breasts.'

Cities were razed and depopulated, prisoners slain or ordered to march as a shield before the army, in full battle formation. Even cats and dogs were killed. Marching through Azerbaijan, the invaders sacked the Christian kingdom of Georgia in 1221, flattening the capital of Tiflis (Tbilisi). Through the Caucasus and the Crimea and along the Volga they advanced, routing Bulgars, Turks and Russian princes as they hugged the northern shores of the Caspian Sea. Another siege was mounted against Urganch, homeland of the shahs. After seven months of resistance, the city was stormed. Artisans, women and children were gathered to one side and enslaved. The remaining men were put to the sword. Each of Genghis's soldiers was ordered to execute twenty-four prisoners.

North of the Oxus the Mongols fell upon the ancient city of Termez, where legend has it that a woman begged to be spared the massacre, telling her captors she had swallowed a pearl. Her stomach was ripped open and the gem removed, prompting Genghis to order his men to disembowel every single corpse. Balkh, the fabled former capital of the Bactrian empire, collapsed before the Mongol onslaught, followed by the city of Merv, where the forces of Tuli, another of the warlord's sons, reportedly slew seven hundred thousand.* Herat, Nishapur and Bamiyan likewise folded. In the dying months of 1221, Jalal ad-din, who had led the resistance to the Mongols after the ignominious flight of his father Mohammed, was defeated at the battle of the Indus, which marked the end of the campaign. In 1223, Genghis returned east. He died four years later, ruler of an empire which spanned an entire continent from China to the gates of Europe.

Though none of his successors was possessed of such savage genius, the Mongol conquests Genghis initiated were vigorously expanded by his sons and grandsons. The territories he had won were distributed according to custom. Tuli, the youngest son, received his father's seat in Mongolia. Jochi, the eldest, received lands farthest away from Karakorum, west of the Irtish river in what later became the regions of the Golden Horde, the Russian khanate which is discussed in Chapter 2. Ogedey, the third son and future Great Khan, or royal leader above all his brothers, was given the *ulus* (domain) of western Mongolia. Genghis's second son Chaghatay received Central Asia as his inheritance. It became known as the Chaghatay ulus, the western half of which formed the Mawarannahr in which Temur grew up.

By 1234, Ogedey's conquest of the Chin empire was complete. The 1240s and 1250s saw Mongol rule spreading west across southern Russia into eastern Europe under the leadership of Genghis's fearsome grandson Batu, founder of the Golden Horde. At the same time,

---

* This figure, like many from the medieval chronicles, should be treated with a degree of caution. Scholars consider the population estimates and reports of the numbers killed in battles to be routinely inflated in these sources.

another grandson, Hulagu, was conquering his own territories by the sword, establishing an empire which included Georgia, Armenia and Azerbaijan in the west, Baghdad and the Fertile Crescent in the south, and ranged as far east as Khorasan, eastern Persia. Founder of the Ilkhanid dynasty of Persia, Hulagu was helped in his conquests by Mongol troops belonging to his brother Great Khan Mönke, together with detachments from both Batu and Chaghatay. United, the khanates proved invincible.

History suggests it is easier to carve out an empire than preserve it, and the fate of Genghis's successors proved no exception to the rule. With the death of Great Khan Mönke in 1259, the great age of Mongol conquest ground to a close. In 1260, the Mongol army was defeated at the battle of Ain Jalut by the Egyptian army under Baybars, who became the first Mamluk sultan later that year. Africa closed her doors forever to the pagan invaders from the east. The Sung empire of southern China fell to Genghis's famous grandson Kubilay in 1279, but by that time the Mongol empire had been torn apart by infighting for two decades. Instead of uniting to extend their dominions in the west, the Golden Horde and the Ilkhanid dynasty had embarked in 1262 on a long series of wars over the pasturages of Azerbaijan and the Caucasus. At the same time in the east, the house of Tuli was disintegrating as Kubilay and his brother Arigh Boke fought a four-year civil war for the imperial throne. As the thirteenth century drew to a close, the Chaghatay ulus found itself at war with the three other Genghisid dynasties. The empires which the Ruler of the Universe had bequeathed to his sons were at each other's throats.

☙❧

Genghis had been dead for more than a hundred years by the time of Temur's birth, but the legacy of the Mongol conquests still hung over this land of desert, steppe and mountain. Many of the practicalities of daily life had undergone little transformation, and nomadism remained dominant in most of the regions Genghis had conquered. As John Joseph Saunders wrote in his classic account of the period, *The History of the Mongol Conquests* (1971), 'Nomadic empires rose and fell with astonishing swiftness, but the essential features of the steppes remained unchanged for ages, and the description by Herodotus of the Scythians of the fifth century before Christ will apply, with trifling variations, to the Mongols of the thirteenth century after Christ, 1,700 years later.'

For centuries the Mongols had driven their flocks and herds across the endless, treeless steppe, roaming from pasture to pasture in migrations whose timing was dictated by the seasons. Sheep and horses satisfied virtually all their needs. From sheep came the skins to fashion clothes, wool to make the *gers* they lived in, mutton and cheese to eat, milk to drink. Horses provided mounts for hunting and battle, as well as the powerfully intoxicating fermented mare's milk, or kumis. Though their ways of life were utterly different, though both sides regarded each other with suspicion, born largely from the predatory instincts of the wandering horsemen, the nomads and the settled populations of the towns and cities of Central Asia came together from time to time to trade.

Among the most prized products for the nomads were the metals with which to forge weapons. Tea, silks and spices were luxuries. Such trade predated Genghis by many centuries. Central Asia had existed as a crossroads between East and West ever since the Silk Road – 3,700 miles from China to the Mediterranean ports of Antioch and Alexandria via Samarkand – came into being around the beginning of the first century BC. By the time of the Mongols, there were at least another three major trade routes linking East to West. First there was the sea route from south China to the Persian Gulf. Another artery began in the lower Volga, clung closely to the Sir Darya and then headed east to western China. Finally, there was the northern ·

route which from the Volga-Kama region cut through southern Siberia up to Lake Baikal, where it diverted south to Karakorum and Peking. Eastbound along these routes came furs and falcons, wool, gold, silver and precious stones. Westward went the porcelain, silks and herbs of China.

If nomadism was one feature of life which remained virtually unchanged from the thirteenth to the fourteenth centuries, the military was another. Mongol men were all, almost by definition, soldiers, since any under the age of sixty were considered fit for service in the army. There was no concept of civilian men. In a desolate landscape, survival itself – primarily by the hunting of meat – demanded the same set of skills required on the battlefield. Military techniques were learnt from the earliest age. As soon as a boy could ride, he was well on his way to becoming a soldier. In the saddle, he learnt to master his horse absolutely and to manoeuvre it with the greatest finesse, to gauge the distance between himself and his quarry, and to shoot with deadly accuracy. It was the perfect training for a mounted archer, the backbone of Genghis's army armed with the composite bow of horn, sinew and wood. As Gibbon remarked, 'the amusements of the chase serve as a prelude to the conquest of an empire'.

Genghis organised his army according to the traditional decimal system of the steppe: units of ten, one hundred, one thousand and ten thousand soldiers, a system which Temur retained. Soldiers were not paid other than in plunder from the enemies they defeated and the cities they stormed. Tribes which had once been hostile were deliberately divided into different units, thereby undermining tribal loyalties and creating a new force united in its loyalty to Genghis. This was in addition to his imperial guard of ten thousand, which functioned as the central administration of the empire. Temur would follow a similar strategy as he sought to weld together an army from the disparate tribes of Central Asia. There was continuity, too, in the tactics employed on the battlefield, particularly in the use of

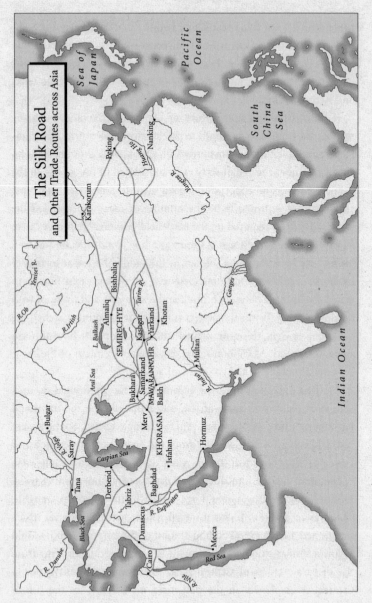

The Silk Road
and Other Trade Routes across Asia

encirclement and the Mongols' favourite device of feigned flight, which was the undoing of many an enemy.

Religion was worn lightly by the Mongols. It consisted of the simple worship of Tengri, a holy protector in the eternal heavens, in whose name divine assistance was sought and victories celebrated. There were no temples, nor organised worship as it is understood today. Horses were often sacrificed to Tengri, and were killed and buried with a man when he died so he could ride on into the afterlife. Shamans, venerated figures in Mongol society, acted as mediators between the natural and supernatural worlds, falling into trances as their souls travelled to heaven or the underworld on their missions to assist the community. Clad in white, mounted on a white horse, resplendent with a staff and drum, the shaman enjoyed distinguished status among the nomads, distributing blessings to herds and hunters alike, healing the sick, divining the position of an unseen enemy and the location of the most favourable pastures. Religious tolerance has come to be inherently associated with the Mongols, for they demonstrated a remarkable open-mindedness towards the other faiths they encountered.

Gibbon was much taken with this aspect of the Genghis legacy. 'The Catholic inquisitors of Europe who defended nonsense by cruelty, might have been confounded by the example of a barbarian, who anticipated the lessons of philosophy and established by his laws a system of pure theism and perfect toleration,' he wrote. So moved was the magisterial historian he even suggested that 'a singular conformity may be found between the religious laws of Zingis Khan and of Mr Locke'. The Mongols proved less dogmatic than the monotheists who travelled through their lands, be they Christian, Muslim, Jew or Buddhist. In the course of their pouring west across Asia towards Europe, they came to accept the religion of the peoples they conquered, be it Buddhism in China or Islam in Persia and the Golden Horde of southern Russia. This did not prevent them clinging on to vestigial aspects of shamanism, however, one reason no doubt why the great powers of the Islamic world never ceased to consider Temur a barbarian rather than a true Muslim.

If religion left only a light imprint on the Mongols, their contributions to culture were still less visible. Though their artistic achievements have been praised – they were talented carvers in bone, horn and wood, and produced handsome cups and bowls and elegant jewellery – theirs was not a literate world. An illiterate race prior to Genghis, they left virtually no written record of their time. The thirteenth-century *Secret History of the Mongols*, a document of questionable accuracy, is the only substantial survivor. An indication of their sophistication, however, is given by the *yasa*, an obscure body of laws codified by Genghis as head of a growing empire. It remains shadowy, because no complete code has ever been discovered. Historians have had to rely on the numerous references to it in the chronicles. According to Ata-Malik Juvayni, the thirteenth-century Persian historian of the Mongol empire, the *yasa* governed 'the disposition of armies and the destruction of cities'. In practice it was an evolving set of regulations touching on all aspects of life in the horde, ranging from the distribution of booty and the provision by towns and villages of posting stations with horses and riders, to the correct forms of military discipline on the battlefield and how to punish a horse thief (the animal had to be returned to its owner with a further nine horses thrown in for good measure; failure to observe these terms could result in the thief's execution). The *yasa* appear to have governed everything from religion (mandating toleration and freeing clergy of all taxation) to the uses of running water (prohibiting urination or washing in rivers, which were considered sacred).

The descriptions of fourteenth-century Tatars reveal the obvious parallels with the thirteenth-century Mongols who had preceded them. In particular, observers remarked on their physical hardiness and legendary military skills. The Tatars, wrote Ruy Gonzalez de

Clavijo, the Spanish ambassador sent to Temur's court by Henry III of Castile in 1402, could withstand 'heat and cold, hunger and thirst, more patiently than any other nation. When food is abundant, they gorge on it gluttonously, but when there is scarcity, sour milk tempered with boiling water suffices them . . . for their cooking fires they use no wood but only the dried dung of their herds, and it makes the fire for all purposes of roasting and boiling.'

Fighting was in their blood. Famed for their skill as archers, they charged across the steppe on horseback, raining down arrows upon their enemies. 'They were archers who by the shooting of an arrow would bring down a hawk from the hollow of the ether, and on dark nights with a thrust of their spearheads would cast out a fish from the bottom of the sea; who thought the day of the battle the wedding night and considered the pricks of lances the kisses of fair maidens.' They were great hunters, too, forming circles many miles in diameter and then riding inwards, driving all the wild beasts before them to their slaughter. It was a sport which honed their military talents and filled their stomachs, celebrated with wine-drenched banquets that lasted deep into the night. By day they tended their animals, riding out to pastures to allow their horses, camels, goats and sheep to graze. This was the currency of everyday life, and when a man wanted a wife, he bought one with animals or grazing rights. If he was rich, he bought several. Polygamy thrived in the upper reaches of society.

For ordinary men and women, the clothes were coarse and simple, long buckram jackets which protected the wearer from the elements. Silks, fine cloths and gold brocade were the preserve of the princes. In battle they made a formidable sight. Their enemies found them terrifying to behold. Amir Khusrau, an Indian poet who was captured by Temur's hordes at the close of the fourteenth century, recalled their appearance with horror.

There were more than a thousand Tatar infidels and warriors of other tribes, riding on camels, great commanders in battle, with steel-like bodies clothed in cotton; with faces like fire, with caps of sheep-skin, with heads shorn. Their eyes were so narrow and piercing that they might have bored a hole in a brazen vessel . . . their faces were set on their bodies as if they had no neck. Their cheeks resembled soft leather bottles, full of wrinkles and knots. Their noses extended from cheek to cheek, and their mouths from cheekbone to cheekbone . . . their moustaches were of extravagant length. They had but scanty beards about their chins . . . they looked like so many white demons, and the people fled from them in affright.

Conflict between the Mongol khanates of Genghis's successors, which held the lion's share of Asia in an unforgiving grip, was the harbinger of conflict within them. In the late thirteenth century, serious strains began to emerge in the Chaghatay ulus. There were tensions between the settled nobility in the towns and villages, largely in Mawarannahr, which had embraced Islam, and the nomadic, military aristocracy to the east, which rejected it and clung on to their pagan beliefs. These aristocrats, for whom the settled life of the conquered peoples was anathema, came to refer scornfully to their neighbours as *qurannas* (half-breeds or mongrels), an insult returned by the western Chaghatays, who called them *jete* (robbers), or Jats. Within the *ulus*, the geographical divide between east and west – the Tien Shan, or Celestial Mountains, whose peaks soar more than twenty-three thousand feet – was as dramatic as the ideological gulf which separated them. Increasingly, both sides stared across it with hatred in their hearts. Tensions were further escalated by the system of privileges granted to the military by the khan. These imposed crippling burdens on the poorer members of the local population, who were forced to feed, clothe and arm the warriors.

In 1266, the Chaghatay khan Mubarak chose to be enthroned in Mawarannahr, rather than in the nomad camp established by Chaghatay on the river Ili in south-eastern Kazakhstan, several hundred miles to the east, as was customary. For the military aristocracy, this symbolic ceremony, which expressed a preference for one way of life over another, represented a direct challenge to their traditions and authority. Worse, Mubarak was subsequently seduced by the siren calls of Islam, a conversion which sent seismic shocks across the heart of Central Asia and opened a growing chasm between East and West. A *qurultay*, an assembly of Mongol notables, was called in 1269 to determine the future of the *ulus*. In it, the warrior horsemen of the steppe prevailed, ruling against both settlement in the towns and the use of their cattle to tend agricultural land. Instead, the hordes would roam across the steppe and the mountains, grazing their hardy mounts on the pastures in accordance with the ancient ways. Mubarak was summarily dethroned. For the next fifty years, the pagan aristocrats held the ground.

But the seeds of change planted by Mubarak continued to take root even after his ousting. The soil was fertile. The Mongol warlords who had accompanied Mubarak to Mawarannahr, who included the Barlas clan, Temur's tribe, had by the opening of the fourteenth century converted to Islam and been Turkicised. The *qurultay* of 1269, however clear its conclusions, had not proved decisive. The old divisions between East and West, paganism and Islam, pastoralism and a more settled existence, remained, tearing at the fabric of the sprawling Chaghatay ulus.

In time, such pressures told. By the 1330s, the internecine disputes, simmering for several generations, finally boiled over until the fault-line cleft the *ulus* in two. To the west, Mawarannahr. To the east, ruled by a separate branch of the Chaghatay family, Moghulistan – land of the Moghuls – a mountainous territory extending south from Lake Issykul in Kyrgyzstan to the Tarim basin. Though this hostile split occurred at around the time of Temur's birth, its consequences occupied him throughout his career. In fact, with only a few intervals, the Moghuls were his lifelong enemy.

In the early fourteenth century, Mawarannahr enjoyed a brief period of prosperity under Kebek Khan (ruled 1318–26). Echoing the sedentary style of his predecessor Mubarak, he shifted his seat to the fertile Qashka Darya valley and introduced a range of administrative reforms, including his own coinage and, for the first time, a well-ordered tax system. Such behaviour did little to endear him to the nomadic elements within Mawarannahr, who chafed against this imposition of authority. His construction of a palace at Qarshi, in the heart of the Qashka Darya valley, only added to their sense of grievance, but Kebek did not back down.

The strains between the rival sedentary and nomadic populations resurfaced aggressively during the reign of his weaker successor, his brother Tarmashirin. The conflict which had ripped Chaghatay asunder now threatened to engulf Mawarannahr. Still hankering for a return to the old way of life, the nomad aristocracy urged Tarmashirin to honour the policies agreed at the *qurultay* of 1269. To no avail. Rather than compromise, the new khan chose instead to convert to Islam. This provocative act, coming at a time of profound instability, sealed his fate. Like Mubarak before him, he was stripped of power.

Tarmashirin's overthrow by the nomadic clans was an important landmark. It marked the end of real power for the Chaghatay khans of Mawarannahr. From this time they became no more than puppet rulers, installed in office as a nod to the customs of Genghis by the nomadic warlords who replaced them as the true source of power and authority. The battle for the soul of Mawarannahr, for the supremacy of a way of life made famous by the Mongol conqueror, had at last been decided. The settled nobility in the towns and villages had been confronted and overcome. Henceforth, power would reside among the men of the saddle, the bearded warriors whose strength and stamina was legendary.

In 1347, Amir Qazaghan overthrew the Chaghatay khan and seized the reins of power. For a decade he led his warriors into neighbouring territories, plundering and sacking with repeated success. Then, in 1358, on the orders of the khan of Moghulistan, he was assassinated, plunging Mawarannahr into turmoil. The collapse of central control was devastating. The vacuum left by Qazaghan was quickly filled by ambitious local warlords and religious leaders. Mawarannahr was riven by petty rivalries and division. Tughluk Temur, the Moghul khan, prepared to invade.

It was into this maelstrom of feuding fiefdoms, high among the shadows cast by the roof of the world, that Temur was born.

&

A brick kern in the roadside village of Khoja Ilgar, eight miles to the south of the historic Uzbek city of Shakhrisabz, the Green City, marks the birthplace of the Scourge of God. As memorials go, it is an unprepossessing sight, a pile of bricks on a concrete base topped by an inscribed plaque, more like a poorly built barbecue than a monument to one of the world's greatest conquerors. A traveller might expect this to be an important tourism site in Uzbekistan, a young country which has, since independence in 1991, resurrected Temur from the dustbin of Soviet historiography and championed him as its new nationalist figurehead, invincible hero of the Motherland. But this being the heartland of a nation still shaking off the ideological dust of communism and singularly uncomfortable with the new ethos of capitalism, there are no signs of commercialism here. No car park teeming with tour buses. No shops selling Temur T-shirts, key-rings or pens.

The site, instead, is exquisitely rural, as it was when the Spanish ambassador Clavijo arrived in Kesh, as Shakhrisabz was then known, on 28 August 1404. The 'great city . . . stands in the plain, and on all sides the land is well irrigated by streams and water channels, while round and about the city there are orchards with many homesteads', he observed. 'Beyond stretches the level country where there are

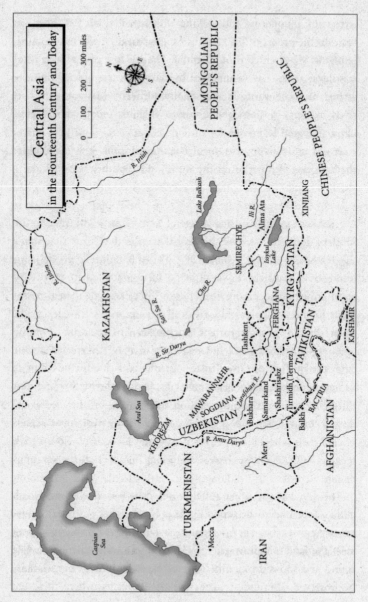

Central Asia
in the Fourteenth Century and Today

0   100   200   300 miles

MONGOLIAN PEOPLE'S REPUBLIC

CHINESE PEOPLE'S REPUBLIC

R. Irtish

Lake Balkash

R. Ishim

SEMIRECHYE

Ili R.

Alma Ata

XINJIANG

Isykkul Lake

KYRGYZSTAN

Chu R.

FERGHANA

Syr Su R.

Tashkent

TAJIKISTAN

KASHMIR

R. Sir Darya

MAWARANNAHR

Aral Sea

SOGDIANA

Zarafshan R.

Bukhara

Samarkand

Shakhrisabz

Tirmidh (Termez)

BACTRIA

KHOREZM

UZBEKISTAN

Balkh

R. Amu Darya

AFGHANISTAN

Merv

TURKMENISTAN

Mecca

IRAN

Caspian Sea

many villages and well-peopled hamlets lying among meadows and waterlands; indeed it is all a sight most beautiful in this the summer season of the year. On these lands five crops yearly of corn are grown, vines also, and there is much cotton cultivated for the irrigation is abundant. Melon yards here abound with fruit-bearing trees.'

This is an appropriate place from which to start on the trail of Temur, to stop and listen for distant echoes of the world conqueror borne across six centuries on the autumnal zephyrs. Already, there are unexpected hints of continuity bridging the historical divide. A small vineyard suggests that though this is a Muslim country, the pleasures of the grape are still observed here, taking one back to Temur's lavish, bacchanalian feasts.

Here in the alternately serene and savage Qashka Darya valley, next to a brick kern and an amiable peasant boy fretting over pilfered melons, it is possible to imagine Temur's early years. This was the rugged terrain in which he grew up, learning the skills of the steppe without which his dreams of world domination would amount to nothing. A local proverb would have been in his mind from an early age: 'Only a hand that can grasp a sword may hold a sceptre.' Self-advancement in this brutal world was inconceivable without excelling in the martial arts.

Surrounded by the snow-capped Zarafshan mountains, he would have galloped wildly across these winter-frozen steppes, accompanied by his band of ruffian friends, sharpening his skills on horseback, imagining great battle charges, lightning raids on an enemy camp, heroic victories and headlong flight. In this fertile valley and among the broad meadows which eased into the lower reaches of the mountains, he would have learnt how to hunt bears and stags. Half a century later, these skills saved his army from certain starvation during one of his most difficult campaigns against the Golden Horde, travelling across what is today a thick slice of Kazakhstan and the southern belly of Russia.

Toughened by the bone-chilling grip of winter and the skin-cracking heat of summer, the young Temur would have learnt to fight like a man in this valley, over the steppes and among the mountains, skirmishing on increasingly daring night-time missions to steal sheep from unwary herdsmen, gathering around him an entourage of like-minded brigands, steadily developing a reputation for courage and leadership which brought him to the attention of the tribal elders.

The sources are generally quiet on Temur's childhood. We can only imagine the vicissitudes of life on the steppes in the early four-teenth century, a world governed by tribal traditions and family relationships, the unending rhythm of the seasons and a fierce struggle to survive amid the unpredictable flux of constantly shifting alliances. Temur himself did little to illuminate the darkness surrounding his early years, taking care only to exaggerate his humble origins, thereby emphasising the glory of his later achievements. Perhaps, as has been suggested, there were signs that the young Temur was destined to be a leader of men. 'At twelve years of age, I fancied that I perceived in myself all the signs of greatness and wisdom, and whoever came to visit me, I received with great hauteur and dignity,' he is supposed to have said.*

---

* The most controversial of sources relating to Temur's life are the supposedly autobiographical *Mulfuzat* (Memoirs) and *Tuzukat* (Institutes). These date back to their alleged discovery in the early seventeenth century by a scholar called Abu Talib al Husayni, who presented them in Persian translation to the Mughal emperor Shah Jahan in 1637. Both the *Memoirs* and the *Institutes* were generally accepted as legitimate historical documents until the late nineteenth century. Major Charles Stewart, who translated them for the London edition of 1830, claimed 'the noble simplicity of diction' and 'the plain and unadorned egotism' that ran through them proved their authenticity. Subsequent generations of scholars have been less impressed. Why, if these documents came from Temur, did neither of the contemporaneous writers Nizam ad-din Shami and Sharaf ad-din Ali Yazdi make any reference to them? Why was the original manuscript – from which al Husayni's translation was made – never retrieved? Finally, how could such an important chronicle, which

Arabshah provides us with another fascinating, though probably overblown, glimpse of Temur as a young man emerging as an inspirational leader among his contemporaries. Again, the value of the description arises from the hostility of the writer, a man less willing than most to acknowledge Temur's qualities.

> *As a youth he grew up brave, great-hearted, active, strong, urbane, and won the friendship of the Viziers' sons of his own age and entered into company with his contemporaries among the young Amirs to such a degree, that when one night they had gathered in a lonely place and were enjoying familiarity and hilarity among themselves, having removed the curtains of secrecy and spread the carpet for cheerful intercourse, he said to them, 'My grandmother, who was skilled in augury and divination, saw in sleep a vision, which she expounded as foreshadowing to her one among her sons and grandsons who would conquer territories and bring men into subjection and be Lord of the Stars and master of the Kings of the age. And I am that man and now the fit time is at hand and has come near. Pledge yourselves therefore to be my back, arms, flank and hands and never to desert me.'*

Whatever the harbingers of greatness, however tough his childhood, Temur vaulted out of obscurity, and into the official histories, in 1360 with a move which exemplified his flair for timing. It was characteristically astute and audacious. Taking advantage of the chaos into which Mawarannahr had fallen after Amir Qazaghan's assassination in 1358, the Moghul khan invaded from the east with a view to reuniting the fractured Chaghatay ulus under his rule. Haji Beg, chief of the Barlas clan that ruled the Qashka Darya valley where Temur lived, decided

---

Temur purportedly wrote for posterity, have remained a secret for 232 years? Until such doubts can satisfactorily be removed, and the *Memoirs* and *Institutes* definitively authenticated, they are best regarded as specious. It should be noted, however, that the state-controlled academia in Uzbekistan – which since the 1990s has been required to support the official Temur revival – considers both to be beyond reproach.

to flee rather than fight. The youthful Temur accompanied his leader as far as the Oxus, where he asked to be allowed to return home. He himself, with a body of men, would prevent the invading Moghuls from seizing more land, he assured his chief.

To judge by what happened next, it is unlikely he ever had such an intention. Contrary to what he had told Haji Beg, he did not lift a sword against the Moghul invaders. Recognising their superior force, he did something infinitely more pragmatic, offering his services to the Moghul khan instead. It was a supremely audacious *volte-face*, but his offer was accepted. Henceforth, he would be the Moghul khan's vassal ruler. At the age of twenty-four, Temur had successfully claimed leadership of the entire Barlas tribe.

To capitalise on his newfound position, he contracted an alliance with Amir Husayn, the grandson of Qazaghan who had emerged as regional strongman and aristocratic ruler of Balkh, northern Afghanistan. Husayn was leader of the Qara'unas tribe. Secretly the two men were pledged to rid Mawarannahr of the Moghuls. Their relationship was cemented with the marriage of Temur to Husayn's sister, Aljai Turkhan-agha. In any event, Temur's submission to the Moghul khan did not last long, for after a bloody purge of local leaders the khan appointed his son Ilyas Khoja governor of Mawarannahr. Temur was not content to be second in command (perhaps Husayn never understood this important distinction). His response was immediate. He and Husayn turned outlaw and went underground.

For the next few years the two partners became highwaymen, bandits and mercenaries, roaming across high Asia with greedy intent. Sometimes they were fortunate and the plunder was rich. More often than not, life was difficult as they found themselves constantly on the move to avoid detection by the vengeful Moghul khan. At one time, said the chronicles, Temur's entire entourage was reduced to his wife and one follower. He reached his nadir in 1362, when he and his wife were imprisoned for two months in a vermin-infested cowshed. These were ignoble beginnings for the man who one day would hold sway from Moscow to the Mediterranean, from Delhi to Damascus.

At some point during this period, probably in 1363, Temur received the injury which left him lame in both right limbs, an affliction which gave rise among his enemies to the scornful nickname Temur the Lame. Most likely he was injured while serving as a mercenary in the pay of the khan of Sistan in Khorasan, in the midst of what is today known as the Dasht-i-Margo (Desert of Death) in south-west Afghanistan. Differing explanations abound. Arabshah, generally the most malicious of the sources, says Temur was a sheep-stealer who stole one sheep too many. Spying the thief prowling about his flock, a particularly watchful shepherd smashed his shoulder with a well-directed arrow, loosing off another into Temur's hip for good measure. 'So mutilation was added to his poverty and a blemish to his wickedness and fury.'

Clavijo, whom we have less reason to doubt as an impartial witness, records how Temur was caught in an ambush:

> *At this time Timur had with him a following of some five hundred horsemen only; seeing which the men of Sistan came together in force to fight him, and one night that he was engaged carrying off a flock of sheep they all fell on him suddenly and slew a great number of his men. Him too they knocked off his horse, wounding him in the right leg, of which wound he has remained lame all his life (whence his name of Temur the Lame); further he received a wound in his right hand, so that he has lost the little finger and the next finger to it.**

---

* On 22 June 1941, Temur's tomb was opened by the Soviet archaeologist Professor Mikhail Gerasimov, who confirmed the injuries to both right limbs. Those who believe in spirits of the dead exercising power beyond the grave made much of the exhumation. Uzbeks had argued vehemently against it, predicting catastrophe if the emperor's tomb was disturbed. Hours after Gerasimov prised it open, the world learnt of Hitler's invasion

He was left for dead, the Spaniard recounted, but managed to crawl to the safety of some welcoming nomads.

Tales grew of his brilliantly inventive tactics in battle during this time, as he struggled both for personal glory and an end to the Moghul occupation of Mawarannahr. Yazdi's *Zafarnama* (Book of Victory), whose honeyed paean is the perfect counterbalance to Arabshah's bitter polemic, repeatedly stresses Temur's military acumen.* In one encounter with his enemy, the Persian wrote, Temur had his soldiers light hundreds of campfires on the hills around the far larger forces of his enemy to convince them they were surrounded. When his adversaries fled, he ordered his men to fasten leafy branches to the side of their saddles to stir up clouds of dust as they gave chase, thereby giving the impression of a huge army on the move. The ruse worked superbly. The Moghuls fled, Mawarannahr was liberated and Shakhrisabz was his. 'Thus fortune, which was always favourable to Temur, caused him to triumph over an army by fire, and to conquer a city by dust.'

&

To this day, the jewel of Shakhrisabz, the monument whose size and beauty so startled Clavijo in 1404, is the Ak Sarai or White Palace. It was, Yazdi reported, 'built so exquisitely fine and beautiful, that no other could compare with it'. Nowhere else is Temur's comment,

---

of Russia. Shortly after Temur's skeleton and that of Ulugh Beg, his grandson, were reinterred with full Muslim burial rites in 1942, the Germans surrendered at Stalingrad.

* The measured voice of Gibbon put the two writers admirably into perspective. On Sharaf ad-din Ali Yazdi: 'His geography and chronology are wonderfully accurate; and he may be trusted for public facts, though he servilely praises the virtue and fortune of the hero.' On Ibn Arabshah: 'This Syrian author is ever a malicious, and often an ignorant enemy: the very titles of his chapters are injurious; as how the wicked, as how the impious, as how the viper etc.'

'Let he who doubts our power look upon our buildings,' so emphatically confirmed. With twin entrance towers rising two hundred feet from the ground, flanking a grand portal arch 130 feet high, this was his greatest palace. Masons and thousands of other craftsmen had been toiling on its construction for twenty years by the time Clavijo arrived, and the building continued daily.

From the fabulous entrance several archways, encased in brickwork and blue patterned tiles, gave onto a series of small waiting chambers for those granted an audience with Temur. Beyond these galleries another gateway led to a courtyard a hundred yards wide, bordered by stately two-tiered arcades and paved with white marble flagstones, at the centre of which stood an ornate water tank. Through the next archway lay the heart of the palace, the domed reception hall where ambassadors craned their necks to admire the magnificence of the craftsmanship and swallowed nervously before they met the Terror of the World.

'The walls are panelled with gold and blue tiles, and the ceiling is entirely of gold work,' noted the incredulous Clavijo. It is clear from his breathless narrative that the Spanish envoy was not expecting anything like this untold splendour. Nor at this time would any other European, for whom the Orient was a dark, barbaric world. 'From this room we were taken up into the galleries, and in these likewise everywhere the walls were of gilt tiles,' Clavijo continued.

> We saw indeed here so many apartments and separate chambers, all of which were adorned in tile work of blue and gold with many other colours ... Next they showed us the various apartments where Temur was wont to be and to occupy when he came here with his wives; all of which were very sumptuously adorned as to floors and walls and ceilings ... we visited a great banqueting hall which Temur was having built wherein to feast with the princesses, and this was gorgeously adorned, being very spacious, while beyond the same they were laying out a great orchard in which were

planted many and diverse fruit trees, with others to give shade.
These stood round water basins beside which there were laid out
fine lawns of turf. This orchard was of such an extent that a
very great company might conveniently assemble here, and in the
summer heat enjoy the cool air beside that water in the shade of
these trees.

These were the opulent gardens of an emperor maintaining a self-consciously Mongol court in the tradition of Genghis Khan. Shakhris-abz, the Green City, was entering its golden age. In 1379, said Yazdi, 'The emperor, charmed with the beauties of this city, the purity of the air in its plains, the deliciousness of its gardens, and the goodness of the waters, made it his ordinary residence in summer and declared it the second seat of his empire.'

Ak Sarai palace, more than any other built by Temur, was designed to impress, to demonstrate, in the words of the Kufic inscription on the eastern tower, that 'the Sultan is the shadow of Allah [on earth]'. Legend describes how Temur, infuriated by the curtailed inscription 'the Sultan is a shadow' on the western tower, flung the craftsman responsible from the top of the palace. Other inscriptions paid elaborate tribute to the Tatar's shining qualities. 'Oh Benefactor of the People, long may you rule like Sulayman. May you be like Nuh in longevity! May this palace bring felicity [to its tenant]. The Heavens are astonished at its beauty,' read one. 'The Sultan binds his enemies with [the chains of] his good deeds,' thundered another. 'Whosoever turns to him gains satisfaction. The fame of his good deeds, like a sweet odour, is ubiquitous. His goodness is evident. His face is clear and his motion agreeable.' How tiny visitors would have felt as they passed through the portal. What a way to put one's visitors in their place, to make them aware, if any doubts remained, that they were in the company of one of the greatest leaders on earth.

The portal towers one sees today have been trimmed down to 120 feet by a combination of war, greed and the passage of time. Yet, even at less than 60 per cent of their original height, they rise majestically, dominating their immediate surroundings in an architectural creation that marries strength with finesse, elegance with simplicity. Towards the top of the towers, above the turquoise and navy-blue Kufic inscriptions of 'Allah' and 'Mohammed' – which to the untrained eye appear only as pretty geometric patterns – the devastating curve of the arch begins. No sooner has it begun its sweep across the heavens than it is instantly cut off by a chasm of sky. Each tower stands in dramatic isolation.

The scale is overwhelming. But what must it have looked like in its full fantastically decadent glory, when the gold-encrusted roof reached to the stars, when Temur's various wives – Clavijo counted eight during his stay – sashayed through the banqueting hall in their rustling silk dresses to take their places reclining among sumptuous cushions and brocades in a garden of pristine lawns and fruit trees, amid the streams and fountains? Here among the luxurious tents and awnings, lined with silk in summer and fur in winter, illuminated at night by the soft flicker of lamps, the song of their voices would have floated up towards the stars.

The restorers have been at work here, and new tiles have replaced those which have not survived, but the essentially ruined state of the palace has been maintained. Temur's most lavish monument is now little more than two foreshortened towers, sunk in the earth like the tusks of a giant beast brought to ground. But it is this very ruination that adds to the grandeur of the impression, a reminder that the original building was of a size and splendour beyond our imagination. Or, as an unusually flummoxed Clavijo put it, as workmen milled around him, still busy after all those years working on the palace, 'such indeed was the richness and beauty of the adornment displayed in all these palaces that it would be impossible for us to describe'.

It is still possible, sweating and panting in the streaming heat, to climb to the top for a vantage point over Shakhrisabz. (How much harder it would have been in Temur's time, when the towers stood at their full height.) Farther afield to the south, the monumental blue dome of the Kok Gumbaz Mosque, built by Temur's grandson Ulugh Beg in 1435–36, interrupts the leafy skyline. Another, smaller blue dome, a junior member of the family, sits next to it. Corrugated-iron roofs, pockets of blinding light, sizzle in the sun. Birds wheel and soar overhead on the thermals.

Directly in front of the Ak Sarai palace, halfway down Victory Park, stands a statue of Temur. He stares into time with a far-off gaze, a symbol of strength and authority, protector of Shakhrisabz. He wears a simple crown. A large belt with a circular embossed buckle is fastened across a calf-length tunic trimmed with paisley patterns. A curved sword is fastened to his left side. A flowing gown hangs from his shoulders. The solid boots emphasise the sense of permanence and power.

Nowadays, dwarfed by the statue and monumental plinth, regularly-spaced processions of bridal parties make their way towards it, laying flowers at Temur's feet and having themselves photographed beneath the Father of the State. The end of each ceremony is marked by the popping of a bottle of Uzbek champagne. No sooner does one party depart than another arrives. It is a pleasant picture: young couples standing respectfully in front of the giant figure of Temur, framed by the ruined towers of his palace in the background. The women seem joyful, however nervous their smiles. But the men without fail look deadly serious, scowling into the cameras as though they would rather be somewhere else.

Late on a sun-spattered October afternoon, several hundred yards away from Temur along the sprawling Ipak Yuli street which cleaves Shakhrisabz in two, a throng of elderly men adjourn to a local *chai-khana* (tea-house), where they sit languidly on cushions on a raised *topchan* (wooden platform), away from their wives and families. All wear the traditional *chapan* gown, some striped in bright purples and indigos, others black and faded. Some wear them as capes, with the distinctive long sleeves hanging down empty almost to their knees. Others have rolled up the sleeves. White, grey or black turbans or the more elaborate embroidered *doppes* perch on their heads like decorative nests. Most have beards, long manes of silver that they stroke from time to time, as unhurried as the passing of the seasons. Clustered together around glasses of *kok chai* (green tea), these men in their ancient costumes are remnants from another era, guardians of history, surrounded on all sides by a younger generation – clad in shell-suits, baseball caps and trainers – which has no time for the sartorial traditions of old.

The tea-house is a fitting place for the elders to make their stand, for this is where the past – and the trail of Temur – begins in Shakhrisabz. Ipak Yuli street is a historical feast which begins with the delicate appetiser of the fourteenth-century Malik Azhdar Khanaqah, originally a refuge for wandering Sufi dervishes, later one of the town's Friday mosques, and in Soviet times a simple museum. The procession of dishes continues with the fifteenth-century baths nearby, now under restoration. Next comes the Koba Madrassah (religious college), formerly a seat of learning teeming with rows of boys learning the Koran. Sometime in the last few years it careered into capitalism and evolved into a courtyard crammed with market stalls selling fake designer jeans, cheap shoes and trainers. Farther down the principal street, thrusting into the skyline with the arrogance of beauty, is the Dorut Tilovat, Seat of Respect and Consideration, whose centrepiece is the most extravagant dish of all, the Kok Gumbaz Mosque visible from the Ak Sarai palace, built by Ulugh Beg, Temur's grandson, the astronomer king.

This was the first place to which Clavijo was taken on his arrival in Shakhrisabz, when the mosque was still unfinished. 'Here daily by the special order of Temur the meat of twenty sheep is cooked and distributed in alms, this being done in memory of his father and of his son who lie here in those chapels,' he noted. Plied with vast quantities of meat and fruit, the Spaniard heard how Temur's cherished son Jahangir had been buried there, together with the emperor's father Taraghay. Temur himself was going to be laid to rest beneath this dome, Clavijo was told.

The restorers have been at work here too, and the portal is ablaze with glimmering blue tiles. Local legend says Temur's father and his spiritual Sufi adviser Shaykh Shams ad-din Kulya are buried beneath ancient onyx carvings in one of the surviving mausolea from the Barlas funeral grounds. Nearby is a small domed chamber which houses four tombstones belonging to Ulugh Beg's kinsmen. A hollow has been worn into the Kok Tash (blue stone) from centuries of parents pouring water onto it for sick children or relatives to drink. The stone contains medicinal salts.

After this tombstone calm, the main market is an explosion of activity. Farmers have come to town with their wives and children to sell their produce. They squat in the dust over wooden crates and metal buckets crammed with tomatoes, onions and apples. Peasant women in cheap patterned dresses and bright headscarves dust off their produce and arrange it in neat piles. Shaven-headed boys stand by makeshift trolleys, ready to cart off loads for anyone who requires a porter. Large awnings have been erected to shade mountains of melons the size of cannonballs. This, at least, has not changed, for Clavijo remarked on exactly the same phenomenon. 'The water melons there are as large as a horse's head ... the very best and biggest that may be found in the whole world,' he wrote. Some are being loaded onto the back of a lorry, thrown carefully by a man on the ground to a boy in the vehicle. Wrinkled women hold forth behind a stone counter selling soft cheese, scooping their products into pretty pyramids and vying with each other to attract customers.

Long counters are given over to sweets, nuts and piles of pasta, biscuits and exotic spices. Sacks of *semechka* sunflower seeds lie open, delved into at will by passing strangers. Men, women and children pick up handfuls, expertly bite down the middle of the seed, spit out the outer covering and chew the tiny kernels as though they are the choicest delicacies rather than the poor man's snack. Fruit and vegetables lie on the ground and on counters, wherever there is space. Here, as in Temur's time, there are peaches, pears and pomegranates, plums, apricots, apples, grapes and figs, potatoes, peppers and onions. Some stalls specialise in plastic bags of pre-cut carrots for use in *plov*, an oily dish of rice, meat and vegetables. Butchers with huge cleavers chop away at cuts of meat that would be consigned to the rubbish bin in wealthier countries. Carcasses hang from hooks, dripping pools of blood into the dust. It is a place of perpetual motion. People come and go on foot, on bicycles, on trolleys, carts, donkeys and horses. Those who wish to escape the sun have adjourned to a small eatery, whose front is covered several layers deep in bicycles. Under the gallery men chew on *shashlik* kebabs or plates of *manty*, mutton and onion dumplings topped with *smetana* sour cream. Some of them congregate like soldiers around a cauldron of *plov*, steaming away on a fire.

Life is hard in Shakhrisabz, as it is throughout Uzbekistan. The lustre that the town enjoyed in Temur's time, six centuries ago, has virtually disappeared. The once luminous jewel of an ever-expanding empire has become a crumbling ruin in a forgotten former Soviet backwater mired in corruption and poverty. The glory of Shakhrisabz has long gone. Only the ruins, and the gleaming statue of Temur, suggest it ever existed.

In 1365, on the banks of the Amu Darya, Temur stood a very long way indeed from glory. His ally Amir Husayn had just deserted him on the battlefield in his first serious reversal. A growing sense of resentment and rivalry was starting to emerge between the two men. It came to life at the fateful battle of the Mire.

Ilyas Khoja, the former governor of Mawarannahr, had invaded again. His army was close to Tashkent when he encountered the forces of Temur and Husayn. Battle was joined as the heavens opened. Amidst thunder and lightning the rain poured down, turning the ground into an illuminated quagmire which swamped man and beast alike. Pressing hard against the Moghuls, Temur seized the upper hand and signalled for Husayn, nominally his commander, to bring forward his men and finish off the enemy. Yet Husayn held back. The Moghul forces rushed to take advantage of this fatal mistake and swarmed through, cutting men down on all sides. Ten thousand were killed. Temur and Husayn fled south across the Amu Darya. It was an ignominious ending.

It was also instructive. For a man like Temur with ambitions far beyond this small theatre of war, it sowed the seeds of doubt into his alliance with Husayn. How reliable was a man who refused to fight alongside his partner in battle when the fighting was at its most critical? In Temur's mind, he had been betrayed. It is unlikely, in any case, that either Temur or Husayn considered this a permanent alliance. That, after all, was the way of the steppes. Alliances were regularly made and just as promptly broken. In the short term, however, the partnership continued. A year after the battle of the Mire, Temur and Husayn celebrated success with their brutal overthrow of the independent Sarbadar leadership of Samarkand and installed themselves as the new rulers.* Officially, as before, Husayn, the nomad aristocrat, grandson of Amir Qazaghan, was the senior man.

---

* The Sarbadars had established an independent state in Khorasan in the 1330s. They took their name from the word for a gibbet or 'gallows-bird'. Rather than accept the rule of the hated Mongols in Mawarannahr, they were prepared to go to the gallows resisting them. One of their most

But already Temur was winning a personal following. His amirs and soldiers, encouraged by his generosity in distributing plundered treasures, loved him. Husayn, by contrast, was mean-minded. To recoup the heavy losses he had incurred in the ill-fated battle of the Mire, he raised a punitive head tax on Temur's amirs and followers. It was so exorbitant, said the chronicles, that it was completely beyond their means. Temur was reduced to offering his horses, and went so far as to give Husayn the gold and silver necklaces, earrings and bracelets belonging to his wife Aljai, Husayn's sister. Husayn recognised the family jewels as he tallied up the levies, but was only too happy to pocket them. His avarice did not escape notice. Temur's star, however, was on the rise.

The alliance between the two aspiring warlords had been sealed with the marriage of Temur to Aljai. Her death at this time, which represented the final severance of family ties, now looked like a harbinger of destiny. From 1366 to 1370, the two men duly opted in and out of temporary alliances, now uniting against Moghul invaders, now resolved each to exterminate the other. With every year that passed one thing became increasingly clear: the vast lands of Mawarannahr were not big enough to encompass their rival ambitions.

Temur used these years profitably. He consolidated his popularity with his tribesmen and cast a shrewd eye over those other sections of society whose support he would need if he were to govern alone: the Muslim clergy; the nomad aristocracy of the steppe; merchants; agricultural workers; the settled populations of towns and villages, hurt by endless conflict. Husayn, on the other hand, progressively alienated his subjects with onerous and capricious taxes. His fateful decision to rebuild and fortify the citadel of Balkh was a provocative

---

notable victories came in Samarkand, where they successfully overcame the siege of Ilyas Khoja's forces. Hovering like vultures around the weakened city, Temur and Husayn moved quickly to exploit this favourable development and seized power.

gesture to the nomad aristocracy who opposed settlement and saw in its broad walls and defences the rise of Husayn's power and the decline of their own.

Temur continued to win more and more followers to his cause. The Moghuls had been successfully repelled. Now he set his sights on removing the last obstacle to supreme power in southern Mawarannahr.

Eventually, the time arrived. At the head of his forces, Temur rode south in 1370, crossing the Amu Darya at Termez (with covetous eyes he would march this way again in 1398, taking his armies across the roof of the world to war with India). Here he met Imam Sayid Baraka of Andkhoi, 'one of the most illustrious lords of the house of the prophet', according to Yazdi, a Muslim sage from Mecca or Medina who was in search of equally illustrious patronage. Having earlier been rebuffed by Husayn, Baraka turned instead to Temur, who proved more receptive to the older man's advances. The white-bearded cleric could not have harmed his chances by foretelling a magnificent future for Temur and handing him a standard and a kettle-drum, traditional emblems of royalty. 'This great Sharif resolved to spend all his days with a prince whose greatness he had foretold,' wrote Yazdi, 'and Temur ordered that after his death they should be both laid in the same tomb, and that his face should be turned sideways, that at the day of judgement, when every one should lift up their hands to heaven to implore assistance of some intercessor, he might lay hold on the robe of this child of the prophet Mahomet.' (On his death, Temur was laid to rest in a tomb at the feet of his spiritual guide, a position of unprecedented modesty for the mightiest of monarchs.*)

---

* Though his tomb was later removed to the Gur Amir mausoleum of Samarkand, where he was interred next to Temur, a shrine to Imam Sayid Baraka remains to this day in Andkhoi, a small town in the remote north-west corner of Afghanistan, several miles from the border with Turkmenistan. A humble building with a whitewashed façade and brown

Assured of Allah's protection, Temur pressed on south, where his army surrounded Husayn's capital of Balkh. Fighting raged between the followers of the two protagonists. Eventually, the city walls were forced and Temur's marauding troops cut loose. Isolated inside his citadel, Husayn watched his enemy advance until at last he appreciated the imminence of his own ruin. Throwing himself on Temur's mercy, he promised to leave Mawarannahr for the *haj* (pilgrimage) to Mecca if his former brother in arms spared his life. But it was too late for contrition.

Husayn's death, when it came, bordered on the farcical. Doubting Temur's promises of quarter, he first hid inside a minaret until he was discovered by a soldier who had climbed the tower in an effort to find his lost horse. The officer encountered a trembling Husayn, who tried to bribe him with pearls. The soldier reported his discovery but Husayn escaped again, this time hiding in a hut. Happened upon by watchful soldiers once more, he was finally handed over to his arch-rival. Pontius Pilate-like, Temur refused to condone his killing – he had given his word that Husayn's life be spared – but did nothing to stop Kay-Khusrau, one of his chiefs who had a blood feud with the ruler of Balkh, from carrying out the deed.

The reckoning had come. Temur was triumphant. His greatest rival had been eliminated. Balkh was robbed of its treasures and razed to the ground, prefiguring the rapine, slaughter and destruction that awaited the rest of Asia.

Not least among Temur's victory spoils was Husayn's widow, Saray Mulk-khanum. Daughter of Qazan, the last Chaghatay khan of Mawarannahr, she was also a princess of the Genghis line. It was customary for a victorious leader to help himself to the harem of his defeated opponent. Temur wasted little time in availing himself of

---

mudbrick domes, it is one of the few historical monuments to have escaped the destruction caused by more than two decades of war.

the privilege. Taking Saray Mulk-khanum as his wife bolstered his legitimacy (the three other wives he inherited were a pleasant bonus). Henceforth, and for the rest of his life, he styled himself Temur Gurgan – son-in-law – of the Great Khan, on the coins which bore his name, in the Friday prayers and in all ceremonial functions.

Temur was as avid a collector of wives as he was of treasures and trophies from his many campaigns. Although little is known about how many he had, and when he married them, from time to time they surface in the chronicles and then just as abruptly sink back into the depths of obscurity. We know that Saray Mulk-khanum was his chief wife, the Great Queen, a position she owed to her distinguished blood. Others followed. In 1375 he married Dilshad-agha, daughter of the Moghul amir Qamar ad-din, only to see her die prematurely eight years later. In 1378 he married the twelve-year-old Tuman-agha, daughter of a Chaghatay noble. Temur's voracious appetite for wives and concubines did not lessen noticeably during his lifetime. In 1397, towards the end of his life, he married Tukal-khanum, daughter of the Moghul khan Khizr Khoja, who became the Lesser Queen. By this time, according to the hostile Arabshah, the ageing emperor 'was wont to deflower virgins'. In terms of numbers of wives, Clavijo's account is probably the most accurate. He counted eight in 1404, including Jawhar-agha, the youthful Queen of Hearts whom Temur had just married well into his seventieth year. An unknown number of others had predeceased him.

In the wake of Husayn's defeat and execution, and in deference to the traditions of Genghis, by which only a man of royal blood could aspire to supreme command, Temur installed a puppet Chaghatay khan, Suyurghatmish, as nominal ruler. This was no more than a formality. All knew that power lay with Temur alone. 'Under his sway were ruler and subject alike,' Arabshah recorded, 'and the Khan was in his bondage, like a centipede in mud, and he was like the Khalifs at this time in the regard of the Sultans.'

The realities of the power-sharing arrangement were underlined in a dramatic ceremony of enthronement. With the blessing of the *qurultay* of Balkh, Temur crowned himself imperial ruler of Chaghatay on 9 April 1370.* Majestic in his new crown of gold, surrounded

---

* In selecting Balkh as the place of his enthronement, Temur was emphatically demonstrating his new supremacy in a famous seat of power which had attracted both Alexander the Great and Genghis before him. Balkh, known by eighth- and ninth-century Arabs as the Mother of Cities, is a place of great antiquity. Zoroaster was preaching fire-worship here sometime around 600 BC. Its position north of the Hindu Kush mountains and south of the Amu Darya made it a strategically important toehold in Afghanistan, and from 329 to 327 BC it served as Alexander's military base. In the first centuries after Christ, when Buddhism was thriving in Afghanistan under the Kushan dynasty, numerous pilgrims flocked to its many temples. By the seventh century its architectural renown was such that the Chinese traveller Xuan Zang could claim it boasted three of the most outstanding monuments in the world. The invasion of the Arabs, bringing Islam in their wake, lent further lustre to Balkh as mosques and madrassahs sprang up in abundance. By the ninth century there were forty Friday mosques within the city walls and Islamic culture was flourishing. Balkh also became an important centre of Persian poetry. Many consider Maulana Jalaluddin Balkhi, the thirteenth-century mystic known to Western readers as Rumi, to be the greatest Sufi poet ever.

> *A moment of happiness,*
> *you and I sitting on the verandah,*
> *apparently two, but one in soul, you and I.*
> *We feel the flowing water of life here,*
> *you and I, with the garden's beauty*
> *and the birds singing.*
> *The stars will be watching us,*
> *and we will show them*
> *what it is to be a thin crescent moon.*
> *You and I unselfed, will be together,*
> *indifferent to idle speculation, you and I.*
> *The parrots of heaven will be cracking sugar*
> *as we laugh together, you and I.*
> *In one form upon this earth,*
> *and in another form in a timeless sweet land.*

It was, predictably, the dark storm of Genghis Khan that swept away forever these days of glory and romantic poetry. In 1220, at the head of

by royal princes, his lords and amirs, together with the puppet khan, the new monarch sat solemnly as one by one his subjects humbly advanced, then threw themselves on the ground in front of him before rising to sprinkle precious jewels over his head, according to tradition. Thus began the litany of names he enjoyed until his death. At the age of thirty-four he was the Lord of the Fortunate Conjunction, Emperor of the Age, Conqueror of the World.

His greatness, said Yazdi, was written in the stars:

> When God designs a thing, he disposes the causes, that whatever he hath resolved on may come to pass: thus he destined the empire of Asia to Temur and his posterity because he foresaw the mildness of his government, which would be the means of making his people happy . . . And as sovereignty, according to Mahomet, is the shadow of God, who is one, it cannot be divided, no more than there could have been two moons in the same heaven; so, to fulfil this truth,

---

ten thousand soldiers, the Mongol warlord rode into Balkh and ravaged it completely. In 1333, more than a century later, Ibn Battutah found Balkh 'an utter ruin and uninhabited, but anyone seeing it would think it inhabited on account of the solidity of its construction. The accursed Tinkiz destroyed this city and demolished about a third of its mosques on account of a treasure which he was told lay under one of its columns. He pulled down a third of them and found nothing and left the rest as it was.' By the eighteenth century, Balkh had recovered sufficiently to become the seat of the governors-general of Afghan Turkestan. In 1866, however, after catastrophic outbreaks of cholera and malaria, the city was abandoned in favour of nearby Mazar-i-Sharif to the east.

Today it is a quiet backwater, but the echoes of Temur, fainter with each passing century, still remain. The blue-ribbed dome which sits atop the shrine of the fifteenth-century theologian Khwaja Abu Parsa, with its corkscrew pillars and stalactite corbels, recalls the imposing magnificence of late Temurid architecture. The badly damaged monument looks down on the tomb of Rabia Balkhi, the first woman of her time to write poetry in Persian. She died when her brother slashed her wrists, furious to discover she had been sleeping with a slave lover. Her last poem, it is said, was written in her own blood as she lay dying. Since 1964, when her tomb was discovered, young lovers, especially girls, have come to pray at her tomb for guidance in their own tangled affairs of the heart.

God destroys those who oppose him whom providence would fix upon the throne.

Had they been consulted, the countless millions who lost their lives over the course of the next four decades – buried alive, cemented into walls, massacred on the battlefield, sliced in two at the waist, trampled to death by horses, beheaded, hanged – would surely have differed on the subject of the emperor's mildness. But they were beneath notice. No one, be he innocent civilian or the most fearsome adversary, was allowed to stand in the way of his destiny. The world would tremble soon enough. Temur's rampage was only just beginning.

2

Marlowe's 'Scourge of God'

1370–1379

'Our quivering lances shaking in the air
And bullets like Jove's dreadful thunderbolts
Enrolled in flames and fiery smouldering mists
Shall threat the gods more than Cyclopian wars;
And with our sun-bright armour, as we march,
We'll chase the stars from heaven and dim their eyes
That stand and muse at our admired arms.'

CHRISTOPHER MARLOWE,
Tamburlaine the Great

While a ten-year-old Temur was learning the martial skills that would make him such an accomplished warrior, three thousand miles to the west one man bestrode the battlefields of Europe. For any child with a taste for romantic knights and heroic endeavours, his is a stirring story, his royal tomb an arresting sight.

Edward the Black Prince lies in Canterbury Cathedral close to the top of Pilgrims' Steps, their stones worn smooth by centuries of feet and bended knees. Boys and girls cling on to the protective bars which surround him, peering through for a better look at the recumbent figure of the prince in full armour. As a schoolboy in Canterbury, I used to do the same, hurrying through the echoing nave before assembly to snatch a few minutes in front of his tomb. How could this slim, neat little man have been such a champion of war six centuries earlier, I wondered, picturing the charge of knights on horseback, the volleys of arrows scything through the sky and the flashing sword-strokes that could hack a man to pieces. His head rests on a fabulous helmet, surmounted by a roaring lion, his hands clasped together on his chest in prayer, sword by his side. He gazes into the heavens, past his knightly achievements, his gauntlets and scabbard, the surcoat and shield emblazoned with the golden lions and fleurs de lys of England.

The Black Prince is perhaps the most glamorous symbol of the European age of chivalry. His career dazzled as brightly as the bejewelled swords which won him such fame and glory in France. In 1346, at the age of sixteen, he led the right wing of his father King Edward III's army to a brilliant victory at the battle of Crécy, where he won his spurs in style. A decade later, he routed the French again at Poitiers, capturing King John II and taking him back to England as his prisoner. He won England new lands in France as prince of Aquitaine, returned Pedro the Cruel, the deposed King of Castile, to his throne, and suppressed rebellions with brutal efficiency. Wherever he went his exploits resonated with the martial thunder of the Middle Ages.

However impressive it may be to schoolboys with their colouring books, castle sets and computer games, the warfare of the fourteenth century spelt only misery and poverty for most of Europe. Historians have long referred to this period as 'the calamitous century', in which famine, war and disease cut swathes through the population. The evangelising glories of the Crusades were already a memory. Christendom had lost its possessions in the Holy Land by the close of the thirteenth century and Outremer, the cherished land overseas, had ceased to exist.

Life was a trial for poor peasants and rich rulers alike, as hereditary monarchies struggled to maintain their royal lines and fend off rival dynasties. For most of the century, England and France, the two great powers of the continent, were locked in conflict, consumed by the Hundred Years' War which emptied their coffers and depleted their chivalry. Both were perilously divided into feuding fiefdoms, their kings undermined by the machinations of the nobles. In France the struggle for the disputed throne allowed the dukes of Orléans, Bourbon, Brittany and Anjou, together with the counts of Foix and Armagnac, to wield power like princely states. The duchy of Burgundy grew steadily from a royal province into a dynasty and a prosperous empire with its own ambitions. For much of this period the French kings were toothless tigers, harried on all sides by disloyal nobles, wandering mercenaries and revolting peasants.

Across the Channel, England faced her own difficulties. Edward III's illustrious fifty-year reign, an exercise in military adventurism and repudiation of papal authority, came to an end with his death in 1377, a year after his son and heir the Black Prince had died. The premature demise of the knight who had twice humiliated the French meant that the throne passed to the king's nine-year-old grandson, Richard II, who was poorly placed to continue Edward's expansionist forays. War had impoverished the country, which was in no mood to countenance another huge demand on its resources. The deeply unpopular poll tax led to the Peasants' Revolt of 1381. The century ended inauspiciously with the youthful king's removal from the throne in 1399 and his murder a year later. It was all the usurper Henry IV could do to keep his kingdom together, beset by the rebellions of the Scots and the Welsh, supported, as ever, by the French.

Nor was the fighting restricted to these northern kingdoms. Europe was awash with petty wars, in thrall to the vogue for military and dynastic adventure. In the quieter periods between the major campaigns of the Hundred Years' War, 'free companies' or bands of mercenaries roamed the continent, torching towns and extorting the countryside, spreading misery and destruction wherever they rode. 'Without war you cannot live and do not know how to,' Sir John Chandos, the Black Prince's lieutenant, reprimanded a group of their captains. Southern France, Italy and Germany teemed with these perennial soldiers who refused to go home. Italy herself was riven by conflict, spurred on by the famous *condottieri*, soldiers of fortune like Sir John Hawkwood, captain-general of Florence, and, later, Francesco Sforza, ruler of Milan. The protracted hostilities between Guelphs and Ghibellines degenerated into wider, equally ruinous, factionalism. Ruled by despots, the great cities scrambled to enlarge their dominions. Naples and Florence tore themselves apart, the trading city of Genoa sank into decline. To add to these economic woes, the once mighty banks of Bardi and Peruzzi collapsed in the 1340s, bankrupted by the defaulting English king, Edward III.

The situation was hardly better in Spain and Portugal where, despite the reconquest of most of Muslim al-Andalus the previous century, disunity and disorder ruled. Aragon was prey to repeated civil wars in which the nobles competed for the crown while, to the west, the death of Alfonso XI of Castile in 1349 – carried off by the plague – triggered another European fight for the succession, this time between Pedro II and his bastard brother Henry, Count of Trastamara. Two more decades of war followed.

And then, of course, there were the horrors of the Black Death, which spread west along the trade routes from Asia and coursed through Europe like poison. By 1347 it had reached Constantinople, Rhodes, Cyprus and Sicily, moving onwards into Venice, Genoa and Marseilles. A year later it infected Tuscany, central Italy and England. By mid-century it was ravaging Scandinavia, penetrating as far north as Iceland and Greenland. One-third of the population of Europe was wiped out by a disease so terrifyingly ghastly many felt it was a heaven-sent punishment for the sins of the world.

'I do not know where to begin describing its relentless cruelty; almost everyone who witnessed it seemed stupefied by grief,' wrote the Sienese chronicler Agnolo di Tura del Grasso, who buried five of his children with his own hands. 'They died almost immediately; they would swell up under the armpits and in the groin and drop dead while talking. Fathers abandoned their children, wives left their husbands, brothers forsook each other.' Dogs dragged hastily-buried corpses into the streets and gorged on them before collapsing themselves. 'Nobody wept for the dead, since each was awaiting death; and so many died that everyone thought that the end of the world had come.' The Black Death killed an estimated twenty-five million people, precipitating an agricultural crisis due to the severe shortage of labour to farm the land. The accompanying breakdown of law and order only added to the havoc left in its wake.

While war, plague and famine sapped Europe internally, external threats were also beginning to mount. Christendom's eastern frontier was under pressure as the weakening Byzantine empire faced attack from the Ottomans. One by one it started to lose its possessions, first in Asia Minor with the fall of Brusa and Nicaea, later and more ominously with Adrianople, Gallipoli and Thessalonica. In 1389, a Christian army under the Serbian king Lazarus was crushed at Kosovo by a Turkish army led by Sultan Murad I. By 1394, Constantinople itself was under siege. Two years later, Christendom roused itself from its sickbed for a final assault on the Muslim foe and put its last Crusader army into the field at Nicopolis, on the banks of the Danube. It was cut to pieces. Europe shuddered to consider what the resurgent infidel planned next. Islam was on the march.

If matters on the European mainland were unpromising, hopes of heavenly salvation seemed equally fraught. Though the Church began the fourteenth century confidently, with Pope Boniface VIII proclaiming in his *Unam Sanctam* bull of 1302 that 'the spiritual power excels in dignity and nobility any form whatsoever of earthly power', it steadily lost much of its authority during this period. Besieged by the dangers of warring Italy, the papacy withdrew shortly afterwards to Avignon on the banks of the Rhône, from where a succession of French popes plotted wars in the papal states and pacification in Europe, the necessary prelude to taking up the fight against the Muslims of the East. They were remembered, and resented, more for the staggering size and ostentation of the papal palace, and the punitive taxes which went to pay for it, than for their commitment to the defence of the faith or the spiritual nourishment of their flock. Then, in 1378, disaster struck as the Church split over the election of the irascible Italian Pope Urban VI. Another Frenchman, Clement VII, was elected to replace him, precipitating the Great Schism. For the next four decades, one pope presided in Rome while another, the anti-pope, held sway in Avignon. The prestige of the papacy sunk further.

The Europe of Temur's time, then, in Muslim eyes at least, was little more than a barbarian backwater. Church and state were divided and weak. The age of imperial adventure had expired, not to be revived until the later fifteenth century. Edward the Black Prince might have cut a dashing figure on the battlefields of Europe, but the Islamic world scarcely registered this sorry land of the infidel. The real treasures of conquest were not to be found in what the Koran referred to as the *dar al-harb* (the abode of war), home of the unbelievers. They lay in the East. As Bernard Lewis wrote: 'For the medieval Muslim from Andalusia to Persia, Christian Europe was still an outer darkness of barbarism and unbelief, from which the sunlit world of Islam had little to fear and less to learn.'

⚬⚬

Europeans were no more impressed by the Oriental heathens. Temur's whirlwind conquests went largely unnoticed in the West until, in 1587, a fire-and-brimstone Tamburlaine sprang onto the Elizabethan stage like a thunderbolt from the heavens.

Temur's neglect at the hands of Western historians, which continues to this day, allowed Marlowe's bloodthirsty Tamburlaine to provide the enduring popular image of a magnificent, God-defying Oriental despot, fearless in conquest, unforgiving in triumph, yet simultaneously capable of scaling the poetic heights with his beautiful lover Zenocrate. It is one of history's small ironies that a man who took such care to ensure his place in posterity by having his civil and military record meticulously chronicled should find his posthumous reputation in the hands of an Elizabethan playwright with a taste for the sensational.

Brilliant in battle, unvanquished on the world stage, Temur's efforts to secure the recognition he so richly deserved came to nothing. 'These cares were ineffectual for the preservation of his fame, and these precious memorials in the Mogul or Persian language were concealed from the world or, at least, from the knowledge of Europe,' wrote Edward Gibbon. 'The nations which he vanquished exercised a base and impotent revenge; and ignorance has long repeated the tale of calumny which had disfigured the birth and character, the person, and even the name, of *Tamerlane*. Yet his real merit would be enhanced rather than debased by the elevation of a peasant to the throne of Asia.'

Passed over by historians, Temur has fared little better on the stage. Though Marlowe's play is more than four hundred years old, productions have been remarkable for their extreme rarity. *Tamburlaine the Great* went through the seventeenth, eighteenth and nineteenth centuries without a single recorded performance. One problem is the play's length: it is really two full-length plays, rather than one. Another is the potentially monotonous series of conquests and slaughter, which continue, as they did historically, until Tamburlaine's death. C.S. Lewis famously described the play as 'a hideous moral Spoonerism: Giant the Jack Killer'. Suffice it to say that the plot is not as complicated as it could be. As a result of these and other difficulties, the first professional production of modern times came in London as late as 1951, when Tyrone Guthrie directed Donald Wolfit in the lead role with the Old Vic company. A quarter of a century later, Peter Hall chose the play to open the Olivier Theatre at the National, with Albert Finney in the lead role. Hall judged *Tamburlaine* variously as a 'Boy's Own Paper story', 'an immoral Morality play', 'the first atheist play' and 'the first existential play'. 'One thing I know very strongly about *Tamburlaine* now,' he wrote in 1976. 'It reeks of the theatre as the circus reeks of sawdust and horse shit.' Yet theatre-goers still had to wait until 1993 for the Royal Shakespeare Company's first production of the play, directed by Terry Hands in Stratford. It was worth the wait.

Audiences were captivated by Antony Sher's snarling barbarism in the lead role, an explosive and athletic performance which rejoiced in the tyranny and bounding majesty of what one reviewer called 'the megalomaniac's megalomaniac'. While the sultan Bajazeth and his Turks strut awkwardly across the stage on golden stilts, Tamburlaine swings in Tarzan-like, kicking Bajazeth to the ground. In victory he glorifies in sneering sadism, rubbing his fingers in Bajazeth's sweaty hair, licking them and offering them to Zenocrate to smell. Bathed in blood, he mocks the famished, caged sultan and encourages his henchmen to urinate on scraps of reeking bread with which they taunt him. Then, with a leering grin, he cuts off one of the sultaness's fingers. Marlowe's virgins of Damascus, yet more victims for the 'scourge of God', become flaxen-haired children sweetly proffering posies. If the 1993 production proved anything, it was that with an actor of Sher's stature, together with careful editing – in this case *Tamburlaine* was whittled down to three hours – opulent costumes and imaginative special effects, Marlowe's most sensational play could be big box office. There was another, more enduring, lesson to be taken from Tamburlaine, a critic noted: 'As events in the Middle East and elsewhere continue to show, we ignore him and his descendants at our peril.'

Had Temur lived long enough to see *Tamburlaine the Great*, he might conceivably have been gratified by his dramatic depiction (though he would certainly have objected to the use of his derisive nickname). Marlowe's Tamburlaine is one of the most intensely realised warrior heroes of the stage. Shakespeare's Henry V and Coriolanus seem poorer creatures by comparison.

For Tamburlaine rises beyond the mortal sphere. As the Persian lord Theridamas remarks on first seeing this 'Scythian shepherd' early in Act I:

> *His looks do menace heaven and dare the gods,*
> *His fiery eyes are fixed upon the earth . . .*

Tamburlaine, the audience rapidly discovers, is interested only in omnipotence:

> *I hold the Fates bound fast in iron chains,*
> *And with my hand turn Fortune's wheel about,*
> *And sooner shall the sun fall from his sphere,*
> *Than Tamburlaine be slain or overcome.*

After routing his Arabian and Egyptian enemy at the close of Part I, he explains his victory to the Soldan of Egypt, who is mourning the loss of his throne. The god of war has resigned to Tamburlaine, the defeated Egyptian is told, and will soon make him 'general of the world'. Even Jove suddenly looks 'pale and wan', fearing Tamburlaine is about to dethrone him. Not content with comparing himself favourably to the gods, he throws down the gauntlet to the Prophet Mohammed, burning the Koran and daring him out of the heavens:

> *Now, Mahomet, if thou have any power,*
> *Come down thyself and work a miracle.*
> *Thou art not worthy to be worshipped*
> *That suffers flames of fire to burn the writ*
> *Wherein the sum of thy religion rests.*

For Elizabethan audiences this was shocking stuff, blasphemy in the eyes of the authorities and an affront to properly Christian sensibilities. Gossip was already afoot concerning Marlowe's supposed atheism, heresy and dissolute life, dangerous charges at a time when the authorities were rounding up those suspected of libel, sedition or even 'unsafe' opinions. Contemporary critics rounded on the play as a glorification of impiety. In his prefix to the largely forgotten *Perimedes the Blacksmith* (1588), Robert Greene condemned Marlowe for 'daring God out of heaven with that Atheist Tamburlan'.

On 12 May 1593, the popular playwright Thomas Kyd was arrested and tortured. He wrote a letter, almost certainly under duress, condemning Marlowe's 'monstrous opinions' and his tendencies to 'jest at the divine scriptures, gibe at prayers, and strive in argument to frustrate and confute what hath been spoke or writ by prophets and such holy men'. A shady character called Richard Baines, another informer, wrote of Marlowe's 'damnable judgement of religion and scorn of God's word', including wild allegations that the playwright professed 'That Christ was a bastard and his mother dishonest,' 'That if there be any god or good religion, then it is in the papists,' 'That all Protestants are hypocritical asses' and that Christ and John the Baptist were sodomites. Such testimonies had the desired effect. On 18 May, the Privy Council issued a warrant for Marlowe's arrest. He was stabbed to death in the notorious Deptford tavern brawl less than two weeks later.

Tamburlaine the Great provided plenty of ammunition to Elizabethan critics, as it does to this day. Joseph Hall, Fellow of Emmanuel College, Cambridge, and later Bishop of Exeter and Norwich, accused Marlowe of gross populism and pandering to the rabble – 'He ravishes the gazing Scaffolders' – in *Virgidemiarum* (1597). Ben Jonson joined the chorus of disapproval: in *Discoveries*, posthumously published in 1640, he argued that there was nothing in plays like *Tamburlaine* except 'scenicall strutting, and furious vociferation, to warrant them to the ignorant gapers'. Wonderfully unconcerned by such high-minded criticism, audiences thrilled to what quickly became a phenomenally popular play. To this day, on those rare occasions when it is staged, they still do, alternately shocked and seduced, appalled and entranced, by the brutal machinations of this exotic tyrant.

Whatever the Elizabethan authorities thought about Marlowe's atheism, *Tamburlaine* was otherwise thoroughly in keeping with the zeitgeist of the era. It posed questions about colonisation and king-ship, rebellion and religion, all the vicissitudes of power. This was a time of vigorous English expansion and growing self-confidence, the birth of a military and mercantile nation with dreams of empire and the ambition to project its might across the globe. Marlowe's numerous references to hemispheres, meridian lines and poles, to continents known and unknown, perfectly reflected an age of exploration and commercial endeavour across the seas, personified by Sir Francis Drake, the man who circumnavigated the world in 1577–80 and calmly finished his game of bowls on Plymouth Hoe before routing the Spanish Armada in 1588. Just as Tamburlaine thunders across the world from conquest to conquest, so England, led by her heroic queen, was steadily emerging as a great power on the world stage. In Elizabeth's famous speech to the English troops at Tilbury on the eve of their engagement with the Armada, there are unmistakable shades of *Tamburlaine* (written only a year previously): '. . . [I] think foul scorn that Parma or Spain, or any prince of Europe, should dare to invade the borders of my realm; to which, rather than any dishonour shall grow by me, I myself will take up arms – I myself will be your general, judge, and rewarder of every one of your virtues in the field.'

Little surprise that for all the authorities' disapproval, the play enjoyed such a remarkable success in its own time. It was so well known that in 1629, more than forty years after its first performance, prisoners pulling carts of sewage through London's streets were taunted with one of the celebrated lines from the play – 'Holla, ye pampered jades of Asia,' the very words which Tamburlaine jeers at Bajazeth's two sons, whom he has harnessed to his chariot.

Different eras have naturally judged Marlowe's Tamburlaine – as well as the real-life conqueror – through different prisms. Nineteenth-century military historians, not least the British, tended to lionise the Tatar for his prodigious military skills, and wrote admiringly of his successful campaigns while downplaying his cold-blooded massacres. In the twentieth century, his career was viewed less enthusiastically. John Joseph Saunders wrote in 1971 that 'Till the advent of Hitler, Timur stood forth in history as the supreme example of soulless and unproductive militarism.' In 1996, the historian Leo de Hartog judged Temur a parochial sadist.

Not surprisingly, different cultures have also reached radically different verdicts. Within the *dar al Islam*, the Muslim world, Temur is a household name, usually revered as a great conqueror and propagator of the faith. In Christian Georgia, which he ravaged half a dozen times, he is spoken of with dread and remains the country's greatest anti-hero. In the Soviet empire, he was removed from the history books, the authorities fearful of the nationalism he might inspire among the subject populations of Central Asia. When he was mentioned, it was only as a savage barbarian and despot. In post-Soviet Uzbekistan, as we shall see, Temur has been rehabilitated and championed as the father of a new nation. In the West he languishes in the depths of obscurity.

Likewise in the theatre, the play that could disgust Elizabethan literary critics was equally able to confirm the prejudices of their late-nineteenth-century successors. Arthur Houston, professor of political economy at Trinity College, Dublin, excused the excesses of *Tamburlaine* on the grounds that 'The principal characters are Eastern barbarians, proverbially prone to the extremes of passion, and addicted to the use of hyperbolical expressions. Marlowe in my opinion has been rather under-rated.' Swinburne admired Marlowe's poetic gifts, but George Bernard Shaw considered him 'a fool' who catered to a 'Philistine and ignorant' public. In our own time, Edward Said accused Marlowe's 'Oriental stage' of preparing the ground for Christendom's jaundiced view of Islam as the 'Other'. More than four centuries after it was first brought to stage, *Tamburlaine* remains as capable as ever of generating storms and controversies.

The play can be understood as a paean to empire, an ode to atheism, a celebration of commerce, exploration, social mobility and individualism, a mockery of royalty and hereditary authority, and a defiance of foreign power – for Tamburlaine read Elizabeth, for Bajazeth's Turkey read Catholic Spain – yet these various layers of interpretation are not what most impress. *Tamburlaine the Great* is as much about sheer performance as it is about principles. Should there be any doubt, Tamburlaine's voice, a blast of sound and fury, seizes the attention at the beginning of the first act, and from that moment never lets go.

The set-pieces are engrossing. Marlowe had immersed himself in the most recent scholarship, using sources such as Pietro Perondini's *Life* of Temur (1553) and George Whetstone's *English Mirror* (1586), and was familiar with the conqueror's career. Although sometimes on uncertain ground historically, his dramatisations of some of its highlights are powerfully drawn. They have become the stuff of legend. Drama and history coalesce in the confrontation between Tamburlaine and Bajazeth, 'emperor of the Turks'. A landmark in the conqueror's career, it becomes a pivotal encounter in the play. Long before the two sworn adversaries even enter the battlefield, Marlowe gives the Ottoman great billing to intensify the scale of the looming encounter. Before battle is joined they meet in person, accompanied by their courtly entourages, and trade insults like boxers before a championship fight. Bajazeth calls Tamburlaine a 'Scythian slave', and swears by the holy Koran that he will make him 'a chaste and lustless eunuch' fit only for tending his harem. The Tatar shrugs off the threat, telling the Turk that 'Thy fall shall make me famous throughout the world!' Which indeed it did.

Battle is brief and devastating. Tamburlaine trounces Bajazeth and imprisons him in a cage, taunting him and his wife to distraction and suicide. Marlowe uses the rout of Bajazeth to emphasise the immutability of fate. Nothing is allowed to stand in the way of Tamburlaine's inexorable rise to glory. This is a man of magnificence, cruelty, military genius, overarching pride and sensuality, whose sense of his own power knows no bounds. He finds his peer group not on earth but in the heavens. After defeating Bajazeth, he styles himself 'arch-monarch' of the earth, 'the Scourge of God and terror of the world'.

The play echoes to the crash and thunder of arms. It has, as one critic put it, an 'astounding martial swagger'. But Marlowe's Tamburlaine is as much a poet as a warrior (testament, though the playwright might not have known it, to Temur's artistic and intellectual interests). If adversaries on the battlefield provoke his fiery wrath, it is his beloved lover Zenocrate who inspires his passion, unleashed in a sparkling stream of poetry which lifts the play into a higher sphere.

> *Ah, fair Zenocrate, divine Zenocrate,*
> *Fair is too foul an epithet for thee,*
> *That in thy passion for thy country's love,*
> *And fear to see thy kingly father's harm,*
> *With hair dishevelled wipest thy watery cheeks;*
> *And like to Flora in her morning's pride,*
> *Shaking her silver tresses in the air,*
> *Rainest on the earth resolved pearl in showers,*
> *And sprinklest sapphires on thy shining face,*
> *Where Beauty, mother to the Muses, sits,*
> *And comments volumes with her ivory pen,*

> Taking instructions from thy flowing eyes,
> Eyes, when that Ebena steps to heaven,
> In silence of thy solemn evening's walk,
> Making the mantle of the richest night,
> The moon, the planets, and the meteors, light.

Later, she falls sick, and Tamburlaine is consumed by the darkest grief. The bloodstained emperor is the poet-lover once more.

> Black is the beauty of the brightest day;
> The golden ball of heaven's eternal fire,
> That danced with glory on the silver waves,
> Now wants the fuel that inflamed his beams,
> And all with faintness and for foul disgrace,
> He binds his temples with a frowning cloud,
> Ready to darken earth with endless night.
> Zenocrate, that gave him light and life,
> Whose eyes shot fire from their ivory bowers,
> And tempered every soul with lively heat,
> Now by the malice of the angry skies,
> Whose jealousy admits no second mate,
> Draws in the comfort of her latest breath,
> All dazzled with the hellish mists of death.

But nothing can save her. Lying in her bed of state, surrounded by kings and doctors, her three sons and her husband, she dies. A distraught Tamburlaine rails against 'amorous Jove' for snatching her away from him, accusing the god of wanting to make Zenocrate his 'stately queen of heaven'. The martial imagery and force of language return in his distraught response, but for once they are born of desperation and tragic futility.

The play closes with Tamburlaine's death. Even here, at the end of his life, there is no regret or repentance, no sense that he is being defeated by a greater force. Instead, he calls for a map and points to this and that battlefield around the world, reliving his great victories in front of his sons. There is time to crown his heir Amyras, and then nature achieves what none of Tamburlaine's earthly foes could manage. At the final moment, in the throes of death, his arrogance does not desert him:

> *Farewell, my boys! My dearest friends, farewell!*
> *My body feels, my soul doth weep to see*
> *Your sweet desires deprived my company,*
> *For Tamburlaine, the scourge of God, must die.*

As a dramatist, Marlowe is guilty of all the usual sins: exaggeration, historical infelicities, geographical inaccuracies, sensationalism. Yet his Tamburlaine is a triumph of imaginative genius. Nowhere else has the Tatar been so brilliantly conceived, so passionately realised. The grandeur of the poetry, the sweeping cadences of the line, the constantly unfolding military drama, all keep the audience rapt. It is little wonder that Marlowe, rather than the historians, holds the key to the popular image of Tamburlaine, with the full flash and fury of his God-defying protagonist. In the play, as in life, the 'Scythian shepherd' transcends all earthly limitations, embarks on a crushing career of conquest, and destroys everything in sight. Marlowe's Tamburlaine rises even higher than his historical counterpart as a figure of boundless power. His is an irresistible, unworldly force that lifts him above his fellow mortals towards the heavens. He tramples over our moral universe, butchering innocent virgins, slaughtering wholesale, all the while consciously setting himself up as a rival to the gods whom he despises for their weakness. As his contemporaries recognise only too well, this is a man

> *That treadeth Fortune underneath his feet,*
> *And makes the mighty god of arms his slave.*

However great his ambition, however broad the stage on which he sought to make his mark, it is doubtful that the real Temur entertained such elevated comparisons in 1370. The titles he had gained, though magnificent, were deceptive. Master of a small swathe of Central Asia, beset on all sides by hostile forces, Temur was neither Emperor of the Age nor Conqueror of the World. It would take several decades of constant campaigning before he could make such exalted claims.

Mindful of Mongol tradition, which he never tired of using to bolster his position, Temur's priority on acceding to the throne was the reunification of the fractured Chaghatay empire. Demonstrating the astute opportunism which would sustain him through numerous challenges over the course of his career, he sought to place himself in the line of rulers harking back to Genghis Khan. His marriage to Saray Mulk-khanum had already eased him, albeit somewhat tenuously, into that position. Now he intended to capitalise on that auspicious beginning by restoring the diminished empire to its former glory. These lands, bequeathed to Genghis Khan's second son, Chaghatay, had disintegrated in the vortex of conflict. To the north-west, the fertile region of Khorezm, formerly within the Chaghatay ulus, now lay independent under the Qungirat Sufi dynasty. To the east, Moghulistan, once also an integral part of the *ulus*, was now a direct enemy whose continued depredations against its western neighbour, Mawarannahr, Temur was resolved to end.

For the next decade he led campaigns against both, now attacking the Moghuls in the east, now taking his armies north into Khorezm. There were expeditions farther afield, too, but for now the priority was to expand and consolidate his base. Today, constant warfare may seem a futile waste of resources, but in Temur's time it was the most effective way of retaining the loyalty of the nomadic tribes, uniting them under the banner of plunder and booty. There were regular challenges to his authority, however, from tribal leaders who resented the loss of power occasioned by his rapid rise. Such moves were frustrated by Temur's clever consolidation of his armies. He and Husayn had amassed powerful forces during their alliance, and on Husayn's assassination they were transferred to his command. He therefore presided over an impressive body of fighting men, including the Qara'unas armies, the largest in Chaghatay. Further support came from the settled populations, for whom war was anathema, stability and prosperity a cherished dream. They understood, as feuding tribal leaders would not, that only a strong ruler could impose the peace that would allow them to flourish.

Temur led his first expedition against his eastern neighbours in 1370, the year of his enthronement. His adversary was the Moghul leader Qamar ad-din, who had succeeded the assassinated Ilyas Khoja. This first campaign was indecisive, though sufficiently successful for Temur's forces to return laden with plunder. Qamar ad-din would remain an irritant for years to come. Though there were more note-worthy campaigns against the Moghuls – the next came in 1375 – their chief evaded capture. Legend tells of an incident during one of these expeditions through the Tien Shan mountains, high above Lake Issykul in what is today Kyrgyzstan. Pursuing Moghul archers over the San-Tash pass, each one of Temur's soldiers was ordered to pick up a stone and place it on a pile. Once they had routed their enemy they returned, each soldier collecting a stone and taking it back with him to enable Temur to calculate his army's losses. By the time his men had left the mountains, a towering cairn still remained, so heavy were the casualties. In the late 1370s, more expeditions took Temur's men into Moghulistan, and by 1383, when another heavy defeat was inflicted on the Moghuls, Qamar ad-din was in his dotage, militarily speaking. He was ousted by Khizr Khoja, son of the former Moghul khan Tughluk Temur, in 1389, although that was still not the last of him. The following year, taking advantage of Khizr Khoja's flight from Temur's armies, he tried to seize power again, only to be chased back once more. The last we hear of him, possibly apocryphally, is sometime around 1393 when, unable to keep up with his retreating army, he was left in a forest by his officers with several concubines and enough food for several days. He was never seen again.

Temur's eastern question was resolved more or less permanently shortly afterwards, when Khizr Khoja came to terms with his more powerful neighbour and was recognised as Moghul khan. The relationship between the two was settled in 1397, when the Moghul khan gave his sister Tukal-khanum to be Temur's wife. In tribute to her royal blood she became his second queen and was known as Kichik Khanum, the Lesser Lady. As Temur's power and riches grew with each season of military campaigns, the size of his household and the number of his wives and concubines swelled in proportion.

During these years, Temur was also actively engaged in bringing his northern neighbour Khorezm to heel. Ostensibly the reason for conflict here was the restoration of the Chaghatay empire as it had been left to Genghis Khan's second son. There was another equally, if not more, compelling reason to pick a fight. Khorezm straddled the caravan routes linking China to the Mediterranean, and therefore enjoyed great prosperity. Bringing the region back into the Chaghatay orbit would restore huge revenues, which in turn would fund further expansion. If Temur could annex the region, securing his borders to the north, he would be free for the first time to lead his armies beyond the borders of the Chaghatay ulus.

This strategy of keeping his armies constantly employed and consistently rewarded was one which Temur pursued for the rest of his life. It was specifically intended to minimise tribal opposition to his leadership. For as long as the traditional political culture of the *ulus*, with its pattern of shifting alliances and intermittent conflict, remained intact, Temur was vulnerable. His task was to weld a fractious confederation of tribes, governed by time-honoured traditions of hierarchy and authority, into an army loyal to his person. A strong centralised leadership weakened the tribal leaders' positions. Unless they were recompensed for this loss, Temur could not count on their continued support. Only by leading the tribes out of the *ulus* to victories abroad could he end, or at least minimise, internal *ulus* politics, and retain their loyalty. Thus, as the American historian Beatrice Forbes Manz put it: 'For the business of politics he now substituted that of conquest.'

This was Temur's highly effective, long-term approach. From a more immediate perspective, Khorezm was a prize worth seizing. Kat and Urganch, its two capitals, were great cities. The latter mightily impressed the world traveller Ibn Battutah, who reported that its markets were so teeming with merchants and buyers that during one foray into the town he was unable to move, such was the jam of humanity passing this way and that. 'The city abounds in luxury and excellent plenty, and its beauties make a fine show,' wrote Arabshah.

Khorezm was a land rich in natural produce. Foodstuffs, particularly cereals and fruits, grew in abundance. Melons and pomegranates were a local delicacy, as was game, in the form of roasted pigeon, fowl and crane. Drawing on the water from the Amu Darya delta, large crops of cotton were harvested in the fields. Flocks of sheep grazed on the plains, herds of cattle on the Aral marshlands. The markets were well stocked with costly animal skins, noted the tenth-century Arab geographer Mukaddasi, some from the Bulgar country of the Volga to the north-west. There was marten, sable, fox, two species of beaver, squirrel, ermine, stoat, weasel, hare, and goatskins. Grapes, currants, sesame and honey were also to be found in profusion, in addition to the gorgeous carpets, cotton and silk brocades, and cloaks destined for export. There was no shortage of military supplies. Armies could be readily equipped with swords, cuirasses and bows. The bark of white poplar, a local speciality, was highly prized as a covering for shields. Hunters came to market to choose from hundreds of handsome falcons. In addition to these products and activities, Mukaddasi discovered a thriving slave trade in Khorezm.

Turkish boys and girls were either bought or stolen from the steppe nomads, converted to Islam, and later despatched to Muslim countries where they frequently rose to high positions.

Most, if not all, of this lucrative trade was bypassing turbulent Mawarannahr. Temur's course was set. As a prelude to invasion, he sent a letter to Husayn Sufi, leader of Khorezm, demanding the return of the Chaghatay lands. Back came a reply. Since Khorezm had been conquered by the sword, its ruler proclaimed, only by the sword could it be taken away. The predictable rebuff handed Temur the *casus belli* he had been looking for. His army rumbled north in 1372. After fierce fighting, the city of Kat fell. One of his first significant victories, it also bore what would become the hallmark of his military actions against recalcitrant cities. All the men of Kat were butchered, their wives and daughters thrown into slavery. The city was plundered and torched. This was the moment for Husayn to surrender, but, encouraged to prolong his resistance by one of Temur's tribal chiefs, he opted instead for battle.* Defeated again, he retreated to Urganch, and died soon afterwards in humiliation. Yusef Sufi, his brother, succeeded him and, recognising his enemy's superior strength, came to terms, promising to send Husayn's daughter Khan-zada as a wife for Temur's first son Jahangir.† This was a noble offer, for she was

---

* The chief whispering in Husayn's ear was none other than Kay-Khusrau Khuttalani, the same man to whom Temur had handed over Amir Husayn for execution in 1370, to satisfy an outstanding blood feud. Kay-Khusrau paid for his subsequent desertion to the Sufis of Khorezm. When captured, he was handed over by Temur to Amir Husayn's family, who executed him in turn. This was typical of Temur's acuity in tribal dealings. In both cases he kept his own hands clean.

† The obscurity surrounding the names and numbers of Temur's wives clears up slightly when it comes to his sons. Temur's first-born, Jahangir, was born in around 1356 when Temur would have been twenty. His mother's name, according to the sixteenth-century historian Khwandamir, was Narmish-agha. Omar Shaykh followed, with Miranshah, the third son, born in 1366. Shahrukh, the youngest, was born in 1377.

both beautiful and of royal blood, granddaughter of Uzbeg, khan of the Golden Horde to the north. She was, wrote Arabshah, a maiden 'of the highest rank and greatest wealth, sprung of distinguished stock, of brilliant beauty, more beautiful than Shirin and more graceful than Waladah'.

Temur returned south to Samarkand and waited. No bride arrived. More interested in war than weddings, Yusef retook Kat in defiance. A second expedition was mounted against him in 1373. This time Yusef came to terms, and southern Khorezm passed into Temur's hands. Khan-zada was duly sent south with a caravan carrying prodigious gifts for her new family. There were untold treasures of gold and rich gems, fine silks and satins, ornate tapestries, even a golden throne. Flowers and carpets were strewn along the route to her betrothed and the air was heavy with perfume. Through the crowds of wide-eyed peasants gathered to watch this extraordinary procession the veiled princess moved silently on a white camel, her beauty hidden from impious eyes. A company of swordsmen mounted on their chargers accompanied her, the rest of her lavish retinue – camels loaded high with gifts, handmaidens in constant attendance – following in their wake. It was a magnificent sight.

But Jahangir's marriage did not last long. In about 1376, returning to Samarkand from another expedition against the Moghuls, Temur was greeted by a very different, more ominous, procession. A group of nobles, men like Haji Sayf ad-din Nukuz, one of his oldest and most trusted amirs, advanced slowly on horseback to meet him. Shrouded in black cloaks, their heads and faces streaked with dust, they were in mourning. Jahangir, stricken by sickness, was dead.

'All the great lords of the empire, the Cheriffs and others, were clothed in black and blue garments; they wept bitterly, covered their heads with dust in token of sorrow, beat their breasts, and rent themselves according to custom,' Yazdi reported. 'All the inhabitants with their heads uncovered, and with sackcloth and black felt about their necks, and their eyes bedewed with tears, came out of the city, filling the air with cries and lamentations.'

Temur was inconsolable. Jahangir, his eldest son, just twenty years old, was his great pride and heir. From his early teens he had played a leading role in his father's political and military affairs; already his military prowess, the talent which Temur prized above all others, had marked him out as a future leader. A fearless warrior, he had even led Temur's advance guard during one expedition against the Moghuls. In the course of his short life he had found time to father two young sons. Mohammed Sultan became the emperor's favourite. In later life he took on Jahangir's mantle as Temur's heir. His were the fabulously arrayed troops who in 1402 led the Tatar army into battle against Sultan Bayazid at Ankara. Another son by a different princess, Pir Mohammed, born a month after Jahangir's death, though less dependable, would also endear himself to his grandfather on account of his courage and valour.

Temur sank into the blackest despair. No soft words, no expressions of sympathy, could alleviate the pain. Trusted amirs and princes were harshly dismissed. 'Everything then became melancholy and disagreeable to him,' wrote Yazdi, 'and his cheeks were almost always bathed in tears; he clothed himself with mourning, and his life became uneasy to him. The whole kingdom, which used to be overjoyed at the arrival of this great emperor, was turned into a place of sorrow and weeping.'

Jahangir's death was a watershed from which Temur took a long time to recover. Although he would outlive many of his closest contemporaries – amirs and comrades in arms, learned men, religious and spiritual advisers, not to mention members of his own family – and gradually steeled himself against the deaths of those dearest to him, the loss of his first son affected him keenly. It marked a temporary end to his military campaigns. Samarkand no longer bristled with the hum of armies preparing for war. The *tovachis*, the aides-de-camp who were responsible for conscription, invariably among the busiest of Temur's senior officers, now fell silent.

If military affairs had receded from the immediate horizon, politics soon intruded. A shabby, unkempt refugee arrived in Temur's court. Notwithstanding his ragged appearance, Tokhtamish was a prince of the royal house of Genghis Khan. He had fled from Urus, khan of the White Horde to the north, and murderer of Tokhtamish's father. Now in exile, determined to avenge his father's death and, although Temur did not yet know it, ambitious for the leadership of a reunified Golden Horde, Tokhtamish threw himself on Temur's mercy.

> *'If we wish to enter upon a branch of inquiry which seems utterly wanting in unity, to be as disintegrated as sand, and defying any orderly or rational treatment, we can hardly choose a better one than the history of the Asiatic nomads.'*
>
> HENRY HOWORTH, *History of the Mongols*

To understand Tokhtamish and the khanate he aspired to lead, it is necessary to return to the Mongol conquests of the thirteenth century. The Golden Horde, or Dasht-i-Kipchak as it was then known, had been carved out by Batu, second son of Genghis Khan's eldest son Jochi. In accordance with the custom of the steppe, Jochi had received territories farthest from the heart of the empire in Karakorum. These ranged west from the river Irtish in Siberia 'as far as the soil has been trodden by the hooves of Mongol horses', according to the marvellously vague definition of the thirteenth-century Persian historian Juvayni. The uncertainty underscored the fact that the gift of these lands was theoretical, as they had yet to be fully conquered. Jochi died in 1227, however, shortly before his father. His eldest son, Orda, received western Siberia and the corridor of land sandwiched between the Amu Darya and Irtish rivers, a territory called 'the eastern Wing of the Ulus of Jochi', later known confusingly as both the White Horde and the Blue Horde. It fell to Batu to consolidate his hold on the lands immediately to the west – the westernmost branch of the Mongol empire, later the Golden Horde – and establish just how far those horses had travelled.

In 1235, he was given his chance. Great Khan Ogedey appointed Batu commander of a 150,000-strong army sent to subdue the Bulgars of the Volga and the Kipchaks. The nomadic Bulgars, among the world's most northerly Muslims, had established a prosperous state whose capital in Bulgar lay near the confluence of the Volga and Kama rivers. Living in tents and breeding cattle, they also traded furs and slaves with Mawarannahr in return for weapons and manufactured goods. The Kipchaks were a powerful confederation of Turkic nomads whose steppe territory, north of the Caspian Sea, stretched west from Siberia to the Danube.

The Bulgars were quickly crushed, their capital destroyed. Bachman, the chief of the Kipchaks, mounted stiff resistance against the Mongols but was eventually captured after a lengthy chase up and down the Volga. Like all defeated adversaries he was ordered to kneel before the victors. 'I have been myself a king and do not fear death,' he replied. 'I am not a camel that should kneel.' He was promptly cut in two.

Batu's forces reached the river Ural in 1237, crossed into Russia and laid waste to every city from Moscow to Kiev, taking advantage of the hopelessly weak and divided Russian princes. The cities of Ryazan and Kolomna in the western reaches were so thoroughly sacked, wrote an anonymous chronicler, that 'no eye remained open to weep for the dead'. Other towns simply disappeared from the map altogether. Kiev fell shortly before Christmas 1240, its Byzantine churches torched to the ground, the saintly bones they harboured burnt in contempt.

Plundering and massacring as they advanced to the gates of Europe, the Mongol army marched into Poland in 1241. In a region utterly unknown to them, thousands of miles from home in the depth of winter, they overcame the Polish feudal chivalry – like the Russians, enfeebled by divisions – through the superb military acumen of Subedey, Genghis's veteran commander. Krakow fell on Palm Sunday. In a subsequent battle outside what was later known as Walstadt, the Mongols collected nine sacks containing the ears of the defeated Germans and Poles. Silesia was similarly devastated before Batu's hordes turned their attention to the kingdom of Hungary, which fell after catastrophic casualties in the region of sixty-five thousand at the battle of Mohi. Contemplating the Mongols' onward advance into the heart of Europe, Emperor Frederick II despatched a letter to the kings of Christendom appealing for contributions to a common army. His request met with a deafening silence. Pope Gregory IX published his own appeal in August 1241, but died shortly afterwards. The continent lay vulnerable before the Mongols.

By 1242 Batu's army was camped outside the walls of Neustadt, south of Vienna, and Christendom stood on the brink of disaster. There were further forays into Croatia and Albania. It is said that the Mongols' depredations in Hungary prompted Queen Blanche of France to ask her son Louis IX what action should be taken against them. 'If these people, whom we call Tartars, should come upon us, either we will thrust them back into Tartarus, whence they came, or else they will send us all to heaven,' he predicted. Fortunately for the kingdoms of Europe, it was not to be. In an extraordinary piece of good luck, the continent was saved by news of Ogedey's death the previous December.

The Mongol army had already been riven by disputes between Batu and rival Mongol princes, harbinger of a more lasting and damaging split between the houses of Jochi and Tuli on the one hand and those of Ogedey and Chaghatay on the other. A struggle for the succession in Karakorum now appeared likely, a consideration which would have weighed heavily with Batu, who wanted to ensure that the candidate most favourable to his interests ascended to the throne. He therefore decided to return to participate in the *qurultay* to appoint the new Great Khan, in the event a matter which took several years to resolve. His horde turned eastwards and Europe survived. Had Ogedey lived longer, the Mongol empire would almost certainly have reached the shores of the Atlantic.

'At a distance of more than seven centuries,' wrote John Joseph Saunders, 'the historian is still struck with wonder at this extraordinary campaign. Whether one considers the geographical scope of the fighting, which embraced the greater part of eastern Europe, the planning and coordination of movement of so many army corps, the clockwork precision whereby the enemy was surrounded, defeated and pursued, the brilliant manner in which problems of supply were solved, or the skill with which Asian armies were handled in an unfamiliar European terrain, one cannot fail to admit that the Mongol leaders were masters of the art of war such as the world scarcely saw before or has seen since.'

Following the end of the European invasion, and in anticipation of further Mongol divisions, Batu's priority was to establish his own kingdom or *ulus*. From 1242 to 1254 he built his capital, Old Saray, on the east bank of the Akhtuba, a tributary of the Volga, sixty-five miles north-west of Astrakhan. After his triumphs in Russia and Europe, his *ulus* – which had originally consisted of a relatively modest slice of land north of the Caspian – extended to include the vast swathe of territory slanting south-west from Nizhniy Novgorod and Voronezh in Russia to Kiev in Ukraine and the river Prut on the borders of Romania. In the east his horde encompassed Khorezm and the famous city of Urganch.

With Saray as their centre these lands were what became known – though only from the sixteenth century – as the Golden Horde. The khanate took its name from Batu's fabulously embroidered silk tents pitched on the banks of the Volga to receive the defeated Russian princes who were summoned thither to pay him homage. Yellow or gold was, besides, the mark of imperial power. Genghis's descendants were known as the Golden Family, and the Great Khan traditionally held sway from the Golden Ordu, his seat of power.

Though the borders Batu established remained essentially the same until Temur's interventions in the late fourteenth century, after his death in 1255 or 1256 his brother Berke mounted the throne of the Golden Horde and raised another city, New Saray, also on the banks of the Akhtuba, east of Volgograd. New Saray became the capital of the khanate under Uzbeg, whose reign from 1313 to 1341 represented the height of the Golden Horde's power and glory. At this time it started to eclipse the Chaghatay ulus as the principal caravan route linking Asia with Europe. The Genoese and Venetians, those indomitably commercial European pioneers, were allowed to establish colonies in Kaffa and at Tana at the mouth of the river Don. New Saray grew rich on trade in child slaves, silks and spices, salt and corn, wine and cheese. In 1339, the Franciscan envoy brought Uzbeg a superb warhorse as a gift from the Avignon papacy, in recognition of the khan's protection of the Christian communities. In the early 1330s, Ibn Battutah discovered an extraordinarily cosmopolitan city of Mongols, Kipchaks, Circassians, Russians and Greeks, each community living in its own quarter. New Saray was, he considered, counting its thirteen cathedrals and numerous mosques, 'one of the finest cities, of boundless size, situated in a plain, choked with the throng of its inhabitants and possessing good bazaars and broad streets'. Such had been its prodigious growth within a few years that it took the methodical Moroccan traveller half a day to cross from one side of the city to the other.

Uzbeg's son Janibeg ruled until 1357, his reign fatally undermined by the ravages of the Black Death, which killed an estimated eighty-five thousand in the Crimea alone. From this time the Golden Horde embarked upon a steady decline. Batu's royal line came to an end in 1359, paving the way for two decades of civil wars and the simultaneous rise of the hitherto subject Russian princes. From 1360 to 1380, fourteen khans came and went, usually amid scenes of terrible violence. After 1368, when the Mongols were finally expelled from China, the greater Mongol empire was rudderless and unable to resolve the internal disputes of the Golden Horde.

By the time of Tokhtamish's arrival in Samarkand, the Horde had fragmented. Khorezm, formerly part of it, latterly independent, had been brought into Temur's orbit. In the absence of central authority, local leaders rose to the fore. One of the most powerful was Mamay in the Crimea. Another was Urus, khan of the White Horde, whose lands bordered Moghulistan. He, like his rivals, aspired to lead a reunified Golden Horde restored to its former might.

The leadership of this region was a vital consideration for Temur, for since the conquest of Khorezm it bordered his empire immediately to the north. Fomenting continued unrest in the White Horde by supporting Tokhtamish, a domestic rival to Urus, made eminent sense. It would distract Urus from his larger designs of consolidating the Golden Horde, which threatened Temur's embryonic empire to the south.

&

No expenses were spared, therefore, when the dishevelled Tokhtamish presented himself in Samarkand. Temur greeted him as his son and threw a sumptuous banquet to welcome him. He gave him gold, precious jewels, new weapons and armour, magnificent belts, cloths, furniture, horses, camels, tents and pavilions, kettle-drums and slaves. To help establish him, he was given lands on Temur's northern borders and an army to further his designs.

Twice Tokhtamish attacked Urus and twice he was repelled. Each time, Temur made good his losses and re-equipped him without complaint. When an ambassador arrived from Urus demanding the surrender of the fugitive, Temur's response was swift: he joined battle alongside Tokhtamish. After stalemate in the frozen steppes, Temur and Tokhtamish were at last victorious. Urus died, his louche and incompetent successor was overthrown soon afterwards, and in 1378 Tokhtamish was installed as khan with Temur's support. From that time he dedicated himself to bringing the entire Golden Horde under his control.

No sooner had Temur resolved this northern question – for now – than news reached him that a former adversary had mounted a rebellion. In Khorezm, Yusef Sufi, no doubt ruing his decision to become Temur's vassal, had elected to regain his independence. Reneging on formal agreements, though he himself practised it unswervingly throughout his campaigns, was anathema to Temur when encountered in an enemy. It demanded punitive retaliation.

The city of Urganch was surrounded. Arabshah described it as a ravished maiden: 'To the beautiful virgin he sent in a suitor and besieged her and reduced her to the utmost distress, tightening the garments of the throat at the neck of her approaches, so that his nails were almost fixed in her lappets.' As the siege engines and mangonels massed around the city walls and set about their destructive work, a desperate Yusef sent a message to Temur: 'Why should the world face ruin and destruction because of two men? Why should so many faithful Muslims perish because of our quarrel? Better that we two should find ourselves face to face in open field to prove our valour.' A time and a place for the duel were suggested.

It was an ill-considered approach to a man who, though lame in his right side, had always thrived on combat. Temur accepted the challenge. Methodically, piece by piece, he donned his duelling armour. The circular embossed shield was secured on his left arm. From his left hip hung his long, curved sword. Only after he had mounted his charger did he put on his black and gold helmet.

Fearing disaster, his amirs crowded round, pleading with him not to undertake such a rash mission. There was no need for such a display of personal bravery, they pleaded with him. It was their duty to fight on the battlefield. The emperor's job was to command from the throne. The old amir Sayf ad-din Nukuz rushed forward, grabbed the horse's reins and remonstrated with his leader. Temur would not countenance any opposition. He made as if to strike his aged retainer and then broke free. Taking a last look at his assembled amirs, he roused his horse with a cry, spurred it forward and galloped off towards the moated city of Urganch, leaving his panic-stricken followers coughing in the dust.

In front of the city walls, under the incredulous stare of scores of archers, any one of whom could have killed him with a single well-placed arrow, Temur announced himself. He had come to accept Yusef Sufi's challenge. He was met with silence. Yusef had never expected Temur to pick up the gauntlet thrown down in the heat of the siege, yet here he was, alone and unprotected. It was a gesture of outstanding bravery and blind recklessness. Humiliated in front of his own men, Yusef cowered in his inner rooms. He had no intention of going out to meet Temur in a duel to the death.

The Tatar looked up with contempt at the massed ranks of archers on the ramparts. 'He who breaks his word shall lose his life,' he shouted, and with that he was gone. Passing back through the lines of siege engines across the empty plain, he returned to a tumultuous reception from his men. Yusef, if he ever heard his enemy's last words, must have been haunted by them. Within three months he had fallen sick and died. The outlying provinces were plundered and ravaged by Temur's hordes who moved across the plains like devouring locusts. Urganch, the city of plenty, now belonged to Temur.

The sacking of Urganch in 1379, though cataclysmic for Khorezm, did not bring to an end the history of Temur's involvement with the city. His empire was one of conquest followed, often years later, by reconquest. A formal empire like that of Rome was neither his model nor his ambition. Trade, and the peace and stability needed to promote it, always weighed heavily in his calculations, but they were of secondary importance to the overwhelming principle of conquest.

Conquest required armies, armies required soldiers. And soldiers had to be paid and rewarded for their efforts. A map of his campaigns remains the most eloquent statement of Temur's boundless ambition, his relentless drive, his limitless energy. Lines stretch greedily across Asia, through natural obstacles, across deserts, past powerful enemies, as far west as the gates of Europe on the Turkish coast, as far east as deepest Siberia, from the outskirts of Moscow in the north, across the roof of the world to Delhi in the south. Looking at this map and studying the dates of these campaigns – back-to-back for thirty-five years with only a single hiatus of two years during which Temur remained in Samarkand – it is difficult to counter the argument that keeping his armies on the move, plundering and sacking as they went, was his overriding *raison d'être*.

Had the leaders of Urganch understood this, they might well have cast aside any delusions of independence and opted for a more peaceful existence under the yoke of Temur's empire. But memories must have been very short in the city, for in 1388, only a decade after the last failed revolt, the Sufi dynasty of Khorezm, spurred on by the troublemaking Tokhtamish, now established as khan of the Golden Horde, decided to rebel.

Once more Temur returned to the city, and once more the results were catastrophic for its citizens. If he was cruel in conquest, when revisiting a city he was merciless. Urganch was razed. For ten days he led his men in savagery and slaughter. By the end of it the city which had been 'a place of meeting for the learned, a home for men of culture and poets, a resort of the refined and great', had disappeared. Urganch consisted only of a single mosque. As a mark of his wrath, Temur had barley sown over the ground where once the city had stood. It was his most feared calling card, a reminder that should he wish to do so he could erase an entire city from the face of the earth.

The once fertile kingdom of Khorezm, a prosperous centre of trade and agriculture and a distinguished seat of Arabic learning, is now a neglected corner of the former Soviet empire, a fatally dry and dusty desert province struggling to survive. The aridity of the region, the root of its poverty and disease, finds its echoes in the story of Urganch's last ill-fated tussle with Temur. For in tearing it apart wall by wall and house by house, Temur spared nothing. The sprawling irrigation system, which watered vast numbers of fields and under-pinned all agricultural activity, was ripped up and destroyed. Urganch was left to the desert. Over the years that followed, it gradually recovered, but it never regained its former splendour. In time it was displaced by the neighbouring city of Khiva as the capital of Khorezm.

Today, Urgench, as it is now known, is a grey, open-air Soviet museum, a city of straight lines and stony faces. Its people have been doomed to live in a region condemned to permanent drought, but in their poverty they have nowhere else to go. Lenin, pioneer of the Soviet experiment that helped turn the province into this poisonous dustbowl, has disappeared, but other monuments, such as that honouring the Martyrs of the Revolution, remain in concrete de-fiance. Clues to understanding Khorezm's decline are clustered around the city. Cotton motifs decorate the buildings, the soulless apartment blocks, even the streetlights, paying tribute to the region's main source of income and the architect of its environmental collapse. Under constant pressure since the 1960s, when the Soviet Union earmarked Central Asia as its cotton basin, the two rivers which flowed so freely in Temur's time and fed the Aral Sea have now been bled dry by this most thirsty of crops. Neither the Amu Darya nor the Sir Darya even reaches the sea any longer.

What Temur began in those moments of fury, the Soviets unwit-tingly accelerated. Where the Tatar obliterated the irrigation network, the Soviets expanded it with a vengeance. The ecological disaster they unleashed is widely regarded as the world's worst. The environmental problem is so acute that Urgench, which until recently saw snow in winter and rain in spring, now has neither. Instead, it is warm and dry all year round. Elsewhere in the region summers have become hotter and winters colder. Clouds which once skimmed over the Aral Sea, collecting water which fed the region as rain, now pick up salt instead.

In the space of a generation, the area of the Aral Sea has been halved, the volume of its waters cut by three-quarters. Each year the water level drops by a further three feet, releasing new swathes of contaminated land to the winds scouring its surface. The herbicides and defoliants used to improve cotton yields leach into the evaporating sea until they are left as chemical crusts, disintegrating into dust and then scattered across the region by the gusting north-east winds and recurrent sandstorms. Driven away or simply destroyed, the number of species of mammals in the region has fallen from seventy to thirty, the number of bird species from 319 to 168. The salt content of the Aral Sea has trebled over thirty years, killing all twenty-four species of its fish – including carp, perch, sturgeon and salmon – and dealing a death blow to the city of Muynak, once its largest port, now the graveyard of Soviet hubris. Rusting hulls of fishing boats lie discarded on their sides, a hundred miles from the sea's retreating shores. These vessels are all that remain of the once mighty Aral fleet which in 1921, responding to an appeal from Lenin to help the starving Volga region, caught twenty-one thousand tonnes of fish and sent them north to relieve the famine. In the 1970s and eighties, the annual catch was forty thousand tonnes and more. Now, apart from the negligible quantities of fish with carcinogenic tissue surviving in the scattered salt-water ponds, the sea is empty.

Muynak is a desperate place. The sea has fled under man's assault, uncovering his legacy of contamination to the winds, leaving the town beached on the sand-flats like a tragic shipwreck, a port without a sea. Health problems abound. Tuberculosis and anaemia are common.

Diets are poor. Meat is almost impossible to find and any vegetables grown locally contain traces of harmful chemicals. The water is polluted. Even the air the people breathe is frequently contaminated, as winds whip up chemical dust and pass it into their lungs.

'Fish are our prosperity', reads a sign in front of the tatty municipal building, flanked by painted hoardings on which smiling sailors with bulging muscles unload their catch into the arms of buxom factory workers. On the top floor is the office of the mayor, a corpulent and corrupt man who takes more interest in dubious construction projects and the beautification of his mansion than in the hunger, disease and economic misery of his townspeople.

Even in that most autocratic of empires under Temur, corrupt behaviour by an official was, if uncovered, unlikely to have gone unpunished. Had he served Temur in local government, the present-day mayor of Muynak would probably have been a marked man. In 1404, returning to Samarkand after five years' campaigning in western Asia, Temur learnt that Dina, the city's governor, had been ruling capriciously during his absence. 'His Highness since his return had come to know that this man had betrayed his trust, using his office to misgovern and oppress the people,' Clavijo related. 'He therefore now commanded this Dina the Chief Mayor to be brought before him, and after judgement forthwith he was taken out and without delay hanged.'

The punishment did not end there. The money the mayor had appropriated from the subjects of Samarkand was returned to the imperial treasury. An influential friend who had tried to buy Dina's pardon was also hanged. Another official, a favourite of Temur who had likewise tried to intercede on the mayor's behalf, was arrested and tortured until he had revealed the whereabouts of his entire fortune. No sooner had he done so than he was dragged off to join the governor of Samarkand on the gallows, where he was hanged upside down until dead. 'This act of high justice condemning so great a personage to death, made all men to tremble, and notably he had been one in whom his Highness had reposed much confidence.'

The only employer left in Muynak is the fish-canning factory, but its days are numbered. Back in 1941, when it was founded, the sea was only five hundred yards away, and fishermen deposited their catch at the gates. Now the few fish being processed come from small salt-water lakes in the region, a token, state-directed effort to keep the factory afloat. It hasn't worked. Like the hotel, the canning plant is facing imminent bankruptcy. Salaries haven't been paid for a year. Only a small fraction of the 1,200 workers who packed fish in happier days remain. Most of these look beaten down by the dreadful conditions. Inside, it resembles a dark, damp dungeon. Unlit corridors penetrate deep into the heart of the building. It is freezing, the sort of cold that hurts your head, shoots through your clothes and passes directly into your bones. The walls are filthy. Just visible beneath the grime, occasional Soviet-era slogans praising the workers overlook teams of men and women hunched over medieval machines. The whole place stinks of an evil combination of putrefying fish and rusting equipment. At the back of the factory, a group of men with makeshift trolleys congregate in front of a counter full of watermelons, the sort which in Temur's time had so impressed Ibn Battutah ('the very best and biggest' in the world, he thought). It looks like a greengrocer with limited stock – one sort of fruit and no vegetables – but the reality is more depressing. This fish-canning factory in Central Asia's most advanced country has run out of money. It pays its workers in melons.

3

'The Greatest and Mightiest of Kings'

'The character of Temur has been differently appraised by those
who are dazzled by his military achievements on the one hand
and those who are disgusted by his cruelty and utter disregard of
human life on the other.'

EDWARD G. BROWNE, *A Literary History of Persia*

If we are to understand Temur's unparalleled life, his numerous campaigns and victories, the motivation which impelled him halfway
across the world to seek them and the brilliant tactical acumen which
left him undefeated on his deathbed, if we are to appreciate his
love of magnificence, bravery and beauty, his intolerance of laziness,
cowardice and corruption, his lifelong respect for learned men and
religious scholars, the cunning and cruelty which proved fatal to
millions, the generosity and forgiveness which came to the rescue of
so many others – in short, if we are to make sense of perhaps the
greatest self-made man who ever lived, then there is no better place
to begin than with his contemporaries.

The most flattering profile of Temur is provided by the Persian
court historian of the early fifteenth century, Sharaf ad-din Ali Yazdi.
Zafarnama, the Book of Victory, is a veritable panegyric, peppered

with passages singing the emperor's praises, so much so that the reader is inclined to skim through the sycophancy and dismiss Yazdi as a hopelessly servile commentator. But what is interesting about the Persian's ingratiating chronicle is the fact that both he and Ibn Arabshah, Temur's inveterate critic, single out several attributes in common.

'Courage raised him to be the supreme Emperor of Tartary, and subjected all Asia to him, from the frontiers of China to those of Greece,' wrote Yazdi. 'He governed the state himself, without availing himself of a minister; he succeeded in all his enterprises. To everyone he was generous and courteous, except to those who did not obey him – he punished them with the utmost rigour. He loved justice, and no one who played the tyrant in his dominion went unpunished; he esteemed learning and learned men. He laboured constantly to aid the fine arts. He was utterly courageous in planning, and carrying out a plan. To those who served him, he was kind.'*

Arabshah, surprisingly, provided the most valuable portrait of the conqueror. As we have seen, the Syrian was anything but a dispassionate observer, having witnessed at first hand the devastation wrought on his native Damascus by the Tatar hordes in 1401. Appalled by the torture and slaughter of the city's inhabitants, it is little wonder that he succumbed to the temptations of invective in his life of Temur. The recurrent references to his subject as a bastard, viper, demon, despot, treacherous impostor, wicked fool, owl of ill omen and the like do little for Arabshah's credibility as an objective biographer.

Yet Arabshah is a critical character witness precisely because of

---

* Yazdi is by no means alone in providing such a glowing profile. Subsequent writers have also been mesmerised by Temur's blaze of conquests. Military historians, above all, have been overwhelmed. Writing in 1915, Sir Percy Sykes echoed Yazdi's conclusions in remarkably similar language, calling him 'the greatest Asiatic conqueror known in history', 'the bravest of the brave', 'an unsurpassed leader of men and a very god of war adored by all ranks'.

this profound enmity. Nowhere is this more in evidence than in the final chapter of his book, the very heading of which pulls the reader up short. It is entitled 'Of the Wonderful Gifts of Temur and his Nature and Character'. Unlike the preceding chapters, which rarely exceed five pages, and are frequently only one, this runs to thirty-five pages. Its opening passage leaves us with a picture of the conqueror at the end of his life, and is worth quoting from at length. It begins with a physical description:

> *Temur was tall and lofty of stature as though he belonged to the remnants of the Amalekites, big in brow and head, mighty in strength and courage, wonderful in nature, white in colour, mixed with red, but not dark, stout of limb, with broad shoulders, thick fingers, long legs, perfect build, long beard, dry hands, lame on the right side, with eyes like candles, without brilliance; powerful in voice; he did not fear death; and though he was near his [seventieth] year yet he was firm in mind, strong and robust in body, brave and fearless, like a hard rock.*

The Soviet archaeological team which opened Temur's tomb in 1941 found that he was a well-built man of about five feet seven inches, 'tall and lofty of stature' for that time. His lameness was likewise established. An injury to his right leg, where the thighbone had merged with his kneecap, left it shorter than the left, hence the pronounced limp referred to in his pejorative nickname. When walking he dragged his right leg, and his left shoulder was found to be unnaturally higher than the right. Further wounds were discovered to his right hand and elbow. The red colour Arabshah mentions in Temur's colouring may well be a reference to his moustache and beard, traces of which were found still attached to the skull.

'He did not care for jesting or lying,' Arabshah continues. 'Wit and trifling pleased him not; truth, even if it were painful, delighted him; he was not sad in adversity nor joyful in prosperity ... He did not allow in his company any obscene talk or talk of bloodshed or captivity, rapine, plunder and violation of the harem. He was spirited and brave and inspired awe and obedience. He loved bold and valiant soldiers, by whose aid he opened the locks of terror, tore men to pieces like lions, and through them and their battles overturned mountains . . .'

It is as though the dignity and grandeur of Temur's character, suppressed by the Syrian for nine-tenths of the book, is finally too much for him to contain. After the long summaries, and vituperative denunciations, of Temur's campaigns, it is time for Arabshah to deliver his verdict on Temur the man. And suddenly, the language has changed. The conqueror is 'wonderful in nature', his fearlessness is mentioned twice within a few sentences, rather like Yazdi's emphasis of his courage. He is the object of his soldiers' awe. The man who Arabshah has been telling us for three hundred pages revels in wanton cruelty and spilling blood does not, it transpires, tolerate any talk of bloodshed, rape or plunder in his presence. As Arabshah continues, you sense that after all these pages filled with hatred he finds himself, despite his intentions, re-evaluating his subject in a vastly more favourable light. It is a marvellous and highly revealing moment. Temur, he goes on, was:

> A debater, who by one look and glance comprehended the matter aright, trained, watchful for the slightest sign; he was not deceived by intricate fallacy nor did hidden flattery pass him; he discerned keenly between truth and fiction, and caught the sincere counsellor and the pretender by the skill of his cunning, like a hawk trained for the chase, so that for his thoughts he was judged a shining star.

No longer the coarse viper, Temur is the consummate diplomat and politician, masterful in the business of empire, attuned to deceit and subterfuge, a 'shining star' in the intellectual firmament. In his first chapter, Arabshah poured scorn on Temur's lineage. He was born, said the Syrian, into 'a mixed horde, lacking either reason or religion'. Brought up in the nomadic traditions of the steppe, the Tatar spoke both Turkic and Persian fluently, but was illiterate. By the end of his book, Arabshah has arrived at a rather different judgement on Temur's intelligence and his respect for learning.

> *Temur loved learned men, and admitted to his inner reception nobles of the family of Mahomed; he gave the highest honour to the learned and doctors and preferred them to all others and received each of them according to his rank and granted them honour and respect; he used towards them familiarity and an abatement of his majesty; in his arguments with them he mingled moderation with splendour, clemency with rigour and covered his severity with kindness.*

Temur's harshest critic, the man who had seen his great city reduced to ashes, its men and women raped and butchered, is at pains to stress that the Tatar was no mindless, uncouth, heathen tyrant. Temur liked to gather the most illustrious minds about him. Few could expect mercy when he torched a city, but scholars, poets, men of letters, Muslim clerics, *shaykhs*, dervishes and divines, artists and architects, miniaturists, masons and skilled craftsmen of all descriptions were invariably spared.

If soldiers were his first love as an emperor, Temur's admiration for holy men and men of letters came a close second. Under his rule Samarkand attracted – voluntarily and otherwise – Asia's most distinguished minds, and this at a time when high culture in that continent shone more brightly than in benighted Europe. From Baghdad came Nizam ad-din Shami, author of the original *Zafarnama*, the inspiration for Sharaf ad-din Ali Yazdi's later work of the same name. Persian scholars thronged to the conqueror's court. There was Sa'd ad-din Mas'ud at Taftazani, one of the celebrated polymaths of his era, a theologian, grammarian, lawyer and exegetical teacher. He was joined by Ali ibn Mohammed as Sayyid ash Sharif al Jurjanj, the mystic and logician, and Abu Tahrir ibn Yaqub ash Shirazi al Firuzabadi, the renowned lexicographer. Lutfallah Nishapuri, the poet laureate and panegyrist of Temur's son Miranshah, was highly regarded by Temur. Another poet, Ahmed Kermani, author of the *Temurnama* (Book of Temur), was on intimate terms with the emperor, while eminent scholars like Djezeri, compiler of one of the most respected Arabic dictionaries, were frequently granted high office. There were many foundations and endowments for colleges and mosques, schools and hospitals. And at the centre of this extended academic and cultural web sat Temur, distributing patronage like a spider spinning its web.

In 1401 there occurred one of the most fascinating meetings of minds of the age when the great Arab historian Ibn Khaldun was presented to the Tatar during the siege of Damascus. After staying in Temur's camp for a month, he left with a profound respect for 'one of the greatest and mightiest of kings', not to mention a commission to write a history of North Africa. Temur impressed him with his knowledge of the history of the Tatars, Arabs and Persians: 'He is highly intelligent and very perspicacious, addicted to debate and argumentation about what he knows and also about what he does not know.' Arabshah also took note of Temur's interest in history: 'He was constant in reading annals and histories of the prophets of blessed memory and the exploits of kings,' he wrote. The emperor even established a new position of Story-Reader in his court. Practical disciplines such as mathematics, astronomy and medicine were particularly favoured.

Prefiguring Yazdi's uncritical comments, Arabshah goes on to express his admiration for Temur's persistence and determination: 'When he had ordered anything or given a sign that it should be done, he never recalled it or turned thence the reins of his purpose, that he might not be found in inconstancy and weakness of plan or deed.' Yazdi puts it rather more flatteringly: 'As Temur's ambition was boundless, and the least of his designs surpassed the greatest actions in the world, he never abandoned any one of his enterprises till he had completely finished it.'

Famously brilliant at manoeuvring his armies to victory on the battlefield, Temur was no less skilful at marshalling his forces on the chessboard, where his cool calculation, audacity and control undid the grand masters of his day. Even here he was exceptional, observed Arabshah. 'He was constant in the game of chess, that with it he might sharpen his intellect; but his mind was too lofty to play at the lesser game of chess and therefore he played only the greater game, in which the chess board is of ten squares by eleven, that is increased by two camels, two giraffes, two sentinels, two mantelets [war engines], a vazir and other pieces.'*

The longer Arabshah dwells on Temur's character, the more highly he seems to extol his virtues, until, towards the end, he observes simply: 'He was called the unconquered lord of the seven climes and ruler by land and sea and conqueror of Kings and Sultans.' But there is a last sting in the tail. Summoning back his deep-seated resentment, he damns the Tatar on one important account: 'He clung to the laws of Jenghizkhan . . . on whom be the curse of Allah,' he rasps. 'Temur must be accounted an infidel and those also who prefer the laws of Jenghizkhan to the faith of Islam.' Arabshah was right to recognise the tension between the two motivating principles behind Temur's life of conquest. What he failed to appreciate was that Temur's political and religious ideology was a shrewdly calculated amalgam of the *yasa*, or customary laws, of Genghis Khan on the one hand and Islam on the other.

Temur drew freely from both Islam and the laws of Genghis to

---

* To this day this most demanding of games is known as Tamerlane chess.

justify his actions, be they military conquest or domestic political arrangements. He was, above all else, an opportunist. At his coronation in 1370 he installed a puppet Chaghatay khan as his nominal superior, in deference to the traditions requiring the khan to be of royal blood. Thereafter a khan presided over Temur's expanding empire: first Prince Suyurghatmish and, from 1388, his son Sultan Mahmud. For all Temur's pomp and power, and even at the height of his majesty, he never styled himself a khan. He was instead Temur the Great Emir, or Temur Gurgan, son-in-law of the Great Khan through his marriage to Saray Mulk-khanum, and it was in these names and that of the Chaghatay khan that coins were minted and Samarkand's authority acknowledged in the *khutba* (Friday prayers) throughout his lands. But no one, certainly not Arabshah, doubted where the real source of power lay.

Temur was no infidel. Islam governed his military career in the same way that Christianity provided the ideological propulsion for the Crusaders during their bloody sojourns in the Holy Lands. The Crescent always surmounted Temur's royal standard, and it was under the banner of Islam that his conquests were prosecuted. That Islam and wholesale slaughter were incompatible bedfellows was beside the point. The same could be said of the Christian faith and the Crusaders.

Just as he borrowed from the traditions of Genghis, so Temur dipped freely into the laws of Islam, picking up and retaining those aspects of the faith he found useful, disregarding those which were inconvenient. He had no time, for instance, for the Prophet's recommendation of a maximum of four wives for a man. More important, despite a lifetime's wanderings, he never found time to honour one of the five pillars of Islam, the pilgrimage to Mecca, a badge of honour for dutiful Muslims who can afford the journey. He did not shave his head, nor did he wear a turban or the robes prescribed by the faith.

Temur's interpretation of *jihad*,* or holy war, cast further doubt on his credentials as a good Muslim. In his eyes it justified the use of force and savagery against virtually anyone. It was one thing to launch a holy war against the infidels of Christian Georgia, as Temur did several times (on one campaign he even forced King Bagrat to convert to Islam). It was quite another to put fellow Muslims to the sword. As high-born leaders, lowly soldiers, desperate women and innocent children all discovered to their cost, professing the faith of Islam was no guarantee of safety from Temur's armies. Muslim Asia, after all, was their stamping ground. They swept through its heartland – across what are today Turkey, Iran, Iraq, Syria, Azerbaijan, Uzbekistan, Afghanistan, Turkmenistan, Tajikistan, Kyrgyzstan, Kazakhstan, Pakistan and India – raining down death on the sons and daughters of the Koran. Who could count the nameless millions of Muslims who perished at their hands? These were the people who suffered his worst atrocities. Two thousand were piled on top of one another and cemented alive into towers of clay and bricks in the city of Isfizar in 1383. In Isfahan, holy city of Persia, seventy thousand were slaughtered in 1387; the sacking of Baghdad in 1401 left ninety thousand dead, their heads cemented into 120 towers. Damascus and Aleppo witnessed unimaginable horrors. And yet this was a man who aspired to the title of Ghazi, Warrior of the Faith.

Christians, Jews and Hindus – the infidels who should have felt the full force of the sword of Islam – escaped lightly by comparison. Only occasionally, as though to make up for his massacres of brother Muslims, did Temur unleash his wrath on them. In 1398, shortly before joining battle against the (Muslim) sultan of Delhi, he gave

---

* The word is used here in the sense of the lesser *jihad*, meaning holy war, rather than the greater *jihad*, by which the Prophet Mohammed exhorted his followers to fight a personal struggle against vice, passion and ignorance, to improve themselves as human beings and demonstrate their commitment to Islam.

orders for a hundred thousand mostly Hindu prisoners to be killed. Two years later, he had four thousand Armenians buried alive in Sivas, this time sparing its Muslim population.

There was an arbitrariness to Temur's atrocities that belied his claims of holy war. Sometimes, as in Afghanistan and parts of Persia, he explained his rampages as an attack on the Sunni creed of Islam.* In Mazandaran, also in Persia, by contrast, cities were razed to punish Shi'a dervishes. Then again, Temur could just as easily pose as protector of the Shi'a tradition. In Damascus, Arabshah's fellow citizens were put to the sword ostensibly on account of their hostility to the Shi'a. In 1396, Temur looked south for his next conquest. 'The sultans of Delhi have been slack in their defence of the Faith,' he told his amirs before leading his troops across the towering Hindu Kush mountains to sack that city. In 1404, he rallied his troops for his last campaign. Once more the banner of holy war was raised, this time against the infidel Ming emperor.

Temur's observation of the Muslim faith was based on pragmatism rather than principle. Although he came from a conventional Sunni tradition, his Sufi credentials were bolstered through his patronage of the Naqshbandi order, centred in Bukhara, and his cultivation of the Sufi *shaykhs* of Mawarannahr and Khorasan, who enjoyed a prominent position in his court, none more so than Shaykh Baraka of Andkhoi.†

---

* Sunni Islam, the most widely followed, orthodox sect of Islam, stressed the original dynasty of the caliphs, while the Shi'a faction, which broke off in 661, supported the rival dynasty of caliphs begun by Ali, son-in-law of the Prophet. Sunni and Shi'a Islam are united only by three core doctrines: the oneness of God, and belief in both the revelations of the Prophet and resurrection on the Day of Judgement.

† Sufism is a mystical orientation within Islam, its followers dedicated to following an inner way or spiritual path to bring them closer to God. The soul is regarded as able to reach out from the physical body to the divine spheres. The many varied techniques of Sufism tend to revolve around rhythm, repetition and endurance, whether through recitation of certain phrases or through singing and dancing. The whirling dervish, who

Temur also buried family members in handsome tombs next to the shrines of distinguished Sufis. But if the hints of his Sufist sympathies were strong, signs of support for the Shi'a were hardly lacking either. The most striking is to be found on his tombstone in the Gur Amir mausoleum in Samarkand, where an elaborate and largely invented family tree traces him back to Ali, the son-in-law of the Prophet. In another nod to Shi'ite tradition, Temur displayed special attention to the descendants of the Prophet throughout his life. It is just as difficult for modern scholars to pin him down on his religious allegiances as it was for his contemporaries. Temur was a chameleon. Whatever worked or furthered his cause in any way was good. This was a cynical interpretation, certainly, but what his message of *jihad* lacked in intellectual coherence and consistency, it made up for in the sheer projection of force. It was, quite simply, the creed of conquest.

It was in the public displays that Islam shone brightest. The five daily prayers were a regular feature of life at Temur's court. Wherever he campaigned, with him went the imams and the royal mosque, a sumptuously appointed pavilion made of the finest silk. From it came the ululating cadences of the *muaddin*, calling forth the faithful to prayer. One of Temur's most practised routines was to prostrate himself on the ground and offer up prayers to the Almighty prior to

---

reaches a trancelike state by spinning ever faster to the accompaniment of music, is perhaps the best-known example of Sufism in practice. The original whirling dervish, it is said, was none other than Rumi, the Sufi mystic and poet.

> *As waves upon my head the circling curl,*
> *So in the sacred dance weave ye and whirl.*
> *Dance then, O heart, a whirling circle be.*
> *Burn in this flame – is not the candle He?*

Sufism remains strongest in Egypt and Sudan, particularly in rural areas, but has declined in popularity to the extent that today there are only an estimated five million followers within the entire Muslim world.

joining battle. This was done in full view of his princes, amirs and soldiers, and served as a reminder that God was on his side, a message reinforced by the dutiful religious leaders who always accompanied the armies on their campaigns.

Pre-eminent among these was Shaykh Sayid Baraka, whom Temur had met in Termez during the early years of rivalry with Husayn. In 1391, as Temur's army stared across the Kunduzcha river at the ranks of Tokhtamish's soldiers, Baraka picked up some dirt and flung it at the enemy. 'Your faces shall be blackened through the shame of your defeat,' he roared. 'Go where you please,' he continued, turning to Temur. 'You shall be victorious.' Once again the emperor's mounted archers rode to triumph.

It was a straightforward, symbiotic relationship. The priestly entourage owed its position to Temur, and in return for this generous patronage assured him – and the soldiers – of the Almighty's support for whatever military campaign His servant on earth might propose. Sycophantic clerics, if called on, would justify any action. As Hilda Hookham put it in her 1962 biography: 'With the blessing of the *shaykhs*, Temur could lead his hordes against all the kingdoms of the seven climes, destroying infidels because they were not Muslims and Muslims because they were not faithful.'

Obsequious court writers like Yazdi, in the service of one of Temur's grandsons, later fulfilled the same purpose. 'We have a tradition of Mahomet,' he observed, 'wherein he assures us that he was the child of the sword, and that the most happy moments which he passed with God were when he had the sword in his hand; and he adds, that paradise itself is under the protection of the sword: which demonstrates that kings are not peaceable possessors of the throne, but when they are victorious; and that subjects cannot enjoy quiet in their families, but by the protection of the sword of their prince.'

Yet the Lord of the Fortunate Conjunction was just as likely to consult astrologers as holy men for the opportune moment to strike.

Their duty was to determine the disposition of the planets. In practice this meant delivering the verdict the emperor wanted to hear. His response to their deductions was governed, as ever, by expediency. If the astrologers failed to reach the desired conclusion, they were ignored. When, at the gates of Delhi, they decided the omens were unfavourable for attack, Temur simply reverted to Islam. 'Neither fortune nor affliction depends on the stars,' he replied with severity. 'I confide myself to the care of the Almighty, who has never yet abandoned me. What does it matter if the planets are in this or that relationship?' As the astrologers retreated in shame, he promptly took out his copy of the Koran and opened it, conveniently, at a passage which indicated that victory was assured. It was.

Temur saw no contradiction between bloodshed and Islam. The transition from slaughter on the battlefield one day and quiet reflection in a mosque or shrine the next posed no moral difficulties for him. Days after ravaging Delhi so utterly it took the city a century to recover, he strode calmly into the beautiful mosque on the river Jumna to give thanks for his victory. In Baghdad, as his soldiers put the finishing touches to the 120 towers of skulls, while the Tigris ran red with blood and the air was putrid from rotting corpses, Temur was visiting the tomb of the venerated eighth-century imam Abu Hanifa, chief of one of the four orthodox sects of Islam, 'to implore the intercession of this saint'. In his understanding that appearances were everything, and with his instinct for choreographed expressions of piety, Temur demonstrated a profoundly modern approach to the politics of his day.

Wine was another subject on which Temur revealed his ambivalence towards religion and his preference for Mongol custom. Strictly prohibited by Islam, it was generally not permitted in his court. But there were numerous exceptions when it flowed freely: at the lavish Tatar banquets held to celebrate a victory in battle; during a family wedding; or on the conclusion of Ramadan. The Spanish ambassador Clavijo was one witness among many to bacchanalian orgies which owed more to the heathen traditions of Genghis Khan and the Mongols than the strictures of Islam. A beautiful cup-bearer was assigned to each man at the feast, the Spaniard noted. Her duty was to ensure that the guest's golden goblet was kept full at all times. Refusing a toast, in which the entire contents of the vessel had to be downed, was considered a serious breach of etiquette and a sign of discourtesy towards the emperor. Teetotallers generally discovered a sudden affection for the grape on such occasions. Feasts invariably ended in a drunken blur. Those warriors who could still stand would grab a companion for the night and stagger back to their tents. There was nothing Islamic about that.

Moments like these betrayed Temur's genius for the popular gesture. Sometimes these were designed to underline his position as an Islamic leader, such as *zakat* (the giving of alms), the observation of Ramadan or the prohibition on eating pork. At other moments it was the laws of Genghis he chose to honour, reassuring his followers that the traditions of the steppe were supreme. He was highly intelligent, ambitious, manipulative, cynical and exploitative. The question whether he was a good Muslim or whether he abided by Mongol customs misses the point. Temur was interested in either code insofar as it supported his designs of conquest. What is important to appreciate is the skill with which he managed to use now one, now the other, to his advantage. And this in turn testifies to his outstanding capacity for leadership.

Nowhere were these talents so much in evidence as with his armies. The foundation of his empire, the men by whom kingdoms were won or lost, Temur's mounted archers were governed by a combination of iron discipline and lavish reward. They knew they could be cut in half, hanged, run through with a sword or otherwise executed for cowardice, treachery or unlicensed plunder. They also understood that unswerving loyalty to Temur on and off the battlefield was the most likely path to riches.

Temur's generosity, referred to throughout the sources, was one of the causes of his victory over Husayn during their struggle for supremacy in Mawarannahr in the late 1360s. Where Husayn was greedy and loath to share the spoils of battle with his soldiers, Temur was generous to the point of self-impoverishment. While the amir of Balkh was happy to see Temur pay a punitive head tax with jewellery belonging to his wife, Husayn's own sister, Temur regarded as a priority the reward of his supporters. This was not out of any sentimental regard for their prosperity and comfort. It was merely the most effective method of retaining their allegiance in a political system notorious for shifting, opportunistic alliances. The chronicles are full of tales of plunder, with soldiers staggering home under the weight of ransacked goods at the head of vast caravans of enslaved prisoners. Temur's reputation for largesse served his military ambitions admirably. It also won him defections from his enemies. At times, such as the battle of Ankara in 1402, these defections were instrumental to his victories. In 1391, after his first defeat of Tokhtam-ish, he distributed priceless gifts to his soldiers in thanks for their courage on the battlefield. Yazdi related how:

> He distributed robes of honour, and belts adorned with precious stones, to the princes, Emirs, Cheriffs, and all the lords and officers of his army: he also honoured with his favours the generals and captains of his troops, as a recompense for their fatigue, and in joy of his victories. But the pleasure which the great warriors received, when Temur applauded their actions, was inexpressibly great; in this charming retreat he sent them in cups of gold the most delicious wines by the hands of the most beautiful women in the world.

Both discipline and reward came to depend upon the emperor himself rather than the tribal leaders at the lower level. Temur deliberately appointed men from the ranks of his personal followers, including family members, to positions of high command. This was done to undermine the traditional system of armies being led by tribal chiefs, the main source of potential opposition to him – or, *in extremis*, outright rebellion. It resulted in the formation of a new military class directly loyal to his person, free from the political constraints of the tribe. These men enjoyed hereditary positions, which meant that in time, through their sons and grandsons, as well as his own, the numbers of Temur's personal followers steadily increased. As his power grew and the size of his armies swelled from captured forces and fresh conscription, the authority of this new elite went from strength to strength, while the influence of the tribal leaders waned in parallel.

The organisation of Temur's armies would have been recognised at once by Genghis Khan, for it followed the structure of the Mongols'. There was a left wing, a right wing, the centre and the advance guard. The smallest unit of men was ten soldiers, an *onlik*, led by an *onbashi*. Ten of these groups formed the *yuzlik*, under the next rank of *yuz-bashi*, officers denoted by the kettle-drums slung across the saddles of their outriders. After this came the *binlik*, a body of a thousand troops under the command of a *binbashi*. The most senior rank beneath Temur was the amir who presided over ten thousand men, a *tuman*, whose insignia was the *tuk*, a long lance with a horse's tail fastened at its tip.

Temur always heaped rewards on those who had shown particular valour on the battlefield. Acts of outstanding bravery were commemorated in the official court chronicles. Promotion depended above all on one's military conduct. An *onbashi* would be made a *yuzbashi* after performing some heroic action, while the commander of a hundred became the commander of a thousand. The most senior officers were granted the ultimate title of *tarkhan*, a position harking back to the days of Genghis Khan. This conferred on them a number of important privileges, among which the most valuable was the permanent exemption from taxes. Unlike any other soldier in Temur's armies, the *tarkhan* was entitled to keep everything he plundered. Everyone else had to make over a share of his spoils to the emperor. The *tarkhan* was also immune from criminal prosecution. Only after he had committed the same crime nine times was he answerable to justice. Perhaps the ultimate prize was his access to Temur at all times.

It was the responsibility of the aides-de-camp, the *tovachis*, to ensure that the soldiers were properly equipped. Once conscripted, each man had to report for service with a bow, a quiver containing thirty arrows, a shield and enough grain to feed a horse for a year. For every two cavalrymen a spare horse was required, and each *onlik*, the body of ten soldiers, had to bring a tent, two spades, a pickaxe, rope, hide, an awl, an axe, a saw and one hundred needles. The Tatar foot-soldier carried a bow, an axe, a dagger, a sabre and a small round shield, wooden with an iron rim, hung at the hip. In winter he wore black sheepskins, coloured kaftans in summer, over either tight or baggy trousers and boots. On his head he sported a tall hat made of fur, felt or sheepskin. There was a comprehensive range of secondary weapons, including maces and varieties of swords, knives and shields. The richer soldiers had helmets, single-edged sabres and coats of mail for themselves and their horses. The Tatar composite bow, the main arm on which Temur's armies depended, was a formidable weapon, considerably longer than the Persian, Turk or Indian versions.* It fired a heavier arrow with a shorter range.

---

* The Central Asian composite bow, made from horn, wood and sinew, was one of the most devastating bows ever created. Historians have rightly made much of the English longbow, scourge of the French at the battles of Crécy and Agincourt in the Hundred Years' War, but the composite bow was a superior weapon by far. Unlike the longbow, which was about six feet in length, it was extremely short, varying between forty and fifty inches. This portable size made it an ideal weapon for a mounted archer, who, unlike the longbowman on the ground, did not become obsolete against a charging enemy after only one or two shots. Moreover, despite

Temur's soldiers made much use of another destructive technology. Greek-fire, invented in the seventh century, was a gelatinous incendiary mixture, fired at one's enemy through bronze tubes. Its original composition is unknown, a closely guarded secret handed down from one Byzantine emperor to another, but it is thought to have been made from a combination of flammable materials such as sulphur, naphtha, quicklime and pitch in a petroleum base. Since it ignited spontaneously and could not be extinguished by water, it was a profoundly effective weapon, sowing panic among those who faced it.

In battle, the principal tactics and techniques employed by Temur were horse-archery, envelopment of his enemy where possible, and, a particular favourite, used with enormous success, feigned flight. At Aleppo, for example, his men staged a deliberate retreat, leading the Syrians right behind their lines, where they were fallen upon and utterly routed. The Tatars, wrote an observer at the outset of the fourteenth century, 'are for the most part victorious over their enemies; yet they are not afraid to turn their backs in a fight if it is to their advantage ... Their manner of fighting is very dangerous, so that in one Tatar battle or skirmish there are more slain or wounded

---

its small size, its curved frame provided a draw just as long as that of the longbow, and a range double that of a wooden bow of similar weight. The longbow had to be the height of a man to withstand the strain of the long draw. The more advanced technology of the composite bow, which used three different materials, avoided such constraints. Although designs changed over the years, and from region to region, the composite bow had a wooden core which formed the frame and determined its final shape. On the side facing the archer was a layer of buffalo horn, which could withstand great compression. The opposite side – facing the target – was covered with sinew, which could withstand high levels of tension. These were bonded together with glue, given a covering of tree bark, skin or leather, and then coated in paint or lacquer to protect the hygroscopic weapon from the elements. A reflexed bow, it curved sharply forward when at rest, stretching back considerably when drawn. In the hands of Temur's mounted archers, who used bronze thumb rings to give them maximum draw on the bowstring, the weapon was used to brilliant effect.

than in any great conflict between other nations, which results from their archery, for they shoot strongly and surely, being indeed so skilful in the art of shooting that they commonly pierce all kinds of armour, and if they happen to be routed they flee in troops and bands so well ordered that it is very dangerous to follow or pursue them, because they shoot arrows backwards in their flight, often wounding both men and horses that pursue them.'

Men predominated in the lines, but war was by no means their exclusive preserve, as Arabshah noted.

> There were also in his army many women who mingled in the mêlée of battle and in fierce conflicts and strove with men and fought with brave warriors and overcame mighty heroes in combat with the thrust of the spear, the blow of the sword and shooting of arrows; when one of them was heavy with child and birth pangs seized her, while they were on the march, she turned from the way and withdrawing apart and descending from her beast, gave birth to the child and wrapping it in bandages, soon mounted her beast and taking the child with her, followed her company; and there were in his army men born on the march and grown to full age who married and begot children and yet never had a fixed home.

A leader of impressive intellect and infinite cunning, Temur placed a premium on good, timely intelligence, the lifeblood of his many campaigns. A vast network of spies fanned out from Samarkand across his lands and into the kingdoms and empires of those he sought to conquer. Well represented among them were the Islamic orders, itinerant monks, dervishes, *shaykhs* and Sufis. 'He was of rare temper and depth so deep that in the sea of his plans the bottom could not be touched, nor could one reach the high peak of his government by a smooth or rough path,' wrote Arabshah. 'He had placed through his realm his informers and in other kingdoms had appointed his spies; and these were amirs like Atilmish, one of his allies, or learned fakirs, like Masaud Kahajani, his chief minister, or traders seeking a living by some craft, ill-minded wrestlers, criminal athletes, labourers, craftsmen, soothsayers, physicians, wandering hermits, chatterers, strolling vagabonds, sailors, wanderers by land, elegant drunkards, witty singers, aged procuresses and crafty old women.'

These men, women and children brought back news from across Asia, from the prices and availability of various commodities to the state of an enemy kingdom, the names of its military leaders and nobles and the mapping of its lands and cities. 'One skilful plan can perform the service of a hundred thousand warriors,' Temur was reported to have said.

To aid the flow of information, Temur, like the Mongols, used a system of posting stations known as *yams*. Up to two hundred horses were kept at each regularly staged post and stable, the costs met by the local population. Clavijo, who witnessed their operations at first hand while on his way to the emperor's court, left a typically detailed description of how zealously the envoys and couriers went about their work on behalf of the emperor. Such was the importance accorded government business that if any envoy riding a tiring mount came upon other riders with fresher horses, these were required on pain of death to dismount and hand over their animals to the messenger and his entourage. No one was spared this inconvenience: the Spaniard was told that on one occasion Temur's eldest son and his attendants were forced to surrender their horses to envoys en route to Samarkand.

The information and intelligence contained in his envoys' despatches was highly valued and jealously guarded by Temur. They were under strict orders to ride full tilt around the clock. 'Temur indeed sets much store that those he sends and those who come to him should ride post day and night,' Clavijo recorded. 'So doing they may easily cover fifty leagues in the twenty-four hours, though by thus riding they will kill two horses. But this may be, rather than to take three days over that journey: for he deems speed to be much to his service.' This was no exaggeration. Such hard riding inevitably took its toll, the unsightly evidence plain for all to see: 'By the roadside many were the dead horses we saw during our journey, which had thus been ridden to death and the carcass abandoned: the number indeed a marvel to note.'

※

It is hardly surprising, given the range of his military triumphs, the part of the world from which he came, and the conscious emulation, when it suited him, of the traditions inspired by his illustrious predecessor, that Temur should find himself compared with Genghis Khan. History's verdict has been divided, with the rival camps occupying the ground staked out for them by the original protagonists, Arabshah on the one hand and Yazdi on the other.

In a recent history of Russia and the Mongols, Leo de Hartog found Temur both cruder and crueller than Genghis.

> Temur was as merciless as the Mongol world conqueror had been, but his subtle methods were often characterised by sadism, which had never been present in Genghis Khan. In the field of religion there were also great differences between the two. A parochial Muslim, Temur had little understanding of other faiths, while the shamanistic Genghis Khan was particularly tolerant towards other religions.

In fact, it is not at all clear that Temur was as merciless as Genghis. There are numerous stories of acts of clemency on his part. Cities which surrendered quickly, such as Herat, Urganch and Baghdad, tended to be treated far more leniently than those whose resistance occasioned casualties among Temur's soldiers and required an all-out assault. Those which opted to rise against him, however, could expect little quarter. As for the destruction which followed his every campaign, Temur was much more likely than Genghis to spare both men and monuments; and even when he did not he frequently had the same cities his men had razed to the ground rebuilt in the interests of trade and agriculture.

That Temur was cruel is beyond question. But to accuse him of sadism is to indulge in unfounded speculation which owes more to the prejudices of the twenty-first century than the values of the fourteenth, when human life was held far cheaper than it is today. Temur was no exemplar of cruelty. When the Mamluk sultan Baybars took Antioch in 1263, for example, he had the sixteen-thousand-strong garrison slaughtered and the hundred thousand inhabitants sold into slavery. The massacres Temur committed were neither for his amusement nor pleasure. They were carried out to strike terror into his opponents' hearts, to rid his newly conquered territories of opponents, and to minimise the risks of rebellion.

The charge of religious intolerance is likewise wide of the mark. Temur used Islam primarily as an instrument conferring prestige and legitimacy on his actions. The charge of parochialism is one that not even his detractors, least of all Arabshah, would have recognised. Temur's was the politics of the expedient. In an age when the Crescent and the Cross faced each other across the Aegean and the Mediterranean like the standards of hostile armies, it was Temur, and not the Ottoman sultan, who made friendly overtures towards the Christian princes of Europe. In Temur's thinking the practicalities of trade between Europe and Asia could outweigh the traditional, deeply held religious antagonism between Christendom and the lands of Islam. He was a man of vision, his intellectual horizons as broad as the steppes across which he led his armies to victory.

Arminius Vambery, the nineteenth-century Hungarian traveller and philologist, was better able to put Temur in historical perspective. He dismissed comparisons with Genghis. 'Those who would rank Temur side by side with a Chinghiz, as a mere savage, wilful tyrant, are doubly in error,' he wrote. 'He was pre-eminently an Asiatic soldier who used his victories after the fashion of his time and country.'

Genghis had delegated civil and military command. After his early conquests, he directed his sweeping campaigns from his headquarters in Karakorum. Temur, a more reckless commander, had no interest in holding back from the fray. Samarkand, though the imperial capital, came to know him as an absentee emperor, forever appearing with untold riches plundered from the great cities of Asia, celebrating his victories at famously sumptuous banquets that could last several months, before disappearing again on campaigns of up to five years. Unlike Genghis, Temur was rarely absent from the battlefield, where he frequently threw himself into the action at great personal danger.

Sir John Malcolm, the nineteenth-century soldier, statesman and historian, provided one of the best appreciations of Temur's military charisma: 'Such a leader as Temur must have been idolized by his soldiers ... he was careless of the opinion of other classes in the community. His object was fame as a conqueror; and a noble city was laid in ashes, or the inhabitants of a province massacred, on a cold calculation that the dreadful impression would facilitate the purposes of his ambition.'

But whatever their respective styles on the battlefield, perhaps the most striking difference was evident off it. By today's standards, Temur was a nomadic conqueror. He was constantly on the move. Hardly had he finished one campaign than his armies were assembled for another. Genghis and his Mongol hordes would, however, probably have viewed Temur's career with disdain, for in Samarkand the Tatar had built a permanent capital, a concession to the way of life of the despised settled population, and a violation of the nomadic tradition cherished by the warriors of the steppe. Temur's beloved city, the Pearl of the East, betrayed his love of opulence. The splendid mosques and madrassahs, the parks and the palaces, each of them a wonder of the world, revealed an appreciation of artistic excellence and architectural beauty that was entirely foreign to Genghis. Both men unleashed havoc across half the known world, put millions to the sword and razed to the earth cities standing in their path. But only Temur saw fit to rebuild, for he was a creator as much as a destroyer. This marked him out as a different breed of conqueror altogether. Much of his life was spent honouring the ancient traditions established by his Mongol predecessor, but by the time he died Temur was his own emperor, in thrall to no other man. Samarkand was the greatest expression of this individuality. It was a tribute to his undefeated military career and a monument to his imperial vanity.

Over four decades the city soaked up Temur's offerings like an avaricious mistress. There was gold, silver, precious stones, marble, exotic beasts, fabulous cloths, silks, tapestries, slaves and spices; yet still she was not satisfied. Each time he returned with more, she sent him back out into battle. Her glorification required ever increasing spoils from countless victories. Only constant campaigning could deliver them.

By the end of the 1370s, Temur's emerging empire took in the treasures and territories of Khorezm and Mawarannahr. Now, with Samarkand whispering in his ear, his eyes roved westward for more.

4

Conquest in the West

1379–1387

'The world is like an ocean and in the ocean is a pearl, and the pearl is Herat.'

ANCIENT PERSIAN PROVERB

'In Herat if you stretch out your feet you are sure to kick a poet.'

ALI SHER NAWAI

Five hundred miles south-west of Samarkand, a forest of slim minarets rose from the drab desert plain. Herat was, with Merv, Balkh and Nishapur, one of the four great capitals of Khorasan, the Country of the Rising Sun.* Straddling a branch of one of Asia's busiest trade routes, it was a city of antiquity, culture and riches. The Herat river,

---

* Today, Khorasan refers only to the north-eastern province of Iran, but in medieval times it covered a far larger territory. For Arab geographers it encompassed everything from Dasht-i-Kavir, the central desert of Iran, to the borders of China in the east, and to those of India in the south. By the fourteenth and fifteenth centuries, however, it had shrunk to the equivalent of Iranian Khorasan, southern Turkmenistan, and northern north-western Afghanistan.

snaking down from the Hindu Kush mountains of central Afghanistan, wended its way westwards past the throng of mosques and minarets before turning north and petering out in the sands of the Qara Kum desert. Little rain fell in this part of the world, and irrigation was provided by an ancient network of canals. East of the city, the Paropamisus range, an extension of the Hindu Kush, was virtually impassable. In practical terms this meant that Herat lay on the first route running north and south through the mountains west of Kabul.

The city's fortifications reflected its strategic location. The walls were nine thousand paces in circuit, according to Hamd Allah Mustawfi al Qazwini, the fourteenth-century geographer and historian, and around them stretched a suburban girdle of eighteen villages. The powerfully reinforced citadel on a hilltop two leagues north of the city offered further protection from attack. The city reached its apogee in the twelfth century, al Qazwini wrote, when there were twelve thousand shops in the markets, six thousand hot baths and 659 colleges. The population was 444,000.* Apart from the dervish convent, a Zoroastrian fire temple and numerous caravanserais, the many mills 'turned by wind, not by water' particularly impressed him.

More impressive still were Herat's many treasures, admired and envied throughout the region. Most famous were the textiles – fabulous silks, tapestries, hangings, cottons, cushions, cloaks and carpets. The markets thronged with dealers selling metalwork and precious stones – gold, silver, rubies, turquoise, lapis lazuli – and fruit – melons, grapes, pomegranates, apricots and apples. Slaves could be found in plenty. The indefatigable traveller Ibn Battutah found

---

* To give an idea of the size of European towns in the fourteenth century, in Italy only four – Milan, Venice, Naples and Florence – could boast populations of over fifty thousand. Paris had in the region of eighty thousand inhabitants. Cologne, the largest city in Germany, had a population approaching forty thousand, almost identical to that of London.

Heratis 'religious, sincere and chaste' when he visited in the early 1330s. It was, he reported, 'the largest inhabited city in Khorasan', a centre of commerce and culture at a time when Merv and Balkh still lay in ruins after the Mongol invasion of 1221.

In fact, Herat was one of the finest cities in the empire which had been carved out by Genghis Khan's grandson Hulagu, the Buddhist founder of the Ilkhanid dynasty, in Persia, Mesopotamia and Syria during the 1250s, the high point of Mongol expansion. As their name, Ilkhans ('subordinate khans'), suggested, they owed their authority to the Great Khans in Mongolia and China until the close of the thirteenth century.

Moving west from Mongolia at the behest of his brother, Great Khan Mönke, in 1253, Hulagu was given the task of destroying two powerful enemies, both of them Muslim. First were the Ismailis, a radical Shi'ite sect also known as the Assassins, who had established themselves in mountain strongholds south of the Caspian, centred in Alamut, 'The Eagle's Nest'. Mönke's hostility to the Ismailis, according to the missionary William of Rubruck, who was sent to Karakorum by Louis IX of France, derived from the unsuccessful attempt by four hundred Assassins in disguise to kill him in his imperial capital. There is more than a whiff of revenge about Hulagu's subsequent campaign during 1256 and 1257, in which he utterly destroyed the Ismailis, who had terrorised Persia's Sunni leaders for almost two centuries, with consummate ease. As Gibbon dryly remarked, the Mongols' crushing of the Ismailis was a 'service to mankind'.

The second enemy Hulagu was sent to defeat was the Abbasid caliphate in Baghdad, which for five centuries had been the beating heart of Sunni Islam. He arrived before the walls of the venerable city in 1258. After it refused to surrender, it was besieged, stormed and sacked. The numbers of those killed in the onslaught range from Hulagu's estimate of two hundred thousand to the eight hundred thousand suggested by al Qazwini. Either way, the bloodshed was devastating. When it finally came, the caliph's surrender was too late. Though it was the Mongols' custom not to shed the blood of noble enemies, as the caliph discovered to his cost, this did not mean they were spared. The distinguished leader of the Sunni Islamic world was wrapped up in a carpet and trampled to death by horses.

Fresh from this impromptu execution, in 1260 Hulagu continued west into Syria, then ruled by the Ayubid dynasty founded by Saladin the previous century. The ancient cities of Damascus and Aleppo quickly fell, and the Crusader authorities of Antioch and Tripoli lost little time in kneeling before the Mongol invaders. But Syria was destined to remain beyond the boundaries of the Hulagid empire. Once again the momentous death of the Great Khan was to shape world history, as that of Ogedey in 1241 had spared Europe the horrors of the Mongol advance. Hulagu learnt of his brother Mönke's demise in the same year he conquered Syria. The news prompted the inevitable struggle for succession to the Mongol throne between his brothers, and Hulagu withdrew from Syria, leaving only a nominal force behind. Later in 1260, a Mamluk army defeated the Mongols at the famous battle of Ain Jalut in Galilee, a date which in retrospect looks like the pinnacle of Mongol conquest. Though there were repeated attempts to retake Syria, the Ilkhanid territories had by this time reached their limits. To the west, their lands ranged as far as the Euphrates, to the north up to the Caucasus mountains running from the Black Sea to the Caspian, with the Oxus and Punjab rivers marking their easternmost boundaries. Hulagu reigned until his death in 1265, but the Ilkhanid dynasty, a hybrid of Buddhist, Christian and latterly Islamic leaders, lasted until the 1350s (ever since Ghazan's renunciation of Buddhism in favour of Islam in 1295, Persia has been governed by a Muslim ruler).

In sum, Mongol rule was an exceptionally traumatic experience for Persia. According to al Qazwini, a thousand years would not have been enough to repair the damage done by Genghis's initial massacres.

Juvayni, one of the most distinguished official historians of the Mongol period, wrote that 'every town and every village' had fallen victim to repeated pillage and slaughter so severe that the population would never reach even 10 per cent of its former total again. The civilian population of cities such as Merv, Balkh, Nishapur, Hamadan, Tus, Ray, Qazwin, and Herat were systematically put to the sword. In many areas of Persia agriculture was obliterated as peasants fled their land, irrigation channels fell into ruin and the desert reclaimed the once fertile land. This process was only accelerated with the arrival of nomadic Mongol hordes who gravitated towards the best lands as pasturage for their animals.

Historians have judged Ilkhanid rule as a time of cultural efflorescence, when communications between East and West improved through increased trade. Religious barriers were similarly taken down with the steady assimilation of the Mongols – led by their rulers – into the Islamic fold. From this time Persia started to replace Arabic as the language of high culture. Mongol rule also witnessed the birth of official histories of Persia with the writings of Rashid ad-din, chief minister of the Ilkhanate for two decades, Juvayni and Wassaf. With these strengthening cultural cross-currents, Chinese landscape painting began to influence the Persian school of miniaturists, which now embarked on its golden age.

Such cultural benefits to Persia of Mongol rule were all very well. But, as David Morgan concluded in a recent study of medieval Persia: 'We may justly have our doubts over how impressed the Persian peasants, as they did their best to avoid the Mongol tax-collectors, would have been by developments in miniature painting. For Persia, the Mongol period was a disaster on a grand and unparalleled scale.' It is difficult to disagree.

As for Herat, the city proved remarkably resilient, as evidenced by its renewed prosperity by the time of Temur's campaign. This despite the fact that it had been one of the centres worst affected by the

Mongol depredations. Infuriated by an uprising of Heratis after the city had surrendered in 1221, Genghis had issued orders to his general Aljigidey to return and spare no one. Saifi, the fourteenth-century historian of Herat, recorded his command: 'The dead have come to life again. This time you must cut the people's heads off. You must execute the whole population of Herat.' For a week Aljigidey cut down the inhabitants until none remained. Several days later, after he had withdrawn, he despatched a force of two thousand horsemen back to the city to make sure anyone who had gone into hiding was put to death. Another two thousand were killed. Only sixteen survived the final slaughter, Saifi wrote. Such was the devastation about them that they were forced to eat the corpses of men and animals. For four years they found food only by raiding occasional caravans.

With the disintegration of the Ilkhanid dynasty in 1335, Persia fell victim to vicious infighting once more, crumbling into competing kingdoms for the most part disputed by rival princes of the powerful Muzaffarid family. Their control was by no means absolute, however, as other dynasties reasserted themselves in the absence of the Mongols. In Baghdad, the Jalayirid clan held sway, while in Sabzawar (in the north-eastern Iranian province of Khorasan) the Sarbadars clung on to power.

Three hundred miles to the south-east, the city of Herat remained under the control of Malik Ghiyas ad-din Pir Ali, leader of the Kart dynasty which had governed the city and much of modern Afghanistan as vassals of the Mongols since the middle of the thirteenth century. Great patrons of literature and the arts, lavish builders of mosques and fine public buildings, the Karts were largely responsible for creating the wealth and opulence of the city amid the ruins of the Mongol conquests.

This, then, was the city Temur now resolved to conquer.

Galloping across the steppe, fording rivers and threading his way through rocky passes, Temur's envoy delivered a portentous summons to Ghiyas ad-din Pir Ali in 1379. The letter requested his attendance at one of the Tatar's *qurultays*, a formal notification that Temur now regarded the head of the Kart dynasty as a vassal. This would come to be a typical device prior to the invasion of new lands, invariably giving him the *casus belli* he was looking for.

It was an ominous, as well as a galling, message to receive. In former, less auspicious times as a roving mercenary, Temur had been taken into the service of Ghiyas ad-din's father, Malik Muizz ad-din Husayn. When he died, Ghiyas ad-din had continued the cordial relations, marrying off his eldest son to Temur's niece. Now he was being asked to acknowledge the authority of the man who only a few years before had been his father's liege. Stalling for time, he replied that he would freely come to Samarkand, and only required an escort to guide him. Temur's trusted amir Sayf ad-din Nukuz duly set out to accompany him to Mawarannahr, but arrived instead to discover the ruler of Herat fortifying his walls in preparation for the defence of his city. He had no intention of giving up his kingdom.

Temur's course was set. The *tovachis* sprang into action, assembling an army for the first campaign outside its own provinces. Each soldier's equipment was inspected by his commanding officer, who reported in turn to his superior. The amirs, gorgeously turned out in their bright armour, finely embossed shields, long lances and bows, stood out from the dark ranks of their *tumans*, the bodies of ten thousand soldiers. Preparations were meticulous, for like Genghis, Temur planned to the last detail. Spies were sent ahead to scout the lie of the land and assess the strength of enemy lines. Provender was packed and loaded for the horses. Women and families collected their belongings for the weeks and months that lay ahead. Supplies were checked and double-checked until, at last, the army was ready to march. Then the amirs lifted their horse-tail standards and the trumpets and kettle-drums sounded the deafening call to war. The Three-Year Campaign was under way.

South-west the army rode to the garrison town of Fushanj, re-inforced to guard the approach to Herat. Under all-out assault, it fell as soon as the hordes had breached its defences through an aqueduct. The garrison was cut down where it stood. Blood ran through the streets.

Learning of the disastrous news, Ghiyas ad-din retreated behind his city walls, much to the contempt of Arabshah. 'He shut himself in the fortress, thinking that in this way he would be inaccessible – because of the weakness of his counsel and the stupidity and folly which were his ruin,' the Syrian wrote. The city was under siege. Frantically, he tried to muster a defence but the inhabitants of Herat, having heard of the precipitate collapse of Fushanj and the slaughter of its garrison, were in no mood to take on Temur. He had 'encircled the perimeter of the city and its suburbs like the bezel around the stone of a ring, like the halo around the moon, and like flies on sugar', and was not going to release his grip until his demands had been met. A master of psychological warfare, the Tatar offered an incentive to the besieged by letting it be known that all those who refused to fight him would be spared. The proposal was eagerly accepted from within the walls. Only by surrendering promptly would their expensive properties be safeguarded, the Heratis reasoned. Resistance against the Tatar's superior forces was futile. It would only be met by the sword and the flame. Swayed by these considerations and mindful of the marauding hordes who were already undermining his walls, the Kart prince capitulated. Accompanied by the notables of Herat, he offered his submission in a humiliating public ceremony. 'Temur pardoned him and caressed him,' wrote Yazdi, 'gave him a belt of honour, and a belt set with precious stones, and then dismissed him.' The city paid for the lives of its inhabitants with a punitive ransom.

The vast treasures of Herat now belonged to Temur. A carefully established system, intended to minimise losses to his treasury, specified precisely how they were to be taken. It was generally observed with the same rigorous discipline which characterised the command of his armies. First, all the gates in the city walls bar one were sealed – on occasions they were even walled up – to prevent both premature plundering by his soldiers and the smuggling away of portable property by the citizens. Once this had been completed, the torturers and the tax collectors marched in, confiscating property, searching houses, extracting confessions from those suspected of having hidden wealth or knowing other families who had yet to detail their belongings. All goods surrendered were taken to collection centres, where they were registered by the amirs, among whom the ransom money was distributed. The houses of the local aristocracy, which had contributed most of this payment, were generally spared. A military cordon was thrown around their neighbourhood. Only when Temur's officials had completed their requisitions were his soldiers allowed to plunder. If they acted prematurely and were caught in the act, they paid with their lives. Like Genghis, Temur preferred to take a city by ransom, not out of any reticence about shedding the blood of innocents, but from purely economic considerations. Seizing it by force inevitably led to outbreaks of unlicensed plunder and a sharp loss of revenue.

In the case of Herat, the massive operation to extract anything and everything of value went smoothly, and the coffers of the most opulent metropolis in Khorasan were opened to reveal wonderful riches. 'It is remarkable that there were in this city all sorts of treasures, as silver money, unpolished precious stones, the richest thrones, crowns of gold, silver vessels, gold and silver brocades, and curiosities of all kinds,' wrote Yazdi. 'The soldiers, according to the imperial order, carried away all these riches upon camels.' The monumental iron-clad Darvazaya Malik, the King's Gate of Herat, adorned with sculptures and inscriptions, was cut down and taken to Shakhrisabz. Just as their counterparts in Urganch had been taken prisoner after that city's fall, the intellectuals and artisans of Herat – the scholars and churchmen, artists and craftsmen – were rounded up and sent to Samarkand, the second in a lifelong series of forced expulsions intended to glorify Temur's capital with the intellectual and artistic fruits of their labour. Ghiyas ad-din, the defeated Kart prince, was permitted to remain in office as Temur's vassal. Determined that neither he nor the city should ever resist him again, Temur had the defensive walls pulled down.*

Herat had fallen to him with hardly a murmur. A city long revered by the poets, prosperous from trade and rich in culture, had slipped into the net of his empire so easily it must have given Temur pause for thought. Having harnessed the loyalties of the competing tribes of the Chaghatay ulus, he had rewarded them with the plunder of the fallen city, establishing his leadership and expanding his territorial sway in the process. It was the beginning of a long-standing equation, in which the confederation of steppe tribes exchanged their loyalty and military service in return for the fruits of Temur's campaigns. Once united, the soldiers offered Temur the opportunity to win new lands by the sword. He offered them the chance to enrich themselves and to win distinction and lucrative promotion on the battlefield. This coalescence of interests was the central pillar sustaining Temur's long career. Herat offered other lessons, too. If he could achieve such

---

* Despite these precautions, the people of Herat rebelled against Temur only two years later. This time the conqueror sent his son Miranshah to quash the uprising, a task he completed with brutal efficiency. The members of the Kart royal family were executed and towers piled high with the skulls of the dead. The city never rebelled again. In 1389 Miranshah killed Pir Mohammed, the last survivor of the dynasty. According to one story, he cut off the prince's head in the middle of a high-spirited banquet, an act he later blamed on the vast quantities of wine he had consumed.

success beyond his borders without even engaging his men in battle, what greater trophies awaited when they were put to the test? There was time to contemplate this question during the hard winter months that followed, when the Amu Darya and Sir Darya rivers turned to ice and Temur and his men encamped in the snowy pastures around Bukhara.

Spring, the beginning of the campaigning season, would bring the answers. The push west, scarcely started, would continue. Herat was no isolated event. In the words of the German historian H.R. Roemer, it was instead 'the prelude to one of the greatest catastrophes in the history of Iran'.

❊

The forest of minarets which greeted the fourteenth-century visitor to Herat is no more. Steadily cut back over the centuries, it has dwindled until only the smallest copse remains. From afar, the tapering towers loom from the mountain-bound plain like industrial chimneys. After the rigours of six hundred years, they totter dangerously, alternately silhouetted against the skyline and submerged in the blowing dust that makes the approach to Herat such a dramatic journey. Close to, it is not chimneys they resemble but rather the arthritic fingers of a giantess, petrified in death, clutching at the sky from the bowels of the earth.

These towers are almost all that is left of the architectural heart of Herat. South of the Injil canal stand the remains of its most outstanding monument. The Musalla complex, a mosque and mausoleum, was built between 1417 and 1437 by Queen Gawhar Shad, wife of Temur's son Shahrukh. Appropriately, since her name means 'Joyful Jewel', this was the high point of Temurid art and architecture, a dazzling fusion of form and colour which paid tribute both to Allah and to His powerful servant on earth. Four minarets, elegant columns of turquoise more than a hundred feet high, shone like bright beacons, marking the corners of the queen's *musalla*, or place of worship, dominating a smaller cluster of minarets beside them. Here stood Herat's first great congregational mosque, a monument which married colossal proportions with the most elegant taste, replete with dancing frescoes and arabesques, its exceptionally fine glazed brickwork a lustrous façade against the dreary desert. Linking the four principal minarets were four galleries, or *iwans*, looking out onto a central courtyard. Bold Kufic inscriptions ran around marble plaques at the decagonal base of each minaret, giving way, as the eye travelled up towards the sky, to sparkling lozenges of blue flowers and amber petals outlined in white faience. In these arid lands the iridescent blue was a refreshing reference to water and a homage to the heavens. Today, the forlorn minarets retain only a smattering of this polished armour, and among the war-torn debris of the site it requires a truly giant leap of imagination even to begin to picture the monument in its all but vanished glory.

It was in Herat, and Samarkand, that one of the Temurids' most remarkable and enduring cultural legacies was bequeathed to future generations. Since Khorasan lacked sufficient supplies of both wood and building stone, the great majority of structures were built from baked brick. This greatly restricted the sculptural possibilities, but did allow for a shining sheath, or revetment, of coloured tiles to enliven the sun-dried surfaces. On this Masjid-i-Jami, the mosque for Friday prayers, the exquisite blue-and-white tile mosaics were laid in such profusion that not a plain terracotta brick was visible on the entire exterior, an astounding achievement in a monument of these dimensions. For once Robert Byron, that most opinionated and least excitable of travel writers, was pulled up short, calling it 'the most beautiful example in colour in architecture ever designed by man to the glory of his God and himself'. Hyperbole, perhaps, but high praise from a man who wrote that Rembrandt left him with 'an unremitting sense of disgust', and who had dismissed Shakespeare's entire canon as 'exactly the sort of plays that I would expect a grocer to write'.*

Next to the minarets, a ribbed dome of azure blue, the defining Temurid architectural signature, topped the squat mausoleum of the queen, murdered in 1457 when she was well into her ninth decade. These glazed blue tiles of Herat became the model throughout much of Asia. The simplicity of the mausoleum's exterior belied the profusion of decoration in the interior, where floral patterns and bands of white calligraphy ran riot. To this day, the three-dimensional ornamentation is of superb complexity. Arches, squinches, domes and stalactite niches trace their shapes across the walls in harmony, painted in ancient hues of terracotta, gold and the faded blue of crushed lapis lazuli from the mines of Badakhshan, in northern Afghanistan.

Unlike much of the devastation wrought on the historical monuments of Afghanistan, the desolation of the Musalla complex cannot be blamed on domestic feuding or age-old tribal warfare. Byron was horrified to learn that his own countrymen were responsible for its destruction. At the height of the Great Game in 1885, Russian troops attacked Afghans south-east of the city of Merv. Fearing a subsequent advance on Herat, which would give St Petersburg access to the Kandahar road and allow it to open a railroad right up to the Indian border, British officers ordered the demolition of most of the buildings in the complex, which occupied a site in the north of the city

---

* Byron's languid peregrinations through Asia in 1933–34 left him with a profound appreciation of the Temurids' artistic and architectural achievements. Queen Gawhar Shad, wife of Shahrukh, particularly intrigued him. 'I feel some curiosity about Gohar Shad,' he confessed, 'not on account of her piety in endowing religious foundations, but as a woman of artistic instinct. Either she had that instinct, or she knew how to employ people who had it. This shows character. And besides this, she was rich. Taste, character, and riches mean power, and powerful women, apart from charmers, are not common in Mohammadan history.'

ABOVE LEFT Temur's birthplace in Khoja Ilgar, near Shakhrisabz, south of Samarkand.

ABOVE RIGHT Temur stares down Victory Park, Shakhrisabz. The ruins of his monumental Ak Sarai or White Palace are visible in the background.

LEFT Shakhrisabz market. 'The watermelons there are as large as a horse's head,' wrote Ruy Gonzalez de Clavijo, Spanish envoy to Temur's court, 'the very best and biggest that may be found in the whole world.'

ABOVE Balkh, northern
Afghanistan. In 1370, Temur
was enthroned in the city
made famous by Alexander
the Great.

ABOVE RIGHT Christopher
Marlowe's 'Scourge of God'.
The National chose
Tamburlaine the Great to open
the Olivier Theatre in 1976.

*'His looks do menace heaven
and dare the gods,
His fiery eyes are fixed upon
the earth…'*
Antony Sher as a bloody
Tamburlaine in the RSC's
1993 production.

The Registan, Samarkand. In 1888, George Curzon, the future viceroy of India, judged it 'the noblest public square in the world. I know of nothing in the East approaching it in massive simplicity and grandeur; and nothing in Europe…which can even aspire to enter the competition.'

The Ulugh Beg Madrassah, Samarkand, a tribute to Temur's grandson. 'This magnificent façade is of such a height it is twice the heavens and of such weight that the spine of the earth is about to crumble,' reads an inscription on the portal.

Inside the magnificent Tillya Kari Madrassah, Samarkand.

ABOVE The Temurid signature. Azure blue domes in Shah-i-Zinda, Samarkand's city of the dead. In these arid lands the iridescent blue was a refreshing reference to water and a homage to the heavens.

LEFT A sun-baked dome in Shah-i-Zinda, Samarkand.

Detail from a blue ribbed dome, Samarkand.

Detail from a minaret, Samarkand. The scrolling Kufic script contains the words 'Allah' and 'Mohammed'.

A wedding party in Samarkand. From the early 1990s, it has become *de rigueur* for newlyweds to pay their respects to Temur, symbol of independent Uzbekistan.

Temur's forces attacking a fort. An illustration from Sharaf ad-din Ali Yazdi's *Zafarnama*.

ABOVE Bukhara, Temur's second city, the 'Dome of Islam'. The famous Kalon Minaret is visible on the left.

RIGHT Kalon Mosque, Bukhara. Genghis Khan was so overawed by the 150-foot Kalon Minaret that he spared it when razing the city in 1219.

BELOW Herat citadel. Temur stormed the city in 1379, his first conquest in the west.

from where the anticipated assault would come. In fact, the Russian advance never materialised, but 'the most glorious productions of Mohammadan architecture in the XVth century, having survived the barbarism of four centuries, were now rased [sic] to the ground under the eyes, and with the approval, of the English Commissioners'. Only nine minarets were left standing.

What man had started, nature continued. Earthquakes in 1931 and 1951 accounted for the loss of three more minarets. Then, in 1979, a century late, the Soviets invaded Afghanistan and Herat's monuments were in the line of fire once again. One more minaret was felled, another received a direct hit from an artillery shell, the hole now used by nesting birds. The pounding stripped the minarets of more of their colour. Floral mosaics, brilliant lozenges of white and light blue, tumbled to the earth, joining the scattered remnants of sparkling faience prised from the towers by five centuries of sand and wind. The Soviets even laid mines around the minarets to prevent Ismail Khan, the local warlord, retaking the city. Those minarets which escaped the destruction once overlooked the magnificent madrassahs of Gawhar Shad and Sultan Husayn Baiqara, the last of Herat's Temurid rulers. Today they preside over mostly bare ground, the isolated mausoleum and a handful of shacks and rusting steel containers converted into shops.

Late one afternoon, I walked through the crowded markets towards the one edifice which still dominates Herat on raised ground in the north of the Old City. Rearing up from the desert earth were the smooth walls of the Qala-i-Ikhtiyaruddin, the citadel beneath which Temur's armies, and those of Genghis Khan before him, had fought their adversaries. Built in sun-dried bricks in its present form by the fourteenth-century Kart prince Fakhr ud-din, restored by Temur's son Shahrukh a hundred years later, it has seen empires and dynasties rise and fall. Over the centuries it has been home to the Ghaznavids, the Seljuks, Ghorids, Mongols, Temurids, Safavids, and even the Taliban, who used it as an army base and arsenal.

Looking at its massive ramparts, buttressed with bulging corner towers and dotted with holes from where the garrison could defend itself, it was not difficult to understand why Ghiyas ad-din had retreated behind them so promptly as he considered his chances of holding out against Temur's siege. Its elevated position and the imposing strength of its defences give it an air of utter invulnerability. Had the Kart prince not surrendered in a timely fashion to Temur, who knows whether the citadel would have survived to this day. The ruthlessness with which the Tatar crushed resistance from other cities suggests it would have disappeared from the face of the earth.

A monumental Kufic inscription in mosaic-faience, three feet high, originally dominated the wall beside the north-west tower. 'AL-MULK LI'LLAH' (The Kingdom is God's), it proclaimed in alternating dark-green and amber letters, visible to all high above the city. If the citadel owed its inspiration to the Almighty, it became, in the fourteenth century, a tribute to Temur. When Shahrukh restored it with baked brick and stone, the fifteenth-century panegyrist Hafiz-i-Abru penned the following lines to the founder of the Temurid dynasty, sections of which appeared on the tiles of the citadel.

> Until the day of judgement the world will not be empty of the
>   descendants of Temur Khan
> From that purer lineage, so excellent a race will follow that one
>   conqueror will follow after another
> Where a pearl should be, they will not see other than pearls; they should
>   not look for anything other than gold from a gold mine
> The King of Islam, Shah Rukh Bahadur, the world has become
>   resplendent with his justice
> [He is] so magnificent that the stars are like his army, he is the
>   commander of his nobility which reaches the summit of the heavens
> The world is trifling compared to his power like the surging sea. The
>   heavens are an atom and his outlook is luminous
> May the world be adorned with his descendants, may the world be
>   perfumed with his race . . .

*The prosperity of the world comes from his sound rule. Just as one
    attains heaven by proper devotions
They laid the foundations of this lofty citadel
In an auspicious time and a favourable horoscope
Rabi II 818 hijrat [1415–16] . . .
First they assigned a location for Herat
So that five gateways were fixed in it
See those five doors of the five towers of its fortress
And consider them gates of victory
Know the proof of the permanence of the building
Regard it well even if you are meticulous
(Your kingdom) will be increased and it will not be destroyed
This prosperity will remain until the day of judgement
The engineer placed within and without it muqarnas, mansions and
    round towers
The stars are proud of its architecture
Its completion has brought glory to the army
In elegance like the aivan of Kisra
In solidity like the dam of Sikandar
In the completeness of its strength like the aivan of Kaivan
The passage of time will not destroy it
It will not be subject to the damage of calamities
Calamities cannot touch the king
From the top to bottom it is beautiful and decorated
Its corners are golden and bejewelled
Its essence is like life in the pillars of the universe
Its splendours are like light in the eyes of the stars*

A surly Taliban soldier on duty told me that both the citadel and the
museum it housed were closed, but after a little encouragement, and
the promise of a tip, he agreed to show me around the ramparts, on
which nine gun emplacements had been mounted. As we clambered
up the steep, dusty track he stopped every few moments to show me
another piece of ordnance. There were grenades, bullets live and
spent, machine-gun rounds, piles of rockets and mines. He picked
up an old grenade, pulled at the ring, and made as if to throw it at

me. Then, seeing my horror, he disappeared behind a wall and threw a large stone onto an unexploded landmine. There was, mercifully, no explosion. He sniggered and continued up the path.

From the ramparts and their jagged towers Herat stretched before us. Women paced through the market, a blue blur of burqas. Children guided goats through the crowds, struggling to avoid the throng of cyclists. Pigeons wheeled in the sunset. Mina birds squawked from treetops in an evening chorus joined by barking dogs below. Peddlers pushed makeshift trolleys along, selling scrap metal and pieces of plastic. Sheep entrails hung over the bicycle handlebars of a mobile butcher like flourishing maroon balloons. A cloth merchant reclined sleepily in the entrance to his shop. Next door a tailor in a coloured skullcap sat cross-legged, busily cutting and sewing. A row of tur-baned 'white-beards', the elders of Herat, sat on a mosque rooftop talking among themselves while they waited for the call to prayer. On the mud roofs around them, boys of all ages ran here and there, shouting and chasing each other wildly amidst the smoke drifting upwards from the kitchens below. Many were flying home-made kites (in contravention of one of the Taliban's many bans), and a myriad coloured cut-outs fluttered in the breeze, gathered around the sinking sun like excited moths. In the distance, lights were being turned on in the thirteenth-century Masjid-i-Jami, the principal Friday mosque. Inside, in pride of place, stood the vast bronze cauldron, four feet in diameter, from which worshippers were served sweet drinks during the reign of the Kart princes in the fourteenth century. In the woven light, Herat was a kaleidoscope of beige and green, bursts of trees amid the subdued colours of the desert. The occasional blue dome, testament to the city's ravishing Temurid legacy, added a flash of azure to the scene. Farther off, hovering over Herat like a dark cloud, was the black-crayon smudge of the Paropamisus mountains.

Then it came. First a crackling, croaky whirr, an amplified intake of breath and then, rising above the static, the melodious voice of the *muaddin* calling the faithful to the *maghrib*, or evening prayer. '*Allahu akbar, Allahu akbar*, God is great, God is great,' he intoned, and the white-beards started to stir. The twin minarets of the Kherqa Mubarak Mosque at the foot of the citadel seemed to stiffen in response. As the call continued, a tide of men, swelling by the minute, flowed across the city towards the mosques. '*Haya alas-saleh, haya alas-saleh*, come to prayer, come to prayer,' the voice chanted. On the streets the men hurried along dutifully, 'encouraged' by the Taliban religious police, the most feared members of the Ministry for the Promotion of Virtue and Prevention of Vice.* '*La ilaha illa'llah*, there is no god but God,' and the white-beards descended carefully from the roof to pray. Across the city the minarets from various generations loomed like saluting exclamation marks.

Few cities have suffered such recurrent disasters as Herat. The catalogue of its misfortunes reads like a history of Afghanistan in miniature, doomed by tribal rivalries and foreign interventions which continue to this day. In 667, Arab armies introduced Islam at the point of the sword. The Ghaznavid Sultan Mahmud annexed the city in 1000. Two centuries later, in 1206, Herat fell to the Khorezm Shah invading from the north. Scarcely had it recovered from that attack than Genghis Khan and eighty thousand of his Mongols flattened it again in 1221, slaughtering all but sixteen of its inhabitants. In 1381, Herat prudently bowed before Temur's armies, sparing itself the worst of his outrages, only to rebel two years later with fatal consequences for the Kart dynasty. On behalf of his father, Miranshah duly put the city to the sword. Babur, Temur's most illustrious descendant, founder of the Mughal empire in India, was unable to save the city

---

* Under Taliban rule, the Masjid-i-Jami, Herat's Friday mosque, one of the greatest buildings in the Islamic world and among Afghanistan's most important historical monuments, was closed to all non-Muslims. Mosque officials enforced this ban zealously, out of fear, they said, of beatings by the dreaded religious police.

from the Uzbek empire-builder Shaibani Khan, who seized it in 1507.

The eighteenth century was no stranger to war and intrigue in Herat. Ahmed Shah Durrani, known as the Father of Afghanistan, waged war on the city in the late 1740s as he carved out the new country. Another army marched on Herat in the last decade of the century, when the city found itself the centre of a power struggle between rivals within the Sadozai Shah dynasty. In 1818 it was Persian forces, stretching their tentacles east, who assaulted the city. They returned twenty years later and Herat was under siege for ten months, a bitter experience repeated in 1863 when Amir Dost Mohammed captured the city, his final act in unifying Afghanistan before his death a month later. Peace still proved elusive for its westernmost capital, however, as ruling family divisions returned to the fore. In 1881, Amir Abdur Rahman was fighting his cousin Sardar Ayub Khan for its possession. Before the decade had ended, the British were tearing out its historical heart, a harbinger of the damage inflicted by the Soviets when they invaded the following century. Twenty years after that the Taliban held the reins of power and Herat, like the rest of Afghanistan, was on its knees again. In the spring of 2001, as the Taliban – to the horror of the world – were dynamiting the two-thousand-year-old monumental sculptures known as the Buddhas of Bamiyan, officials destroyed any historical artefacts considered sacrilegious. Pre-Islamic sculptures, outstanding examples of their kind, were among the casualties. In late 2002, Herat returned to the rule of local warlord Ismail Khan. Amid the confusion and chaos of war, more ancient relics were plundered from the city's museum.

Yet somehow all these centuries of destruction and the horrors of the Taliban regime have failed to subdue this desert city. Staring down on it from the restored citadel, its greatness seemed undiminished. The Taliban were merely the latest and by no means the nastiest scar on its surface, a short-lived experiment that barely merited a mention in the city's long history. The ancient cultural centre would outlive these philistine warriors of Islam just as she had seen off other invaders before. The bright home-made kites, scraps of paper and plastic taut in the wind, careered merrily across the sky like totems of hope.

Another evening, as dusk started to steal down from the sky, throwing a wonderful honeyed veil over Herat, I arranged to visit some of the city's shrines with two of its most distinguished elders. Maulavi Said Mohammed Omar Shahid, president of Herat University, and Maulana Khudad, president of the council of mullahs, were both in their sixties. Like many Afghans who had endured the twin evils of war and malnutrition, they looked considerably older, their withered walnut faces peering out from pristine white turbans.

Together we walked north of the Musalla complex to the shrine of the fifteenth-century Sufi poet Abdur Rahman Jami, the last great classical poet of Persia. It was a mournful, windswept site, as romantic as the poetry which had thrilled, inspired and saddened so many in his lifetime, so many more in the centuries since his death. The tomb itself was of simple design, protected from the sun by an elderly pistachio tree. Overhead, banners, pendants and flags of green, white and yellow flapped like sheets in the streaming wind. A group of teenage boys, strangely silent, had also come to pay their respects. Jami, one of Herat's most famous sons, was the most celebrated poet of his generation. His literary influence and the beauty of his verses coursed through the continent.

> *When your face is hidden from me,*
> *Like the moon hidden on a dark night,*
> *I shed stars of tears*
> *And yet my night remains dark*
> *In spite of all those shining stars.*

This tomb in a corner of benighted Afghanistan was just one small piece of the vast cultural legacy bequeathed by Temur. Poetry, painting, calligraphy, architecture and craftsmanship, all had flowered under his watchful eye, a tradition continued still more lavishly by his descendants. From the blood of his conquests and the cut of his sword had issued a cultural renaissance that bore his name and would never be forgotten. Herat, Shahrukh's imperial city of the Temurids, was another Samarkand, doted on by his queen, Gawhar Shad, wildly generous patron of the arts. Kindled by Temur, the fires of Temurid culture, one of the most important epochs in Persian history, flamed through Asia. Jami kept these fires alive, but his death in 1492 marked the end of the golden era of classical Persian poetry. In one moment the Temurid cultural blaze was extinguished.*

I asked Maulavi Said whether, given this great legacy, he considered Temur a hero. He looked horrified. 'No! Definitely not. He was a killer and an invader, a bloody man and a barbarian. He did nothing for culture here. It was his son Shahrukh who made up for all his father's destruction by supporting the arts. Temur's family was civilised but he was just a thug.'

His elderly companion shook his head but said nothing. We moved on to Gazargah, the fifteenth-century shrine complex built by Shahrukh several miles east of the city. Past the mulberries and rose bushes beggars young and old swarmed around the ornate portal created by

---

* Like his predecessor Hafiz, Jami did not hide his light under a bushel. He claimed never to have met anyone who could best him in an argument, one reason presumably why he refused to acknowledge the obligations of a pupil to any teacher. He described himself as a great poet, a great scholar and a great mystic, a master of all literary genres and subjects: lyrical and romantic poetry, exegesis of the Koran, analysis of the divine mission of the Prophet Mohammed, Arabic grammar, rhyme, prosody and music. In his own words: 'My verses have achieved so much fame in the whole world that a minstrel begins singing with my verses. If the caravan of my verses reach Fars, souls of Sa'di and Hafiz welcome it. If they reach India, Khusraw and Hasan come out to receive it. Sometimes the Emperor of Constantinople Rum sends his greetings to me while at other times, Cheepal sends messages to me from Hind.'

the Persian architect Quram ad-din Sherazi, towering so high it was visible from Herat. Some had made this place their home, and shuffled about in ragged cloaks and blankets. Inside were hundreds of headstones. The most ancient, smooth with age but with many of their beautiful inscriptions intact, leaned precariously in the ground like twisted teeth. Elderly men with unkempt beards, little changed in dress or appearance from the times of Temur, sat cross-legged and quiet, whispering thanks for any alms given by visitors. A few yards behind them stood a fifteen-foot marble pillar from the mid-fifteenth century, finely carved, a model of the highly skilled craftsmanship which Temur so actively supported. Nearby was another exceptional monument, the nineteenth-century tomb of Amir Dost Mohammed. We paused by the shrine of Khoja Abdullah Ansari, eleventh-century Sufi poet, philosopher and patron saint of the city,* set in the shade of an old ilex tree and the once gleaming blue *iwan*, an arched niche within an eighty-foot wall surmounted by a domed turret at either end. Patches of blue glaze survived at the lower level of the *iwan*, but most of the decorative tiles had fallen like winter leaves, leaving a dull beige façade.

While we walked slowly among these funerary monuments Maulana Khudad resumed our conversation where we had left off. He disagreed with his colleague's damning verdict on Temur. 'From my point of view he was certainly a hero. Generally, those who called him a barbarian came from the West. Temur was spreading Islam and they didn't like it so they denigrated him.'

---

* Robert Byron, as ever, had his own counter-intuitive views on this celebrated saint. 'Khoja Abdullah Ansari died in the year 1088 at the age of eighty-four, because some boys threw stones at him while he was at penance. One sympathises with those boys: even among saints he was a prodigious bore. He spoke in the cradle; he began to preach at fourteen; during his life he held intercourse with a thousand sheikhs, learnt a hundred thousand verses by heart (some say 1,200,000) and composed as many more. He doted on cats.'

He cast a mischievous glance towards his old friend and continued. 'Though at first he wreaked havoc in Herat, he also brought great benefits and honoured Islamic scholars like Mohammed Said Sharif Gurgani, Maulana Saad ad-din Taftazani and Maulana Razi. His children and grandchildren – men like Shahrukh, Sultan Baysunqur, Ulugh Beg and Abu Said – served Islam greatly. In Temur's time there were 350 madrassahs just in Herat. One of them, the Mirza Madrassah, had forty thousand students, many of them foreign. Four thousand graduated every year. The whole thing was supported by Temur. And it wasn't just Islam which benefited. He had great creative vision. For example, he built twelve huge irrigation canals around Herat which changed agriculture here forever. And just think of the great artist Bihzad, who worked at the court of Sultan Husayn Mirza.* And of course, then there was the emperor Babur, who founded the

---

* Born in the late fifteenth century, Bihzad first entered the service of Ali Sher Nawai, the statesman, poet, father of the Chaghatay language, generous patron of the arts and friend of Sultan Husayn Mirza, before graduating to royal appointments. Though little is known about him, he worked in Herat, ushering in a new style of Persian miniature painting which was characterised by firm lines, strong colours, unprecedented detail and exquisite delicacy. His work is now regarded as marking the high point of the Islamic miniaturist's craft and a major influence on Persian painting. Writing around 1523, the historian Khwandamir left this glowing profile of his contemporary: 'He sets before us marvellous forms and rarities of art; his draughtsmanship, which is like the brush of Mani, has caused the memorials of all the painters of the world to be obliterated, and his fingers, endowed with miraculous qualities, have wiped out the pictures of all the artists among the sons of Adam. A hair of his brush, through its mastery, has given life to the lifeless form . . . At the present time, too, this marvel of the age, whose belief is pure, is regarded with benevolence by the kings of the world and is encompassed with the boundless consideration of the rulers of Islam.' Bihzad's magnificent illustrations can be seen in Yazdi's *Zafarnama*. They include fascinating pictures such as 'Temur granting audience on the occasion of his accession', 'The Building of the Great Mosque in Samarkand', 'Destruction of the remnant of the Kipchak army', and 'The Assault on the fortress of the Knights of St John at Smyrna'. After the capture of Herat by the Safavids in 1510, Bihzad moved to Tabriz, and possibly Bukhara.

Mughal empire in India. None of this would have happened without Temur.' He shot a defiant glare at his friend again. 'This was not an ordinary man. He was a man of war, yes, but of culture, too. We will always remember him for these fine buildings. My friend is not right. For Herat, Temur was the greatest hero the city ever knew.'

&

With Herat conquered and the winter snows thawing amid the first hints of spring, Temur resumed his heroic ambitions in the west. 'Asia trembled from China even to the borders of Greece,' wrote Yazdi, and well it might. In 1382, the Tatar armies rumbled north-west towards Mazandaran, the province immediately south of the Caspian Sea. Protected both by the Elburz mountains, with summits of up to seventeen thousand feet, covered with thick forest, and by treacly swamps, it was inauspicious terrain for an invader, but after stiff resistance Amir Wali, the local ruler, was defeated and forced to offer his submission. Four years later, Mazandaran rebelled. Temur was well positioned to deal with the challenge, having recently begun the first of his three major campaigns in Persia. He wrote a letter to Amir Wali demanding his surrender. Alone among his chiefs, Amir Wali refused to comply, despatching pleas for assistance to Shah Shuja Muzaffar, who ruled Fars in the south, and Sultan Ahmed of Baghdad and Azerbaijan. No help arrived. Amir Wali was forced to join battle without his allies, conscious that defeat spelled certain death.

'When the armies were in sight of each other and blows of javelins, swords and spears were being dealt indiscriminately, Shah Wali withstood some time his adverse fortune; then he turned his back after deciding upon withdrawal and flight,' wrote Arabshah. He was subsequently captured and lost his head, literally. It was brought to Temur's throne in a gesture which paid tribute to the *yasa* of Genghis Khan.

Mazandaran's fall in 1382 was followed a year later by an act of calculated brutality by Temur. Once again it was inflicted on a city which had rebelled, and once again the price was calamity. Isfizar, a city south of Herat, fell, and two thousand inhabitants were taken prisoner. Rather than execute them on the spot, Temur chose instead to make an example – if any were needed – of the consequences of rebellion. A tower was constructed, though this time the prisoners who went into it were not dead. 'There were near two thousand slaves taken who were piled alive one upon the other with mortar and bricks, so that these miserable wretches might serve as a monument to deter others from revolting,' wrote the unsympathetic Yazdi.

Invigorated by this dreadful act, Temur led an army of one hundred thousand into Sistan, the south-western province of Afghanistan. Zaranj, its prosperous capital, mounted a valiant defence. Such was the ferocity of the fighting that Temur felt impelled to throw himself into the heart of the battle, at great personal risk. When his horse was shot from beneath him, he vowed revenge. Sistan already held painful memories, for this, most probably, was where he had received the wounds that left him lame in both right limbs, either while fighting as a hired sword in the service of the local khan or – the more prosaic version – when caught in the act of stealing sheep. Whatever his feelings, Zaranj felt his fury, and the capital of a fertile province known as the Garden of Asia and the Granary of the East was pitilessly razed. Arabshah wrote that the residents of Zaranj sued for peace, which Temur granted on condition they surrender all their weapons. 'And as soon as they had given this guarantee, he drew the sword against them and billeted upon them all the armies of death. Then he laid the city waste, leaving in it not a tree or a wall and destroyed it utterly, no mark or trace of it remaining.' Men, women and children perished in the slaughter, echoed Yazdi, 'from persons of a hundred years old, to infants in the cradle'. Windmills, agricultural lands and, worst of all, dykes and irrigation canals, were destroyed. In time, the desert moved to reclaim what it had lost, the sands swept in, and the once green province gave way to the Dasht-i-Margo (Desert of Death), the Dasht-i-Jehanum (Desert of Hell) and the Sar-o-Tar (Place of Desolation and Emptiness). To this day the region remains poverty-stricken and deserted.

From Zaranj, Temur swung east to the southern Afghan city of Kandahar, which fell to him in 1384, its governor thrown in irons and hanged. No sooner had he seized Kandahar than he abruptly doubled back on himself, marched west halfway across Persia and, after the feeble flight of its ruler Sultan Ahmed, accepted the surrender of Sultaniya in the same year.

This was a development of enormous significance. Sultaniya was an important commercial centre, a 'great city', as Clavijo reported on his arrival on 26 June 1404, twenty years after it had passed into Temur's dominions. Founded in about 1285 by Arghun, the sixth Ilkhanid ruler of Persia, who was attracted by its abundant pastures and used it as his summer capital, Sultaniya became the seat of empire under his son Mohammed Oljeytu Khudabanda in 1313. The city was expanded aggressively, the outer walls increasing from twelve thousand paces in circumference to thirty thousand. At its heart stood a powerful square citadel with heavy fortifications, built of cut stone with walls broad enough for several horsemen to ride abreast on their ramparts. Sixteen towers looked down onto an encircling moat beyond the outer walls, decorated with turquoise tiles, Arabic inscriptions and pictures of horsemen fighting heads of lions.

Oljeytu intended Sultaniya to become a fully functioning capital, no mere royal camp. He duly embarked on a terrific building spree, ordering his courtiers to design graceful palaces and gardens. The vizier Rashid ad-din built an entire quarter of a thousand houses. Another, Taj ad-din Ali Shah, built a lavish, ten-thousand-dinar palace called Paradise, its doors, walls and floors studded with pearls, gold, rubies, turquoise, emeralds and amber. A city of monuments made from baked brick, stone and wood sprang up on the desert plain,

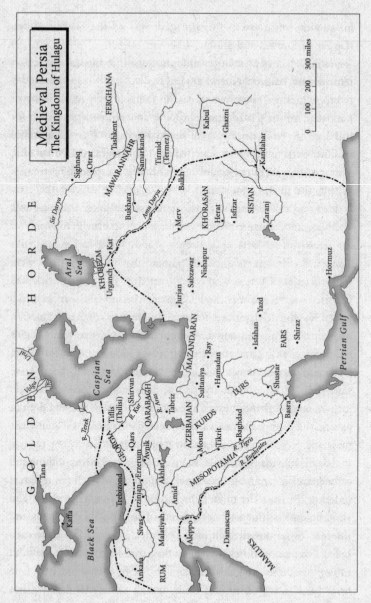

Medieval Persia
The Kingdom of Hulagu

0   100   200   300 miles

GOLDEN   HORDE

Sir Darya

Sighnaq
Otrar
Tashkent   FERGHANA

MAWARANNAHR
Samarkand
Bukhara   Tirmid
(Termez)
Amu Darya   Balkh

Kabul
Ghazni

Kandahar

Aral
Sea

KHOREZM
Urganch   Kat   Merv   KHORASAN   SISTAN
Herat
Isfizar   Zaranj

Caspian
Sea   Jurjan   Sabzawar   Nishapur

Ural   Hormuz

Volga   MAZANDARAN
Ray
Yazd   FARS
Shirvan   Sultaniya   Isfahan   Shiraz
R. Kur   Hamadan   LURS
Tiflis   Tabriz
(Tbilisi)   QARABAGH   R. Aras   Shustar
R. Terek   Qars   AZERBAIJAN   Basra   Persian Gulf
Tana   Avnik   KURDS
Erzurum   Akhlat   Mosul   Tikrit   R. Tigris
Trebizond   Arzinjan   Baghdad
Kaffa   GEORGIA   MESOPOTAMIA   R. Euphrates
Sivas   Malatiyah   Amid
Black   Sea   Aleppo   Damascus
Ankara   RUM   MMLUKS

luxuriously decorated with bronze doors, inlaid window grilles, marble revetments and mosaic faience.

The most famous architectural creation, however, was Oljeytu's monumental octagonal tomb, 120 feet in diameter, which alone today recalls Sultaniya's illustrious past. The tomb complex, which incorporated a mosque, madrassah, hospital and *khanaqah* (a hostel for travelling dervishes), was one of the grandest pious endowments of its time. Octagonal in plan – a reference to the eight gates of Paradise – the rectangular burial chamber projected from the southern *iwan*. Within the portals, courtyards of white marble dazzled the eyes, which were drawn inexorably towards the giant shadow-making dome and the eight minarets which guarded it at each of the corners of the upper terrace. Beneath the dome stood two storeys of eight-bay arcades. A third opened onto the exterior. Inside, four bays were especially elaborately decorated in geometric patterns of brick and delicate strips of glazed and unglazed terracotta. A dado of hexagonal glazed tiles divided the chamber into two. Above it, the entire interior, including that of the dome, was covered in plaster, painted with decorative patterns and inscriptions. It was a truly imperial creation.

'The total of those who worked on the foundations was ten thousand men,' wrote the fourteenth-century Mamluk biographer al Yusufi. 'Five thousand moved dirt, and five thousand cut and dressed stone. There were five thousand wagons to move rock and other materials, for which there were ten thousand donkeys. They made a thousand kilns for brick, and a thousand kilns for lime. Five thousand camels transported wood, and two thousand persons were assigned to cut wood from the mountains and other places. Three thousand smiths were employed to work sheets of metal, windows, nails and the like. There were five hundred carpenters, and five thousand men laid marble. Supervisors were appointed over them to urge them on in the work.'

Trade, meanwhile, flourished. Although its population was less than that of Tabriz, capital of Azerbaijan to the north-west, Sultaniya was 'a more important centre of exchange for merchants and goods', said Clavijo. According to the Ilkhanid chronicler Abul Qasim al Kashani, the city had more than ten thousand shops filled with bales of Chinese brocade, small boxes, cups, ewers and a host of other materials. In June, July and August each year, weary camel caravans trudged in from the deserts laden down with spices – cloves, nutmeg, cinnamon, manna and mace – from India and Afghanistan, cotton and taffeta from Shiraz and silks from the southern shores of the Caspian.* 'The city then is in a state of great commotion, and immense are the customs dues that accrue to the Treasury.' Merchants from Persia, Genoa and Venice gathered to buy the cloth; large quantities were also exported to Syria, Turkey and the Crimea. Sultaniya was also a centre of the trade in pearls and precious stones. From China came pearls, mother of pearl and rubies, shipped to the port of Hormuz in southern Persia. Here they were expertly drilled and strung and exported 'to all parts of the western world'. Many were loaded onto camels for the sixty-day caravan journey to Sultaniya where they were bought by merchants 'from Christian lands' and from Turkey, Syria, and Baghdad.

Such was the city's size and strategic importance, straddling a major east–west trade route, that Pope John XXII set up an archbishopric at Sultaniya in 1318. Archbishops were appointed until 1425.

---

* Clavijo, though he greatly admired the fabulous silks of Sultaniya, was inconvenienced by the tremendous heat of the region. His comments, which anticipate the complaints of British tourists holidaying abroad by some six hundred years, are particularly interesting from a Spaniard based in Castile. 'These countries where silk is made are all so hot that any strangers who go there suffer much from sunstroke, which indeed at times may kill; they say that the stroke goes straight to the heart, causing first vomiting and then death. To the sufferers their shoulders will seem to burn, and they say too that those who escape with their lives ever afterwards are yellow in the face or grey, never regaining their natural complexion.'

By the time Clavijo arrived, shortly before Temur's death, Sultaniya had passed its apogee. The outer defensive walls had gone, he reported. The city was losing its importance. In the seventeenth century, the Persian ruler Shah Abbas moved his capital to Isfahan and Sultaniya's decline accelerated. Today, the metropolis is long gone, whittled down over the centuries to the point where Oljeytu's tomb looks down upon nothing more than an insignificant mud-brick village in northern Iran.

For Temur, the importance of seizing Sultaniya was by no means exclusively commercial. Of far greater consequence was what its capture represented. It is easy now to overlook the milestones in his military career. Sometimes the victories seem to merge into a remorseless blur of savagery and slaughter. But though it seems to have been largely neglected by the court chroniclers and historians in subsequent centuries, the taking of Sultaniya represented a definite landmark both in the scope of Temur's ambitions and in his ability to fulfil them. His successes until this point, though impressive, were essentially domestic achievements. Herat represented the first foray abroad, militarily decisive but still tentative in purely geographical terms, rather as though Temur were testing the waters before he plunged in deeper. The temperature evidently suited him, because that challenge had been overcome with contemptuous ease.

Herat ushered in a new era of conquest. Henceforth, for practically the rest of Temur's life, spring would herald a new campaigning season. Winter was a time for hibernation and planning the next target for his armies. His first campaign was instructive. First Kandahar crumpled and then, in one fell swoop, he had led his men across the Persian deserts to seize the prize of Sultaniya, a thousand miles west of Samarkand, without so much as a battle. As an entrance onto the international stage it was a move of astonishing audacity, a trumpet blast to the world and an announcement, in the most dramatic terms, of Temur's empire-building intentions. In fact, with a more or less united confederation of tribes under his single command, all hungry for reward, it was imperative for him to lead them beyond their borders – beyond Mawarannahr and the Chaghatay ulus – to new triumphs abroad. This, indeed, was the only way to retain their allegiance and service. Steppe tribesmen traditionally would remain loyal to a leader only for so long as he proved victorious on the battlefield. Temur understood this acutely. Any analysis of his career necessarily dwells on the observation that essentially it was one long campaign, punctuated with only the briefest of interludes. Quite simply, he needed to keep his armies on the move.

These initial manoeuvres, from the fall of Herat to the bloodless defeat of Sultaniya, also demonstrated his capacity to surprise, a key weapon in his armoury and one that he would employ throughout his campaigns. They also revealed his willingness to use terror to project and increase his power through Asia. The razing of Zaranj and the extermination of its population were inspired by what Temur saw as the need to acquire a reputation for complete ruthlessness, as a man who, if challenged, would unleash every instrument of cruelty and destruction at his command. It was in his interests for this reputation to filter across the continent. Equally, the events at Zaranj were intended to show other would-be opponents the futility of resistance to this unstoppable force. The skulls severed from the corpses of his defeated opponents – soldiers and civilians, men, women and children alike – should be understood in this context of terror. Far better, both for Temur and the cities and dynasties which blocked his expansion, that they surrender quickly and be spared. Defiance would only meet with the swiftest and most terrible retribution. Little wonder that Sultan Ahmed had no stomach for the fight as Temur marched into his lands. The loss of Sultaniya was a great blow. Once assimilated into Temur's emerging empire, it steadily assumed a greater political role to match its commercial pre-eminence. By the time Clavijo passed through, it had taken its place as the capital of Persia.

If Temur had learnt any lessons from his seizure of Herat and Sultaniya, it was this: that issuing unexpected ultimatums, reinforced by the rapid manoeuvring of his armies across great distances and the threat of massive, terrifying force in the style of Genghis Khan, was a potent strategy. As Arabshah put it: 'He ran to the ends of the earth, as Satan runs from the son of Adam and crept through countries as poison creeps through bodies.'

Tempted by Tabriz after seizing Sultaniya, Temur returned instead to winter in Samarkand, to rest his soldiers and allow them to enjoy the fruits of their endeavours. In his absence came disturbing news. Tokhtamish Khan, his one-time protégé, had thrust south from the Golden Horde of Russia and sacked Tabriz himself. From Temur's perspective, this was an unacceptable development. His earlier acts of friendship had been thrown back in his face. Had Tokhtamish already forgotten how Temur had clothed him so richly when he had arrived destitute in the Tatar's court in 1376? How Temur had financed repeated military campaigns to win him his kingdom in the north, even fighting alongside him until he was installed as khan of the Golden Horde? Such ingratitude so soon augured badly. The sweeping steppes of Asia, its wide deserts and snow-capped mountains were beginning to look too small to encompass the rival ambitions of the two warrior princes.

⚙

In taking Tabriz, the khan of the Golden Horde had issued a direct challenge to the Unconquered Lord of the Seven Climes. It was not in Temur's character to let it go unanswered. Had the city been of little consequence, it is probable he would have acted no differently. The point was that Tokhtamish had announced his ambitions overtly. Failure to respond decisively would have represented, in Temur's mind at least, an admission of weakness and an invitation to further attacks.

In any case, the Azerbaijan capital was one of the greatest cities in the world outside China. It stood at the centre of the busiest international trade routes. Merchants and caravans streamed through on the Khorasan road running east from Baghdad as far as the frontier with China. Others arrived from Cairo, Constantinople and Trebizond in the west, from Damascus, Antioch and Aleppo in Syria. Pilgrims and merchants travelled the well-trodden path from Mecca north to Baghdad and Tabriz, while from India came more itinerant traders, crossing overland from the port of Hormuz.

The city walls measured twenty-five thousand paces (compared with nine thousand in Herat and ten thousand in Samarkand), encompassing a vast population in the region of 1.25 million, based on the two hundred thousand households recorded by Clavijo.* Travellers competed with each other for superlatives when they arrived at this booming metropolis. Marco Polo described Tabriz in around 1270 as 'a great and noble city' teeming with a cosmopolitan crowd of Armenians, Nestorians, Jacobites, Georgians and Persians. Writing at the turn of the fourteenth century, the Persian historian Rashid ad-din commented on the throng of 'philosophers, astronomers, scholars, historians – of all religions, of all sects' gathered in Tabriz. There were Indians, Kashmiris, Chinese, Uighurs, Arabs, Franks, Turks and Tibetans. The city's prodigiously stocked markets, arranged according to the various trades and products – jewellery, musk, ambergris, silks, cottons, taffetas, unguents, lacquers from China, spices from India – were the envy of all.

'I entered the town and we came to a great bazaar, one of the finest bazaars I have seen the world over,' gasped Ibn Battutah. 'Every trade is grouped separately in it. I passed through the jewellers' bazaar, and my eyes were dazzled by the precious stones that I beheld. They were displayed by beautiful slaves wearing rich garments with a waist-sash of silk, who stood in front of the merchants, exhibiting the

---

* Such figures, as has been noted, are considered exaggerated today.

jewels to the wives of the Turks, while the women were buying them in large quantities and trying to outdo one another.'

Tabriz was fantastically rich. 'This city, I tell you, is the finest in the world, for trade,' observed Friar Oderic, writing in the early fourteenth century. 'Every article is found here in abundance. It is so marvellous that you would scarcely believe everything unless you saw it . . . The Christians of this place say that the revenue it pays to its emperor is greater than the revenue all of France pays to its king.' In 1341, the treasury's revenues from Tabriz amounted to almost nine million dinars, a staggering total for the time.

Such prosperity was evident in the magnificence of its mosques, madrassahs, palaces and hospitals, resplendent with marble, limestone and glazed blue tiles. Clavijo, the most diligent of eyewitnesses, was taken by the sheer number and quality of the public buildings, lavishly decorated with mosaics of blue and gold. The city owed its architectural grandeur both to the prosperity generated by trade, he was told, and to a thriving culture of one-upmanship among its architectural patrons.

> All these fine buildings had been erected in days past when there had been living in Tabriz many famous and rich men who had vied each with his neighbour as to who should build the finest house, each spending willingly his wealth in what he did. Of such buildings we visited especially one, a great palace that stands surrounded by its own wall most beautifully and richly planned, and within this building were twenty thousand rooms and separate apartments.

It was an elegantly planned city, with good roads, plenty of open spaces and many caravanserais for passing merchants. Clavijo and his entourage spent nine days there, handsomely entertained by Temur's *darugha*, the governor or mayor. Like those travellers before him, the Spaniard admired the markets and luxuriated in the steaming bath-houses which he thought 'the most splendid' in the entire world. Fed by the river which irrigated the outlying fields, open channels of water gurgled through the streets, providing refreshment for the merchants haggling furiously in the bazaars with women draped in white sheets, their eyes hidden behind veils of horse hair: 'In the streets and squares of this city there are many fountains, and in summer they fill them with pieces of ice, and put brass and copper jugs near them, so that the people can come and drink.'

This, then, was the city which Tokhtamish, thundering through the alpine meadows of the Caucasus, had seized so suddenly and which now, in the spring of 1386, attracted Temur's attention. The khan of the Golden Horde, said the dutiful Yazdi, had sacked the city with a ninety-thousand-strong army of 'infidels of a cruel and merciless nature'. They had 'pillaged the place and exercised all imaginable cruelties and abominations: the desolation was universal, and all the riches, treasures, and rarities which had been amassed there during a great many years were consumed in less than six days'. The Persian chronicler obligingly supplied the religious justification for Temur's move on Tabriz. 'The emperor having advice of this devastation was incensed at the violence and tyranny which had been exercised against the Mussulmans,' he wrote. A crime had been committed against Islam.

&

In Samarkand, where Temur had returned after seizing Sultaniya, the glacial winds of winter had given way to the pleasant zephyrs of spring. The mountains had shed their snowy coats and the Zarafshan (Gold Spreader) river was bursting its banks, watering the orchards and vineyards that lay all around the city. The streets hummed with activity. From the treasury came the din of crashing metal as swordsmiths went about their business. Hundreds of craftsmen and metalworkers, rounded up and imprisoned as Temur spun his web

of empire, sweated in workshops fashioning body armour and helmets for the army. In the bazaars, saddlemakers reeking of tanned
hides and oil gossiped with merchants about the forthcoming season,
comparing notes on the imperious government couriers riding
through on horseback with despatches and instructions. Temur, it
was said, was assembling an army for a Three-Year Campaign in
Persia, his most ambitious undertaking yet. The *tovachis* were busier
than ever, gathering the forces, procuring supplies and checking that
the soldiers were properly equipped. Confidence was high among
these war-hardened tribesmen. Over the course of the long winter
they had eaten and drunk and spent their way through much of last
season's plunder from the fall of Herat and Sultaniya. The family
coffers were almost bare. It was time to leave Samarkand again to
make war in distant kingdoms. These men placed great faith in their
leader. They did not doubt for an instant that he would win them
new treasures. He had never failed them yet. There was no reason to
suppose he would now. Final preparations were made, the baggage
caravans were counted and recounted and the amirs announced their
readiness to the man who would conquer the world. One by one the
horse-tail standards were lifted. With a roar, Temur's army marched
west again.

The mountain tribes of Lurs, south of Sultaniya, were first to feel
the Tatars' steel. They had been ransacking the pilgrim caravans which
plied the routes to and from Mecca, an outrage which demanded
retaliation. After a forced march at the head of a select body of troops
from the main army, Temur attacked. The tribesmen were shattered.
'They were flung headlong from the tops of mountains,' Yazdi
reported.

The richest prize still awaited. From Lurs, the army marched north
towards Tabriz. An ill-prepared Sultan Ahmed started mustering
forces to defend the city, but it was too little too late and his attempt
came to nothing. With Temur's army at the gates, once again he

disappeared in ignominious flight, leaving the city to take its chances. A detachment of Temur's men was sent after him and pursued him closely – Arabshah called him an 'opportunist fugitive' – but he managed to escape. Without its leader, Tabriz had little option but to surrender. Out trooped the city's notables, the amirs and religious leaders, less magisterial now that their protector had abandoned them to the Scourge of God. In front of Temur they sued for peace and pleaded for their lives. Tabriz, since it had surrendered without a struggle, was spared. Seizing one of the greatest cities in the world had not cost Temur a single soldier.

Instead of putting the citizens to the sword, he punished them with a huge ransom. For the rest of the summer he and his army remained in Azerbaijan while local leaders arrived to pledge their loyalty to the new ruler. Skilled craftsmen, artists, mathematicians and scientists were once more despatched east, joining colleagues from captured lands to adorn Temur's growing capital of Samarkand. Such was the importance of Tabriz within his expanding dominions that it was conferred to the rule of Mohammed Sultan, youthful son of the late Jahangir, Temur's beloved first-born who had died a decade earlier.

Clavijo's portrait of Tabriz, observed eighteen years after Temur had won it, is valuable for a number of reasons. It is one of the few detailed accounts we have of it at that time, and one of the only descriptions of a city under his rule. As Harold Lamb noted in his 1928 biography of Temur, the Spaniard's testimony undermines the arguments of those who would dismiss the conqueror as 'an architect only of pyramids of skulls and as a barbarian destroyer'. Tabriz was clearly flourishing architecturally, economically and intellectually within his empire. The picture of a smouldering pile of ruins – far more the signature of Genghis than of Temur – could hardly be further from the truth.

As a rule Temur made a distinction between those cities that

surrendered without resistance – which were spared – and those that
cost him dearly, in terms of time, effort and the lives of his soldiers
– which were ravaged. But even when he unleashed his hordes, he
still tended to spare the cities' public buildings – mosques,
madrassahs, schools and shrines. And even in those instances where
he gave his men free rein to burn and pillage, more often than not
the architects, builders and craftsmen were later ordered in to repair
the damage. Teams of soldiers were left behind to restore canals,
encouraging the devastated agricultural economy with a view to
maximising future tax revenues. Temur's Persian panegyrist made a
point of mentioning this, of course, for it was much to Temur's credit
as a man of the holy book. 'The Alcoran remarks that the rebuilding
of places is one of the most glorious actions which princes can
perform in this world, and which conduces most to the good of
society,' Yazdi wrote with typical complacency.

Temur had no intention of turning back after these rapid gains.
This was no time to exchange the challenges of campaigning for the
comforts of Samarkand. After Tabriz he abruptly called a halt to the
westward advance and pushed north instead. On a map this decision
to march his men into the mountains of the Qarabagh, rather than
continuing west along easier territory, looks odd, particularly given
the inhospitable season, but it was a direct response to the gauntlet
thrown down by the khan of the Golden Horde who had led his
army south through the Caucasus to seize Tabriz. By incorporating
this unruly region into his empire Temur intended to ensure that
Tokhtamish could never repeat such mischief again. No one could
be allowed to show the slightest mastery over Temur. His will was
supreme.

There was another incentive to attack, though this would have
weighed less heavily with him. Georgia was an unsightly island of

Christianity amid the mighty seas of Islam. Conquering it was an opportunity to win favour as a Ghazi, or warrior of the faith. King Bagrat the Great must be forced to see the error of his ways. 'God hath recommended to Mohammed to excite the Mussulmans to make war on the enemies of their religion, because it is the most excellent of all actions,' noted Yazdi, ever ready to please his paymaster, 'and the Alcoran praises above all others those who risk their fortunes and lives in such a war.'

Winter had fallen. 'The violence of the cold was extraordinary, and the air was full of ice and frost,' said the chronicle, but still the marches continued. Dreaming of the summer pastures of Samarkand, the soldiers struggled across freezing plains, urging their exhausted horses over ground that had been churned into a quagmire. Into the mountains they stumbled, hauling their vast quantities of equipment behind them.

At the Georgian capital of Tiflis (Tbilisi), the Tatars encountered a vigorous defence. Both the city walls and the citadel were heavily fortified. The Georgians were also famously resilient soldiers. These were not the sort of people to surrender their city without a fight like the cowardly Sultan Ahmed of Azerbaijan. Calmly, Temur ordered the siege machines to be prepared, and the assault was launched. When the walls had been weakened he rallied his men with the terrible cry, 'Allahu akbar, God is great,' the signal to storm the city. With sword in hand he led the army into Tiflis, where the defiant king was captured, put into chains and brought before his new master. Later, after divisions of the Tatar army had subdued the region, razing towns and castles before them, Bagrat was given another audience with Temur in which the compelling truth of Islam was impressed upon him. The Georgian king was no less opportunist a ruler than Temur, and it did not take him long to see the wisdom of conversion. In front of his victorious opponent, he declared: 'La ilaha illa'llah, Mohammedan rasul' Allah', there is no god but God and Mohammed is his Prophet,' the seven words which identify one as a Muslim. Bagrat underwrote his loyalty to Temur by presenting him with a coat of mail said to have been forged by the prophet David.

Pleased by Bagrat's show of devotion and repeated professions of loyalty, Temur granted him his freedom as a vassal king. It was to prove a fairly short-lived treaty. Georgia was the most rebellious region within Temur's empire. In 1393, six years after his first triumphs here, the conqueror was campaigning again in the Caucasian mountains. By then, Bagrat had died and his son Giorgi VII had succeeded him on the throne. Like his father, he too required a show of arms to concentrate his mind. In all, Temur mounted six campaigns against Georgia. He was still fighting there as late as the autumn of 1403, a stooped old man of sixty-six.

The fifteenth-century chronicle of T'ovma Metsobets'i, a native of the region north of Lake Van (close to the Turkish border with Armenia), described that first campaign in the most apocalyptic of terms. Like Arabshah, Metsobets'i had felt at first hand the dislocation and devastation brought by Temur's armies, repeatedly having to flee for his life at this time. 'A man named Tamerlane, holding the faith and precepts of the obscene Mahomet, precursor of the Antichrist, appeared in the East, in the city of Samarkand, merciless, cruel, treacherous, filled with all the evil, impurity and stratagems of the tempter Satan,' he began. En route to Georgia, Temur and his army 'tormented the entire multitude of believers with starvation, the sword, enslavement, and with unbearable tortures and bestial behaviour they made the most populous district of Armenia uninhabited. Many people were martyred and were worthy of the crown; they are known only to the One Who receives them, Christ our God.' North the Tatars continued into Georgia, bloodshed attending their every advance. 'Temur took booty, plunder, and countless captives. No one can relate the disasters and bitterness of our people. Going with numerous troops to the city of Tiflis, he took it and captured countless people; and it is believed that those killed outnumbered those left alive.'

More troublesome news reached Temur that winter. Tokhtamish had mounted another expedition into the strategically important Darband region on the western shores of the Caspian Sea, a corridor which controlled access into Temur's newly won lands – Georgia, Armenia and Azerbaijan of today – from the north. The Tatars clashed with the vanguard of the invaders and a number of the soldiers of the Golden Horde were taken prisoner. Rather than killing them in cold blood, Temur set them free and sent them back to their master with a message reminding him of his obligations and the treaty between the two men. 'How comes it that your prince, whom I regard as my son, uses me so ill as to send an army into this country, without any provocation given him?' Temur asked. 'For you know there is between us a certain relationship like that between father and son. And why is he the occasion of the loss of so many thousands of Mussulmans?' It is unlikely Temur expected a conciliatory reply. The khan's recent manoeuvres suggested that filial respect for his southern neighbour was far from his mind. On the contrary, the relationship between the two appeared to be growing ever more hostile. With each year that passed, full-scale war between the two would-be world conquerors seemed the most likely outcome.

❧

As the first buds and blossoms of spring arrived in the rugged pastures of the Caucasus on the shores of the Blue Lake in 1387, Temur, his great amirs and the massed hordes who fought so furiously in his name stirred like a hibernating giant awakening from the winter sloth. Queen Saray Mulk-khanum, Temur's chief wife, and other members of the royal household who had helped warm the emperor's bed during these freezing months departed for Samarkand. What lay ahead did not concern them.

During three decades, the timetable of Temur's campaigns rarely changed. In the winter months the soldiers were stood down, returning to their families across the empire, heavily laden with the booty of the last season. As the cold months passed and the temperatures started to rise, as the frozen lakes thawed, the troops braced themselves for the emperor's next campaign. For the best part of thirty years, spring habitually meant one thing: war.

From Armenia the army marched west, seeping into Asia Minor like poison. Perhaps Temur already envisaged a confrontation with one of the greatest rulers in the world, Bayazid I, the Ottoman sultan on whose borders he was close to trespassing. But for now his sphere of action lay slightly to the east, in an unruly region held by feuding Turkmen tribes. Word came to Temur that they had been massacring caravans of pilgrims en route to Mecca, another pretext to raise the banner of *jihad*. Erzerum and Arzinjan quickly fell to him. High on a rocky peak the impregnable citadel of Van, 'which had never been conquered by any sovereign', represented a more difficult challenge. Yet it surrendered after just two days. The defenders of the fortress who refused to join their prince in submission were overrun after a siege of twenty days. Those who were not butchered by the sword met an even more dreadful fate, tied by the hands and feet and hurled into the abyss, a thousand steps below, to their destruction.

This procession of victories marked the western limits of Temur's Three-Year Campaign. As abruptly as he had pushed north from Sultaniya, he now swept south across Azerbaijan, riding back into Persia at the head of his army of mounted archers. Such unexpected changes of direction, employed regularly during his campaigns, consistently wrong-footed his enemies. Temur was a brilliant military tactician. Unaware of his approach, oblivious to the threat, sultans, kings and princes suddenly found their cities, castles and armies under attack without warning. The element of surprise achieved formidable success.

This time Temur had another target in sight. Glittering on the desert plain like a brooch of emerald and sapphire, its cool waters and lush orchards equally inviting, lay Isfahan. It was, reported Ibn Battutah, 'one of the largest and fairest of cities', a place of plenty and splendour. Its architecture was graceful, its markets thick with merchants, famed for hundreds of miles. Watered by the Zayandeh river, it was a fertile oasis surrounded by limitless horizons of sand and salt. 'It is rich in fruits, among its products being apricots of unequalled quality with sweet almonds in their kernels, quinces whose sweetness and size cannot be paralleled, splendid grapes, and wonderful melons,' wrote the Moroccan traveller. 'Its people are good-looking, with clear white skins tinged with red, exceedingly brave, generous, and always trying to outdo one another in procuring luxurious viands.' Arabshah agreed. Isfahan was 'a great city, full of excellent men and teeming with nobles'.

Although an early proponent of *blitzkrieg*, Temur liked to justify his military actions before they began. A pretext was needed before he could lay claim to Isfahan. He did not have to cast about for one for long. Prior to leaving Samarkand on this Three-Year Campaign, he had received a highly unusual letter from Shah Shuja Muzaffar, the ruler of the Persian province of Fars, with whom he had previously contracted an alliance. After a decadent life indulging heavily in wine and women, the patron of the poet Hafiz was now on his deathbed, from where he entrusted the protection of his remaining family to Temur.

'Great men are aware that the world is the theatre of inconstancy,' Shah Shuja's letter began:

> Men of learning are never given to trifles – nor transitory pleasures
> and beauties – because they know the passing of all things ... As
> to the treaty between us, deigning never to break it, I look upon
> the gaining of the Imperial Friendship as a great conquest, and
> my chief wish – dare I say it – is to have in my hand this treaty

*with you at the Day of Judgement, so that you should not reproach
me with breaking my word . . . Now I am called before the tribunal
of the Sovereign Master of the Universe, and I thank the Divine
Majesty that I have done nothing for which my conscience can
reproach me – notwithstanding the faults and sins which are insep-
arable from life and the depraved nature of man – and I have
tasted all the pleasures I could reasonably expect during the fifty-
three years I have stayed upon the earth . . . In brief, I die as I
have lived, and I have abandoned all the vanities of the world.
And I pray God to give his blessing to this monarch [Temur] as
wise as Solomon and as great as Alexander. Although it is not at
all necessary to commend to you my loved son Zayn al Abidin –
God grant him a long life under the shadow of your protection –
I leave him to the care of God and your Majesty. How could I
doubt that you will keep this treaty? I also beg of you to say the
final prayer for your devoted friend, who is happy in departing
out of this life in friendship with you, that through the prayers of
a Prince so great and fortunate, God may be merciful to me and
raise me up among the saints. This is what we pray your Majesty
to carry out, as our last will, for which you will be answerable in
the next world.*

The Muzaffarid prince gave Shiraz, capital of Fars province, to his
son and heir Zayn al Abidin. The old man's nephew Shah Yahya
received Yazd, his brother Sultan Ahmed inheriting Kirman. Isfahan
was bequeathed to his valiant nephew Shah Mansur. The letter and
Shah Shuja's will gave Temur just the opportunity he was waiting
for. Testing the loyalty of his new vassal, he summoned Zayn al Abidin
to swear loyalty to him at his travelling court. The prince failed to
present himself.

Suddenly the Tatar hordes were lined up in full battle formation
before the walls of Isfahan. It was a terrifying sight for its governor
and citizens, who knew Temur's reputation only too well. A false move
and the city would be turned to ashes. Rushing out to pre-empt certain
slaughter, the governor and his officials offered their surrender. Temur

accepted, on condition the city pay a typically heavy ransom. Once this had been agreed, he rode into Isfahan with a magnificently arrayed entourage to inspect his latest acquisition.

Tension gripped the city. No one knew what Temur would do next. Gossip, rumour and wild speculation coursed through the bazaars. Some said Isfahan was going to be spared, and that Temur would soon be on his way after seizing the ransom. Others, mindful of previous outrages, expected the city to be torched, and retreated into their cellars, determined not to move until the conqueror and his army had left.

A new governor was appointed, and then, as suddenly as he had arrived, Temur wheeled around, spurred his horse and galloped back to his camp outside the city, well pleased with the day's events. Night fell and the cloak of darkness descended on Isfahan. An uneasy peace bristled in the streets. Tatar officers guarded the gates to the city, reinforced within the walls by a garrison of soldiers. No one else was allowed entry. Camped outside after several months on the march, seventy thousand hungry and exhausted soldiers thought longingly of plunder, picturing the sexual and gastronomic pleasures that surely awaited them, and wondered what the morning would bring.

Some time in the night, according to Yazdi, Isfahan awoke to the noise of a blacksmith beating his drum and urging his fellow citizens to fall upon the Tatar soldiers stationed inside the walls. Gripped by fear and moved by hatred, they rose up against their new conquerors and the garrison of three thousand was slain. In a matter of minutes the massacre was complete. Toasting their success, the hot-blooded rebels swore that Isfahan would remain free. But the celebrations did not last long. The first flush of victory quickly receded, replaced by the chilling realisation that Temur would certainly avenge these killings, carried out in defiance of a treaty agreed with the city elders. No quarter could be expected from him now. With this recognition that they had signed their own death warrants rather than liberated Isfahan, the mood of the warriors changed and their limbs started to tremble. And then another silence, heavy with dread, hung over the roofs of the city.

At dawn, wrote Arabshah,

> *Temur perceived that evil crime; and Satan puffed up his nostrils and he forthwith moved his camp and drew the sword of his wrath and took arrows from the quiver of his tyranny and advanced to the city, roaring, overthrowing, like a dog or lion or leopard; and when he came in sight of the city, he ordered bloodshed and sacrilege, slaughter and plunder, devastation, burning of crops, women's breasts to be cut off, infants to be destroyed, bodies dismembered, honour to be insulted, dependants to be betrayed and abandoned, the carpet of pity to be folded up and the blanket of revenge to be unfolded . . . then he loosened the reins of the cutting sword in the fields of their necks and made their graves in the bellies of wolves and hyenas and the crop of birds; and the whirlwinds of destruction did not cease sweeping them from the trees of existence, until they counted the number of dead, who were six times more than the people of Nineveh.*

Temur ordered the killing of every man, woman and child. Seventy thousand lost their lives in the bloodbath. Each division of the army, from the detachments of ten and one hundred to the *tumans* of ten thousand, was ordered to bring back a certain number of heads, and the *tovachis* were appointed to count them. At first, Yazdi observed, there was great reluctance among the soldiers to murder fellow Muslims in cold blood. Many bought heads from more willing executioners. Heads changed hands for twenty dinars apiece until the soldiers lost their scruples and the torrent of slaughter raged unabated through the city; the price plunged to half a dinar. Those who had escaped the initial slaughter, hiding in their houses, crept out at night and fled through the snow. They were hunted down the following morning and butchered where they stood.

No mercy was shown Isfahan's children. Schiltberger, the Bavarian squire captured and taken prisoner by Temur's army at the battle of Ankara in 1402, described what happened after the slaughter inside the city walls.

> *Then he ordered the women and children to be taken to a plain outside the city, and ordered the children under seven years of age to be placed apart, and ordered his people to ride over these same children. When his counsellors and the mothers of the children saw this, they fell at his feet, and begged that he would not kill them. He would not listen, and ordered that they should be ridden over; but none would be the first to do so. He got angry and rode himself* [amongst them] *and said: 'Now I should like to see who will not ride after me?' Then they were obliged to ride over the children, and they were all trampled upon. There were seven thousand.*

The familiar totems of Temur's wrath sprang up around the city like an unholy halo of death. The historian Hafiz-i-Abru walked halfway round Isfahan shortly after the bloodshed and counted twenty-eight towers of fifteen hundred heads each.

In the final weeks of 1387, Temur was celebrating the peaceful surrender of Shiraz, two hundred miles to the south. There was reason to be content. Like Herat, Tabriz and Isfahan, the city had emptied its coffers to him, this time for a crippling ransom of ten million silver dinars. In the mosques, Temur's name was read in the *khutba* – the sermon in Friday prayers – as the new sovereign. The rival princes of the Muzaffarid dynasty were now vassal kings. Victory letters were despatched to Samarkand commemorating, in florid prose, the sweep of his triumphs. The lion's share of the empire carved out by Hulagu now owed its allegiance to the upstart sheep-stealer-turned-emperor from Samarkand.

It was in Shiraz, according to a popular story, that the poet Hafiz, the brightest star in the literary firmament, was summoned before Temur to explain himself. He had written a verse which had come to the Tatar's attention and displeased him mightily.

If that unkindly Shiraz Turk would take my heart within her hand,
I'd give Bukhara for the mole upon her cheek, or Samarkand.

Temur's voice, though calm, was full of menace. 'I have subdued with this sword the greater part of the earth. I have depopulated a vast number of cities and provinces in order to increase the glory and wealth of Samarkand and Bukhara, the ordinary places of my residence and the seat of my empire; yet you, an insignificant individual, have pretended to give away both Samarkand and Bukhara as the price of a little black mole setting off the features of a pretty face.'

It was a dreadful moment for Hafiz. His life hung in the balance. A careless answer would cost him his head. 'Alas! O Prince,' he replied, 'it is this prodigality which is the cause of the misery in which you see me.'

Far from offending Temur, the poet's reply amused him. Instead of ordering his immediate execution, he presented him with extravagant presents and asked him to stay in the imperial court.

☙

These weeks of courtly pleasures were suddenly interrupted. From Samarkand, eleven hundred miles away, came desperate news. Mawarannahr was under attack. The heart of the newly won empire was besieged. Prince Omar Shaykh, Temur's eldest surviving son, had only narrowly escaped death on the battlefield. Enemy forces had surrounded Bukhara. Some were marauding in the Qashka Darya valley, where Temur had been born. Soldiers were laying waste to towns and villages. The palace at Qarshi, one of the defining symbols of the Chaghatay empire, had been razed to the ground. Worse still, the Jats, Temur's long-standing adversaries in Moghulistan, had wasted no time in joining the rebellion, accompanied by the Sufi shah of Khorezm.

It was a bitter blow. By the mid-1380s, Temur ruled, or rather had conquered, lands stretching west from Samarkand as far as Georgia and the fringes of the Ottoman empire. Although much of these territories would require periodic reconquest, it was Temur, and no other man, who could justifiably claim to be emperor over them. But while he had been winning these new lands with the sword a thousand miles away in the west, a hostile army, taking advantage of his absence from the seat of empire, had struck decisively in the east. His adversary had mounted a lightning raid where it was least expected, using precisely the sort of tactics which Temur himself had employed with such success. The brilliantly executed manoeuvrings had completely wrong-footed the master of warfare. Now, after years of peace and plenty, Samarkand, his beloved capital, was under threat. It was the most serious challenge he had ever faced. Failure to confront and overcome it would spell the humiliating end to his career of conquest.

But what made the news even harder for Temur to stomach was the identity of his enemy. The grating irony was that it was the very man whose incursions had prompted him to campaign in the Caucasus to shore up his western defences. Here was an adversary of an altogether different nature, of far greater mettle, than those Temur had faced and defeated before, an audacious warrior in his own mould. The one-time protégé had unleashed his sword against his former mentor. The son had turned against his adopted father. Tokhtamish, khan of the Golden Horde, wanted war.

5

The Golden Horde and the Prodigal Son

1387–1395

'Then Temur came into those parts with a great army, nay, a turbid sea, whose soldiers carried flying arrows, sharp swords and quivering spears and were ravening lions and furious leopards, all of warlike spirit, which takes vengeance on the enemy, stoutly defends its own flag and its allies and homes and its prey and its lairs and covers with the sea of war him who opposes its waves and breakers.

'Therefore Toqtamish sent to the lords of his subjects and the magnates of his peoples and the dwellers in sandy places and inhabitants of the borders and chiefs who were his kinsmen and leaders of the right and left of his army, whom he summoned and called to meet the enemy and wage war and they came clad in the long robe of obedience and hastening from every high mountain; and there assembled hosts and tribes of horse and foot and swordsmen and javelin-throwers and archers and attackers and defenders and warriors and slayers with the sabre and skilled archers and wielders of spears, who would not miss the mark compared with the sons of Tual, skilled spearmen. When they take their weapon and aim at what they need, they strike the mark whether sitting or flying.

'Then Toqtamish rose to fight, ready for onslaught and battle, with an army numerous like the sands and heavy like the mountains.'

AHMED IBN ARABSHAH, *Tamerlane*

Temur, as he hurried back east to Samarkand to protect his homeland, must have cursed his earlier foreign policy in the north. He had used Tokhtamish as a pawn in the succession game against Urus, khan of the White Horde.* A blood feud already existed between those two men. Urus had murdered Tokhtamish's father and was now concentrating on enlarging his empire, a direct threat to Temur's dominions immediately to the south. At the time, distracting Urus from these grander designs by keeping him mired in internecine conflict within the White Horde had seemed eminently sensible. For as long as Urus was fighting a domestic rival, he was prevented from reunifying the fragmented Golden Horde under one ruler, and was therefore unlikely to emerge on ambitious campaigns beyond his borders.

Temur had groomed Tokhtamish, had educated him in the art of warfare and had armed and equipped him time after time in the second half of the 1370s. Repeatedly defeated at the hands of Urus, Tokhtamish had straggled back to Temur's court, from where, with health and wealth restored, he had returned again and again to the frontline. Temur had even fought alongside him.

How Temur must have regretted these intrigues as relays of messengers galloped into his camp, bringing more details of the damage suffered during Tokhtamish's invasion of Mawarannahr. In terms of its immediate objectives, his policy had succeeded. Urus had been emasculated. But Tokhtamish, in his wake, had proved too powerful. By 1378, he had succeeded his arch-rival as khan of the White Horde. By 1380, he was installed as leader of the combined hordes in the flourishing capital of Saray on the Volga. Two years later, his armies overran and torched Moscow. Tokhtamish now presided over the

---

* From the mid-fourteenth century, the Golden Horde had started disintegrating under internal pressures. The province of Khorezm had been reunited under the Sufi dynasty, while in the south-east, Urus, descended from Genghis Khan's eldest son, Jochi, presided over the regions bordering on Moghulistan, known as the White Horde.

restored Jochi ulus, the Golden Horde, original patrimony of Genghis's eldest son.

These lands, the northernmost and westernmost Mongol territories, which stretched from the Danube in the west to the Irtish in the east, were populated by an unruly and exotic cast of nomadic peoples of Turkic origin – Bulgars, Kazaks, Kyrgyz, Alans, Kankalis and Mordovians – known simply as the Kipchaks, the men of the desert, whose steppes formed the centre of this fluid movement of the tribes. The Horde reached as far as Khorezm in the south-east, its south-western borders marked by the northern Caucasus, Crimea and Moldo-Wallachia. In the north-west it included the lands of the Volga Bulgars and Mordovians. A vast swathe of steppe, it boasted well-maintained trade routes and excellent pasturage for the nomads' animals.

The fringes of Temur's empire and those of the Golden Horde were particularly blurred in two areas: Khorezm in the east and, more particularly, Azerbaijan in the west. These spots were potential flashpoints, the more so given the expanding arc of both Temur and Tokhtamish's ambitions. That Tokhtamish had pushed on farther south into the bosom of Temur's empire – he had even had the temerity to lay siege to Bukhara – into lands over which he held no conceivable hereditary claim, was an outrage and an intolerable insult.

When discussing the looming conflict between the two men it is important to remember that Tokhtamish, unlike Temur, could claim the most illustrious descent. He was a prince of royal blood, who traced his lineage back to Genghis through Tokay Temur, son of Jochi. Once he had seized power, therefore, he had the right to style himself khan, a title forever prohibited to Temur by the conventions of the steppe.

Whatever hospitality he had received from Temur, it would not have been unreasonable for Tokhtamish to regard the Tatar as an impostor on the Asian stage, a minor noble at best. If anyone was

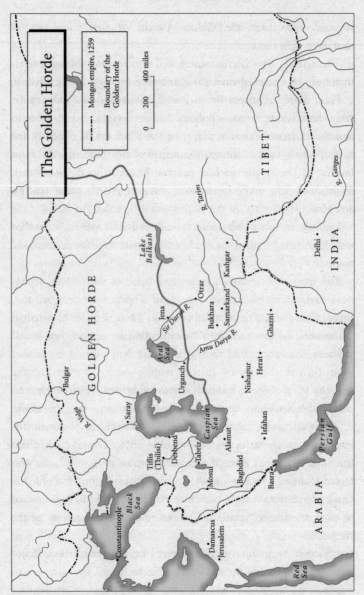

The Golden Horde

Mongol empire, 1259
Boundary of the
Golden Horde

0   200   400 miles

TIBET

R. Tarim

R. Ganges

Delhi

INDIA

Lake
Balkash

Kashgar

Otrar

Jena

Sir Darya R.

Samarkand

Bukhara

Ghazni

GOLDEN HORDE

Amu Darya R.

Bulgar

R. Volga

Aral
Sea

Urganch

Nishapur

Herat

Saray

Caspian
Sea

Isfahan

Alamut

Persian
Gulf

Tiflis
(Tbilisi)

Derbend

Tabriz

Mosul

Baghdad

Basra

Black
Sea

ARABIA

Constantinople

Damascus
Jerusalem

Red
Sea

to reunite the fragmented Mongol empire, it was he and not his upstart rival in the south. The older enmity between the Jochids and the Hulagid empire of Persia, where Temur had already announced his intentions by making great inroads, merely reinforced this conviction.

From Temur's perspective, war with Tokhtamish was now inevitable. For as long as his aggressive northern neighbour was free to launch attacks on Mawarannahr, his empire-building of necessity had to stop. This suited neither his objectives nor those of his Tatar hordes, as predictable as ever in their lust for booty and riches. Tokhtamish had to be neutralised and eliminated. There was no acceptable alternative.

Before he set about his preparations for this campaign, Temur first wanted to establish how the khan of the Golden Horde had managed to penetrate so far south. His attention to detail and discipline was, as ever, meticulous. Why, he wanted to know, had the imperial armies not driven Tokhtamish away? What explained the shameful defeat of Prince Omar Shaykh's forces at Otrar on the Sir Darya? How could Tokhtamish have humiliated Temur in the conqueror's own lands? Bukhara, the heart of Islam, had almost fallen to these enemies of the faith. Temur glowed with fury at the thought of it. An inquiry was held. Temur's son was found to have led his men bravely, and escaped any charge of cowardice. One warrior, who had fought like a lion, was handsomely rewarded with land and the most distinguished title of *tarkhan*. Another commander, however, who had fled from the battlefield when the fighting was at its most furious, was forced to suffer a highly unusual and embarrassing punishment. His beard was shaved, his face was painted with rouge and he was forced to put on woman's clothing. Then, 'after having received severe reproaches for his cowardice', he was made to run barefoot through Samarkand, to the general hilarity of the citizens and the more subdued emotions of the soldiery.

For now, war would wait. More than a year elapsed from Temur's

arrival in Samarkand in the autumn of 1388 to the departure of the
imperial armies on their mission to extinguish Tokhtamish. As always,
there was the business of empire and family to attend to first. Khorezm, above all, had to be taught the price of rebellion. Urganch was
savagely erased from the map, fields of barley planted on its ruins.
More happily, a number of marriages were celebrated within the
imperial family. Brides were found for Prince Omar Shaykh and the
eleven-year-old Shahrukh, later bearer of the Temurid flame, together
with the emperor's cherished grandsons Pir Mohammed and
Mohammed Sultan, the heirs of Jahangir, Temur's first-born who had
predeceased him. In the Paradise Garden pavilions were erected, lined
with elaborate carpets and hangings. Amidst this splendour, among
pearls and rubies, gold and silver, the royal princes were married to
princesses who were, said the chronicle, as fabulously beautiful as
the *houris* of paradise.*

The amirs were stood down, the soldiers released from duty and
instructed to return to their families until the return of spring and
another campaigning season. Peace descended on Mawarannahr
and the citizens, reassured by the arrival of their emperor after the
traumas of invasion, slept soundly once again. And then, just as
Samarkand was slumbering through the deep snows of winter, came
more chilling news, almost too improbable to believe. Tokhtamish,
at the head of a formidable army, was bearing down on Mawarannahr
again. His forces had already crossed the Sir Darya and showed no
signs of halting despite the vicious conditions. Panic-stricken, Temur's
advisers counselled against retaliation. This was not the time to

---

* The *houris* are the stunning dark-eyed virgins who await every Muslim
man in the heavenly afterlife. Their youth and celestial good looks are
everlasting, their virginity renewable at pleasure. They are referred to in
the Koran in a number of suras: 'As for the righteous, they shall be lodged
in peace together amid gardens and fountains, arrayed in rich silks and
fine brocade. Even thus: and We shall wed them to dark-eyed *houris*'
(Sura 44: 51–54).

engage the enemy, they argued. The main body of the imperial army had retired for the winter, out of reach and scattered across the empire. Even with those soldiers who remained at hand, the weather was simply too hostile to contemplate military action. The snow was too deep for the horses. Far better to sit it out in Samarkand until the advent of spring. Tokhtamish, besides, would only be exposing himself and his men to the harsh elements while skirmishing relatively harmlessly in the outlying areas. The losses would be minimal. There was nothing to be gained from attacking now, ill-prepared and motivated by rage.

There can be no doubt Temur's pride had been stung. It was not in his nature to let such an attack go unanswered. He would not countenance any delay. Besides, retiring now would contravene his long-held military principle never to fight a defensive war. It was his enemies, not his own men, whom he forced to defend themselves behind walls, and the result was always the same: a devastating rout. He would not subject himself or his armies to such ignominy. The khan of the Golden Horde had attacked at the most unexpected and inhospitable time of year. The Tatar would make him pay for it. The invader would be expecting Temur to act as his most trusted amirs had suggested, by withdrawing to the south and avoiding battle. Ignoring this advice, he assembled an army from Samarkand and Shakhrisabz and moved north by night marches. The horses struggled ahead fitfully, with snow up to their bellies. Temur's army reached the vanguard of Tokhtamish's forces and succeeded in driving them back across the Sir Darya. And then the skies whitened and the air was full of stinging snow, hurled at the rival armies by the ferocious winds. Visibility disappeared altogether. Horses lost their way, falling constantly in the drifts. The men shivered within their tents, comforting themselves with already long-distant memories of warm nights at the family hearth. As quickly as it had begun, the expedition ground to a halt.

The spring of 1389 brought further indecisive skirmishing. Before he could embark on an all-out campaign against his northern adversary, one which would doubtless take many months, Temur first crushed the rebellion that had broken out in Khorasan and then drove back the Jats of Moghulistan, his long-standing enemy to the east. Driven by the time-honoured principle that my enemy's enemy is my friend, the Moghuls, under their new ruler Khizr Khoja, had done all in their power to assist Tokhtamish against Temur. Pacifying Khorasan – with typical brutality – secured the Tatar's western flank. The offensive against the Moghuls, pressed home emphatically until Khizr Khoja turned tail and fled into the mountains, removed the eastern threat. The road to Tokhtamish was now clear.

A *qurultay* was called near Shakhrisabz in the valley where Temur had been born, at which the amirs and their army officers, from the proud *binbashis*, commanders of one thousand, to the most junior *onbashis*, commanders of ten, gathered to hear the emperor's plans. The scale of the festivities reflected the importance of the campaign. 'There was another magnificent feast by Temur's order, the expenses of which were prodigious great,' Yazdi recorded. 'The princesses and ladies were all adorned with the richest jewels; the earth was covered with carpets of gold, China brocades, and embroidered pieces of work enriched with pearls, rubies and other precious stones: the cups, which were presented by the most beautiful women in the world, were of pure rock crystal, worked with all the delicacy and fineness which can be expected from the skill and industry of the most ingenious artists of past ages.'

Orders were given to expand the forces at the leader's disposal. Temur wanted to put an army of two hundred thousand into the field. The Tatar did not underestimate his former protégé. He already had good grounds to respect his military talents.

It is clear from the chronicles that of all Temur's opponents over the years, Tokhtamish was the warrior he most admired. The court records confirm how highly the Tatar valued the victories over him. The two campaigns and great battles against the khan of the Golden Horde are painstakingly detailed by Yazdi. We know more about these expeditions than most of the others: the great hardships faced by Temur's weary army as it marched north across the barren steppes; the feint and counter-feint of master and disciple, father and son, as the two armies faced each other across the river Terek; the course of the battle as first one side, then the other, snatched advantage; the wild celebrations which concluded the campaign.

In a sense the khan of the Golden Horde was Temur's reincarnation, for the younger man had learnt his military skills directly from his more experienced neighbour. Like Temur he was a leader who possessed cunning and guile in abundance. But Tokhtamish's status as Temur's arch-enemy was due also to geographical factors. His ambitions represented the most serious challenge to Temur's supremacy in Central Asia. There were other great contemporary sovereigns, but none breathing down his neck so closely. Their empires were distant: the Ottoman Sultan Bayazid I ruled far to the west, the Ming emperor held sway thousands of miles to the east.

At Shakhrisabz the *qurultay* was dismissed and the amirs and *tovachis* departed to attend to their armies. By the end of 1390, Temur was ready to depart. The Moghuls were no longer an immediate threat in the east. Khorasan had been subdued. The army had been assembled and well supplied for the campaign ahead. As a first step towards his enemy, Temur led his men two hundred miles north. Then he called a halt as the first snows of winter spiralled down from colourless skies. The emperor and his army would winter in Tashkent.

෴

In the late fourteenth century the city of Tashkent, or Shash as it was then known, was a pale shadow of the modern capital of Uzbekistan, and Temur had very little to do with it. Samarkand was the seat of his empire, Bukhara his religious capital. As his conquests expanded from this nucleus, they incorporated an ever-growing number of cities famed throughout Asia and the rest of the world. Tashkent, by contrast, is mentioned only rarely in the chronicles. There are several references to it in Yazdi, but they say little other than that Temur camped in the pastures outside the city prior to, or on his return from, one of his many campaigns; there is certainly nothing to show that he paid the place any particular regard. Nor is there any record that he left his mark there architecturally, no mosques or madrassahs, parks or palaces.

Though history reveals the little esteem in which he held the city, in the early twenty-first century Tashkent is at the forefront of a powerfully orchestrated Temur revival. Right in the heart of the capital, in the centre of a cool, tree-lined square, is a life-size statue of a man on horseback. The pose is regal and military. The sculptor has captured the moment of a great leader in action. The warrior wears a beard and a handsome crown. His right arm is raised aloft in a gesture of control, perhaps addressing his troops or surveying the sweep of his empire. His expression is imperious, the look of a man accustomed to command. The loose folds of his cloak catch the wind and billow behind him. With his left hand he reins his horse in tightly, catching the beast in mid-stride, snorting, its head sharply bowed, its left foreleg treadmilling the air. On his left side sits a long, gently curved sword, secured above a circular embossed shield. Massive boots with protective plates rest in huge stirrups. A richly decorated blanket covers the horse's back, edged with rows of hanging squares and pendants. Beneath the reins runs an elaborate girdle with matching fringes. Strength is engraved in every sinew of the stallion. In his thunderous chest and powerfully built legs. In his vigorous mane and pricked ears. In his voluminous tail gathered into an ordered bunch. Even in the veins running across his prodigious testicles. At the foot of the marble plinth that bears man and beast lies a tired bunch of flowers, a small donation from an anonymous admirer. On the plinth itself are the words 'Strength in Justice', set in bronze. And above them, in larger letters, the name of the man on horseback: Amir Temur.

Across the square, its blue ribbed dome recalling, though to a much inferior degree, the dazzling Temurid cupolas, is the Amir Temur museum, a relatively new circular building whose crude roof, complete with *faux* crenellations, is propped up by a series of insubstantial columns. At ground level square doors fill the lower half of tall marble arches set against a background of faded salmon. The upper half of the arches contain plain decorations that pay scant homage to the fine craftsmanship demanded by Temur.

Looking at the building on a bright September morning, I couldn't help thinking that if the Tatar's architects and masons had built it in his honour, they would have lost their heads. 'If you want to judge our strength, look at our monuments,' Temur had said. The verdict here would have been entirely unflattering. The museum lacks any sense of solidity or durability. His monuments were of an unparalleled magnificence. Built on a colossal scale, in which monumentality became virtually the official creed, they towered over everyday lives in unearthly splendour. They were built to last, and, with few exceptions, that is precisely what they did.

Buildings have always been windows onto a nation's soul, an indication of strength and style, imagination, sense of beauty and financial muscle. They are direct expressions of the values of the cultures and civilisations which design and produce them. They speak of everything from scale and proportion to vision and technology. In their various forms they suggest concepts of harmony and comfort, the desire to please or impress, shock or inspire. It is no coincidence that some of man's greatest monuments are those that reach out to the heavens and pay tribute to his God. Religion has produced masterpieces as utterly diverse as the Aztec Templo Mayor, Canterbury

Cathedral, the Parthenon, Herod's Temple in Jerusalem, the Shwe Dagon Pagoda in Rangoon and the Great Mosque at Samarra, Iraq. Many of the finest architectural creations are possessed of a permanence that marks them out from the ordinary. There is a monumentality about, say, the Pyramids of Giza or the Coliseum in Rome, the Great Wall of China or even, in more modern times, some of the financial institutions of London and Wall Street, that bespeaks power, confidence and prosperity, man revelling in his abilities to create. In the Muslim world, one thinks of the many glories of Islamic architecture, buildings like the Alhambra in Granada, Isfahan's Imam Mosque, the Ibn Tulun Mosque in Cairo, the Taj Mahal, the *medinas* of Meshed, Fes, Damascus, Aleppo and Bukhara, all designed and built with painstaking care by the most talented craftsmen using the richest materials available, in the service of often cruel but culturally and artistically enlightened rulers.

In any assessment of Temur it is vital to stress his contribution in this field, if only because he gave birth to one of the most glorious architectural epochs in history, which lasted more than a hundred years after his death. It says much about him as a man, about his understanding, all but unique in an unlettered nomad of the steppe, of the possibilities of art and architecture in a settled urban centre. Genghis, by contrast, is remembered today only for his legendary destructive powers. He flattened, but he did not build. This museum in the heart of Tashkent, though it celebrates a leader who bequeathed Asia this rich architectural legacy, though it stands in a corner of the square which bears his name, is in a very different and inferior league from its more illustrious Islamic predecessors. Even Temur's plainest and most humble mausoleum would have put it to shame.

Inside, the centrepiece on the ground floor is a panel in which Temur is holding a *diwan* or council. Beneath the dais on which he sits are several courtiers humbly prostrated before him. A host of domes and great monuments stand behind him, next to a lion, a stylised sun and Temur's arms, consisting of three circles arranged thus:

$$\begin{matrix} \circ \\ \circ\circ \end{matrix}$$

Together with the motto '*Rasti Rusti*' – 'Strength in Justice' – this symbol may have represented Temur's power encircling south, west and north. Clavijo was told that it 'signifies that he Temur is lord of all Three Quarters of the World'. A more likely explanation is that Temur simply appropriated it from Persian heraldry, in which rings representing strength and unity were engraved on the tombs of the Sassanids. The panel is illuminated by a bright gold chandelier of impressive size, suspended from the great dome above. Around the base of the cupola are a number of Temur's sayings, some of which have been inexpertly translated into English:

> *Honesty and faithfulness people and army strengthen the state.*
> *The work which can't be done by hundred thousand cavalries can be*
> *done by one correct arrangement.*

But the best clue to understanding this museum and how it fits into the broader question of Temur's contemporary renaissance comes at the top of a grand marble staircase, where the following words have been written alongside a portrait of the pudgy Uzbek president, Islam Karimov:

> *If someone wants to understand who the Uzbeks are, if somebody*
> *wants to comprehend all the power, might, justice and unlimited*
> *abilities of the Uzbek people, their contribution to the global devel-*
> *opment, their belief in future, he should recall the image of Amir*
> *Temur.*

It was Karimov, supported by suppliant academics, who effected Temur's resurrection. On 1 September 1993, as part of the second anniversary of Uzbekistan's independence, the president unveiled the statue of Temur in the centre of Tashkent. 'Today, thanks to the return of independence and sovereignty, the great Amir Temur has returned to his Motherland,' he told the crowd. 'The Uzbek people, trapped for so many years in the clutches of the colonial vice, are no longer deprived of the opportunity to honour our great compatriot and render to him his historical due.'

It was a long, revealing dedication speech. 'For many years,' Karimov continued, 'the name of Amir Temur was degraded and blacked out from the pages of our history in order to remove the self-awareness from the soul of the Uzbek people, in order to destroy the people's sense of national pride and increase its sense of dependence and subordination. But the Uzbeks have not forgotten their ancestors and heroes – they have guarded them in their soul like sacred objects . . . There is no doubt that this image of our great ancestor, erected in the very heart of our beautiful capital – beloved, ancient Tashkent – will forever evoke a feeling of immense pride in our people.'

The museum had been hastily constructed three years later, in time for the celebrations of the conqueror's 660th anniversary in 1996. Temur had ridden to the rescue of a communist leadership swaying in the wind after the rapid unravelling of the Soviet Union. The liberating storm had spread from Moscow, engulfing the Soviet republics one by one. In 1991, independence gusted into Tashkent, foisted on a bewildered leadership by events beyond its borders and entirely beyond its control. The solid ground on which Karimov had stood throughout his career was suddenly torn from beneath his feet. For years a communist supremo, he now needed repackaging. He and his henchmen cast about for new symbols of power and legitimacy. Who better to bolster his claim to leadership than Temur, rebranded as an Uzbek hero, the irresistible warrior whose name had been alternately suppressed and vilified for seven decades by the Soviets? He was no longer the destructive tyrant the Soviets had labelled him in their implacable determination to erase any nationalist symbols that might undermine the union. Temur was now the glorious saviour of Uzbekistan, and the answer to all of the challenges facing an emerging regional power.

He took his place, then, on the marble plinth in Tashkent's central square as the latest in a succession of ideological or nationalist symbols. Before Temur, Marx had scowled down on passers-by. Before Marx, it had been Stalin. Before Stalin, Lenin. Before Lenin, Konstantin Kaufmann, governor-general of Russian Turkestan. The Scourge of the World was in good company.

The irony of this rehabilitation of Temur was that in its heavy-handed crudeness and utter intolerance of dissent it bore all the hallmarks of a Soviet-era campaign. Take this, for example, from *Khalq sozi*, the official organ of Karimov's People's Democratic Party.

> *His Highness Amir Temur is a symbol of national greatness. One of the fundamental slogans of our independence, one of the bases of our national unity . . . is 'Uzbekistan – the future great state'. For a nation with a great past, the future also can only be great. The deeds of the great Amir Temur in state-building, his political wisdom and fearlessness are reflected in the principles of today's policies. It is well known that this dignified and just ruler always dealt with the world with good and kind intentions. And our independent republic, from its very first steps, has announced the very same goals – to conduct itself in the world with kindness and goodwill . . . The policies of our President, directed at giving due respect to the spirit of our ancestors, teach us all to be worthy of these qualities embodied by Amir Temur.*

State-sponsored academics published encomiums on the hero of the motherland. Where once the Soviet establishment had humiliated and ruined those Uzbek academics who dared question the official picture of Temur as savage barbarian, now Karimov's government leaned heavily on anyone casting doubt on the new, sanitised orthodoxy of

Temur as symbol of the state.* Streets and squares were named after him. Throughout the country young couples celebrated their marriages in front of statues of him, laid wreaths of flowers before him. His picture appeared on the highest-denomination banknotes, on newspaper mastheads and street hoardings. The president appeared in portraits alongside him, and encouraged favourable comparisons with him. 'Strength in justice' was the new government mantra.† The

---

* In September 2000, I interviewed Professor Omonullo Boriyev, a specialist on Temur, in Tashkent. He told me that in 1968 Ibrahim Muminov, president of the Uzbek Academy of Sciences, had published a book on Temur. Although the publication coincided with UNESCO's celebrations of Temurid culture in Samarkand, its timing proved disastrous. 'Of course, he was fired immediately. The Central Communist Committee of Uzbekistan issued a resolution removing all copies of his book. Everything he had written about Temur and his role in Central Asia was censored and ridiculed. The Soviets mobilised other historians to destroy his career, and that was the end of that. There was no way for any Uzbek writer or historian to celebrate Temur. Instead, all that was published were books and articles in which you saw Temur the barbarian, Temur the destroyer, Temur the tyrant and so on.' Muminov's treatise, a revisionist attempt to set the record straight by questioning Temur's official pariah status, dropped like a bombshell on the platitudinous world of Uzbek academe. Professor Boriyev's views, however, were typical of the new, equally rigorously enforced, orthodoxy. 'Temur was without equal in history,' he told me. 'Now we are independent there is great interest in him in Uzbekistan. The people respect him very much. Streets, schools and villages are named after him, there are more and more statues of him erected across the country. School pupils and university students can now learn the truth about our hero through the conferences arranged by the Amir Temur Fund.' I asked him what he thought about President Karimov comparing himself with the peerless Tatar. He looked uncomfortable. 'If the president compares himself with the best, and aspires to that, can that be a bad thing?' What of Uzbekistan's neighbours? The Uzbek rehabilitation of Temur as national hero must have been somewhat unsettling for those countries – Turkmenistan, Kazakhstan, Kyrgyzstan, Tajikistan and Afghanistan – whose lands had once fallen under his sway. 'That is a question for the politicians,' he replied.

† The case of award-winning Uzbek poet and writer Mamadali Makhmudov provides an insight into what 'Strength in justice' means in practice for some people under Karimov's government. Like Temur, the Uzbek

proliferation of Temurabilia in Tashkent and throughout Uzbekistan, albeit hijacked by the state, was a heartening discovery. Six hundred years after his death and in the unlikeliest of circumstances, Temur was back.*

&

If you take the underground to Chorsu, the old city of Tashkent, and walk down a winding lane, past rows of mud-baked houses from where the myriad sounds of family life filter out into the gloaming – a mother reprimanding her shrieking child, a man repairing his ancient Lada, saucepans clattering – eventually the lane becomes a street and the street becomes a road and you find yourself in Khast

---

president does not tolerate opposition on any level. Makhmudov was arrested on 19 February 1999, three days after a series of bomb explosions aimed at Karimov rocked Tashkent. He was charged with threatening the president and the constitutional order, and sentenced to fourteen years in prison. His chief crime appears to have been links to the Erk opposition party, outlawed by the government since 1993. The following are excerpts from his testimony smuggled out of court in 2000: 'I was taken for interrogation by men in disguise. They put a mask on me and [kept me] handcuffed. After questioning, they dragged me across the floor half dead, back to my prison cell ... They hit me with batons and kicked me until my body was covered with blood. There was no healthy part left on me. My body turned black and blue and swelled up. My hands and legs were burnt. My nails turned black and fell off. I was hung for hours with my hands tied behind my back. I was given some kind of injection and I was forced to take some kind of syrup. In the cold of the winter, there were times when I lost consciousness – then they poured cold water over me. They stuffed something smelly up my nose. In wet clothing, in my icy prison cell, I spent the days and nights all alone in unbearable suffering ... They told me they were holding my wife and daughters and threatened to rape them in front of my eyes.'

* Temur could even be invoked in the war on terror, held up as a paragon of statesmanship and guarantor of law and order. As one member of the Uzbek Academy of Sciences wrote: 'That which Amir Temur valued most – well-being, prosperity and, above all, peace and harmony – has been placed at the head of our independent republic's agenda to safeguard against disorder and disturbance.'

Imam Square, the heart of Muslim Tashkent. On your left is the sixteenth-century Barak Khan Madrassah, a religious school founded by a Shaybanid ruler of Tashkent and descendant of Temur. It is a towering edifice with Koranic inscriptions running across its fine façade amid a medley of blue-tiled mosaics, and it is home to the Mufti of Uzbekistan, spiritual leader of the country's Muslims. Directly opposite the madrassah is the Tillya Sheikh Mosque, which dates from the same era and, although a less notable building from the outside, is Tashkent's chief Friday mosque.

Inside, after you have passed through the open courtyard, opened the door directly opposite you, walked down a carpeted corridor past the library, which holds a collection of eighty-five thousand books and manuscripts dating back to the earliest days of Islam in this part of the world, you reach a small room which contains the mosque's greatest treasure, one of the most remarkable and famous books in the world and one of Temur's most enduring gifts to posterity.

In a climate-controlled glass case, its ancient pages opened like the wings of a butterfly, sits the Holy Koran of Othman, an encyclopaedia-sized volume. It is the oldest Koran in the world. The librarian, a diminutive middle-aged man with glasses who, were it not for the absence of a beard, would look the archetypal Islamic scholar, will tell you it was written in 646 by the third caliph, Othman, son-in-law of the Prophet Mohammed. Well over thirteen hundred years old, the pages of gazelle skin are worn beyond measure by the passage of time. But despite the attrition of the centuries, the verses of the Koran, written in a strong and elegant hand, still dance across the ancient leather.

The librarian, if you press him, will tell you that before Othman, the Koran had been committed to memory by early Muslims and recorded variously on scraps of wood, camel bones, leaves, odd pieces of leather, even rocks. After Mohammed's death in 632, Abubakr, the first caliph, arranged for all the known suras (verses) to be written down by scribes. It was Othman who summoned the four most distinguished Koranic scholars of his time and ordered them to be collected together and written down in one volume. This book, prepared in the holy city of Medina, became the definitive version of the Koran, superseding anything that had gone before. Othman used it as his personal Koran. Other copies were made, but none of them survives in its complete form.

The history of the Othman Koran is a tale of piety and politics, intrigue, murder, conquest and greed. The first half of Othman's twelve-year reign as caliph was marked by peace and administrative reform. The *dar al Islam*, the realm of Islam, stretched from Morocco in the west to Afghanistan in the east, and in the north the call to prayer was heard as far as Armenia and Azerbaijan. During the second half of his reign, a rebellion arose and there were calls for Othman to resign. Reluctant to shed Muslim blood, he did not crush the uprising although he had the power to do so. Eventually the rebels surrounded his house in Medina and, after a long siege, on 17 June 656, a mob broke in and murdered him at the age of eighty-two. Othman, so the story goes, was reading a verse from his copy of the Koran at the time: 'And if they believe even as ye believe, then are they rightly guided. But if they turn away, then are they in schism, and Allah will be thy protection against them,' a verse that neatly anticipated the seismic split within the Muslim community which arose on Othman's murder and in due course resulted in the rival Sunni and Shi'a communities. Deep in the Othman Koran, a dark stain spreads across the pages. 'This is the blood of Othman,' says the librarian in a hushed whisper. 'His throat was cut while he was reading the holy book.'

Othman's life was over, but the adventures of the book he had laboured so hard to produce were only just beginning. There are many versions of what happened next. According to one of the most popular, Othman's successor, Ali, took the Koran to Kufa in Iraq, where it remained for several hundred years. In the fourteenth century, Temur retrieved it after his conquests in the region and brought it to the Nur Madrassah in Samarkand. There it lay for half a millennium, if you believe the librarian, until the nineteenth century and the advent of the Great Game, the elegant but deadly war between Victorian Britain and Tsarist Russia for supremacy in Central Asia, a conflict fought by the bravest, most brilliant spies and military officers on both sides amid the high mountain passes and the brutal, opulent courts of local potentates. Russia expanded south (by the end of the Great Game, the British and Russian frontiers, originally two thousand miles apart, separated by tracts of desert and the world's highest mountains, lay only twenty miles from each other), and in 1868 the Othman Koran was delivered to Tsar Alexander II by General von Kaufmann, governor of Turkestan, and added to the imperial library in St Petersburg. But the Muslims of Turkestan petitioned Lenin to return the book to them, and after many attempts they were successful. The Othman Koran arrived in Tashkent, where it spent much of the twentieth century in the history museum. In 1989 it was transferred to the Tillya Sheikh Mosque, where it remains to this day.

It is kept in a tiny room in a humble mosque in a forgotten country, but the Othman Koran still attracts an impressive cast of international VIPs. 'Madeleine Albright, Hillary Clinton, Vladimir Putin, the leaders of Iran, Turkey, Egypt and the Emirates, have all been to see the Koran recently,' the librarian will tell you proudly. 'And without Amir Temur, it wouldn't be here today.'

Still the snows fell from leaden skies. Soldiers pulled their black sheepskins tightly round their throats against the invading cold. There was nothing to be done. It was just a matter of sitting out the dreadful winter. No one expected any action until spring. But in January 1391, without warning and at the coldest time of the year, instructions were issued from the imperial tent. The Lord of the Fortunate Conjunction had ordered the army to march north. Tokhtamish was to be found and engaged. So far there had been only indecisive skirmishes. Now Temur was resolved to settle the issue in battle.

There were mutterings of discontent in the ranks. Many could scarcely believe the reports running through the camp. What was the emperor thinking of? Moving an army of two hundred thousand halfway across Asia in these conditions was suicidal. But these murmurings remained subdued and discreet. The army knew better than to question Temur's commands. The emperor's will was law.

The decision to hunt out the khan of the Golden Horde amid a raging winter, and in some of the most inhospitable terrain imaginable, looked like sheer folly. In terms of logistics alone, it beggared belief. There was no way of knowing where or when Temur would happen on Tokhtamish's army. All he could be certain of was that it was bigger than his own. The route ahead was famously barren, so much so that once you had crossed the Sir Darya river, north of Tashkent, you entered a vast tract of land called the Hunger Steppe. There were sandy deserts, empty plains, rivers and mountains to cross. The main army and the long supply convoy would be struggling in deep snow and dangerous ice from the start. How could this great body of men and women be provisioned for a campaign that might require it to operate in such inauspicious country for months on end? The plans invited disaster.

But as Temur viewed the situation, he felt he had no choice. Twice Tokhtamish had invaded, first Temur's western dominions and, more recently, the centre of his empire in Mawarannahr. In so doing he had announced his intentions all too clearly. Until he was removed from the field, he would remain a threat to the empire. As for the most appropriate strategy for dealing with him, if Temur were to strike from the west, as he had started to do in the Caucasus, he would merely open the way for Tokhtamish to attack in the east, bearing down on Mawarannahr once again, only this time with far worse consequences. In the event of another invasion of his lands, Temur stood to lose both his seat of empire and his army to his rival. Far better to regain the offensive, however difficult the expedition might prove, than to fight a defensive and unpopular war on his own territory, where the damage would be great. There were no treasures for the army, bedrock of his authority, to gain by staying at home. The prizes awaited, as ever, beyond his borders. There was also the added element of surprise, always a favourite weapon in Temur's armoury, to take into consideration. The khan of the Golden Horde had attacked Temur where and when he least expected it. Now, in the snowbound depths of winter, Temur intended to return the compliment.

Stealing up on Tokhtamish, catching him unawares in the sloth of winter, would be a formidable undertaking. He had his spies, too, and there is little reason to believe they were any less effective than those of Temur. Certainly they must have given him timely intelligence of his adversary's movement north, for not long after the Tatar army had left behind the Sir Darya, envoys arrived from the court at Saray, presenting Temur with nine magnificent horses – this was considered an auspicious number – and a royal falcon, beautifully bejewelled. The talk was of forgiveness and mercy, not war. Tokhtamish, the emerging warlord, was now a humble model of contrition: 'Your majesty has always acted the part of a father towards me; you have always nourished and brought me up as your son, and the favours I have received from you are innumerable. If my wicked proceedings and the war I have carried on by the instigation of some malicious persons, which has been my misfortune, and of which I repent and am ashamed, can once more find pardon from the clemency of my lord, this will be an addition to the obligations I owe to him.' In short, Tokhtamish was ready to be 'a submissive and obedient servant' to his former mentor.

There was a long silence. The ambassadors in their fine silks did their best not to fidget nervously. This was no declaration of war they brought, nor any calculated insult to Temur, but still the role of messenger was not without its dangers, and who knew how the emperor would react? At last, long after the silence had become unbearable, he fixed them with his imperious gaze and made his reply.

> When your master Tokhtamish was wounded and fled from the enemy, I received him like a son. I took up his cause and made war on Urus Khan on his behalf. I sacrificed my cavalry and equipment, which were lost that hard winter. However, I continued to support him, and placed this country in his hands. I made him so strong that he became khan of the Kipchaks, and he mounted the throne of Jochi. But when fortune had begun to smile on him, he forgot his obligations to me: and without thinking how a son ought to behave towards a father, he took the opportunity, while I was occupied with the conquest of the kingdom of the Persians and the Medes, to betray me, sending troops to ruin the borders of my empire. I pretended to take no notice, hoping that he might be ashamed of his action, and in future abstain from such extravagances. But he was so drunk with ambition, that he could not distinguish good from evil. He sent another army into my country against me. It is true that as soon as we marched against him, his advance guard fled at the very dust of our approach. Now, when Tokhtamish has heard of our march, he begs pardon, because he knows no other way to save himself from the punishment he deserves. But since we have seen him break his word and violate his treaties so often, it would be imprudent to trust his word. With the aid of God we shall carry out the resolve we have made. If, however, he speaks the truth and wants peace with all his heart, let him send to us Ali-Beg, his minister, who can then negotiate with our chief amirs.

Temur recognised the khan's overture for what it was, merely a ruse to forestall him. He knew this because these were his very own tactics.

Later, he would try something similar on Tokhtamish himself. The conflict between the two men, marked by constant manoeuvring and deception, crushing force and honeyed diplomacy, was among the most fascinating of Temur's career, because they were so well matched.

The ambassadors were left in no doubt as to Temur's intentions. He saw no reason to turn back. It was up to Tokhtamish how he chose to proceed. The march north, meanwhile, would continue.

By the first week of March, Temur's army passed Yasi and Sabran in what is today Kazakhstan. Yasi, renamed Turkestan in the sixteenth century, was a thriving town on the caravan route, its markets home to merchants trading tiger skins, gold and silver from Persia, porcelain from China, astrakhan, glassware, Siberian deer, lynx and the ubiquitous silks. In the latter half of the 1390s, with the campaigns against Tokhtamish behind him and another wedding to look forward to – his latest wife was Tukal-khanum, a beautiful princess and daughter of the Moghul khan Khizr Khoja – Temur revisited Yasi and rebuilt a memorial complex there in honour of the holy Sufi dervish Khoja Ahmed Yasevi. To this day it remains one of the great examples of medieval architecture in Central Asia, a blaze of blue domes, ribbed and smooth, intricate tiled portals decorated with ivory and a riot of Islamic calligraphy, designed and constructed on a monumental scale. The main dome has a diameter of almost sixty feet. The saint's reputation was such that three pilgrimages to the mausoleum were considered equivalent to a pilgrimage to Mecca. It still attracts large numbers of pilgrims each year.

Onto the Hungry Steppe Temur's army now advanced like a falling shadow. Bristling with tension, the mounted archers pressed on in forced marches, still hoping to surprise and fall upon Tokhtamish's forces. But around them the horizon was limitless, and instead of the massed ranks of Kipchaks they stared instead at dry ground with only the meanest grazing for the horses. It was a dispiriting sight.

After three weeks in these vast plains, wrote Yazdi, 'the horses were so fatigued with the great way they had gone, and the scarcity of water, that they were reduced to extremity'.

By April, after crossing the Sari Su river, they were among the Ulugh Tagh mountains. Here Temur ordered an obelisk to be erected as 'a lasting monument to posterity'. It recorded the size of the army he was leading against Tokhtamish Khan, king of the Bulgars, and the date of its arrival in these mountains. It was indeed a gift to posterity – the obelisk was discovered in Kazakhstan in the 1930s – but it was also a distraction, perhaps deliberate, from the increasingly dire situation in which the army now found itself.

After almost four months' march from Tashkent, Temur's scouts scanned the horizon in vain for their enemy. Tokhtamish's men had melted away into the farthest recesses of the steppes and, just as the amirs had worried all along, the army was now fast running out of supplies. The price of a sheep from the travelling market that accompanied the expedition had soared to a hundred dinars. Soon there were none left. Officers of all ranks were given orders 'that no one on pain of death should bake in the camp either bread, pastry-work, mutton, pies, tarts or anything proper for boiling'. Struggling across difficult territory, shattered by the forced marches, the soldiers had to subsist on the most meagre rations. First it was a thin meat stew. Then, as the meat ran out, the stew became a broth. When the supplies of flour were practically exhausted, the broth became even thinner and the men were sipping miserably at a mixture of water and herbs, one bowl a day, if they were lucky. Fanning out across the plains, they fell on anything remotely edible. Herbs, roots, wild grasses, occasional eggs and rats were all seized greedily, supplemented by horsemeat whenever an animal succumbed to the desperate conditions. It was no way to provision an army about to fight its most testing battle deep behind enemy lines. The grumbling grew louder.

The men were at their weakest. Although in the course of their campaigns they had grown used to adversity, they were not accustomed to these levels of privation. Fears started to grow that Tokhtamish's Kipchaks, well provisioned, well rested and entirely familiar with the terrain, would choose this moment to rise from the shadows and cut them to pieces.

It was a desperate time for Temur, and a critical test of his leadership. He faced either a rebellion from his starving soldiers or, as they beat a frantic retreat towards Mawarannahr, certain defeat by the Golden Horde, whose spies had already been joined by a number of deserters from Temur's camp and who were well aware of his parlous position. Retreat or rebellion. Neither were words in Temur's vocabulary. Since defeating Husayn in 1370, he had known only triumph. One by one his opponents had crumpled before him. Now he stood on the brink of catastrophe.

The first priority was to feed his men. Tokhtamish, as he had already proved so cleverly, could wait. Summoning his senior officers, Temur gave commands for a Tatar hunt. Riders galloped off to the amirs of the left and right wings, instructing them to lead their men forward steadily in a half-circle. Those soldiers in the centre remained where they were. The distance between the wings in this army of two hundred thousand was so great that it took two days just to complete the circle. When the men of the left wing joined with those from the right, encompassing an area of many square miles, orders were given to close in. The men marched inwards, each dreaming of the next meal of meat. Before them ran startled deer, hares, wild boars, wolves and antelopes, probably elk too, since the chronicle mentions a type of gazelle the Tatars had not seen before, as large as a buffalo.

When the circle had shrunk to the required size, the order was given to halt. Temur rode in first, as was customary. Despite the lameness on his right side, he was a superb shot and an excellent horseman. Riding full tilt at one moment, almost stationary the next, he unleashed his arrows at his quarry. To loud cheers from his men, he brought down a number of deer. Once the emperor had had his sport, it was their turn. For hours the hunt continued. The slaughter was immense that day, the dinner sumptuous. For days to come, the camp was wreathed in smoke as the heavy smell of game rose into the night sky from bubbling cauldrons. All the worries were quickly forgotten. The grumbling subsided.

With his army well fed and approaching the borders of Siberia, Temur chose this moment to order a general review of his troops, a move calculated to instil discipline and confidence. When the army of two hundred thousand had been brought into formation, the splendidly dressed emperor appeared before them on horseback, wearing a gold crown encrusted with rubies and carrying an ivory baton tipped with the carved golden head of a bull. Starting his review with the left wing, he made sure the soldiers were all properly equipped with a sabre on their left side, a half sabre on their right, as well as a lance, a mace, a dagger and a leather shield, each man carrying a bow with thirty arrows in his quiver. The horses were decorated with tiger skins.

There was a carefully arranged choreography and score to accompany the review. When Temur arrived in front of each *tuman* of ten thousand, the amir, be he senior officer, son or grandson of the emperor, dismounted, threw himself to the ground, kissed the earth, told his ruler what excellent condition the troops were in, and sang his praises with elaborate compliments. 'Let all the world be obedient to Temur: from faithfulness and duty, we will always be ready to sacrifice our heads and our lives at the feet of his majesty's horse,' said Birdi Beg, leader of a *tuman* in the left wing. Prince Omar Shaykh pleased his father with the good order of his men and the congratulations he lavished on Temur's conquests from the frontiers of China to the Caspian. Temur, said Yazdi, was also impressed by the Hazaras of Sulduz, battle-hardened warriors with their bows, arrows, nets, clubs, lassoes, maces and scimitars. Next he passed on to the right wing, commanded by his son Miranshah. For two days the review lasted, at the end of which Temur pronounced himself content with the state of his army.

After all the recent hardships, the successful hunting expedition had galvanised the men. From the emperor's great kettle-drum came a roar of thunder across the plain, picked up and echoed by the drums of the divisions. Banners and standards fluttered over this immense fighting force. Fists were clenched and arms were raised. Over the drumbeats came another deafening roar, this time the cry of war, '*Surun! Surun!*', running from the tip of the left wing to the end of the right. A bristling half-silence fell once more over the army, and in the cold grey of dawn it moved north in battle formation.

Unknown Siberia lay ahead. It was an empty place, whatever the time of year. Ibn Battutah named it the Land of Shadows. 'No one sees the people who live in this place,' he wrote. 'Here the days are long in summer and the nights are long in winter.' Would this be where Temur happened upon his enemy, or was Tokhtamish, always several marches ahead, luring the Tatars onwards to their destruction? The alien landscape, dense with fog and sodden underfoot, offered no clues to these men of the south.

Only scouting parties, sent ever deeper into enemy territory, would resolve the issue. Mohammed Sultan, the emperor's grandson and favourite, pleaded to be sent on such a mission. Temur consented and, once the astrologers had determined the most suitable time and date at which the young man should begin, he set out in the last week of April.

Traces of human life started to reveal themselves. First of all a track, which led to the still-warm embers of half a dozen fires. The news was sent back to Temur who despatched a detachment of expert scouts to join the party. North they galloped, scouring the plains for telltale signs, until they reached the Tobol river, a tributary of the Irtish which flows into the Arctic. On the far bank they saw more fires, seventy of them, and another set of horse tracks, but no other indications of life.

Shaykh Daoud, a Turkmen with a reputation for great bravery, was sent to bring back more definite news. After riding for two days he came upon some thatched huts and hid himself away during the night. The next morning a man rode out, and was instantly seized by the Turkmen and taken to Temur. Although he knew nothing of Tokhtamish or his army, ten days before he had seen a group of ten armed horsemen camping nearby. The scent was becoming stronger. Temur sent an advance party of soldiers to find and capture the horsemen. When surrounded, they resisted fiercely but prisoners were taken and new intelligence extracted. The first skirmish had been fought.

The great Tatar army now wheeled west towards the enemy. On 11 May it reached the Ural river. Ever suspicious that the guides could be leading his men into an ambush or other misadventure, Temur disregarded the crossing places they suggested and instead swam his men and horses over at less obvious locations. The situation was not yet hopeless, but with each day that passed it was becoming increasingly dire. More than four months out of Tashkent, and still the Tatars had not engaged the Horde. Time, as the historian Harold Lamb understood, was now of the essence. 'Temur's long march to the north would puzzle a modern strategist, but this was warfare without rules and without palliation,' he wrote. 'To display weakness or to leave himself open to a surprise attack by the Horde would have been fatal. He knew that unseen eyes had watched his advance and that the Khan was well informed of his movements. Time meant everything to Temur, who must force the Horde to battle, or bring his own army into cultivated land before the end of the summer; delay was Tokhtamish's finest weapon and he made full use of it.'

Another week of hard marching saw Temur's weary men at the Samara river. Here a party of scouts rejoined the main body of the army with news that they had heard the enemy. At last, battle was getting closer. Prisoners started to be brought in, each of them carrying intelligence of some value. One was delivered by Temur's zealous grandson Mohammed Sultan. Another captive reported how, until deserters from Temur's army joined the Kipchaks, the khan of the Golden Horde was not even aware of his enemy's approach. They had enraged him with their warning that the Lord of the Fortunate Conjunction was marching north at the head of 'an army more numerous than the sands of the desert or the leaves of the trees'.

As the two armies manoeuvred in search of advantage and the Tatars braced themselves for the long-awaited encounter, the order went out not to light any fires at night. At each camp, the soldiers were instructed to dig defensive positions and mounted guards were assigned to patrol the perimeter. The separate divisions were to remain in battle formation. Warlike music on the drums and trumpets now accompanied the daily marches. 'When this vast multitude began to move, it resembled the troubled ocean,' said Yazdi.

Still there was no sight of the Horde. Moving north, it had devastated the countryside before it, trampling the ground into a quagmire to the misery of the Tatar horses who followed, and systematically stripping the land of what little sustenance it offered. Mists descended on the chilly marshes, lowering the mood in Temur's camp. It was another moment for the emperor to take charge, regain the initiative and inspire his disconsolate forces. First there had been the hunt, then the fabulous review. Now he called his senior officers together once again, gave them words of encouragement and fine robes of honour, and had new weapons distributed among the troops, including armour for man and beast alike, shields and fresh bows and arrows.

Both sides mounted ambushes against one another. Prisoners

flowed this way and that, each with reports of the enemy's where-abouts. In one particularly brutal clash, a number of Temur's officers were killed. A retaliatory raid was launched by the emperor himself, and all those who had fought valiantly were generously rewarded, the bravest receiving the highest honour of *tarkhan*.

Although it was now summer, the conditions were still grim. 'The air was so dark, the clouds so thick, and the rains so great, that one could not see three paces,' the chronicle reported. Then, after a week of pea-soup fog, the skies cleared abruptly. It was the middle of June and the men had been marching for almost five months over a distance of eighteen hundred miles. These sons of the desert had ventured so far north that the long summer days seemed endless. The priests were thrown into confusion by the constant daylight, which completely upset the daily routine of five prayers. With Temur's permission the evening prayer was quietly dispensed with.

Reports were streaming in now of enemy sightings. Temur made final preparations for war. The Tatar divisions moved forward in precise battle formation, based on the traditional plan of a centre and two wings, but with the additions of a vanguard to each wing and a vanguard and reserve for the centre. Mohammed Sultan, apple of his grandfather's eye, was given command of the centre. Sultan Mahmud, son of the puppet Chaghatay khan, led the vanguard of ten thousand before it. Omar Shaykh, who was proving an exemplary officer, commanded the left wing with his troops from Andijan. His brother Miranshah led the right. Sayf ad-din, the aged but most loyal of amirs, commanded the vanguard of the left wing. Temur himself took charge of the rearguard.

Forward they marched, the sunlight shimmering on their armour so that they resembled 'the waves of the tempestuous sea'. And then, as the horizon unfurled before them, out of the dancing light rose the horned standards of the Golden Horde, half a mile away. The enemy, at last, was ready to do battle. Death was in the air, but after all these months of anticipation, hunger, exhaustion, frustration and impatience, the Tatar army felt not fear, but relief. The rhythm of feint and counter-feint, pursuit and calculated retreat, looked as if it had finally run its course. One way or another the fight for supremacy between Temur and Tokhtamish would be settled.

But there was one last ruse to be played. As the two armies faced each other across the divide, Temur gave orders very publicly for his sumptuous tents and pavilions to be unpacked and erected, and his carpets laid out. It was a deliberate show of contempt for the Horde, and an exercise in psychological warfare typical of his imagination and audacity. According to the chronicle, although Tokhtamish's forces were more numerous than the Tatars, this eleventh-hour performance shattered their morale.

※

The early hours of 18 June 1391 did not look much different from a typical summer's dawn in these northern regions. The grey sky, flat and all-consuming, offered only the weariest of light. The cold was the same insistent force as ever, rushing in on the tails of the wind. What was exceptional on this day, though, were the odd shapes and sounds seeping through the gloom. The dark lines of the two armies stretched for several miles into the half-light until they merged with the dark earth and the pale horizon, and disappeared altogether. Here and there angular protuberances rose from this dark mass – a lance, a standard, a guard on horseback. A disturbed hush hung over the lines of war, hinting at calamity.

On the Tatar side, Temur rode out in front of his army, dismounted, kissed the earth and prayed for the assistance of almighty Allah. The soldiers, with quickening heartbeats and throbbing temples, broke out into spontaneous roars of '*Allahu akbar*, God is great.' Imam Sayid Baraka stepped forward to add his blessings to the imminent battle. Around him the drums started to beat and the trumpets sounded their terrible call. The holy man prostrated himself on the ground, recited a passage from the Koran and scooped up some dirt. He faced the Horde and his voice rose to shouting pitch. 'Your faces shall be blackened through the shame of your defeat,' he yelled. Then he turned to the emperor he had served so dutifully for twenty years, and his voice lowered almost to a whisper. 'Go where you please,' he said, 'you shall be victorious.' The drums and trumpets struck up again, rising in a crescendo, the battle-cry '*Surun, Surun*' filled the sky and Asia shuddered as her greatest armies thundered towards each other across the divide. The following words are from Arabshah:

> *Then both armies, when they came in sight one of the other, were kindled and mingling with each other became hot with the fire of war, and they joined battle and necks were extended for sword-blows and throats outstretched for spear thrusts and faces were drawn with sternness and fouled with dust, the wolves of war set their teeth and fierce leopards mingled and charged and the lions of the armies rushed upon each other and men's skins bristled, clad with the feathers of arrows, and the brows of the leaders drooped and the heads of the captains bent in the devotion of war and fell forward, and the dust was thickened and stood black and the leaders and common soldiers alike plunged into seas of blood, and arrows became in the darkness of black dust like stars placed to destroy the Princes of Satan, while swords glittering like fulmi-nating stars in clouds of dust rushed on kings and sultans, nor did the horses of death cease to pass through and revolve and race against the squadrons which charged straight ahead or the dust of hooves to be borne into the air or the blood of swords to flow over the plain, until the earth was rent and the heavens like the eight seas; and this struggle and conflict lasted about three days.*

Battle began with a charge from Temur's right wing under Miranshah against Tokhtamish's left. The fighting was furious but indecisive, with neither side breaking through the ranks of the enemy. Horses careered wildly at each other, their riders unleashing vicious volleys of arrows at their adversaries. At closer quarters, the sabres and scimitars were unsheathed, and steel blades rained down from the sky, slashing through anything that opposed them. In the general mêlée that followed the first attack, Temur seized the advantage on the right flank and in the centre. In response, Tokhtamish directed his right wing against the Tatar left led by Omar Shaykh, detaching it from the main body of the army with the aid of his greater numbers and threatening to engulf it completely. But then, in the heat of the action, just as the men of the Golden Horde looked set to carry the day, confusion suddenly gripped them when they saw that the horned standard of Tokhtamish had vanished from the field. It was the surest sign their leader was dead. In fact he was alive, but had abandoned his men and fled the battlefield, 'seized with fear and despair' as Temur's horse-tail standard bore down on him. Panic descended on the Kipchaks and spread through the ranks. Soon the army that was on the verge of routing Temur's host was itself in headlong flight, chased and cut down without mercy by the rampaging Tatars. 'For the space of forty leagues whither they were pursued nothing could be seen but rivers of blood and the plains covered with dead bodies,' wrote Yazdi. A hundred thousand men and women lost their lives at the battle of Kunduzcha.*

The long march north was over. Temur kissed the earth and offered up thanks to God for delivering him this famous victory. Once more he and his army tasted the sweet fruits of victory. The amirs and princes of the blood stepped forward to congratulate him, sprinkling gold and precious stones over him, as was the custom. The booty was immense. The poorest soldiers plundered more horses than they could take back to Samarkand. There were camels, sheep and cattle. Those Kipchak men and women who had not been butchered were

---

* The battle was fought east of the Volga river between Samara and Chistopol in what is now the republic of Tatarstan.

instantly thrown into slavery. Five thousand boys were chosen for service in the imperial household. The most beautiful girls and women were destined for the harem.

Ruthless in his prosecution of war, Temur was lavish in his celebrations of triumph. Orders were given for a grand festival on the banks of the Volga, on the very plain where Jochi, son of Genghis, had held his seat of empire. Row after row of warriors sat inside the handsome pavilions in front of golden platters heaped with roast horse-meat, toasting their invincible emperor and reliving their battlefield heroics with tall stories. At their elbows stood the most desirable captives, beguiling women dressed in silks, filling their crystal cups with wine, filling and refilling them until, unable to drink any more, the warriors collapsed on the ground or grabbed a companion for the night and staggered heavily back to their tents. For a full month they sank into these blissful excesses, forgetting the fatigues of war, losing themselves in rousing music, bumpers of wine and deep embraces. Tokhtamish, it is true, had escaped their clutches, but his Horde had been shattered. New leaders had been installed in his place, and division sown among the Kipchaks. The threat to Mawarannahr, the land beyond the river, had been removed. Their mission was accomplished.

❦

That should have been the end of Tokhtamish. His struggle for supremacy had been fought and lost. Though the contest on the battlefield had been extremely close for several hours, in the end he had been utterly routed. Most men would have been grateful simply to have survived the slaughter. After that catastrophic reversal, few would have dreamt of resuming a career of conquest. But unfortunately for Temur, the ambitions of the khan of the Golden Horde proved more difficult to destroy than his mighty army.

Three years after the battle of Kunduzcha, Temur was campaigning in the western empire. Persia had reverted to its unruly ways and a rebellion had broken out among the eternally feuding Muzaffarid princes. The troops of Mawarannahr, levied for a new, Five-Year Campaign, left Samarkand in early 1392. Sweeping all before him, Temur blazed through Mazandaran before continuing north-west to reconquer recalcitrant Georgia. From there he marched south, retaking Shiraz and occupying Baghdad without a fight after the battle-shy Sultan Ahmed abandoned his dominions once again.

By 1394, already aware that Tokhtamish was reassembling an army and contracting an alliance with Sultan Barquq of Egypt against Temur, the Tatar was brought disturbing news.* The Kipchaks of the Golden Horde had rumbled south through Georgia and were now laying waste once more to the borders of his empire. A force was sent at once to give battle, but in typical fashion the Horde retired the way it had come, vanishing back into the steppes.

On hearing these reports, Temur must have rued his failure to capture and kill Tokhtamish when their armies had last met. The sultan of Egypt was steadily emerging as an adversary who would have to be dealt with in due course. And after the great gains made during his westward expansion, Temur's empire was beginning to rub uncomfortably close to the lands of the Ottoman sultan. A confrontation there also looked likely. But both these opponents could wait. Having been scorched on the battlefield, Tokhtamish was now emerging phoenix-like from the ashes. He had to be destroyed.

The initial formalities took little time. An envoy was sent to Tokhtamish with a direct ultimatum:

> *After having given God the thanks which are due to the governor of the world; I demand of you, whom the devil of pride hath*

---

* In seeking a treaty with Barquq, Tokhtamish was observing the well-established tradition of the Golden Horde khans by which they allied themselves with the Egyptian sultans and made common cause against the dynasties ruling Persia.

turned from the right way, what is your design in passing beyond your bounds? Who has put you upon such vain undertakings? Have you forgotten how in the last war your country and effects were reduced to nothing? You certainly behave with great rashness, since you oppose your own happiness. Is it possible you can be so ignorant that they who have testified their friendship to me, have been received with respect, and drawn great advantages from the treaties I have made with them, and which I have inviolably observed; while my enemies have not only been under continual disquiets and fears, but also been unable to escape my vengeance, though in the greatest security? You are acquainted with my victories, and are persuaded that peace or war are equally indifferent to me. You have experienced both my mildness and severity. When you have read this letter, do not delay sending me an answer; but let me know your resolution, either for war or peace.

The khan of the Golden Horde was not interested in peace. His character was far too similar to that of Temur, unable and unwilling to settle, ever striving to win new lands by the sword. The greatest difference between them was in their respective talents and fortunes on the battlefield.

Temur wintered near the Caspian, enjoying the company of his wives during these desolate months. In the spring of 1395, as the snows receded, he bade them farewell and sent them home. The pleasures of the imperial pavilion must give way to war.

Another review was ordered. The emperor reminded his amirs and their officers of their glorious triumphs of recent years. Of their conquest of Persia, Iraq and Georgia. Of their earlier destruction of Tokhtamish. This was the last time they would fight the khan of the Golden Horde, he assured them. Never again would this ungrateful princeling dare to trespass on the empire. Victory was, as always, in the hands of Allah, and in His boundless mercy and wisdom He would bless them once more against this treacherous infidel.

Never since the time of Genghis had such a vast army been seen in the region, said Yazdi. The vanguard of Temur's left wing stood at the foot of the Elburz mountains, the right wing on the banks of the Caspian. The order to march in full battle formation was given. The army was not to be surprised by Tokhtamish. Golden eagles circled overhead, high above the forests of juniper trees and maple. Brown bears and wild boars, lynxes and leopards, roamed the landscape in the shadows of Mount Damavand, the dormant volcano.

Skirting the Caspian, the Tatars marched first west, then swung along a gentle arc north. Through the famous Derbend pass they continued, the spot where Tokhtamish had launched his predatory raids on Tabriz exactly ten years before. Once they had passed Georgia and its capital Tiflis, laying waste to vineyards as they moved through, they were in modern-day Chechnya. Here the countryside was far more enclosed than the northern steppes of the Horde, who had less room to withdraw and hide. The elaborate chase on which Tokhtamish had led Temur for five months prior to their last battle could not be repeated in this sort of territory. And so, in April 1395, at the Terek river near what is today the city of Grozny, Temur happened upon his enemy.

The advantage was with Tokhtamish, who held the northern bank after crossing the river at the only available ford. Knowing that Temur was pressing him hard, he guarded the passage to prevent his rival's approach. The Spanish envoy Clavijo recorded the Tatar's subsequent manoeuvres.

> On coming up, Temur, finding that Tokhtamish was in possession of this passage, halted, sending envoys to Tokhtamish demanding why he acted thus, and assuring him that he, Temur, had not come to make war on him, being indeed his good friend, and calling on God to witness that he, Temur, on his part had never intended any aggression against him. Tokhtamish, however, would listen to none of his message, knowing well the guile of Temur. The next day therefore Temur broke up his camp and proceeded to march up the river bank on the south side, seeing which Tokhtamish did

likewise and marched his host along the northern bank keeping pace opposite him. Thus the one following the other, both hosts took the way upstream, and at night camped each over against the other with the river in between. This business went on and was repeated during three days, neither army outstripping the other, but on the third night as soon as his camp was formed, Temur issued orders that all the women who marched with his soldiers should don helmets with the men's war-gear to play the part of soldiers, while the men should mount and forthwith ride back with him to the ford, each horseman taking with him a second mount led by the bridle. Thus the camp was left in charge of the women disguised as warriors, with their slaves and captives under guard, while Temur went back by a forced march the three days' journey to where the river could be crossed.

The most revealing words in this passage are 'the guile of Temur'. The Tatar's first attempt at trickery was brazen. He can hardly have expected it to work. After the history between the two men, after the rout at Kunduzcha, and after his pursuit of Tokhtamish across Asia to the banks of the Terek, his intentions would not have been difficult to divine. For three days, then, the battle of wits continued, the necessary prelude to conflict as both leaders vied for position. Temur only broke this stalemate by deploying the extraordinary device of dressing up the women as soldiers, a plan so far-fetched it is scarcely credible. Had it not been for the many instances in which Temur had already displayed his mastery of the art of warfare – both conventional and psychological – his grasp of the counter-intuitive and his love of highly imaginative risk-taking, we would probably accuse the Castilian of high spirits and credulousness.

As it is, we know much about Temur's talents in these areas from a number of sources. The most remarkable example was given by Archbishop John of Sultaniya, who told the story of a young Temur outwitting his adversary through tactics as ingenious as they were improbable. The event was said to have occurred prior to his coronation in 1370. Summoned by a hereditary khan to submit to his authority or face him on the battlefield, Temur resorted to an elaborate ruse. Since he did not have an army strong enough to deploy on the battlefield, he pretended he was sick. While receiving the khan's envoys, he started vomiting blood copiously, the result, though they did not know it, of consuming a basinful of wild boar's blood. Predictably, the envoys returned to their master with news of Temur's imminent death. Catching the khan and his courtly entourage entirely unawares, Temur promptly defeated them with ease.

On 22 April 1395, battle commenced. The Tatar left wing came under heavy pressure from the start. At the head of twenty-seven regiments of the reserve, and under cover of his archers' fire, Temur charged forward to support it. The counter-attack was so successful that they drove the enemy far back, until they found themselves separated from the main force of the army, heavily outnumbered by the regrouping Horde. The emperor himself was under fierce assault, fighting hand-to-hand as wave upon wave of Kipchaks surged forward against him. 'His arrows were all discharged, his half-pike broke to shatters,' reported Yazdi. Seeing his leader on the point of death, Shaykh Nur ad-din rushed to his protection with a small body of fifty men. Dismounting from their horses, they formed a circle around him, kneeling on one knee and firing volleys of arrows at the Horde. Some of Temur's officers captured three wagons from Tokhtamish's men and used them as a barricade, over which the familiar horse-tail standard stood aloft.

While Temur and his men stood their ground in desperate straits, Mohammed Sultan rallied his right wing, took the fight to Tokhtamish's left and inflicted heavy losses on him, forcing his adversary ever farther back. Amir Sayf ad-din Nukuz, leading the vanguard of the right wing, was hard pressed, his men dismounting under orders and defending themselves behind shields, fending off blows from swords and lances. Eventually, the left wing of the Horde gave way, turned to flight and was chased off the field. Demoralised by this loss, Tokhtamish's centre now faced its opposite number. The two sides fought like 'enraged lions . . . so that the blood flowed in this place like a torrent'. The Horde was first to buckle, at which point Tokhtamish, with his men in disorder all about him, 'shamefully' turned his back on the battlefield and rode for his life. Kicking their chargers for all they were worth, the Tatar horsemen galloped after Tokhtamish and his retreating Horde, hurling down their blades on them and screaming 'Victory!'

This was a defeat from which Tokhtamish never recovered. There was nothing now to stop Temur's men from marching north to avenge his depredations against Mawarannahr. With its army cut down or flying for its life, the Golden Horde was defenceless. It was time for plunder.

Looking at a map charting Temur's various campaigns and the routes taken by his armies, one curiously shaped loop stands out. It is clear that this represents his northernmost venture. From the Terek river, the line of his progress through the Golden Horde swings round in a gentle north-eastern arc towards Astrakhan, thence north again to Saray, capital of the Golden Horde. After continuing towards Moscow, there is an abrupt change of direction and the line thrusts west for more than four hundred miles to the Dnieper river on the shores of the Black Sea. Here it heads first south, then east and finally north once more to form another smaller loop. The advance north continues just beyond the Russian city of Yelets before wheeling round tightly and returning south. From the Terek river to the northernmost point of the campaign, the distance as the crow flies is about 750 miles. Taking into account the frequent changes of direction, the true distance travelled in the Horde after Tokhtamish's defeat is far longer, several thousand miles at least.

It is tempting to infer from this long and arduous march the strength of Temur's ill feeling against Tokhtamish. It is reasonable to assume that he was motivated by a profound desire to avenge his former protégé's disloyal behaviour – for that is how he would have seen it, notwithstanding his own highly pragmatic attitude towards alliances – but that is only part of the story.

In fact, the direct pursuit of Tokhtamish did not last long. Chasing the royal prince, the Tatars first followed the Volga river north until the khan vanished for good into the Bulgar forests. After his disappearance the priority switched to razing the main urban centres of the Horde, and pillaging without mercy. The last time Tokhtamish had been defeated, within three years he had rebounded strongly. If it was not possible for Temur to lay hands on his troublesome adversary, then at least his kingdom must be brought to ruin to ensure that this could never happen again.

The Tatars roamed at will, laying waste the surrounding countryside. Yazdi had Temur marching as far as the Russian capital, Moscow, 'which his soldiers pillaged, as they had done all the neighbouring places dependent upon it, defeating and cutting in pieces the governors and princes of these parts. The Russians and Muscovites never beheld their kingdom in so bad a condition, their plains being covered with dead bodies.' This is inaccurate: Temur did not reach Moscow, for he had richer prizes in his sights.* First, Tana, where the Don river feeds into the Black Sea, a thriving commercial centre with a

---

* According to the Yermolinski chronicles, Muscovites were spared Temur's invasion in large part by the arrival in their city of an icon of the Holy Virgin which worked miracles. Although Grand Prince Vassili I of Muscovy made preparations for a defence of the city, there can be little doubt that had Temur wanted to press on to Moscow, he would have faced little opposition from this comparatively feeble Russian army.

substantial population of merchants from Europe, particularly Venice and Genoa. Reneging on his promise not to harm the population, Temur ordered the Muslims, who were spared, to be separated from the Christians, who were slaughtered.

Tana was a succulent *hors d'oeuvre*, preparing Temur's palate for the main feast which lay several hundred miles east on the southern Volga. When he thought of Saray, capital of the Golden Horde, he remembered the ultimate ignominy Tokhtamish had wrought on Mawarannahr in 1387, when the khan had burned to the ground the famous Chaghatay palace at Qarshi, in the valley where Temur had grown up as a boy.

Saray, reported Ibn Battutah, several decades before the ruin inflicted by Temur, was a city 'of boundless size ... choked with its inhabitants'. The bazaars thronged with metalware, leather, wool, grain, furs, timber and slaves. Now it was summarily torched, its citizens left to freeze in the snow. Under licence from their leader, the hungry Tatar hordes helped themselves to the contents of the city while Temur seized ingots of gold and silver, great quantities of weapons and slaves, flax from Antioch, Russian cloth, silks and sables black as jet, ermine, fox and furs of all description. Such was the quantity that 'it would be tedious to give a detail of all the booty they obtained in this great country', wrote Yazdi.

It was not just the personal vendetta that drove Temur to ravage the Golden Horde so utterly. Apart from the need to sate his exhausted soldiers' appetite for booty, self-interest required him to do so. Determined to ensure that Tokhtamish would never again represent a military threat, Temur understood the need to wipe out his commercial cities and centres of production. A large army required domestic prosperity, and this in turn was dependent on trade. Almost overnight, Saray and Tana, both important centres on the caravan routes leading from the Black Sea through Central Asia to the Ming empire of China, ceased to exist. Urganch, a third stop on the northern trade route, had been razed in 1388. Henceforth, the northern trade route that bypassed Temur's empire was forced into disuse. The caravans diverted south instead, through Persia and Afghanistan into Mawarannahr, thereby transferring the wealth that was once accumulated by Tokhtamish directly to Temur. It was a masterstroke of brutal efficacy.

As his armies eased south towards warmer, more comfortable climes, Temur left behind a devastated Horde. Just as he had planned, and thanks to his support of rival princes, it now fell victim to self-destructive infighting. Arabshah described how the once magnificent khanate became 'a desert and a waste, the inhabitants scattered, dispersed, routed and destroyed'. In the century after Temur's death, the Golden Horde collapsed into independent kingdoms, its splendour gone forever. Defeating his northern rival must have been particularly satisfying for Temur, not least because it was righteous punishment of a man who had sought refuge with him, taken his money and accepted his military supplies and support on the battlefield, only to later turn on his former protector in what was, even in the fluid world of Central Asian alliances, the height of opportunism.

As for Tokhtamish, his ambitions remained as great as they had always been. Only now, his ability to prosecute them had been crushed. It never returned. For the rest of his life he roamed across the windy Kipchak steppes in a futile bid to regain power. His days of conquest were over. He had pitted himself against one of the greatest conquerors the world had ever seen, and he had lost. Temur's stiffest challenge had been overcome. The Unconquered Lord of the Seven Climes, now at the zenith of his glory, remained undefeated.

6

Samarkand, the 'Pearl of the East'

1396–1398

> 'The richness and abundance of this great capital and its district
> is such as is indeed a wonder to behold: and it is for this reason
> that it bears the name of Samarkand: for this name would be
> more exactly written Semiz-kent, two words which signify "Rich-
> Town", for Semiz in Turkish is fat or rich and Kent means city or
> township: in time these two words having been corrupted into
> Samarkand.'
>
> RUY GONZALEZ DE CLAVIJO,
> *Embassy to Tamerlane 1403–1406*

> 'Samarkand, the most beautiful face the Earth has ever turned
> towards the sun.'
>
> AMIN MAALOUF, *Samarkand*

Samarkand roared its welcome as Temur rode into his beloved capital
after an absence of four years. The streets heaved with 150,000 citizens,
all curious to catch a glimpse of 'this great emperor in triumph'. For
several seasons, they had heard only rumours. Temur was sick; he
was on his deathbed; he had recovered and was marching north; he

had been defeated and Tokhtamish was heading south to ravage Mawarannahr.

With her great parks and vineyards, her gardens and orchards in full bloom, Samarkand arranged the most sumptuous decorations to greet the emperor at the head of his army. It was a reception designed to reflect the magnificence of Temur's triumphal procession, when it seemed that half the world trooped into town carrying before it the booty of all Asia. 'On all sides were to be seen garlands of flowers with crowns, amphitheatres, and musicians performing the newest pieces of music to the honour of his majesty,' wrote Yazdi. 'The walls of the houses were hung with carpets, the roofs covered with stuffs, and the shops set off with curious pieces. There was a vast multitude of people, and the streets were covered with velvet, satin, silk and carpets, which the horses trampled underfoot.' Through this gorgeous tableau walked slaves with bowed heads, scarcely knowing where to look as they moved through the astoundingly opulent city of dazzling domes. Behind them rode the mounted archers, endless columns of them streaming into the city in their most luxurious livery, drunk with the tumultuous celebrations whose din seemed to touch the heavens. The rapturous reception was crowned with Temur's proclamation of a three-year tax exemption for his subjects.

Temur had good reason to feel pleased with his achievements. The Five-Year Campaign had been completed in four. Persia had been brought back into line, recalcitrant Georgia had been reconquered, and Iraq had folded weakly before him. Above all, his deadliest enemy, Tokhtamish, had been trounced and the Golden Horde exterminated. Mawarannahr now faced no external threats. With the immense treasures plundered from the campaign being carried into Samarkand on the backs of exhausted horses and camels, the empire was at its zenith.

Temur was now in his sixty-first year. For more than half a century he had braved the elements of Asia on horseback. He had endured the fiercest summers and the most brutal winters, constantly on the move. There were signs that his age was starting to steal up on him. In the summer of 1392 he had been dangerously ill for a month, confined to his bed at the outset of his campaign in the west. Mawarannahr had trembled at his sickness, only too aware that the fate of the empire rested on the shoulders of one man. However great and noble his sons and grandsons – two sons, Jahangir and, more recently, Omar Shaykh, had predeceased him* – none possessed his indomitable will, his fearless leadership and his brilliance on the battlefield. None, surely, could bear the weight of empire alone. During that previous illness, Allah in all His wisdom, grace and compassion had intervened to save Temur, but looking into the years ahead, who could fathom the wishes of the Almighty? The emperor's upright frame was starting to stiffen, his limp was becoming more pronounced and his eyesight less keen. Izrail, the Angel of Death, could not spare him forever.

Such intimations of mortality were to be expected in a man of Temur's years. Many, if not most, men entering their seventh decade would have been starting to withdraw from active life, looking forward to a time of greater ease and comfort during their autumn years. Temur, inevitably, was different. His career of conquest already marked him out from other men. From humble beginnings he had seized control over vast territories of Asia, retaking the former empires bequeathed by Genghis one by one. First he had risen to power at the head of the reunited Chaghatay ulus. Then he had cast his net out to the west, ransacking the Hulagid dominions and hauling them into his empire. Lastly, he had turned to the north and stamped his

---

* Omar Shaykh, ruler of Fars, was killed by an arrow-shot while besieging a fortress in Kurdistan in late 1393 or early 1394. Though this was the second of Temur's sons to predecease him, the Tatar was said not to have betrayed the slightest trace of emotion on learning the news. Omar Shaykh's son Pir Mohammed, Temur's grandson, was installed as ruler of Fars.

authority over the great Jochi ulus of the Golden Horde. Even in the rarefied world of great Asian leaders, he was without equal. Though he was now in his sixties, he betrayed no hint that he had any wish to relinquish the burdens – physical, intellectual, emotional – of empire-building. On the contrary, he was more assertive than ever. He seemed positively to thrive on the business of empire.

Historians have traditionally faulted Temur for his failure to bequeath a long-lasting empire to his successors. Though Babur, his great-great-great-grandson, founded the Mughal dynasty in India – which survived until the nineteenth century – it is true the Temurid empire was short-lived. Within a century of Temur's death, it had ceased to exist. This impermanence owed itself to the highly autocratic system of rule he instituted. In a word, the system was Temur. As Beatrice Forbes Manz explained in her scholarly study of his life, 'His government was that of an individual, who interfered at will in the affairs of his subordinates and demanded direct and complete loyalty from his subjects – loyalty not to his office, nor to his government, but to his person. For the period of his life this administration served its purpose well.'

Temur was able to draw on two parallel structures for the administration of his empire. First there was the Turco-Mongolian system of government, with its hereditary official positions, common to the nomadic empires of his neighbours such as the Golden Horde and the Ilkhanids. Then there was the Persian bureaucracy in the settled lands of the west. The former was tasked with the administration of the court and military affairs, the latter took charge of financial matters, most notably tax collection, though there was considerable overlap between the two.

Persian scribes and Chaghatay amirs worked side by side supervising the provincial courts – or *diwans* – which operated throughout the empire. Their inspections of local government occasionally unearthed instances of embezzlement and corruption, which could be punishable by death. Both could work together, too, in collecting ransom money from defeated cities and registering the contents of their treasuries. Temur retained the military Mongol office of *darugha* – regional governor – and usually granted it to the Chaghatays. At times, however, he appointed religious figures or Persian scribes to the post. These governors were by no means stationary officials bound to stay in their capitals. Instead, they were required to rove widely with the army on Temur's campaigns. As Forbes Manz has underscored, what is most striking about a study of Temur's administration is the vagueness and imprecision of official posts and the duties associated with them. For instance, though it was traditionally the duty of *tovachis* to conscript the emperor's armies – as well as to ensure that they had all the proper equipment in decent order – this prestigious role was not exclusive. Amirs could equally be used for the same task.

In practice, the structure of Temur's government was less important than the fact that power was exercised personally, rather than through institutions. Temur's life was spent in the saddle campaigning. His energies were not given over to formalising the mechanics of government. The authority of the *darughas* and *diwans*, the princes and amirs, all depended directly on the emperor.

Temur had manipulated and subverted traditional tribal loyalties in his rise to power. As emperor, he continued the policy. Tribal chiefs, who could already count on a degree of loyalty from their kinsmen, tended not to be appointed amirs in his army. That would have conferred too much power upon them. Wherever possible, the highest offices were awarded to his sons and grandsons, princes of the royal family. Omar Shaykh, his second son, ruled Farghana, and later the kingdom of Fars. When he was killed on the battlefield in Kurdistan, his lands were given to his son Pir Mohammed, Temur's grandson. Another grandson, also called Pir Mohammed, son of Jahangir, later inherited the kingdom of Ghazni, modern Afghanistan. Miranshah, until his summary removal, was given the kingdom of

Hulagu, covering northern Persia, Azerbaijan and Baghdad. For a time, Shahrukh was governor of Samarkand. Later, he was appointed ruler of Khorasan from his capital at Herat. But no member of the imperial family was ever allowed to become too powerful. Throughout his life, Temur took care to prevent any of the royal princes emerging as a rival to the throne. This jealous guarding of power was such that by the time of his death, his designated successor had been shorn of the personal authority and military resources required to consolidate the realm. Temur's empire was a one-man show.

A nomadic conqueror in the mould of Genghis, he exhibited the same scorn for the settled life of peasant farmers. His energy was remorseless, his career one of constant movement – from city to city, pasture to pasture, through deserts, over mountains, across steppes, along rivers. Time and again, his army marched thousands of miles across difficult country, inflicted bloody defeats on a series of adversaries, returned to Samarkand and, after only the briefest of rests, set out again on a new campaign. The only pause in this frenetic whirlwind came in winter, when camp was made during the harshest months of the year. This was a guiding principle, however, not a rule, and there were times when the implacable Temur ordered his shivering soldiers into action in the depths of January. There were occasions, too, when the amirs urged Temur to slow down, to give his soldiers more time to recuperate from the rigours of the latest expedition. But always the movement continued, a raging blur of mounted archers, piercing arrows and slashing swords leaving smoking ruins, piled corpses and towers of skulls – the instruments of terror – in its wake, with trains of horses and camels bearing off the most fantastic treasures of the world looted from its greatest cities. Only once in his entire career did Temur stop for a significant time in Samarkand. That time was now.

Temur, wrote Harold Lamb, loved Samarkand 'as an old man loves a young mistress'. In fact, it would be more accurate to say he wooed her with the ardour of a young man trying to win the love of a beautiful, older woman. The love affair began in 1366, when Temur was thirty-one and he and Husayn, his then ally, took the city by the sword from the Sarbadars. It was his first significant victory, his first notable conquest, and brought into his orbit a city whose name, like Rome and Babylon, echoed through two millennia. He always cherished this moment as the foundation of his bid to rule the world. From that moment Samarkand occupied an unchallenged position in his aesthetic universe. As Clavijo put it: 'Samarkand indeed was the first of all the cities that he had conquered, and the one that he had since ennobled above all others, by his buildings making it the treasure house of his conquests.'

Temur's first move was to dress his new lover, encircling her with a girdle of fortified walls to protect her from invaders. This was out of character, insofar as it challenged the traditions established by the nomadic Genghis for whom a settled life and its associated infrastructure – towns, markets, agriculture – were anathema. The Mongol, who did not share Temur's romantic associations with Samarkand, had swept through in 1220, arriving before the city to find massive ramparts with twelve iron gates flanked by towers. A guard of twenty elephants and tens of thousands of Turkic soldiers were unable to prevent his hordes from razing both walls and city to the ground. According to tradition, the shamanistic Genghis told the Muslims of Khorezm: 'I am the punishment of God. If you had not committed great sins, God would not have sent punishment like me upon you.' Since that dreadful storm, when the city had been 'drowned in the ocean of destruction and consumed by the fire of perdition', Samarkand had lain unprotected. Temur's building works 150 years later were the first time the outer walls had been restored, an indication of the great esteem in which he held her.

For the rest of his life, Temur hurried across the world, storming, sacking, torching, razing, seizing, all for the greater glory of his adored metropolis. He rampaged through the continent as though nothing else mattered, always returning to adorn her with his latest trophies and embellishments. Captured abroad, scientists and scholars, writers, philosophers and historians congregated in the new academies and libraries he built, adding intellectual sparkle to the city. Temur, said Arabshah, 'gathered from all sides and collected at Samarkand the fruits of everything; and that place accordingly had in every wonderful craft and rare art someone who excelled in wonderful skill and was famous beyond his rivals in his craft'. Priests and holy men preached to their flocks in the mosques, which multiplied like mushrooms throughout the city, their lofty blue domes glimmering among the clouds, their interiors bright with gold and turquoise. Parks sprang up one by one, idyllic oases of tranquillity sprawling through the suburbs. Asia surrendered her finest musicians, artists and craftsmen to the regal vanity of Samarkand. From Persia, cultural capital of the continent, came poets and painters, miniaturists, calligraphers, musicians and architects. Syria sent her silk-weavers, glass-makers and armourers. After the fall of Delhi, India provided masons, builders and gem-cutters while Asia Minor supplied silversmiths, gunsmiths and rope-makers. This was one of the most cosmopolitan cities in the world. Among the Muslim population there were Turks, Arabs and Moors. The Christians were represented by Greek Orthodox, Armenians, Catholics, Jacobites and Nestorians, joined in lifelong servitude by the Hindus and Zoroastrians. Samarkand was a melting-pot of languages, religions and colours, an exercise in imperial splendour and an act of devotion by one man, constant in his love.

Christopher Marlowe's description of 'Samarcanda' was, for once, historically accurate. Attacked for the licence he took in his freewheeling masterpiece *Tamburlaine the Great*, he nonetheless brilliantly evoked the proud and wrathful emperor revelling in the great glories of his city.

> Then shall my native city Samarcanda,
> And crystal waves of fresh Jaertis' stream,
> The pride and beauty of her princely seat,
> Be famous through the furthest continents;
> For there my palace royal shall be placed,
> Whose shining turrets shall dismay the heavens,
> And cast the fame of Ilion's tower to hell;
> Through the streets, with troops of conquered kings,
> I'll ride in golden armour like the sun;
> And in my helm a triple plume shall spring,
> Spangled with diamonds, dancing in the air,
> To note me emperor of the three-fold world.

In the heart of this gracious city was the symbol of its strength, the heavily fortified Gok Sarai (Blue Palace), simultaneously a citadel, treasury, prison and armaments factory where the captive artisans and armourers were put to work. The great walls reverberated with the din and clattering of burly men hammering plate armour and helmets, making bows and arrows. Others blew glass for the emperor's palaces, alongside cobblers cutting leather for army boots and sandals. The rope-makers were set to work on piles of flax and hemp – new crops which Temur had introduced to the agricultural lands outside the city expressly to supply the ropes for the mangonels and other siege engines with which he overwhelmed defiant cities and castles. Here also were the archives, the coin-filled treasury, rooms full of Asia's plundered treasures and formal reception halls where the emperor occasionally held court.

For all his restless roaming, Samarkand was the centre around which Temur revolved. During thirty-five years of campaigning, the city invariably marked first the launch and – with ominous regularity for his enemies – the triumphal homecoming of his expeditions. He returned in 1381 after the sacking of Herat, and again in 1384 after taking Sistan, Zaranj and Kandahar in southern Afghanistan. He was back in 1392 after routing Tokhtamish. Samarkand, the Rome of the East, looked on in wonder as its illustrious emperor trampled the universe.

In 1396, after the latest catalogue of victories in Persia, Mesopotamia and the Kipchak steppes, Temur returned once more to Samarkand. Here he remained for two years, substituting peace for conquest while he embarked on his most sustained building projects yet. Peace maybe, but Temur threw himself into the glorification of his capital with all the furious energy of war.

⚇

On 8 September 1404, after a journey of fifteen months and almost six thousand miles from Cadiz, the dust-encrusted Spanish ambassador Ruy Gonzalez de Clavijo rode wearily into Samarkand with his modest entourage. Arriving with the European ignorance of the East that was typical of his age, he was staggered to discover the city was larger than Seville, with a population of 150,000.*

Samarkand was approached through 'extensive suburbs', the awe-struck envoy noted, each one contemptuously named after the great

---

* We have the whims of Black Sea weather systems in November 1403 to thank for Clavijo's brilliantly observed portrait of Samarkand in its finest hour. Clavijo's embassy, which included the friar Alfonso Paez and an officer of the royal guard called Gomez de Salazar, originally intended to meet Temur in the plains of the Qarabagh in the eastern Caucasus, where the emperor and his army were wintering after campaigning in Georgia. The itinerary, however, did not go according to plan. Shipwrecked on the edge of the Bosporus, the Spaniards were forced to wait for four months in Constantinople until more favourable conditions arrived. The following spring they continued their journey to Trebizond on the north coast of modern Turkey. By this time, however, Temur had left for Samarkand, and the envoys were obliged to play catch-up, following him across his Persian dominions to the heart of Mawarannahr. There they remained for three months. It was one of history's most auspicious shipwrecks.

cities of the East that Temur had conquered – Baghdad, Damascus, Cairo, Shiraz and Sultaniya – to demonstrate that by comparison with this imperial metropolis, Pearl of the East, Garden of the Soul, they were no more than provincial backwaters. These outlying districts, densely populated, were neatly laid out with orchards, vineyards, streets and markets in open squares.

> *Among these orchards outside Samarkand are found the most noble and beautiful houses, and here Temur has his many palaces and pleasure grounds. Round and about the great men of the government also here have their estates and country houses, each standing within its orchard: and so numerous are these gardens and vineyards surrounding Samarkand that a traveller who approaches the city sees only a great mountainous height of trees and the houses embowered among them remain invisible.*

Clavijo did not have to wait long for his audience with the Scourge of God. It took place in the evocatively named Baghi Dilkusha, the Garden of Heart's Delight, one of Temur's most fabulous parks, designed and laid out during the emperor's two-year residence in his capital to mark his marriage in 1397 to princess Tukal-khanum, daughter of the Moghul khan, Khizr Khoja. The garden lay a little to the east of Samarkand among the famous meadows of Kani-gil. From the Turquoise Gate in the city walls a straight avenue of pines led directly to the summer palace. In his memoirs, Babur noted its many paintings celebrating Temur's Indian campaign. With three storeys, a glittering dome and a forest of colonnades, it was a building of imperial dimensions.

Within hours of his arrival, the Spaniard handed over to two courtiers the gifts from King Henry III of Castile. Once these formalities were over, he was led forward by new attendants holding him by the armpits. Eventually they came to another orchard, entering via a towering gate beautifully decorated in the finest blue and gold tilework. Past the imperial doorkeepers armed with maces they walked, confronted at once by six enormous elephants with miniature castles on their backs performing tricks at the behest of their keepers. The ambassador and his companions were then led forward by a succession of courtiers in order of seniority, until they were brought before Khalil Sultan, Temur's grandson and son of Miranshah, to whom they handed over the letter from the king of Spain to the Lord of the Fortunate Conjunction. The audience could now begin. The scrupulously attentive ambassador left us this portrait of the most magnificent Oriental despot.

> We found Temur and he was seated under a portal, which same was before the entrance of a most beautiful palace that appeared in the background. He was sitting on the ground, but upon a raised dais before which there was a fountain that threw up a column of water into the air backwards, and in the basin of the fountain there were floating red apples. His Highness had taken his place on what appeared to be small mattresses stuffed thick and covered with embroidered silk cloth, and he was leaning on his elbow against some round cushions that were heaped up behind him. He was dressed in a cloak of plain silk without any embroidery, and he wore on his head a tall white hat on the crown of which was displayed a balas ruby, the same being further ornamented with pearls and precious stones.

The audience passed off successfully, although Temur left the Spaniard in no doubt that he regarded himself as sovereign of the world, referring to the Spanish monarch as 'my son your King'. Henry III, Temur acknowledged, was 'the greatest of all the kings of the Franks who reign in that farther quarter of the earth where his people are a great and famous nation', but that was only in small-time Europe, land of the Franks. Temur's power and riches were on an altogether more impressive scale, hence the paternalistic condescension to a petty princeling of the West.

Clavijo's description of Samarkand in the early years of the fifteenth century, the zenith of Temur's empire, is virtually unparalleled. The envoy, marvelling at the formally laid-out parks and gardens, could hardly believe what he was seeing. There were fifteen or sixteen of them, with names like Garden of Paradise, the Model of the World and Sublime Garden, all with palaces, immaculate lawns, meadows, babbling streams, lakes, orchards, bowers and flowers. There was the Garden of the Square, home to the two-storey Palace of Forty Pillars, then the Baghi Chinar or Plane Tree Garden, where Clavijo saw an extravagantly beautiful palace in the process of construction. Then there was Baghi Naw, the New Garden, lined with four towers surrounded by a high wall a mile long on each side. In the centre of the garden was an orchard and in the orchard was a palace. 'This palace, with its large garden was much the finest of any that we had visited hitherto, and in the ornamentation of its buildings in the gold and blue tile work far the most sumptuous'. Inside were marble sculptures and floors with exquisite mosaics of ebony and ivory. According to Babur, a verse from the Koran was inscribed over the doorway in letters so large they could be read two miles away.

Through this network of palaces and gardens Temur glided like a gilded lion, spending several days in one before moving serenely to another. A week after his arrival, Clavijo was invited to an imperial banquet in another garden planted with fruit trees and paved with paths and walkways. All around him were silk tents with coloured tapestries to provide shade. In the centre of the garden was a richly furnished palace where the Spaniard glimpsed the emperor's sleeping chamber, an elegant tiled alcove with a silver and gilt screen in front of which a small mattress of silk worked with gold thread lay on a dais. The walls were covered with rose-coloured silk hangings ornamented with silver spangles containing emeralds, pearls and other precious stones. Silk tassels rustled in the breeze. In front of the entrance to these chambers were two tables of gold and on them seven golden flasks, two of which were set with large pearls, emeralds and turquoises with balas rubies at their lips. Next to them stood six cups of gold, similarly set with pearls and balas rubies. Clavijo took it all in, entranced.

The Northern Garden, one of Temur's most extravagant creations, was another of the grandiose projects conceived between 1396 and 1398. It was typical insofar as it made use of the finest materials and the most famous craftsmen from the empire. The marble for the palace was imported from Tabriz, the artists and painters from Persia, under the supervision of the celebrated Abdul Hayy, a prize from Temur's capture of Baghdad in 1393. The images in these paintings, like those of the Registan which survive to this day, were a direct challenge to the Islamic prohibition on figurative art, symbolic perhaps of Temur's unrivalled ascendancy, boundless self-confidence and also of his ambivalent attitude towards the faith. These frescoes, wrote Arabshah, represented 'his assemblies and his own likeness, now smiling, now austere, and representations of his battles and sieges and his conversations with kings, amirs, lords, wise men and magnates, and Sultans offering homage to him and bringing gifts to him from every side and his hunting nets and ambushes and battles in India, Dasht [Kipchak] and Persia, and how he gained victory and how his enemy was scattered and driven to flight; and the likeness of his sons and grandsons, amirs and soldiers, and his public feasts and the goblets of wine and cupbearers and the zither-player, of his mirth and his love meetings and the concubines of his majesty and the royal wives and many other things which happened in his realms during his life which were shown in series, all that was new and happened; and he omitted or exaggerated none of these things; and therein he intended that all who knew not his affairs, should see them as though present'.

It was not just the outstanding beauty of these parks and palaces that so moved Clavijo. It was also their sheer scale. During his two years in and around Samarkand, Temur laid out another park, the Takhta Qaracha Gardens, an enclosure so vast, said Arabshah, that when one of the builders working on it lost his horse, the animal roamed about grazing quite happily for six months before he found it again. There were so many fruit trees planted throughout the city that one hundred pounds of fruit 'would not sell for a grain of mustard'.

This was a land of plenty, watered by the Zarafshan river, with fertile soil producing bumper crops of wheat and cotton. Vineyards were plentiful. The grazing was excellent for cattle and sheep. 'The livestock is magnificent, beasts and poultry all of a fine breed,' the envoy remarked approvingly. There were sheep with tails so fat they weighed twenty pounds. Even when Temur and his army were camping in the outlying meadows of Kani-gil and demand for meat was high, a pair of sheep still cost no more than a ducat. Wherever he looked, Clavijo saw food. Although he was teetotal – much to Temur's displeasure – the Spaniard was something of a gourmand, and noted with wonder the range of produce. Bread was available in all parts, while rice was sold cheaply in great quantities. Everywhere there were open squares with butchers selling meat ready-cooked, roasted or in stews, with fowl, pheasants and partridges, fruit and vegetables, including the delicious Samarkand melons, grown in such abundance that many were cured and kept for a year.

During his three months in the city, Clavijo was especially impressed by the well-stocked markets. Standing on the great Khorasan road running east from Baghdad to the border with China, Samarkand had become a major trade centre during Temur's reign, the more so once the northern trade route had been diverted south after his destruction of the Golden Horde. In the bazaars Clavijo saw the furs, leather and linens from Russia and Tartary, the silks, rubies, diamonds, agates, pearls, musk and spices from China. The caravans from India brought nutmegs, cloves, mace and cinnamon, ginger and manna. Syria and Asia Minor provided cloth, glass and metalware. Rich in agricultural produce, Samarkand was also a centre for factories making silks, crêpes and taffetas. Some specialised in making fur linings for silk garments. During a later feast, Clavijo was amazed to see royal pavilions lined with grey squirrel and ermine, 'the most precious fur in the whole world'.

If the Zarafshan watered the city, trade fed it and made it rich. Caravans regularly poured into town bringing plunder from the latest campaign, and tribute was always arriving from the growing ranks of vassal rulers. But commerce, and the taxes it generated for the imperial exchequer, was the backbone of prosperity throughout the empire, and was always attended to by Temur with the greatest care even if, as Clavijo suggested, this was for entirely selfish reasons. 'Trade has always been fostered by Temur with the view of making his capital the noblest of cities,' he wrote.

The Spaniard's four-month overland journey from Trebizond to Samarkand allowed him to observe how trade operated within these lands. It was Temur's boast that a child could carry a purse of gold unmolested from the western borders of his empire to its farthest reaches in the east, a claim Clavijo came close to endorsing with his observation that 'the whole country was at peace under the rule and government of Temur'. As he travelled east towards Samarkand through some of the well-known centres of the caravan routes, he saw for himself the busy markets, astounding architecture and pockets of affluence that thriving trade had brought. 'Tabriz is a very mighty city rich in goods and abounding in wealth, for commerce daily flourishes here,' he wrote, admiring the well-paved streets and squares, the fine buildings decked in blue and gold tiles, the elegant drinking fountains, richly decorated mosques and elaborate bath-houses. On reaching Sultaniya, he saw that this city was an even 'more important centre of exchange for merchants and goods'. It was 'so full of commerce that a great sum in customs is brought in yearly to the Imperial Treasury'.

As he passed through these exotic Oriental cities, each step bringing him closer to the empire's capital, Clavijo must have started to question his long-held assumptions of European supremacy over the savage, uncultured Orient. For several thousand miles he bore witness to the ruthless discipline with which Temur's commands were enforced in towns and villages. 'Wheresoever we might come and whensoever, no matter at what hour, if those of the settlement or township did not forthwith very quickly bring all that was required, they received merciless blows and beatings, suffering the same in a manner that we marvelled to witness,' he observed. Envoys and messengers criss-crossed the empire on charging steeds, taking horses from the regularly-spaced posting stations and riding them so hard their corpses littered the routes. Whoever held sway over such territories must surely be a great emperor.

When he finally reached Samarkand in the first flush of autumn, drained from the travails of the road, Clavijo found it a revelation. 'The richness and abundance of this great capital and its district is such as is indeed a wonder to behold,' he exclaimed. Christendom, he had always believed, was unrivalled in the world. The rout of the Crusaders at the hands of Bayazid in 1396 had certainly challenged his confident outlook, but in his heart he was certain that the sword of Christianity would prevail over these heathens of the East. Now, as he gazed up at the shimmering portals of Samarkand, its gorgeous turquoise domes, its heavenly parks and palaces, he tried to suppress a host of troublesome thoughts. Even before reaching Samarkand he had seen enough of this empire to know that Christendom could boast no equal to the man who ruled these lands. Europe suddenly seemed a small place, a long, long way away.

Sweet to ride forth at evening from the wells
When shadows pass gigantic on the sand,
And softly through the silence beat the bells
Along the Golden Road to Samarkand.
We travel not for trafficking alone:
By hotter winds our fiery hearts are fanned:
For lust of knowing what should not be known
We make the Golden Journey to Samarkand.

JAMES ELROY FLECKER, *Hassan: The story*
of Hassan of Bagdad and how he came to
make the Golden Journey to Samarkand, 1922

There is nothing golden any more about the road to Samarkand. Here and there cottonfields pop up and disappear into the horizon, little changed since the days of Temur, but they tell a tale of sadness rather than romance. Cotton remains the key cash crop of Uzbekistan, where old communist habits die hard. As I approached the city from Tashkent on a clear autumn morning, passing through the drab poverty of the suburbs – originally part of Temur's outlying districts of Baghdad, Damascus, Cairo, Shiraz and Sultaniya – a convoy of more than a hundred antiquated buses filled with young men and women passed in the opposite direction. I asked Farkhad, my travelling companion, who they were and where they were going.

'Oh, they're just students going to pick cotton,' he replied.

I expressed surprise that such punishing work could attract such great numbers of volunteers.

Farkhad looked at me askance. 'Of course they're not volunteers. They have to pick cotton or they'll be kicked out of university by the government. No cotton-picking, no degree.'

He himself had left university prematurely in the days of the Soviet Union because he could not cope with the physically gruelling, compulsory work. Then as now, students who refused to pick cotton were ejected from university without a degree. 'These days it's still the same. Nothing's changed only now it's better hidden. The cottonfields are mostly far away from the main roads, so foreigners like you can't see what's happening.'

The golden road to Samarkand was still tainted with the enduring stain of communism a decade after its collapse in Moscow. When James Elroy Flecker's play first appeared, Samarkand simmered in the Western imagination as the most romantic of cities, distant and exotic – to many minds, it still does. Its very name conjured up images of caravans bearing spices and fabulous treasures, struggling against the fiercest desert sandstorms, of superb palaces and mani-cured gardens stretching enticingly before the eye. It was the essence of opulence and majesty, a blue-domed oasis of grace and serenity in a world of Oriental barbarism. But even in the first decades of the twentieth century these fondly cherished impressions were illusory. The Great Game, an age of elegance and *chutzpah*, was long over. The nascent Soviet empire was spreading south to encompass the former realms of Temur.

In 1917 the Russians seized Samarkand and the red flag fluttered over the great Registan (literally 'sandy place') Square. In 1924 the Uzbek Soviet Socialist Republic was born, and a year later Samarkand was declared its capital, ushering in a new age of progress and modernity. The regime embraced the identikit paraphernalia of the Soviet experiment. Factories, schools, hospitals and high-rise housing sprang up. Broad, tree-lined avenues replaced the clutter of labyrin-thine streets. The site of Temur's Blue Palace became Lenin Square, repository of the new culture in the form of a House of Soviets, an opera house and ballet theatre. The sprawling, disorganised romance of Samarkand was tamed. As for the great monuments of the city, these were to be restored after centuries of abandon.

The Registan, the centrepiece of ancient Samarkand which for half a millennium has shocked visitors with its size and splendour, a trio of monuments rightly regarded as the apotheosis of the city's Temurid architecture, is an ensemble which Temur would not have recognised. Each of its three madrassahs dates from after his death.

The Ulugh Beg Madrassah, named after his grandson, is the oldest of the three – built between 1417 and 1420, more than a decade after the emperor's death – and dominates the western side of the square. Constellations of stars on the towering 110-foot portal pay tribute to the astronomer king, who also numbered mathematics, medicine, music, poetry, history, philosophy and theology among his interests. 'This magnificent façade is of such a height it is twice the heavens and of such weight that the spine of the earth is about to crumble,' boasts a Kufic inscription. Geometric patterns executed in glazed and unglazed brick zigzag splendidly across the exterior walls, a technique known as *hazarbaf*, or 'thousand-weave', tracing sacred names in turquoise cut tiles within borders of navy blue. Mosaic faience, for once, is used sparingly, above all on the intricate entrance *iwan*, while carved glazed terracotta, or *haft rangi*, dominates on the fading three-dimensional sections which make the rope moulding around the *iwan* arch. Smooth surfaces of marble appear from time to time, in the entrance *iwan* and along a low dado inset with strips of dark-blue-glazed tile.

Through this devastating portal the humbled visitor walks with craning neck, confronted at once by a courtyard over ninety feet square, which once housed fifty cell-like rooms on two storeys. Here a hundred of the brightest students pored over their Korans, wrapping themselves tightly against the icy draughts of winter, perspiring in the draining heat of summer. During the most irksome hours of recitation and exegesis, digging their fingernails into their hands to keep awake, they would have cast a weary eye on the portal of the mosque on the south-west side of the court, where an inscription reminded them of the fame of their institution, the greatness of its patron: 'This portal is built to resemble Paradise . . . in it are teachers of the truths of the sciences useful to religion, under the direction of the greatest of sultans.' High above the soft murmurings of the student rooms, among the gusting winds a pair of minarets loomed like watchful sentinels, laced with script in turquoise and navy blue like those of the madrassah on the eastern side of the square. Towards their summits, stretching into the skies, the script grew larger. In bold white letters, bordered with blue, the word 'Allah' ran continuously around the column.

The Ulugh Beg Madrassah remained a teaching school until the late seventeenth century. In the eighteenth, its ignominious fate would have horrified and infuriated its progenitor as the fabled college sunk first into absolute dereliction, then reincarnation as a grain warehouse. In the early twentieth century it returned to its roots, and once more the courtyard echoed to the ululating cadences of Koranic recitations, the sixty students being warned that it was not safe to enter the lecture-room area due to the frailties of the creaking structure.

Directly opposite, squaring up against the Ulugh Beg Madrassah with an equally imposing portal flanked by two minarets, is the Shir Dor ('lion bearing') Madrassah, built two centuries after the Ulugh Beg Madrassah between 1619 and 1636. What the visitor first notices about the portal – apart from its great size, since this applies equally to all three of the Registan's monuments – are the stylised lions prowling after white does in front of two suns with human faces, another defiance of Islamic tradition. Legend has it that the architect paid for this heresy with his life. A similarly florid inscription – 'The skilled acrobat of thought climbing the rope of imagination will never reach the summits of its forbidden minarets' – decorates the portal. A little behind this superb façade, and partially eclipsed by it on either side, are two azure-blue cupolas, hallmark of the Temurid architectural style.

To the north, completing the ensemble, is the slightly later Tillya Kari Madrassah, built between 1646 and 1660. Of lower construction than its neighbours, it stretches farther across the square with a width of 230 feet, its two storeys of *hujra* (student rooms) topped on the western side by another cupola, larger and more dominant this time, resplendent with its sun-catching blue tiles.

The future viceroy of India George Curzon, who visited while a Tory MP in 1888, was one of countless visitors on whom the square made a profound impression. 'The Registan of Samarkand was originally, and is still even in its ruin, the noblest public square in the world,' he wrote. 'I know of nothing in the East approaching it in massive simplicity and grandeur; and nothing in Europe ... which can even aspire to enter the competition. No European spectacle indeed can adequately be compared to it, in our inability to point to an open space in any western city that is commanded on three of its four sides by Gothic cathedrals of the highest order.'

As an architectural set-piece the Registan, in its original state, was one of the brightest gems of the Islamic world. Its pleasing symmetry, the gorgeousness of the portals with their intricate floral motifs and epigraphic patterns, the elegance of the Kufic calligraphy, the rush of colour – azure, green, yellow and dark blue – against the desert beige, above all its sheer scale, are what grab the eye. But Curzon spoke before the Russians, and more recently the Uzbeks, set to work restoring the decrepit monuments. Today there is something inescapably artificial and new about the square. The restoration has been just that little too efficient, the mosaic details just that little too perfect, the blue majolica tiles impossibly lustrous for buildings of this age.

The Registan has become an Islamic Disneyworld, immaculate and almost devoid of flaws. The natural ageing process has been halted, wear and tear frowned upon and attended to in earnest. All this is understandable, given both the neglect into which the buildings had fallen and the desire for tourist dollars, but the effect is sterilising. After a few minutes contemplating the Registan I found myself genuinely relieved to see a wobbly-looking minaret on the Ulugh Beg Madrassah, a fault the restorers had yet to rectify. A policeman sidled up brandishing a key, and offered to take us to the top of Samarkand's Leaning Tower of Pisa in exchange for two dollars.

Temur would not have been able to look down on the Registan from the top of this minaret, because neither it nor the rest of the ensemble had been built during his lifetime. (The vantage point would, however, be used a century later when Babur was fighting the Uzbeks.) But if the chess-playing conqueror had been able to ascend to such heavenly heights, he would have stared down on the crossroads of his capital, not on the Shir Dor or Tillya Kari madrassahs, but on a lofty domed bazaar in which the half-dozen principal roads of his city converged.

These arteries wended their way crookedly past the azure-domed mosques, madrassahs and mausolea, through a series of bazaars, located according to their trade. Here were weavers, ironworkers, goldsmiths, potters, bow-makers and tile-makers, an ever-swelling population of craftsmen from all corners of Temur's burgeoning empire. Eventually the roads emanating from the Registan reached the six gates of the city walls, massive earthen ramparts with a circumference of five miles, surrounded by a deep ditch, that Temur had reconstructed after the devastation wrought by Genghis.

From the top of the minaret Samarkand was a sea of sparkling blue domes and iridescent portals almost as far as the eye could see. Only in the very farthest reaches of the horizon, where the brooding desert lurked on the shores of this ocean, as if ready to reclaim the city in an instant, was the effusion of light dimmed slightly. And there, in the midst of this fulgor of sunshine, several hundred yards north-east of the Registan, just south of the Iron Gate which lay between Afrosiab (ancient Samarkand) and the newly settled quarters to the south, stood the Bibi Khanum Mosque – Mosque of the Mother Queen – Temur's pride and joy.*

The Cathedral Mosque was one of his greatest projects, a vast, towering edifice, among the most colossal monuments ever built in the Islamic world, a fitting tribute to his numerous victories. Its construction began in 1399, when Temur returned to his capital fired with zeal after the lightning assault on Delhi. According to Clavijo, it was 'the noblest of all those [mosques] we visited in Samarkand'. Perhaps in these late years the emperor was growing increasingly aware of his own mortality and decided on a building to honour the Almighty, rather than a secular project as was generally his wont.

It may have been, as Hilda Hookham suggested, that the mosque Temur admired at Firuzabad in India inspired this new mosque. Alternatively, it might have been the Tughluk *masjid* of Jahanpanah

---

* Though both the chronicles and the inscriptions on the Cathedral Mosque attribute its construction to Temur, a popular Samarkand legend has it otherwise. According to this version, it was built by Bibi Khanum, his Chinese princess wife, to surprise him on his triumphant return from India. Warned of her husband's imminent return before the mosque was finished, Temur's wife rushed to the architect to hurry him along. In vain she pleaded with him to redouble his efforts. Seething with passion for this predictably beautiful princess, the architect steadfastly refused to continue his work until she gave him a kiss. 'But all women are the same,' she replied, fearful of the consequences of kissing another man. 'Take one of the slave girls from the harem.' She brought him a bowl of coloured eggs. 'Break any one of these eggs and inside they are all the same.' Unmoved by this analogy, the architect attempted one of his own. Pouring water into one glass and vodka into another, he observed: 'Their colour and shape are identical, but their contents are completely different. There are some women who are cold, like water. Others burn and set the veins on fire, like vodka.' Impressed by his logic, if not his looks, Bibi Khanum consented to a kiss, covering her cheek with her hand. The mosque was finished, but such was the ardour of the lovelorn architect that his kiss burnt an imprint through the princess's hand onto her cheek. When Temur discovered his wife's infidelity, he ordered her to be taken to the top of a minaret and thrown to her death. The architect was also sentenced to death, but sprouted wings and flew to heaven instead.

in Delhi. Another possible inspiration, given the number of years his project took to complete, is the great Umayyad Mosque of Damascus, which Temur had observed while camped in front of the city in 1401. 'From whatever direction you approach the city, you see this dome, above everything, as if suspended in the air,' gasped Ibn Battutah. In Temur's earlier buildings, the domes tended to follow the Persian style – pointed without flowing outwards from their base. The Bibi Khanum Mosque and the Gur Amir mausoleum, with their majestic pomegranate domes, were harbingers of a new style, embraced by the Temurids after the emperor's death and passed on to the Mughals of India, who used it to most notable effect in the Taj Mahal. The style was later exported to Russia, where it is seen in its full glory in the Kremlin.

Clavijo said the Cathedral Mosque was built in memory of the mother of Temur's chief wife, Saray Mulk-khanum; others that it was erected in honour of the wife herself, hence its nickname of Bibi Khanum. The chronicles, for once, are silent on such details, but regardless of the inspiration, it was a project on which Temur unleashed his fearsome instincts for control. Two amirs, Khoja Mahmud Daoud and Mohammed Jalad, were put in charge of the work and sent him daily progress reports. They presided over a huge, highly skilled army of workers, each man selected for his special talents. Master craftsmen from Basrah and Baghdad joined stone-masons from Azerbaijan, Fars and India, crystal workers from Damascus and artisans from Samarkand. Among the greatest surprises for the local population were the ninety-five elephants hauling two hundred blocks of marble from Azerbaijan, Persia and India. The animals, which Temur made a point of showing off both on and off the battlefield, had never been seen before in Samarkand.

In 1404, as the mosque neared completion, the workers were surprised by the arrival of Temur, fresh from his triumphant Five-Year Campaign. The emperor was so unimpressed by the size of the portal that he ordered it torn down at once and new foundations dug. Clavijo reported that the portal was too low, Arabshah that it was dwarfed by the rival façade of the Saray Mulk-khanum Madrassah directly opposite. Whatever the reason, Temur was incandescent with rage. The two amirs responsible for its construction were sentenced to death. Temur reserved the most gruesome pre-gallows punishment for Mohammed Jalad, according to Arabshah.

> *Merely casting an eye upon it* [the mosque], *he pronounced against Mohammed Jalad sentence of death and forthwith they drew him on his face and bound his feet and ceased not dragging him and drawing him over the ground on his face, until in this manner they had torn him to pieces; and Temur took for himself all his servants, children and property. Now he had diverse reasons for that deed, of which this was the chief; the queen, the chief wife of Temur, ordered to be built a college and the architects and geometers judging by unanimous consent that it should be built opposite that mosque, raised its columns high and elevated its structure and lifted its stories and walls above that mosque, wherefore it became stronger than it and stood higher, but since Temur was by nature like a leopard and the temper of a lion, no head was raised above him but he brought it low and no back grew stronger than his but he broke it and he was thus in all things which concerned or touched him. Therefore when he saw the great height of that college and that it bore itself more proudly than the slighter structure of his own, his breast was bitter with anger and he blazed forth and dealt as he did with that superintendent, who did not find the fortune which he had hoped.*

Temur now took personal charge of the construction. Although in poor health and unable either to stand for long or to mount his horse, he had himself carried to the site every day in a litter. His obsession with the work astonished Clavijo.

> *He would stay there the best part of the day urging on the work. He would arrange for much meat to be cooked and brought, and*

*then he would order them to throw portions of the same down to
the workmen in the foundations, as though one should cast bones
to dogs in a pit, and a wonder to all he with his own hands did
this. Thus he urged on their labour: and at times would have coins
thrown down to the masons when especially they worked to his
satisfaction.*

With Temur on site, the building continued night and day. The result
was breathtaking. The carved stone and marble, glazed mosaics and
bright blue and gold frescoes, together with the hangings and silk
carpets, lent the mosque an incomparable refinement. Its scale was
unique, contained within a site spanning 350 feet by five hundred
feet. The portal reached over a hundred feet, outdone only by the
150-foot minarets which lanced the skyline and looked down on a
great courtyard bordered by a gallery of four hundred cupolas supported by four hundred marble columns. Kufic inscriptions from the
Koran traced their way around the base of the majestic dome, so
large they could reputedly be read from miles away. 'The dome would
have been unique but for the sky being its copy; the arch would have
been singular but for the Milky Way matching it,' the court historian
simpered.

The quality and variety of ornament were extraordinary. Large
surfaces were covered with glazed brick-ends in *hazarbaf* technique,
crammed with square Kufic designs paying tribute to Allah and his
Prophet. In places these paeans to the Almighty were traced across
neat arched panels parallel to the ground. In others they cascaded
diagonally down the façades in staccato zigzags beneath a frieze of
jagged crenellations. All of the mosque's visible faces were covered
in this profusion of colour. The entrance portal and sanctuary *iwan*
had panels of mosaic faience, with insets of polished brick and stone
matrices and majolica tiles. A spiral moulding of light blue tiles drew
the eye towards the sky, while carved stone anchored the colossal
structure to the earth.

Inscriptions on the entrance portal honoured Temur, relating how work began in 1399 and was completed in 1403–04. 'The great sultan, pillar of the state and the religion, Amir Temur Gurgan ibn Taraghay ibn Burgul ibn Aylangir ibn Ichil ibn al-Amir Karachar Noyan, may God preserve his reign, was helped (by heavenly favour) to complete this jami [Friday mosque] in the year 806 [1403–04],' read an inscription in carved stone over the main entrance.

By removing the minarets from the top of the massive *iwans* and placing them at the sides like the salients of a fortress gate, Temur was confidently departing from the Ilkhanid style, giving his Cathedral Mosque an unmistakable religious–military aesthetic on a grand scale. What better testament could there be to the man who regarded himself as the Sword of Islam? There were other important architectural innovations. The novel combination of lateral *iwans* with domed units, moving away from the traditional court mosque with its four *iwans*, reappeared in the Masjid-i-Shah of Isfahan and was later exported to the mosques of Mughal India.

But however magnificent Temur's Cathedral Mosque, it had been built too quickly. The emperor's personal intervention, not least his execution of the two amirs in charge of the project, had doubtless caused a frenzy among the workers and foremen. Perhaps they cut corners in their efforts to finish the building and escape the emperor's ire. Perhaps the foundations were too shallow to support such a mighty edifice. The exact reasons are not known, but no sooner had the mosque been completed than it started falling down. It was not long before worshippers, their devout reflections shattered by tumbling masonry, decided to take their prayers elsewhere. Its shell remained, however, and by the nineteenth century the mosque was doubling as a cotton market and stables for Tsarist officers. Bukharan amirs had already plundered it of anything valuable, not least the famous gates of seven metals, which were melted into coins. In 1897 an earthquake hit Samarkand, and the mosque was dealt a lethal blow.

Today, the main body of the mosque remains closed to visitors, its interior dark and dilapidated. Peering through a grille into the gloom, I could make out a cavernous, largely derelict space in which only the most faded, smudged traces of painted plaster and gilt *papier-mâché* remained. Yet still the monument stands proudly erect, remarkable evidence of Temur's princely vision. Restored with more sensitivity than the shiny monuments of the Registan, its twin portal towers taper elegantly towards the heavens. The detail on the façade, as fine as anything in Samarkand, has been retraced in subdued blues and beiges.

From the top of the towers, after paying the requisite bribes, I stared over a burnished Samarkand in the warm streaming wind, past the mosque's immense dome, the azure sheen pockmarked with terracotta where the missing tiles should have been. In the courtyard in front of the portal was a massive lectern of Mongolian marble, given by the astronomer king Ulugh Beg. In former times this had housed the Othman Koran, but when the Russians seized the holy book and carried it off to St Petersburg in the second half of the nineteenth century, it was removed from the crumbling mosque for its own safety and left to fend off the elements in the open air. Far below my vantage point I made out a heavily-built matron and her daughter. The younger woman was crawling around beneath the lectern, getting up, shaking herself down and then disappearing beneath it again. Legend has it that a barren woman who crawls underneath it three times will be blessed with children.

Looking down on the ruined glory of the mosque, I wondered whether its sorry fate had harmed Temur's status and reputation abroad, contributing to the ignorance which generally greets his name in the Western world. Perhaps if it had survived more completely it would have stood as an unparalleled tribute to the greatest conqueror of the Islamic world, reminding all who saw it that though he was a blood-soaked tyrant, he was also a man of vision and culture, a more complex and fascinating figure than either Alexander the Great or Genghis Khan. The monumentality of his architecture, the rationality of its proportions, the quality of the materials used and the craftsmen employed, all were still visible in what remained of this fabulous complex. Yazdi's comments admiring the otherworldly dimensions of the mosque came back to me as I gazed across the city of turquoise domes:

> How marvellously high is the building whose upper rooms are Paradise
> To estimate its loftiness must confound the greatest minds.

For once, the panegyrist was barely exaggerating.

&

If the Bibi Khanum Mosque was Temur's most extravagant religious building in Samarkand, the mausolea of Shah-i-Zinda (the Living King) was his holiest. The site itself, which lay beyond the city walls in the north-east of the capital over the ancient settlement of Afrosiab, predated Temur by several centuries, but under the conqueror's lavish patronage it developed into an important centre for pilgrims, an integral part of his attempt to make Samarkand the Mecca of Central Asia.

Mausolea had existed here from at least the twelfth century, but Genghis's hordes erased them from the face of the earth, with one prominent exception. The solitary survivor of the Mongol invasion and the centrepiece of the complex was the tomb of Kussam ibn Abbas, cousin of the Prophet Mohammed, who is supposed to have arrived in the province of Sogdiana – which included Samarkand and Bukhara – in 676. Brimming with missionary fervour, Kussam was on a mission to convert the Zoroastrian fire-worshippers to Islam. The local population did not take kindly to this foreign preacher, however, and Kussam was promptly beheaded. Notwithstanding his decapitation, the story goes, he managed to pick up his head and jump down a well, where he has remained ever since, ready to resume his reign when the time comes. The Arabs venerated him as a great martyr, and the cult of the Living King was born. Over the centuries, the tomb continued to attract the faithful. 'The inhabitants of Samarkand come out to visit it every Sunday and Thursday night,' wrote Ibn Battutah in 1333. 'The Tatars also come to visit it, pay vows to it and bring cows, sheep, dirhams and dinars; all this is used for the benefit of the hospital and the blessed tomb.'

Temur sought to increase the popularity and prestige of the Shah-i-Zinda by converting it into a royal burial ground. Valiant amirs were also allowed to be buried here, and during the latter half of the fourteenth century the complex developed into one of the prize jewels in Samarkand's architectural crown. Two of Temur's sisters were buried there, together with other relatives and amirs who had loyally served him. It was a feast of fine craftsmanship, masonry, calligraphy and art, a street of the dead awash with all hues of blue majolica tiles. Blue domes glowed like beacons in the white light, while all around them plainer domes of terracotta baked slowly in the sun.

For most of the twentieth century, in a cruel twist of history perpetrated by the Soviets, Shah-i-Zinda languished as an anti-Islamic museum. Now freed from the shackles of communism it is enjoying its latest renaissance as one of Samarkand's most impressive attractions. One afternoon, Farkhad and I took a taxi to the necropolis. Our driver, a retired army officer, was completely unmoved by the government's rehabilitation of Temur: 'You know, in the army now they teach soldiers about Temur, how he was a great warrior, how he won his many battles and how the new army of Uzbekistan fights in his spirit. All this talk of Temur is rubbish. It's all very well mentioning him all the time, but what does any of it mean? The comparisons aren't even accurate. Temur treated his soldiers well. The pensions we get aren't enough to live on. This government can't even feed its own people.'

We filed through Ulugh Beg's elaborate portal and domed entrance halls and stepped into the complex, confronted at once by the familiar blue cupolas which top the Qazi Zadeh Rumi mausoleum, the largest on the site and thought by some to hold the body of Temur's wetnurse. Down a narrow street shaded on both sides by tall monuments stand two of the finest tombs. The first, the mausoleum of Shadi Mulk-agha, built in 1372, housed a niece of Temur – 'This is a garden in which lies buried a Treasury of good fortune, And this is a tomb in which a precious pearl has been lost' reads the inscription framing the door – who had been joined later by the emperor's eldest sister Turkan-agha. Apart from the Rukhabad mausoleum in the centre of town – one of the few monuments in Samarkand that dates to Temur's time – this was the first dome of plain brickwork I had seen, its restrained simplicity forming a counterpoint both to the turquoise sky above and the intricate panels of carved and glazed terracotta and majolica on the portal below. It is justly considered one of the most brilliant examples of early Temurid ceramic revetments, with its entire façade and interior, including the dome, sheathed in tiles in a variety of highly refined techniques.

Inside the shaded tomb, the exuberance of the decoration shows no signs of restraint. Large rectangular panels containing medallions against a background of hexagrams stretch across the walls, framed by borders of knotted Kufic to give the impression of a particularly fine carpet. The interior angles are filled with tumbling *muqarnas* or stalactite ornament. Above them, in the crown of the dome a magnificent star shines forth, its eight points running down into lines which divide the heavens into eight panels, each with a teardrop medallion containing a sun and six planets in red, green and bright yellow.

Directly opposite is the tomb of Shirin Bika-agha, another of the emperor's sisters, erected a decade later, traced with mosaic faience in spiralling floral patterns of blues, yellows, white and green, vying for attention with scrolling vegetal decorations and the ornate ochre calligraphy running across the mosaics. Inside, beneath a double dome, a sixteen-sided drum tapers into an octagonal zone illuminated by shafts of sunlight stealing in through plaster-grille windows of coloured glass to reveal golden murals and a dado of green hexagons and flying cranes, the birds of heaven.

Towards the end of the street lies the Tuman-agha Mosque and mausoleum complex, named after one of Temur's favourite young wives, a twelve-year-old whom he married when he was in his early forties. The Paradise Garden was also designed in her honour. Tuman-agha had the complex erected in 1405, the year of her husband's death, shortly before she was forced to marry Temur's amir Shaykh Nur ad-din by Temur's grandson, Khalil Sultan. The unfortunate woman was widowed again when her second husband was killed by Shahrukh's armies in 1411.

At the foot of a portal twinkling with colourful faience is a carved door and above it the sombre inscription: 'The tomb is a door which everyone must enter.' On the portals of the mosque is the more encouraging reminder: 'The prophet of God, peace be upon him, said, "Hurry with prayer before burial, And hurry with repentance before death."' Within the mausoleum, Temur's bride sleeps beneath a dome of eternal night, a blue sky with scattered stars of gold watching over an idyllic country landscape of trees and flowers.

At the end of the street, past the tomb of Kutlug-agha, yet another of the emperor's wives, is the object of this pilgrimage, the deliciously cool Kussam ibn Abbas Mosque, supreme in the skyline with a trio of grand cupolas. The centre of the edifice, the *ziaratkhona* (pilgrimage room), rebuilt in 1334, two years before Temur's birth, is ablaze with bright tiles. An elegant dado of light blue hexagons encircles the chamber, trimmed by mosaic faience in blue, green and white.

The holy heart of Shah-i-Zinda appears in a small chamber visible through a wooden lattice frame. There lies the grand four-storey tomb of Kussam ibn Abbas, its several tiers loaded with ornamented majolica and crammed with Koranic inscriptions: 'Those who were killed on the way of Allah are not to be considered dead,' reads one. 'Indeed they are very much alive.'

☙

At the bottom of Samarkand's University Boulevard, a cool avenue of tall plane trees leading into Registan Street, is a monumental statue in bronze of an enthroned king. His line of sight stretches down towards the Registan. Even sitting down, Temur is an intimidating fifteen feet tall. His beard is trimmed short beneath a highly orna-mented crown. His arms are crossed over one another and his right hand rests on the hilt of a curved sword held against his left side. A flowing cloak with a bold border covers his broad shoulders and simply-decorated tunic, reaching down to his ankles. Large boots poke out from beneath it. The statue lords it over the boulevard, exactly as the sculptor intended.

This is Samarkand's tribute to Temur, its version of the stirring statue of the emperor on horseback in Tashkent. A dappled light filtered down through the trees and played across the pavement. Down a side street a group of boys were fishing in a pool beside a restaurant. Others were splashing about and swimming in a fountain, the water catching the bright sunlight on their backs. Clusters of students walked and cycled past. Zhigulis and slightly larger Volga saloons, the stock Russian cars which dominate the roads of Uzbeki-stan, rushed by in varying states of repair. A gentle breeze took the sting out of the growing heat.

Two taxis were parked on the side of the road beneath the statue. A petite woman stepped out delicately, taking care not to disturb her wedding dress. Dwarfed by its expanding frills and ruffles, she looked as though she had come off worst in a fracas with a large white meringue. Next to her the groom shuffled awkwardly in an ill-fitting dark suit and adjusted his tie. Once the couple had composed themselves they looked up to the statue of Temur, several steps above road level, and started a slow, deliberate walk towards it. Behind them, their mothers, wearing the traditional Uzbek tie-dyed *ikat* silk dresses, fussed about with the bride and groom's clothes, smoothing down the wedding gown and brushing off stray dandruff from the groom's shoulders, as the growing ranks of the family joined them from other taxis.

The bride and groom led the way up the steps with regal formality. At the foot of the statue the woman laid a bunch of flowers on the marble dais. Then a professional photographer with a Soviet-era camera closed in on the couple and snapped them in front of, and beneath, the austere king staring down towards the centre of his capital with the familiar far-off gaze. More shots were taken of the bride and groom with the rest of the family, and with that the second part of the ceremony was over and the group made their way off. The couple had already been to the register office to get married, and had come to the statue simply to pay their respects to Temur and to seek his blessings.

No sooner had the taxis departed than another convoy arrived. Another meringue and her groom were deposited on the road and the process was repeated all over again. More fussing about the wedding dress. A sombre march up to the statue. Another bunch of flowers. More photos.

As I watched, I realised what a dramatic reversal of fortune these touching ceremonies represented. Who could have foreseen it? Who could have predicted how history would treat Temur? During the six centuries after his death he had been successively neglected by historians, erased by the Soviets, and now revered as the father of his nation. Overlooking his city's greatest monuments, Temur had finally returned from the shadows, restored to his beloved Samarkand.

By the beginning of 1398, Temur had spent almost two years in Samarkand, by his standards an eternity. But this lull in his military campaigns had not been unprofitable, and disguised considerable activity on other fronts. The various architectural works – the fabulous parks and gardens and palaces – lent further lustre to his imperial capital, which had multiplied in size and riches during his reign. Pearl of Islam and Centre of the Universe, Samarkand was now the envy of the world.

These extravagant improvements had occupied only part of Temur's time, however. Always the restless conqueror was looking ahead, gathering intelligence, provisioning his men and planning future conquests. For the first time in his life, his eyes turned east to his most formidable enemy, the Ming emperor of China. War with the ruler of Peking had long motivated Temur. It was the chance to win untold glory by raising the sword of Islam against the infidel in the darkest corners of the world. More important, it was an opportunity to test his power against the mightiest ruler on earth.

With this object in mind, Temur had ordered fortresses to be built in his eastern frontier regions, around Lake Issykul in Kyrgyzstan, in the shadows of the spectacular Tien Shan mountains, and in the neighbouring city of Ashpara. His favourite grandson and designated heir Prince Mohammed Sultan had been given a special detachment of senior amirs and troops and entrusted with ensuring that the land could supply the needs of the army when it marched through en route to China. After overtures to the ever troublesome Moghuls, Temur had concluded a treaty with their khan, Khizr Khoja, a cessation of hostilities celebrated by his marriage in 1397 to the khan's daughter, princess Tukal-khanum. The way east was open.

All these preparations had been set in motion by 1398. It seemed clear where the emperor's driving ambition would lead him and his armies next. But Temur was an unpredictable opportunist. He knew that the kingdom of Delhi, a thousand miles to the south, had been perilously weakened and was in a state of civil war. In 1394 its ruler Nasir ud-din Mohammed Tughluk had died after a rein of six years. The same year, the Angel Izrail descended on his son Humayun after only six weeks on the throne. The premature death triggered violent disputes over the succession. 'The misfortunes of the state daily increased,' wrote the historian Ferishta. 'The *omras* [great lords] of Firuzabad, and some of the provinces, espoused the cause of Nasrut Shah. Those of Delhi and other places supported the title of Mohammed Tughluk. The government fell into anarchy: civil war raged everywhere; and a scene was exhibited, unheard of before, of two kings in arms against each other residing in the same capital.'

Up to this point, with the exception of the periodic campaigns against Moghulistan, Temur had looked west for his military conquests. Preparations had now been set in motion for war with China. While they continued, a lightning raid on Delhi would secure his southern borders and bring fresh plunder from the bulging treasuries of India. There was a third consideration. 'His present resolution [to conquer Delhi] was further strengthened by accounts long since conveyed to him, of the gross idolatry still suffered to extend its pollutions, throughout the countries dependent on both Delhi and Multan,' wrote David Price in an early-nineteenth-century history of India. 'And as the views of this apostle of desolation had been for some time bent on a war of religion, it seemed of little importance whether the current of zeal impelled him south or east.'

For an ageing emperor, the opportunity to earn great honour by fighting a holy war against infidels who had turned their back on Islam was particularly inviting. Considering the extent of his conquests, Temur had yet to feature highly on the Islamic horizon. Indeed, as he looked around his fellow Muslim rulers he must have felt he had not been afforded the status – or the soubriquets – he so richly deserved within the *dar al Islam*. In Cairo, there was the caliph.

In Baghdad, the Protector of the Faithful. Sultan Bayazid, the Ottoman emperor, was styled the Sword Arm of the Faith. These three men regarded Temur as no more than a barbaric pagan.*

There was yet another important motivation at work. To date he had met and overcome the challenge of every enemy he had encountered. Was there indeed a power on earth which could resist him? For a ruler with such a keen interest in history on the one hand and an undefeated military record on the other, it was entirely natural that Temur should wish to pit himself against the great figures of antiquity. Alexander the Great had barely crossed the river Indus. Genghis, having made little headway in India, turned back because of the appalling heat. Neither of these world conquerors had managed even to reach Delhi.

Temur put the idea to his princes and amirs. What was their opinion of this most audacious campaign against an enemy of the faith across the snow-capped mountains? They looked at him aghast. 'The rivers! And the mountains and deserts! And the soldiers clad in armour! And the elephants, destroyers of men!' they trembled. Surely the emperor was not serious about this most dangerous of ideas?

Mohammed Sultan, disgusted by this cowardice, cut short their protestations with an impassioned appeal to their greed and sense of honour.

> *The whole country of India is full of gold and jewels, and in it there are seventeen mines of gold and silver, diamond and ruby and emerald and tin and iron and steel and copper and quicksilver, and plants which are suitable for making clothes, and aromatic plants, and sugar cane. It is a country which is always green*

---

* Temur's armies would in due course make a mockery of these exalted titles. His own claims to greatness within the Islamic world, however, should be viewed within the context of a career in which he directed his butchery primarily against Muslims, rather than Jews and Christians.

and verdant, and the whole aspect of the country is pleasant and delightful. Now, since the inhabitants are chiefly polytheists and infidels and idolaters and worshippers of the sun, by the order of God and his prophet, it is right for us to conquer them.

The emperor's son Shahrukh added his voice to the council. 'India is an extensive country,' he argued. 'Whichever Sultan conquers it becomes supreme over the four corners of the globe. If, under the conduct of our amir, we conquer India, we shall become rulers over the seven climes.'

The emperor smiled benevolently. His mind was made up. His grandson Prince Pir Mohammed Jahangir was sent ahead to put the holy city of Multan (in present-day Pakistan) under siege. The *tovachis* once again turned to the business of raising an army of ninety thousand. Then, in March 1398, the emperor called the traditional *qurultay*, at which he made clear his unswerving intention.

Although the true faith is observed in many places in India, the greater part of the kingdom is inhabited by idolaters. The sultans of Delhi have been slack in their defence of the Faith. The Muslim rulers are content with the collection of tribute from these infidels. The Koran says that the highest dignity a man can achieve is to make war on the enemies of our religion. Mohammed the Prophet counselled likewise. A Muslim warrior thus killed acquires a merit which translates him at once into Paradise. Now that the empires of Iran and of Turan* and most of Asia are under our domination,

---

* Turan, a vaguely defined Iranian term, refers to the land north-east of Iran. According to *The Encyclopaedia of Islam*: 'The Muslim writers, Arabic, Persian and Turkish, have not been logical in the use of the term Turan. But since for the Arab geographers, the land of the Turks began only to the east of the Sir Darya and did not include Transoxiana, it seems that there was a tendency to identify Turan with Transoxiana, i.e. with the lands between the Amu Darya and the Sir Darya ... The term Turan became naturalised in Europe only in the nineteenth century. Its vague character has earned it a certain degree of popularity as applied to ideas where accuracy of definition is out of the question.'

and the world trembles at the least movement we make, Destiny has presented us with the most favourable opportunities. The troops will ride south, not east. India through her disorders has opened her doors to us.

7

India

1398–1399

'If the rulers of Hindustan come before me with tribute I will not interfere with their lives, property or kingdoms; but if they are negligent in proffering obedience and submission, I will put forth my strength for the conquest of the kingdoms of India. At all events, if they set any value upon their lives, property and reputation, they will pay me a yearly tribute, and if not, they shall hear of my arrival with my powerful armies. Farewell.'

LETTER FROM TEMUR TO SARANG KHAN OF DIPALPUR

'It is difficult to take an empire like a bride to your bosom without trouble and difficulty and the clashing of swords. The desire of your prince is to take this kingdom with its rich revenue. Well, let him wrest it from us by force of arms if he is able. I have numerous armies and formidable elephants, and am quite prepared for war.'

SARANG KHAN'S REPLY

Once more the plains around Samarkand echoed to the thunder of arms. A thick pall of dust hung over the army as ninety thousand soldiers manoeuvred into position. Ninety thousand men, awaiting the emperor's command, pondered the battles ahead. Among the veterans there was bluff confidence and a certain heartiness, a resignation to the will of Temur and the expectation, rarely disappointed over the years, of great reward. Temur's generosity to his soldiers was famous the length and breadth of Asia. 'I saw the duration of my power in this,' the Lord of the Fortunate Conjunction is supposed to have said. 'That I should divide among my soldiers the treasures which I had gathered together, both the money and the effects.' This he had done assiduously from his early days as a desperado and mercenary to the height of his glory as emperor. It was one of the reasons he had triumphed over Husayn in 1370. The battle-hardened men remembered the lavish spoils from previous campaigns. If they fought valiantly again, they would win honour and new riches. All knew that a soldier distinguishing himself exceptionally in battle, be he the most junior infantryman or the greatest amir, might be awarded the exalted title of *tarkhan*. It was a prize worth fighting for.

Delhi lay a thousand miles to the south-east as the crow flew. In practice it was much farther, given the complicated manoeuvrings and battles that would have to be fought along the way. Their marches would take them across some of the most treacherous terrain on earth, over the mighty Hindu Kush mountains, known to Arab geographers as the Stony Girdles of the Earth, with twenty-five-thousand-foot peaks soaring into the heavens. Here lived the warlike Kafir tribes which even Alexander the Great had been unable to subdue. As the amirs had warned, there were rivers and deserts which guarded the approach to Delhi. And even if they managed to overcome all these natural obstacles, they would then face the dreadful beasts of India, the colossal armoured elephants of which blood-curdling tales were told. They could uproot trees and houses, crash through walls, impale men on their sword-like tusks and rip heads clean off with their trunks. From lofty castles on their backs, Indian soldiers rained down arrows upon their enemies. Perhaps the emperor in his later years was miscalculating the host of dangers that lay before him.

Ninety thousand interwoven destinies lay on these plains. Some young men, with tightly drawn, implacable features looked forward to war with a quiet assurance. Plucked from small, obscure lives on the steppes, in the towns and villages among the deserts and mountains, all of them steeped in poverty, they knew that by joining Temur's army they were serving some higher purpose.

Amid the smoke of the campfires that glowed like fireflies in the night, among the sweet smell of roast horse and mutton, the talk was all of war. Wizened veterans would have boasted of their past heroics on the battlefield, telling tall stories to credulous neophytes and describing with as much detail as they could muster how they would give these infidels a slow and excruciating death. Others probably spoke of the treasures they would steal from Delhi, the slaves they would make of their enemies and the beautiful women they would despoil. And as these stories dissolved into the night, the silent young men who dreaded this campaign more than anything in their short lives must have struggled to control a mounting fear.

The emperor was troubled by no such doubts. He moved, as he knew, under almighty Allah's protection, raising the sword of Islam against the infidel. His intelligence told him everything he needed to know. Fratricide, rampant since the death of Firuz Shah in 1388, had torn India apart. The country had degenerated into petty kingdoms – Bengal, Kashmir and the Deccan. Delhi, ancient treasure-house of the empire, was locked in internecine conflict. 'Within ten years five kings, the grandsons and the youngest sons of Firuz, followed one another on the throne of Delhi like transient and embarrassed phantoms,' wrote the historian Sir George Dunbar. 'The state of the country was an open invitation to an invader.'

The invitation was accepted, and in March 1398 the order to march south was given. Ninety thousand soldiers – sons, husbands, fathers, grandfathers – said their prayers and set their eyes towards the Great Snow Mountains of the Hindu Kush.

⚜

The M-39 south from Samarkand, which traces the route by which the Emperor of the World led his men to Delhi in 1398, is a notoriously dangerous road, crumbling and potholed in many places, and the annual death toll is heavy. In winter it is particularly unsafe, and reckless driving among the icy passes of the Zarafshan mountains, part of the Pamir range, accounts for numerous lives.

The road starts climbing almost immediately after leaving Samarkand, pressing forward into High Asia and the distant outlines of the mountains, submerged in haze. There are dusty villages lined with white acacias, Persian walnut, pine and plane. Shepherd boys encourage their flocks along with sticks as the Darhom river sweeps past in full flow. Orchards hang in bright blossom. Mud bricks bake in the sun by the roadside. Apricots dry on rooftops. Old men trot along on donkeys, the long sleeves of their *chapan* gowns flapping like birds' wings as they bump gracelessly up and down.

Soon the M-39 is snaking tortuously uphill into the snowy mountains, and the Ladas, the Uzbek taxi drivers' cars of choice (the choice is limited), labour up the 5,500-foot Takhtakaracha pass with engines screaming. The view from the summit of the pass, named after a palace built in 1398 by Temur at Qara Tepe, thirty miles south of Samarkand, is worth the effort. The country opens up magnificently, overlooking the broad Qashka Darya valley which is dominated by a dry riverbed littered with the debris of what must have been a spectacular landslide. Rocks the size of large houses have detached themselves from the upper slopes of the mountains and tumbled down towards the green fields of wheat and cotton and the villages below. Thousands of feet below the pass the road twists suddenly to avoid the latest rockfall. Somewhere down there, way off in the blurred distance, is Shakhrisabz, the Green City, birthplace of Temur.

The immense scale of this country turns one's thoughts to the unfathomable logistical difficulties of Temur's expedition. How to move an army of ninety thousand with twice that number of horses a thousand miles across the roof of the world? The enormous variety of terrain the army had to cover, and the different climates it was required to endure, would have been the undoing of a lesser leader. Between Samarkand and Delhi there were freezing mountain ranges and scorched deserts, great swathes of land where supplies to provision the soldiers simply did not exist. Everything would have had to be carried by horse. How would they have managed at high altitude, stumbling among the precipices with heavy burdens on their backs as slashing rain and snow raged against them? This mountainscape has lost none of its grandeur since Temur led his army across it. It is big, bleak and raw. What the soldiers thought of it at the time we can only guess at. What we do know is that six hundred years later, with conditions vastly improved, taxi drivers cosily insulated in their heated cars still complain bitterly about the dangerous conditions and the icy passes.

South of Shakhrisabz, a dark smudge on the horizon marks the Hissar mountains. The road continues through villages and hamlets, past orchards and ploughed fields, old homesteads and abandoned plots of land. Flocks of sheep graze on the plain beneath the hills, kicking up glittering veils of dust that linger over them. Farmers fork straw into growing mounds. The occasional *yurt* indicates nomadic families still eking out a living in this wild landscape.

Beyond the Hissar mountains, two days' ride from Shakhrisabz, Temur and his army rode through the famous Temur Darwaza, or Iron Gates of Derbend in the Baysun Tau mountains (literally 'turban-wearing', to describe their mantle of snow). These gates earned their name many centuries before Temur's time. Travelling to Termez in 629, the Buddhist monk Xuan Zang remarked on the double set of heavy wooden doors, reinforced with iron and hung with bells, that guarded the mountain pass. By the early fifteenth century, when Clavijo traversed the pass, the doors had disappeared but the Iron Gates retained their name, in addition to their vital role as a customs and immigration post for Temur's empire. As ever, it was the Spanish envoy who left us the most detailed description of the place at that time.

> The mountain range . . . is very lofty and the pass that traverses it is a narrow cleft where the passage seems to have been cut through by the hand of man, with the mountain wall on either side rising vertical to an immense height. The roadway itself is quite level, passing deep down in the cleft. Here in the midst of surrounding heights stands a village, and the place is known as the Iron Gates. In the whole length of this mountain range there is no other pass to cross it, save this one, which is thus the Guard House of the Imperial city of Samarkand. It is only by this one pass that all who travel up to Samarkand from India can come: nor can those who go down from the Imperial City voyaging to India travel by any other route. The lord Temur is sole master of these Iron Gates, and the revenue is considerable to the state from the customs imposed on all merchants who come from India going to the city of Samarkand and to the regions beyond.

The Iron Gates also represented an expression of Temur's power, for one thousand miles west of the Caspian Sea lay another Temur Darwaza, guarding the Derbend pass through which Tokhtamish had launched his raids on his rival's territories. All the land in between the two Iron Gates, as Clavijo recorded, was controlled by one man. 'Between these Gates of Samarkand and those Gates of Derbend indeed is a distance of at least 1,500 leagues of land and of this great territory, as you must know Temur is lord. He is master of both these Iron Gates, and the Iron Gates of Derbend yield him a very considerable yearly tribute from customs, as do those of Samarkand.'

As he passed through the Iron Gates south of Samarkand, bound for war against the sultanate of Delhi, Temur might have remembered an auspicious journey along the same road twenty-eight years before. In 1370, he rode this way en route to Balkh and a final confrontation with his rival Husayn. Now he sent his prayers towards most compassionate Allah, asking for divine protection in his latest task to defend the faith.

Today, the Iron Gates are a disappointment. A roadside sign marks the Temur Darwaza on a downward slope of the road, in what can best be described as a very minor escarpment. It would not be stretching the bounds of geographical terminology to call this a gorge – it would be breaking them completely. Clavijo's lofty mountains are nowhere near. There is no 'narrow cleft' and the village itself has long disappeared. I asked the taxi driver and the other passengers what had happened to the famous pass through the towering gorge. No one could tell me.

&

At Derbend, the M-39 checks its south-easterly meanderings and heads south with new purpose. It bisects the pretty village of Sairob, whose main claim to fame is a pair of ancient plane trees which would have been mere four-hundred-year-old saplings when Temur's army passed this way. One of them is eighty feet high and has a huge hollowed trunk – with a thirty-five-foot perimeter – you can easily walk into. In 1920 it was the village soviet, where the elders gathered and pontificated over the issues of the day. In 1936, after a spell as a regimental library, it became a village shop. Today it lies empty. Across the road, at the foot of a sprawl of stone cottages which line the hillside, is a spring. According to local legend, the dark grey fish which throng the waters are holy, and therefore protected. Anyone who dares to eat one will die instantly.

Past Sairob the last contours of the Hissar mountains soon splutter out, until the road is slicing south across desert plains towards the ancient city of Termez, the Amu Darya, and Afghanistan. Several miles north of Termez, Uzbekistan's southernmost town, a sign by the road points towards the Hakim at Termezi mausoleum, its most important historical site, a complex containing a tenth-century mausoleum, a twelfth-century mosque and a fifteenth-century *khan-aqah* (dervish hostel).

The monuments honour Abu Abdullah Mohammed ibn Hassan ibn Bashir al Hakim at Termezi, a Sufi mystic and jurist who was, mercifully, given a more concise nickname. 'On account of his deep knowledge and cleverness the contemporaries named him Al Hakim, i.e. a wise person,' reads a marble plaque inside the mausoleum. It goes on to praise his 'honest labour and sacrilegious [sic] life', a reference to his prolific literary output – four hundred or so works, including *The Secrets of Holy Trips* and *Rare Stories about the Prophet Rasul*. Educated in Balkh and already a *haj* at twenty-seven (a title conferred upon those Muslims who have made the pilgrimage to Mecca), Hakim at Termezi led a life of irreproachable holiness until his death in 869. The marble plaque which tells his life story was provided by Temur's son Shahrukh in the fifteenth century.

The most striking feature of the complex is not the individual monuments – handsome enough in their own way, but bland by comparison with those of Samarkand and Bukhara – but the setting. Only yards behind the mausoleum, past flowerbeds teeming with daisies and rich red gladioli, is an electrified fence, on the inside of which stands a second fence of barbed wire. Behind these lies one of the most memorable sights in Central Asia.

Arab geographers of the Middle Ages referred to it as the Jayhun, and included it with the Tigris, Euphrates and Jaxartes (Sir Darya) as one of the four Rivers of Paradise. For much of its 1,800 miles the Oxus of antiquity, the Amu Darya of today, forms the northern border of Afghanistan. It is the longest river in the region. Tumbling down from the Pamir mountains, it is destined to end its course dribbling weakly into the sands far short of the Aral Sea it once fed. But it is not so much the geographical facts which impress, more a sense of this river's place in the history of Central Asia, its role in tumultuous centuries long past.

It is difficult to say exactly why – the romantic setting undoubtedly plays a part – but as soon as you see this steaming band of silver for the first time you understand at once that with all its suggestions of mystery, adventure, history, empire-building and war, with all its redolence of Alexander the Great and Genghis Khan, and the memories of the ancient cities which lined its banks and those of its tributaries – Bukhara, Samarkand, Termez and Balkh – this is one of the great rivers of the world.

&

When Temur arrived in Termez, or Tirmidh as it was then known, in the spring of 1398, the city was rising from the ashes left by Genghis Khan in 1220. For centuries it had thrived at the crossroads of Asia, a prospering Silk Road emporium, with caravans streaming through en route to the markets of Khorasan and India to the south. Well before Islam arrived, Termez was a cradle of Buddhist civilisation, brought across the mountains of Afghanistan by the currents of trade and embraced by King Kanishka of the Kushan dynasty in the second century.* Xuan Zang, the Buddhist monk who passed through the Iron Gates on his way to Termez, counted more than a dozen monasteries during his visit to the city. Within the city walls, that ran for

---

* King Kanishka (78–144) was the greatest king of the Kushan dynasty that ruled over the northern part of the Indian subcontinent, Afghanistan and parts of Central Asia. He is remembered above all as a great patron of Buddhism. A cosmopolitan and tolerant king, he presided over an era in which trade with the Roman empire and the exchange of ideas between East and West flourished. The fusion of these two worlds was best exemplified in the Gandharan school of art, in which Greco-Roman classical lines found new expression in images of the Buddha.

seven miles, were something like 1,100 monks. Zang reached Termez shortly before Buddhism was swept brutally off the stage by the Arab invasion in the dying years of the seventh century. Termez duly transferred its religious devotions to Islam and was integrated into the territories of Transoxiana.

In the tenth and eleventh centuries, though surrounded by great mountains and almost a thousand miles from the nearest coastline, the city found unlikely fame as a port. The boats it built and exported plied the length of the Oxus. By 1333, when Ibn Battutah arrived, a century after the Mongol sacking, new Termez was 'a large and beautiful city, abounding with trees and water', not to mention a palace, a prison, a fine canal, and city walls with nine gates. Its markets heaved with merchants and customers seeking the city's famous soaps and perfumes. 'It abounds in grapes and quinces of an exquisite flavour, as well as in flesh-meats and milk,' the Moroccan continued. 'The inhabitants wash their heads in the bath with milk instead of fuller's earth; the proprietor of every bath-house has large jars filled with milk, and each man as he enters takes a cupful to wash his head. It makes the hair fresh and glossy.'

Visiting Termez in 1404, Clavijo failed to remark upon the shine and bounce of local hairstyles, but still thought it a 'great city'. 'We were liberally entertained, all our needs being amply supplied,' he noted approvingly.

The following centuries saw Termez alternately conquered and destroyed by rival warlords, including Temur's son Shahrukh and his grandson Ulugh Beg. The strategic importance of its position on the Oxus marked it out as a glittering jewel to be seized by one or other ambitious empire-builder. By the nineteenth century, Termez found itself a Russian bulwark against British expansion during the Great Game, when both sides sought to maintain Afghanistan as a buffer state between their empires, using dashing multilingual spies and bribery to advance their cause. In 1937, Fitzroy Maclean's high-spirited arrival shed some light on a forgotten Soviet outpost; but Maclean aside, the city was effectively beyond limits to foreign travellers.*

The town's strategic appeal reasserted itself in 1979, when Soviet tanks first rolled into Afghanistan. For the next decade Termez was the command centre for the Red Army invasion. It was one of the USSR's most inglorious military adventures, however, and in 1989 Termez watched in disbelief as soldiers straggled back across the Oxus after a humiliating retreat. Her *raison d'être* snatched away again, the town quietly staged her own withdrawal from the world stage and sank back into obscurity. Today all that remains of Moscow's tragic imperial blunder are unhappy memories and rows of rusting artillery guns in front of the old fort. Termez is a poverty-stricken ghost town stranded on the sandbanks of the Oxus.

---

* Fitzroy Maclean, the British army officer, envoy of Winston Churchill, writer, politician, spy and fearless traveller, reached Termez after a long and riotous train journey whose only refreshments consisted of untold quantities of vodka and 'pink Soviet sausages'. In *Eastern Approaches*, the classic story of his adventures in Soviet Central Asia, he described his unlikely mission to cross the Oxus by boat from Termez into Afghanistan. Predictably obstructive, the Soviet authorities advised him to return several thousand miles to Moscow overland and then fly to Kabul rather than attempt the river crossing. The unstoppable Maclean favoured the more direct approach. Finding a suitable vessel to make the journey was no easy matter. The boat he finally chose, 'which rejoiced in the name of *The Seventeenth Party Congress* . . . was handicapped by the absence of an engine or motor of any kind'. Its captain was a singular character who informed Maclean he was learning English from a book entitled *London from the Top of an Omnibus*. 'For purposes of conversation, however, his knowledge of the English language seemed to be limited to the one cryptic expression: "Very well by us" of which he was inordinately proud, and it was to repeated shouts of "Very well by us!", heartily reciprocated by myself, that some time later I embarked on *The Seventeenth Party Congress*.' The crossing completed, the crew were counted to ensure no one had fled, and without further ado 'the remarkable craft started off stern first for the Soviet Union as if the whole capitalist world was infected with the plague'.

To follow Temur's route into Afghanistan you must cross the Oxus. In 1398, this was not a problem for the Conqueror of the World. Whenever he wanted to cross a river, he ordered a bridge built. As soon as he and his army had reached the other side, the structure was immediately dismantled. The Oxus was a defining, semi-closed border for his empire, as Clavijo reported.

> None may be given passage from the province of Samarkand to go into the lands to the south of the river unless he has been granted a permit and warrant. This must declare whence he has come and whither he is about to go: and such permit is necessary even though he be a free born native of Samarkand. On the other hand any persons who wish to pass the river going into the Samarkand province may do so unhindered and none need show any warrant for the passage. All the ferry-boats thus have guards stationed in them, set there by order of Temur to oversee and control the passage.

Northbound traffic was welcomed. Southbound departures were not tolerated. There were good practical (and somewhat sinister) reasons for this.

> The true reason why these guards have thus been set here is that Temur . . . has brought to Samarkand in captivity from his wars an immense concourse of folk to people this province of his, causing them to migrate hither from all the conquered provinces. This he has done to repopulate the country of Samarkand and to ennoble the same, and the order above given is that none shall escape him to return home to the place whence they have been brought captive.

In the early twenty-first century, the southbound traveller faced similar difficulties. The so-called Bridge of Friendship linking Uzbekistan to Afghanistan had been closed for two years. Tashkent was no friend of the Taliban. Fearful of Afghanistan exporting radical Islam across the Oxus, the Uzbeks had sealed their side of the bridge.

I made a plea for permission to continue my journey across the border. Beyond the Oxus Afghanistan loomed temptingly in the haze. The commander of the military base, an ethnic Uzbek with large shades, four stars on his epaulettes and an inscrutable air, arrived in a Jeep. 'You have come to a prohibited area without permission and your visit has been recorded,' he told me peremptorily. 'You must leave at once.'

'Sir, the journey I am making is in honour of the great Amir Temur, symbol of your new independent Uzbekistan. I am researching a book on this historical hero. It is essential I cross the Oxus to pay tribute to his mighty conquests.'

He removed his shades and shot me a hard look. 'I don't give a shit about Temur or your book. This is a restricted area. Your time at the border is over. Get out of here. Goodbye.'

෧෧

Temur, of course, was confronted by no such governmental obstruction in 1398. He was the government. Swiftly crossing the Oxus, he led his army south-east past Balkh, scene of his coronation in 1370. For 150 miles they marched on until they reached Andarab, from where the Stony Girdles of the Earth rose before them in all their dreadful splendour. Here Temur left the main body of his army and took a smaller mounted fighting force thirty miles east. As snow fell around them, they crossed the Khawak pass which at 12,600 feet was the natural defence of the marauding Kafir tribes. Since, in Yazdi's words, 'the great Temur always strove to exterminate the infidels, as much to acquire that glory, as to signalise himself by the greatness of his conquests', it was only natural that he should now turn his attention to this warlike race.

Here on the roof of the world, amid the icy peaks and passes of the Hindu Kush, the weather deteriorated rapidly. Temur's men were hardy warriors from the desert and steppe, but of these terrible conditions they had no experience. Horses slipped and stumbled to their deaths. Casualties were high. Travelling by night to avoid losing their foothold on melting ice, the expeditionary force pressed on. In places they came upon precipices which were impassable without ropes. At one, Temur's men had to lower the aged emperor a thousand feet on a litter. They tried the same with the horses, but only two survived, and Temur was forced to walk on foot like the humblest infantryman. The whole body of men was now unmounted. Still he would not call a halt. Whatever the difficulties, and they were mounting by the day, the mountain infidels had to be subdued before he would turn his thoughts to Delhi.

At last the small force reached the home of the Kafir tribes and stormed their mountain stronghold. The fighting was fierce and Temur lost many men, said the chronicle, a guarantee, if only the Kafirs knew it, that he would be merciless in victory. Surrender came too late for them, however, and before long the snows of the Hindu Kush were marked with spreading stains of blood and the trademark towers of skulls. Only now would Temur rejoin his main army and resume his southerly progress.

By August they had reached Kabul, where Temur paused to attend to the business of empire. Ambassadors arrived from the Kipchak princes Idigu and Kutluk-oghlan, who had fought with Temur against Tokhtamish. They repented for their past disobedience when, contrary to their agreement to bring their armies back to Temur, they had 'wandered in the desert like thieves without a home', and expressed their hope that the gracious emperor would 'forget all our sins and faults and cross out with lines of forgiveness the pages of our wrongs'. Another envoy arrived from his former adversary Khizr Khoja, the Moghul khan, pledging his allegiance.

The highlight of Temur's stay in Kabul was the presentation by Shaykh Nur ad-din of all the wealth plundered from Persia in the Five-Year Campaign which had concluded two years previously, in

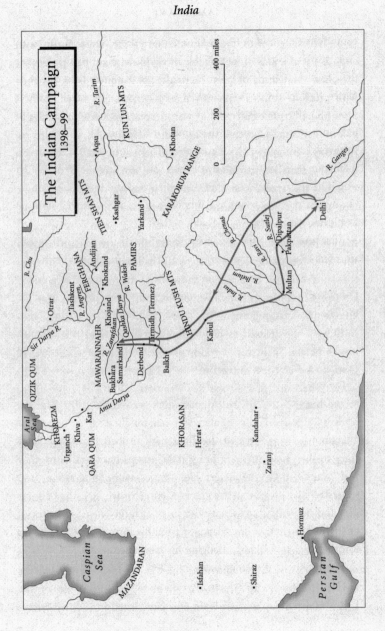

The Indian Campaign
1398–99

400 miles

200

0

R. Tarim

KUN LUN MTS

• Aqsu

• Khotan

KARAKORUM RANGE

TIEN SHAN MTS

• Kashgar

R. Ganges

• Yarkand

• Delhi

R. Chu

PAMIRS

R. Sutlej

R. Chenab

• Andijan

FERGHANA

• Dipalpur

• Khokand

R. Waksh

R. Ravi

R. Jhelum

• Pakpattan

R. Angren

• Tashkent

Khojand

Tirmidh (Termez)

HINDU KUSH MTS

R. Indus

• Multan

Sir Darya R.

• Otrar

Qashka Darya

• Derbend

• Samarkand

R. Zarafshan

MAWARANNAHR

Kabul

QIZIK QUM

• Bukhara

• Balkh

• Kat

Amu Darya

Aral Sea

• Urganch

KHOREZM

• Khiva

QARA QUM

KHORASAN

• Herat

• Kandahar

Caspian Sea

• Zaranj

MAZANDARAN

• Hormuz

• Isfahan

• Shiraz

Persian Gulf

1396. 'He brought with him an immense treasure,' wrote Yazdi, 'with abundance of jewels of inestimable price; likewise animals proper for the chase, and birds of prey; leopards, gold money, belts enriched with precious stones, vests woven with gold, stuffs of all colours, arms and all sorts of utensils for war, Arabian horses with saddles of gold, great camels, several carriages and riding mules, fine stirrups, the straps embroidered with gold and silver; umbrellas, canopies, pavilions, tents and curtains of scarlet and all colours.'

It took the secretaries of the *diwan* three days just to record all these treasures – 'the fingers of the book-keepers grew weary with the writing' – and two days for Temur to see them pass before him in review. As a morale-booster for the troops, of course, this magnificent ceremony was difficult to outdo. Those soldiers who had been dreading the battles that lay ahead now turned their thoughts to the pleasures of plunder. Up to this point everything had gone according to plan, just as the emperor had assured them. The defeat of the wild Kafir tribes, warriors who had refused to bow before Alexander, had been sudden and complete. There was no reason to expect the battles which awaited them to be any less successful. They had crossed the roof of the world. The worst of their journey was over.

⚬⚬

Twenty-first-century Kabul is a ruined city, its historical monuments prised apart, bombed, shot at, plundered, smashed, swept away by centuries of conflict. The past has been forcibly erased by the present. It is a city of derelict palaces, destroyed factories, devastated parks and gardens, hollowed houses, broken mud walls, torn-up roads and shattered lives. Here are the familiar victims of conflict, the veiled widows, beggars young and old, amputees, unemployed men, victims of landmines, sick, malnourished children, proud, poverty-stricken fathers, the flotsam and jetsam cast up by the retreating tides of war. It is a modern-day reincarnation of a city visited in fury by Temur.

After the debacle at Termez, I had entered Afghanistan via Pakistan. Without much hope of success I picked my way through the subdued corridors of Kabul University's damaged cubist sixties buildings to Professor Abdul Baqi, Afghanistan's only specialist on Temur, an elderly man with a blunt nose, full lips and obligatory white beard.

When I asked him what Temurid secrets the city could offer, he smiled sadly. 'I'm afraid you won't find much in Kabul,' he said. The ancient Balar Hissar fortress was a military base closed to visitors. What little Temur had built in the city had long since disappeared.

My disappointment was obvious. A long silence followed.

'You know, there is one thing you should see while you're here,' the professor eventually added. 'Go to Babur's Gardens. They were designed by Temur's most famous descendant. You'll find his tomb there.'

Laid out in the middle of the sixteenth century, Babur's Gardens occupy a large rectangular sweep of ground on the western slopes of Mount Sher-i-Darwaza. One of the grandest horticultural projects the city had ever seen, the gardens were a striking reminder of Temur's magnificent cultural legacy. Today they offer a valuable glimpse into how a city like Kabul would have looked in its full Temurid bloom. The natural adornments were of a grace and sophistication no longer found, an aesthetic triumph built on a scale which blended monumentality with harmony.

From the moment he conquered it in 1504 and made it the first seat of his empire, Babur loved Kabul with a passion, so much so that he asked to be buried in these gardens. Much of his memoirs, a fascinating window into the late Temurid world, is devoted to describing the city. The climate was perfect. 'If the world has another so pleasant, it is not known. Even in the heats, one cannot sleep at night without a fur coat.' Then there were the 'heady' local wines, 'famous for their strength'. Like his world-conquering great-great-great-grandfather, Babur was a prodigious drinker of some renown, writing light-heartedly about one evening when he downed so much wine he could barely stay on his horse. 'Very drunk I must have been, for, when they told me next day that we had galloped loose-rein into camp carrying torches, I could not recall it in the very least.'

When he was not quaffing the fine local wines, Babur was something of a naturalist. He counted thirty-two varieties of wild tulips on the mountainsides and admired the fecundity of the fields and orchards, which produced 'grape, pomegranate, apricot, apple, quince, pear, peach, plum, almond and walnut' in abundance. Oranges, lemons, rhubarb, melons and sugarcane also grew plentifully, and apiaries produced honey. There was no shortage of firewood. Throughout the city and among the valleys of the outlying villages, beneath snow-capped mountains, birds filled the air with their song. There were nightingales, herons, mallards, blackbirds, thrushes, doves, magpies and, most stately of all, cranes, the birds of heaven, 'great birds, in large flocks, and countless numbers'. In the rushing waters of the Kabul river and its tributaries, fishermen took to the banks and 'many are netted and many are taken on wattles fixed in the water'. The city, Babur wrote in a passage which would have interested his ancestor, was 'an excellent trading centre. Down to Kabul every year come 7, 8, or ten thousand horses and up to it, from Hindustan, come every year caravans of ten, fifteen, or twenty thousand heads-of-houses, bringing slaves, white cloth, sugar-candy, refined and common sugars, and aromatic roots. Many a trader is not content with a profit of thirty or forty on ten. In Kabul can be had the products of Khorasan, Rum, Iraq and China, while it is Hindustan's own market.'

New parks, palaces and mosques sprang up during Babur's reign as he sought to beautify the city, just as Temur had done in his own capital. Trees were planted on a rise he named the Four Gardens in memory of the Samarkand he had left behind. One of them, known as the Great Garden, had been seized by Temur's grandson, Ulugh

Beg. Babur bought it from its then owner and described it in some detail in his memoirs. A river descended from the mountain,

> *with gardens green, gay and lovely on either bank. Its water is quite pure and so cold that it need never be iced to drink ... Around this enclosure large plane trees spread their shade, making pleasant sitting places beneath, and through it runs a perennial stream, large enough to turn a mill wheel. I ordered its winding course to be made straight ... Lower down there is a fountain called the Revered Three Friends, with oak trees growing on hillocks at either side ... On the way down from this fountain towards the plain many places are covered with the flowering Arghwan [Judas] tree, which grows nowhere else in the country ... If, the world over, there is a place to match this when the Arghwans are in full bloom, their yellow mingling with red, I do not know it.*

As late as 1977, Nancy Hatch Dupree, an expert on the cultural heritage of Afghanistan, wrote admiringly of Babur's Gardens:

> *On entering, the first structure to meet the eye is the charming summer pavilion built by the Amir Abdur Rahman (1880–1901). It is shaded by magnificent plane trees so beloved by the Moghuls [Mughals]. From the graceful pillared veranda one looks down upon terraced gardens dotted with fountains. Inside, the ceilings are beautifully painted in the style of the late nineteenth century ...*

Two decades of fighting had changed the place beyond all recognition. Dupree's description was of another world. Babur's Gardens were no more than a giant slope of wasteland overlooking a visibly shattered city. Mortars had ripped into the park and craters had replaced flowerbeds. The neat lawns which once stretched down towards the city had disappeared altogether. Fountains had been smashed and removed. The once magnificent plane trees were charred trunks, hacked down and burnt as precious firewood.

My guide in the gardens was Shukur, an Afghan in his early thirties.

He had fled to Pakistan after both his parents were killed in a rocket attack on Kabul sixteen years earlier. He used to visit the gardens regularly with his family, he told me, but had not returned to the capital since his parents' death. Seeing the extent of the damage to Babur's beloved gardens was a powerful shock. As we surveyed the desolation around us he grew tearful. 'There used to be lots of plane trees here,' he said, pointing to another charred trunk. 'There were flowerbeds filled with flowers, everywhere there were bushes. Many families came here for picnics in the afternoons and weekends. It was a very beautiful place. It's all gone now. Fighting has killed everything.'

We continued up the barren slope to Babur's tomb, next to a badly damaged marble mosque built by the Mughal emperor Shah Jahan in 1646. Next to it was an empty swimming pool with a broken diving board. In the nineties, the 'charming' summer pavilion remarked upon by Nancy Dupree succumbed to the ravages of war.

The tomb itself consists of a simple slab of marble on a raised platform grazed by random bullets. Above it are these words:

> *Only this mosque of beauty, this temple of nobility, constructed for the prayer of saints and the epiphany of cherubs, was fit to stand in so venerable a sanctuary as this highway of archangels, this theatre of heaven, this light-garden of the God-forgiven angel king whose rest is the garden of heaven, Zahiruddin Mohammed Babur the Conqueror.**

---

* According to another epitaph: 'In the year 937, on the 6th of the 1st Jemadi [26 December 1530], as the Emperor was in the Char Bagh [garden near Agra] which he had made, he was seized with a serious illness and bade farewell to this transitory world. Let it suffice to say that he possessed eight fundamental qualities: lofty judgement, noble ambition, the art of victory, the art of government, the art of conferring prosperity upon his people, the talent of ruling mildly, the people of God, ability to win the hearts of his soldiers, love of justice.'

Babur had chosen his burial place with care. It gave the finest views over the city. Warfare had disfigured this picture, and many of the buildings which rose into the skyline were skeletal ruins, beyond repair. Far beneath us on the plain loomed the stark outline of rocket-savaged Habibiya high school, a building which had been hit so many times it looked like a concrete colander. In the distance beyond was the war-torn outline of Darulaman Palace, built for King Amanullah Khan in 1923. Yet for all this, Kabul managed to retain its natural beauty. Beneath a shameless blue sky a veil of haze drifted upwards from the amphitheatre of mountains which girdle the city. Fighting had raged here in recent times, but the flourishing pockets of green suggested that the parks and gardens had weathered the onslaught. Just as it had done since Kabul was founded at least 2,500 years ago, the Kabul river meandered dreamily through the city.

Babur had asked that nothing should cover his grave, so that rain could fall and sun could shine on him. For a long time after his Afghan wife Bibi Mubarika (Blessed Lady) Yusufzai brought his body back from Agra to Kabul, his instructions were honoured. But in the reign of King Nadir Shah (1929–33), a marble stone was installed over the grave, together with a pavilion to protect it from the elements. Ironically, the recent fighting had helped fulfil the last wish of Babur. Gunfire had removed much of the roof, which now contained more rectangles of sky than tiles. It was an oddly inappropriate monument to a man of such genius, but at least it had survived.

'The people who did this had no respect for our history,' Shukur said softly. 'They were not good men. Looting and destroying, that was what interested them. That was all they knew.'

Listening to these wistful recollections, the stories of plunder six centuries after the rampages of Temur's hordes, I recalled Ibn Battutah's description of Kabul. He had passed through in 1332 in the course of his epic peregrinations across the world. Then, as now, destruction was the order of the day. Kabul, he wrote, was 'once a large city; but it is now, for the most part, in ruins'.*

🍥

With the inspection of his fabulous treasures at an end in Kabul, Temur ordered the army to continue south in three divisions. Sultan Mahmud Khan, the puppet Chaghatay ruler whom Temur had installed in 1388 after the death of his father Suyurghatmish, took the left wing towards Delhi. Sulayman Shah led the vanguard to clear

---

* A visit to Kabul in the summer of 2004 was a happier experience. After the departure of the Taliban in late 2001, the Afghan capital was pulling itself together again, helped by an army of NGOs and UN agencies, not to mention the 5,500 troops from thirty-three nations who made up the International Security Assistance Force. Reconstruction was the order of the day, and Babur's Gardens were one of the many beneficiaries of the new climate of peace and development. Through a $3 million restoration programme carried out under the auspices of the Aga Khan Trust for Culture, the gardens were steadily being transformed. What four years earlier had been a barren slope of earth was now green, and getting greener. Five hundred trees had been planted – plane, apricot, apple, mulberry, fig, walnut, pomegranate – and another 1,500 were due to be planted in 2005, including wild cherry, which Babur is supposed to have introduced from north of Kabul, cypresses, hawthorn, roses and jasmine. 'The idea is to restore the original character of the garden,' Ratish Nanda, a conservation architect with the Aga Khan Trust for Culture, told me. 'Babur was always very careful looking after these gardens. Even when he was in India, he continually sent messages to his governor telling him to take care of them, reminding him to look after the plants and sending him very specific instructions.'

Restoration work had been complicated by the fact that for much of the past twenty years the gardens had been on the front line between warring factions. Ordnance was everywhere. In one month alone, Nanda's team uncovered thirty rocket-propelled grenades and thirteen artillery shells. How sustainable the restoration work would prove was anyone's guess. 'Once this project is completed in 2006, our hope is that the local population will protect it, but there is always a worry at the back of my mind,' Nanda admitted. In Afghanistan, peace can never be taken for granted. Without ISAF's presence in Kabul, many fear the city – and the country – would tear itself apart again.

the way through hostile territory. Temur himself ranged south to meet his grandson Pir Mohammed, who was occupied with the siege of the holy city of Multan, in what is today the Pakistani province of Punjab.

By September the emperor reached the Indus, at the very spot, said Yazdi, where Jalal ad-din, king of Khorezm, swam across in flight from the wrathful Genghis. Another bridge was constructed and within two days the army had crossed the great river. But more obstacles lay ahead: first the Jhelum and shortly afterwards the Chenab and Ravi rivers. Fearfully Temur's amirs had warned of the difficulties of overcoming these natural defences which guarded the approach to Delhi. None proved a significant obstacle, however. The army pressed on.

In October Temur stopped at the Sutlej river for his rendezvous with Pir Mohammed. Multan, the City of Saints, had mounted a vigorous defence before it fell to the Tatar invaders. After a siege lasting six months, conditions inside the city were intolerable. 'The inhabitants were in such great want of victuals, that they were constrained to eat unclean things, and even dead bodies,' wrote Yazdi. Outside the city walls, the situation of Pir Mohammed's men had been scarcely better. Racked by disease, the great majority of his horses had perished, prompting a rebellion by the recently conquered local rulers. Only when news of Temur's imminent arrival reached the rebels did they think better of their rising and withdraw in rapid flight. Pir Mohammed was congratulated by his grandfather for subduing the enemy. His reward was thirty thousand fresh horses and the command of the right wing.

Closing in on Delhi, Temur swept through the Punjab, driving all before him. He took particular care to take revenge on those who had risen up against his grandson. One by one whole towns and villages emptied in terror as the conqueror approached, put them to the sword and burnt them to the ground. At Bhatnir, refugees from

Dipalpur and Pakpattan crowded beneath the city walls as Temur's army bore down on them. Their efforts to flee were in vain. Those who escaped the massacre were beaten and carried off as prisoners. The slaughter was so intense the city stank with rotting corpses, the court chronicle reported.

By December, Temur was poised to strike. Everything on the path to Delhi had fallen to him. It only remained to seize the greatest prize. At Loni, north of the city, he set up camp and surveyed the terrain from raised ground above the Jumna river. 'A great city, where men skilled in various arts are gathered; a home of merchants, a mine of gems and perfumes', Delhi lay invitingly before his army. Though she had been perilously weakened by internal division, within her walls was an army of ten thousand horse, between twenty and forty thousand infantry, and 120 elephants equipped for war.

The first skirmish came when Temur's reconnaissance party of seven hundred cavalry was attacked by the forces of Mallu Khan, who was then ruling Delhi through Sultan Mahmud Khan. The Tatars held off the Indians and returned safely to camp, but there were important consequences. First, Temur had managed to tempt Mallu into battle, albeit little more than a scuffle. This augured well. After the interminable siege of Multan, Temur was minded to take Delhi as quickly as possible. He did not want to be forced to sit and wait for the city to surrender from starvation. Far better to lure Mallu into a pitched battle and settle the issue without delay. Second, the rush of troops against the Tatars had been met with roars of approval from the hundred thousand Hindus taken prisoner en route to Delhi. Such was the fervour of their reaction, born out of hopes of liberation, that Temur, fearing a rebellion in his rearguard, gave orders for each and every one to be killed on the spot. The command was to be obeyed on pain of death. Even the holy men travelling with Temur's army were required to act as executioners, and many were their tears as they sent innocent men and women to their deaths in cold blood.

'The history of mankind cannot furnish another example of so horrid an act of deliberate cruelty,' wrote the nineteenth-century historian Sir Malcolm Price, 'yet the being who perpetrated it has been exalted by historians and poets into a demi-god; and several, not contented with ascribing to him that valour, policy, and martial skill, which he undoubtedly possessed, have extolled him for his numberless virtues; and, above all, for his justice and clemency.'

Perhaps this unexpected butchering of captives added to the sense of foreboding within Temur's ranks. Certainly there was real fear among his men. Of greatest concern were the mighty Indian elephants, of which they had heard dark stories in Samarkand and had now seen for themselves in the opening skirmish. Covered in heavy armour-plate, carrying flame-throwers, archers and crossbowmen in protected turrets on their backs, and armed with tusk-mounted scimitars that were rumoured to be poisoned, they made a terrifying sight. Arrows and sabres were no use against them.

'The rows of mighty elephants, clad in complete steel, emptied the brains of the chieftains of their ardour,' wrote the sixteenth-century historian Khwandamir. 'Since they had never seen a battle with elephants, and on the subject of their dreadful aspect, and the power of their deeds, they had heard exaggerated accounts of these strange animals, hence they entertained great fears and regarded the overcoming of the elephants as an impossibility; and the misgivings of the noble and the great on this account had been raised to such a pitch, that at the time of appointing the position of the officers, when his majesty the Sahib-Qiran [Temur] asked the distinguished persons and accomplished scholars of exalted rank, which place they liked . . . [they] answered that their place was to be with the ladies.' It was yet another test of Temur's leadership and tactical acumen. The amirs, officers and men needed to be reassured. A strategy for combating the elephants had to be devised.

Temur ordered his soldiers to dig deep trenches, reinforced with ramparts, to protect their positions. Next, he had men fashion caltrops, three-pronged iron stakes, which were then strewn across the elephants' path. Buffaloes were tied together at the neck and feet by leather thongs and lined up in front of the trenches. Camels were also roped together with wood and dried grass on their backs. The archers were told to concentrate their fire on the exposed *mahouts* who controlled the elephants.

With the preparations complete, attention turned to the court astrologers. Prior to joining battle, it was customary for them to pronounce their satisfaction that the planets were in an auspicious position. This time, whether through lingering fears of the elephants or other less worldly concerns, they expressed unease about the timing of Temur's plans. To no avail. For once, the Lord of the Fortunate Conjunction declared himself in no wise interested in the conjunction of the planets or the state of the heavens. The cowering astrologers were scolded. Temur would not wait for their verdict, favourable or otherwise.

Publicly, he called for his Koran to be brought before him. With marvellous convenience it was opened at a passage proclaiming the annihilation of a people by the perseverance of its powerful enemy. According to Ghiyath ad-din Ali, author of an original Persian diary of the Indian campaign, Temur read from the chapter of Yunis (Jonah):

> *This present life is like the rich garment with which the earth adorns itself when watered by the rain We send down from the sky. Crops, sustaining man and beast, grow luxuriantly: but, as the earth's tenants begin to think themselves its masters, down comes Our Scourge upon it, by night or by day, laying it waste, as though it did not blossom but yesterday ... Those that do good works shall have a good reward, and more besides. Neither blackness nor misery shall overcast their faces. They are the heirs of Paradise, wherein they shall abide forever. As for those that have done evil, evil shall be rewarded with evil. Misery will oppress them (they shall have none to protect them from God), as though*

patches of the night's own darkness veiled their faces. They are the heirs of the Fire, wherein they shall abide forever.

The good news coursed through the ranks. What the stars could not support, the Koran could confirm. Once again Allah had spoken. Delhi was theirs for the taking.

&

On 17 December 1398, the army of Mallu and Sultan Mahmud marched through the gates of Delhi to give battle beneath a heavy sky. The Indian troops drew up with the elephants in the centre, each beast carrying its deadly contingent of men armed to the teeth. Both sides drew into the traditional formation employed by Muslim armies at this time, with left and right wings, a centre and an advanced guard.

Temur had stationed himself on high ground overlooking the field of battle. As was customary in the final few moments before the fighting began, while the tension occasioned by the imminence of bloodshed bristled among the opposing armies, the emperor dismounted, threw himself onto the ground and beseeched Allah for His blessings. He had done all he could. The rest was in the hands of the Almighty.

'So hot a battle was never seen before,' Yazdi reported. 'The fury of soldiers was never carried to so great excess; and so frightful a noise was never heard: for the cymbals, the common kettle-drums, the drums and trumpets, with the great brass kettle-drums which were beat on the elephants' backs, the bells which the Indians sounded, and the cries of the soldiers, were enough to make even the earth to shake.' Amid this terrible cacophony, the skies darkened as Temur's archers loosed their arrows against the Indian right wing. Mallu and Sultan Mahmud responded by directing their left wing and vanguard against the Tatar right, but in a brilliant manoeuvre they were overcome at their flank and rear by Temur's vanguard.

After losing several hundred men in their first charge, they broke in rout. Temur had seized the initial advantage.

Watching the scattered ranks of their left wing in retreat, Mallu and Sultan Mahmud gave a prearranged signal. The plain shook with thunder as the war elephants lumbered forward in tight formation, the heavily-armed men in their miniature castles poised to strike. Pounding the ground as they approached the Tatar lines, the huge armoured beasts struck fear in Temur's men. Following orders, the archers directed their fire at the *mahouts*, but still the elephants advanced.

From his vantage point, Temur saw the commotion caused by the elephants among his men. He had made preparations to deal with these exotic beasts of war. It was time to unveil them. The amirs ordered the camels bearing bundles of dried grass and wood to be driven forward. As the elephants approached, the loads were set alight and the camels rushed forward in panic. Suddenly the elephants were being charged by roaring camels on fire. Their response was instinctive. They wheeled round in terror and charged headlong into their own troops, trampling them to the ground, impaling themselves on the vicious caltrops and causing mayhem among the Indian lines. 'The Indian troops on the left and the right fell on the ground like shadows,' wrote Khwandamir. 'The heads of the Indians were reduced to atoms, they were like coconuts dropped from the trees.'

The valiant Pir Mohammed led a charge at the head of the right wing, and soon the Indians were in full retreat, cut down without mercy as they sought the safety of Delhi's city walls. Another prince, the fifteen-year-old Khalil, distinguished himself by overcoming an elephant, together with its guards, and marching it back as a gift to his grandfather. Temur was so impressed by the young man's bravery that he awarded him the title of Sultan. The sixteenth-century Muslim historian Ferishta wrote disparagingly of the Hindu defence of Delhi: 'The Indians were, in a very short time, totally routed, without making one brave effort to save their country, their lives, or their property.'

The battle was over. 'The sun of victory and triumph rose from the east of his majesty's banners and a whirlwind of happiness powdered the eyes of the enemy with the dust of misfortune,' wrote Ghiyath ad-din Ali, diarist of the Indian campaign. 'So great were the heaps of corpses that the battlefield resembled a dark mountain and rivers of blood rushed across it in mighty waves.'

Temur's Tatars had secured one of their greatest victories. Outdoing both Genghis and Alexander, they had marched across the most forbidding mountains of the world, crossed rivers and deserts and brought one of the richest cities in the world to its knees. Its divided rulers had failed to defend it from the northern invaders. Now its untold treasures lay before them.

As the battlefield smouldered around him, Temur moved smoothly from the pain of war to the pleasures of peace. The day after the battle he entered Delhi in triumph. His standard was erected on the walls of the city and the sumptuous imperial pavilion unfurled and pitched. Into it filed the trembling *sharifs*, *qadis*, court officials and men of letters, confirming the formal surrender of Delhi and pleading for their lives now that Mallu and Sultan Mahmud had abandoned them to the mercy of the conqueror. Beautiful music played around the emperor as he spared them in return for a crippling ransom.

How sweet this victory must have tasted as, one by one, the hundred or so surviving elephants were brought before Temur and made to kneel in submission and bellow their greetings to him. Once they had paid their respects to the new master of Delhi, they were sent to the far corners of his empire, to the princes of the line in Tabriz, Shiraz and Herat, to Prince Taharten at Arzinjan and Shaykh Ibrahim of Shirvan. Messengers accompanied them, spreading news of this famous victory to the farthest reaches of Asia, while in the mosques of Delhi the Friday prayers were called forth in Temur's name.

With these agreeable formalities over, it was time to move on to the serious business of calculating – and then removing – the treasures of the city. Temur's officials were busy collecting money and belongings from the inhabitants of Delhi. At this stage there were no signs of trouble. The surrender of the city had passed peacefully and a ransom had been agreed. Nevertheless, an ominous trend was underway. For several days after the battle, the number of Tatar soldiers entering Delhi rose rapidly. Some were tasked with separating the inhabitants of Delhi, who had been granted an amnesty, from those taking refuge in the city, who had not. Others were engaged in assessing the ransoms to be paid by householders and property-owners. Several thousand besides, said Khwandamir, were inside the city walls to requisition sugar and corn for the troops.

Still others had entered without official sanction. These were soldiers who came to satisfy their curiosity, satiate their sexual appetites or indulge their taste for plunder. When word came that the ladies of the imperial household wished to make a tour of the conquered city, the gates were opened and not locked up again for hours. The numbers of Tatars inside Delhi swelled again. Yazdi's account mentions fifteen thousand soldiers entering the city at this time.

It is impossible to identify exactly what precipitated the chain of events that now unfolded and that would be remembered with horror by Indians for centuries to come. Perhaps it was a single instance of rape or murder that ignited local passions. Maybe all that was required to unleash destruction was a disagreement between one hot-headed Tatar and a furious Indian protecting his property. Whatever the immediate cause, the carnage that ensued was momentous even by Temur's standards. Casting scorn on the Indians' feeble resistance, Ferishta portrays the terrors of a city given over to fire and the sword.

The Hindus, according to custom, seeing their females disgraced, and their wealth seized by the soldiery, shut the gates, set fire to their houses, murdered their wives and children, and rushed out on their enemies. This led to a general massacre so terrible that some streets were blocked by the heaps of the dead; and the gates being forced, the whole Mongol army stormed inside, and a scene of horror ensued easier to be imagined than described. The desperate courage of the Dehlians was at length cooled in their own blood, and throwing down their weapons, they at last submitted like sheep to the slaughter . . . In the city the Hindus were at least ten to one superior in number to the enemy; and had they possessed souls, it would have been impossible for the Mongols, who were scattered about in every street, house, and corner, laden with plunder, to have resisted.

Through the streets the Tatars advanced, chasing the beleaguered Indians into Old Delhi, where they sought sanctuary in the Cathedral Mosque. With a detachment of five hundred men, two of Temur's amirs smashed into the mosque and 'sent to the abyss of hell the souls of these infidels, of whose heads they erected towers, and gave their bodies for food to the birds and beasts of prey. Never was such a terrible slaughter and desolation heard of.' For three days the massacre continued. Yazdi blamed it on what he called the 'ill conduct' of the inhabitants. As a court historian, he was hardly likely to do otherwise. Ghiyath ad-din Ali, who wrote the original report of events at Delhi, recorded how the Tatar soldiers rampaged through the city like 'hungry wolves falling on a flock of sheep or eagles swooping on weaker birds'.

Whatever kindled the conflagration, Delhi, the city of gems and perfumes, was a blazing inferno reeking with the stench of slaughter. Carousing in his tent, celebrating his famous victory with a magnificent banquet in the company of the ladies of the imperial household, Temur was reportedly unaware of the bloodbath. While the amirs in the city were frantically – and unsuccessfully – trying to bring the marauding mob to heel, none of their colleagues apparently dared to disturb the emperor at play. These accounts are somewhat suspect, however, not least because Temur was not a man who lost control. It is doubtful he was not well informed about events within Delhi's city walls. Elsewhere in the sources, much is made of the discipline of his troops, upheld on pain of death. Plunder, until official permission had been granted, was a serious crime. Knowing this, would these soldiers really have dared to cross their emperor?

With or without his sanction, the Tatars helped themselves to the coffers of Delhi. Teeming with treasures, these shocked the soldiers by their sheer opulence. There was gold and silver without end, jewellery, pearls and precious stones, coins and rich clothing; so much, said Yazdi, that words could scarcely describe it all. Above all, there were slaves, the customary trophies of battle – ordinary citizens of Delhi, men and women alike, thrown into servitude directly upon their capture. Many of the Tatars marched out of the city with a column of 150. The poorest soldier seized at least twenty.

For two weeks Temur remained in Delhi, accepting the surrender of local Indian princes and adding their gifts to his lengthening train of treasure. Master craftsmen and the masons of Delhi, renowned for their excellence, were thrown in chains for the return march to Samarkand. The chronicles remark on one present which particularly impressed Temur, a pair of white parrots which for years had graced the antechambers of the Indian sultans.

Then, abruptly, the emperor gave the order to leave. One of the local princes, Khizr Khan, founder of the Sayid dynasty, who claimed descent from the Prophet Mohammed, was quickly installed as Temur's governor of what is today Punjab and Upper Sindh.* Temur

---

* Delhi itself was left without a ruler and, like the rest of northern India, remained racked by internecine conflict among the princes. Mallu Shah and Sultan Mahmud returned to the fray, joined in time by other would-be rulers. By the time Khizr Khan captured the city in 1414, these depredations had taken their toll and the once illustrious kingdom of

was less interested in the administration of empire – history has judged this as one of his greatest failings – than the glory of conquest.

Laden with booty, the army made laborious progress on its northward journey, sometimes as little as four miles in a day. One of Temur's first stops was the celebrated marble mosque built by Sultan Firuz Shah on the banks of the Jumna, where the emperor gave thanks to Allah for his recent success, and which may have inspired Temur's monumental Cathedral Mosque in Samarkand.

This was to be no leisurely return, however. More battles awaited the Tatars, for the *jihad* had not ended. There were still many more infidels to be killed or converted. First the army swung round to the north-east, sacking the stronghold of Meerut before reaching the Ganges and slaughtering forty-eight boatloads of Hindus in addition to an undisclosed number of Zoroastrians. Into the foothills of Kashmir and the Himalayas Temur's forces continued, fighting twenty or so pitched battles and plundering profitably wherever and whenever the occasion presented itself. The Muslim Shah of Kashmir submitted with promises of a vast tribute. The Hindu Raja of Jammu was captured in an ambush and hastily converted to the true faith. An expedition was sent against Lahore to punish a prince who had already submitted to Temur but had conspicuously failed to reappear as instructed. Lahore was seized and the careless prince executed.

By March Temur had satisfied his lust for war and treasure. He said goodbye to the princes of the royal line and gave them permission to return to their provinces. In Kashmir, to the great concern of his amirs and princes, he had been stricken by a tumour on his arm. Now, as he forged north out of Kabul, he developed boils on both hands and feet, so serious an incapacity that he could no longer remain on horseback. His return journey through the lofty Hindu

---

Delhi had shrunk so dramatically that its territories barely extended beyond the city walls.

Kush had to be made in a litter borne by mules. During one day alone, wrote Yazdi, the route was so circuitous the royal entourage had to cross the same river forty-eight times.

In the first days of spring, as the trees blossomed in welcome, Temur crossed the Oxus and at Termez was met by the bulk of the imperial household. Here was the Great Queen Saray Mulk-khanum, his most senior wife, closely followed by Tukal-khanum, the Lesser Queen, and Tuman-agha, his latest and most youthful wife. Here also were two of the emperor's grandsons, Ulugh Beg and Ibrahim Sultan, joined by several of the princesses and a delegation of senior officials from Samarkand. All hurried forward to greet and congratulate the old emperor on his most recent triumph.

The royal party pressed on towards Samarkand in high spirits, stopping for a fortnight at Shakhrisabz where Temur paid his respects at the tombs of the saints and that of his own father, Amir Taraghay. As they neared his beloved capital, thoughts turned to the triumphal entry that lay only hours away. It would be the most spectacular yet.

∴

One thousand miles away, Delhi lay in ruins. The extraordinary wealth amassed by generations of Indian sultans had vanished in a matter of days. Temur had sown devastation across an already damaged kingdom and northern India had suffered one of its most catastrophic invasions. Stores of grain and standing crops had been destroyed. Fields lay empty. Famine and disease were rife. Heaps of putrefying corpses poisoned air and water alike. Towers of rotting heads rose from the rubble. The skies were silent. 'Delhi was utterly ruined and those of its people who were left, died, while for two months not a bird moved wing in the city.'

The Scourge of God had left his terrible mark and darkened the pages of Indian history. It took more than a century for Delhi to recover.

8

'This Pilgrimage of Destruction'

1399–1401

> '"You see me here a poor, lame, decrepit mortal. Yet by my arm
> has the Almighty been pleased to subdue the kingdoms of Iran,
> Turan and the Indies. I am not a man of blood, and God is my
> witness that in all my wars I have never been the aggressor, and
> that my enemies have always been the authors of their own
> calamity." During this peaceful conversation the streets of Aleppo
> streamed with blood and re-echoed with the cries of mothers and
> children, with the shrieks of violated virgins. The rich plunder that
> was abandoned to his soldiers might stimulate their avarice, but
> their cruelty was enforced by the peremptory command of produc-
> ing an adequate number of heads, which, according to his custom,
> were curiously piled in columns and pyramids.'
>
> EDWARD GIBBON, *The Decline and Fall of the Roman Empire*

The crowds gasped as captured elephants, decked out in brilliant
colours, strode through the streets of Samarkand. Few, if any, of the
citizens had ever set eyes on such gargantuan creatures. Fabulous
stories about these great beasts told how they were invulnerable to
swords and arrows, could uproot trees just by running past them

TAMERLANE

and toss man and mount to their destruction with their swinging trunks. As Temur rode past, slaves scattered precious stones beneath his horse's hoofs. Others threw gold dust and pearl seed into the air to honour him. Men and women cheered and clapped and shouted until they were hoarse. Spring sunlight glinted on the blue domes of mosques and palaces that rose throughout the city and on the many minarets tiled in azure majolica. Never had the emperor's triumphal homecoming appeared so exotic and magnificent. After three decades watching Temur depart from the capital on one or other campaign, waiting for news of his battles until, several years later, he reappeared victorious, there was a sense of inevitability about his successful return. All that seemed to change, rising inexorably beyond the mortal sphere, was the scale of his victories and the richness of his plundered treasures. Now India had bared its coffers to him and Samarkand ruled the world.

In a style befitting this latest whirlwind conquest which had taken him a little over a year to accomplish, Temur made a grand, stately progress through his kingdom to celebrate it. After a fortnight holding court in the as yet unfinished Ak Sarai palace at Shakhrisabz, he continued north, first to the rolling lawns and pastures of Takhta Qaracha park, one of Samarkand's most luxurious, thence to the Garden of Heart's Delight. His route was a roll-call of his tireless building works: to the city baths; the Shah-i-Zinda complex of shrines; the madrassah of Great Queen Saray Mulk-khanum; then a further round of park-hopping, from the Garden of the Plane Trees to the Model of the World, Paradise Garden and High Garden.

As Samarkand simmered with excitement at the emperor's return, Temur announced his greatest construction project yet. The Cathedral Mosque would be a tribute both to his countless conquests and to the God who had enabled them. Scores of Indian masons, taken prisoner after the sacking of Delhi, were put to work alongside craftsmen from Basrah and Baghdad, Azerbaijan, Fars and Damascus as well as artisans from Mawarannahr. The mosque was still being built when the Spanish envoy Clavijo arrived in Samarkand in late 1404 to find Temur directing much of the work in person, shouting instructions and throwing chunks of roast meat to the workers sweating in the foundations.

'At length, under his conduct, this great edifice was finished,' the dutiful Yazdi reported. 'It contained 480 pillars of hewn stone, each seven cubits high. The arched roof was covered with marble, neatly carved and polished: and from the architrave of the entablature to the top of the roof were nine cubits. At each of the four corners of the mosque without was a minaret. The doors were of brass: and the walls, as well without as within, as also the arches of the roof, were adorned with writing in relief, among which is the chapter of the cavern, and other parts of the Alcoran. The pulpit, and reading-desk, where the prayers for the emperor were read, were of the utmost magnificence: and the niche of the altar, covered with plates of iron gilt, was likewise of perfect beauty.'

For a while, at least, the Cathedral Mosque marked the apotheosis of Temur's architectural creations. But Yazdi neglected to relate how quickly this monument to the emperor's hubris started to collapse, the result of its hasty construction. As a court historian, this would have been impolitic in the extreme.

※

All of a sudden, the high-spirited celebrations accompanying Temur's return were dramatically interrupted. From the Caspian came dark news in the beautiful shape of Khan-zada, widow of Temur's first-born Jahangir and wife of Miranshah, who ruled the Hulagid kingdom in his father's name. Trembling before the Conqueror of the World, this princess who could trace her ancestry to Genghis told him how Miranshah's behaviour had degenerated appallingly and how he was, as she spoke, plotting to seize Temur's throne. Pleading for mercy and sobbing uncontrollably, she threw herself at the emperor's feet, saying she could no longer suffer her husband's intolerable abuse and would never return to him.

Though shocking, the news did not come as a complete surprise to Temur. Already, on his way back from India, word had reached him of Miranshah's uncontrolled debauchery. There were stories of riotous gambling, of marathon drinking bouts inside mosques, and of gold coins being thrown from palace windows into the hands of frenzied mobs. The state treasury had been bled dry to fund the prince's hedonistic pursuits.* Further evidence of his disturbed mind came with reports that he had desecrated the tomb of the Mongol prince Oljeytu in the famous green-domed mosque of Sultaniya. Another, that of the Persian historian Rashid ad-din, he ordered to be destroyed and the bones transferred to the Jewish cemetery. Other fine buildings throughout the city were also being summarily demolished. Clavijo doubted reports of Miranshah's insanity, however, attributing his bizarre behaviour to nothing more than insecurity and attention-seeking. The Spaniard quoted one report which had Miranshah saying to himself: 'Forsooth I am the son of the greatest man in the whole world, what now can I do in these famous cities, that after my days I may be always remembered?' Indulging in a very personal building spree, according to this account, the decadent prince soon realised that none of his monuments in any way surpassed those of his predecessors.

> Considering this he was heard to say: 'Shall nothing remain of me for a remembrance?' and added 'They shall at least remember me for some reason or other,' and forthwith commanded that all those

---

* These bacchanalian revelries had taken their toll on the prince's health and physique, according to Clavijo, who met Miranshah and was entertained by him in Sultaniya, en route to Samarkand. The Spaniard described him as 'a man of advanced age, being about forty years old, big and fat, and he suffers much from the gout'.

> buildings of which we have spoken should be demolished, in order
> that men might say: that though Miranshah forsooth could build
> nothing, he yet could pull down the finest buildings of the whole
> world.

As for his plotting to succeed Temur, Arabshah had Miranshah writing
a letter to Temur whose contents, if true, would surely have resulted
in his immediate execution. It was time, said the upstart prince with
excruciating directness, for the emperor to make way for the next
generation.

> Certainly through your advanced age and weak constitution and
> infirmity you are now unequal to raising the standards of empire
> and sustaining the burdens of leadership and government and
> above all things it would befit your condition to sit as a devotee
> in a corner of the mosque and worship your Lord, until death
> came to you. There are now men among your sons and grandsons,
> who would suffice to you for ruling your subjects and armies and
> undertake to guard your kingdoms and territory ... You govern
> men, nay also you administer justice, but unjustly; you feed, but
> it is on their wealth and corn; you act the defender, but by burning
> their hearts and ribs; you lay foundations, but foundations of
> afflictions; you go forward, but on a crooked road ...

Whatever the truth of Miranshah's mental state, his military talents,
or rather the lack of them, gave his father greatest cause for concern.
The record of recent years suggested he was ill equipped to rule a
notoriously unruly region populated by Georgians, Turkmens,
Armenians and Azerbaijanis who were invariably loath to recognise
Temur's supremacy. Sultan Ahmed Jalayir of Baghdad, having been
expelled from his capital by Temur in 1393, had reoccupied it the
following year. Miranshah had attempted to drive him out for good
but his mission had ended in ignominious retreat. To the north, he
had been similarly humiliated. Sultan Ahmed's son had been hard
pressed under siege by the Tatars in the city of Alanjiq in Azerbaijan.

Instead of pressing home his advantage and storming the stronghold, Miranshah had been overcome by a rescue party of Georgians. He had lost both his quarry and the city.

Such a poor performance did not commend itself to his father. Although the chronicles report how Temur loved drinking bouts, particularly after great battles, or at weddings and festivals, the difference was that unlike Miranshah, he did not let the drinking get in the way of either winning wars or administering his empire. The answer to the problem was self-evident. Something had to be done with this wayward son.

&

In October 1399, only four months after returning from India, Temur left Samarkand at the head of his army. Mohammed Sultan, his designated successor, whose name was already read out at Friday prayers and minted on the imperial coinage, had been summoned to Mawarannahr to take care of the kingdom in the emperor's absence. Son of Jahangir and Khan-zada, this grandson remained Temur's favourite.*

With barely a summer in which to rest and recuperate, the troops had been levied for a Seven-Year Campaign in the west. Temur was still not ready to press east. His southern borders had been secured with victory in India. To the north, his defeat of Tokhtamish had sown internal dissension in the lands of the Golden Horde and crushed its capacity to challenge him. But there was unfinished business in the west.

---

* Even the invariably hostile Ibn Arabshah acknowledged Mohammed Sultan's qualities. He was, said the Syrian, 'a manifest prodigy in his noble nature and vigour. And when Temur saw in his nature signs of singular good fortune and that in the excellence of his talents he surpassed the rest of his sons and grandsons, he disregarded all of them and turned his mind to this one and appointed him his heir.'

In 1393, when Temur seized Baghdad, Sultan Ahmed had fled to Cairo, where he took refuge at the court of Barquq, sultan of Egypt and Syria. At the time Temur had sent an embassy proposing friendly relations between the two states, but Barquq had imprisoned and murdered the Tatar envoys, the leader of whom was related to Temur by marriage.* Equally provocative was the Mamluk sultan's decision to rearm Ahmed and support his successful bid to retake Baghdad, an alliance he later cemented by marrying one of the Iraqi's daughters.

Temur had come close to engaging Barquq in battle while campaigning in Iraq in 1394 but, with his troops exhausted, had resolved to wait until a more favourable day. Now came news that Barquq had died, leaving his ten-year-old son Faraj at the mercy of various

---

* There are fascinating records of the correspondence, in rhyming couplets, between Temur and Barquq in the aftermath of the Mamluk sultan's murder of the Tatar ambassadors. In one, Temur threatens annihilation of the Egyptian if his rival chooses war over peace:

> *'Our forces are numerous, and our valour is vigorous; Our horses forward dash, our lances deeply gash, our spearheads like lightning flash, and our sabres like thunders crash. Our hearts are as the mountains strong, like sands in number our armies' throng, and we among the heroes and Himyar's kings belong. Our kingdom none can assail, our subjects from harm shall never ail, by our might our rule shall ever prevail. To him who makes peace with us will safety ensue, but he who makes war on us will repent and rue, and he who doth avow of us what he doth not know of us – he is a fool.'*

Barquq's reply, casting scorn on Temur's confused style and rhetoric, was equally direct:

> *'For you were the fires of hell created, kindled that your skins be incinerated . . . For our horses are Barcan, our arrows Arabian, our swords are from Yaman, and our armour Egyptian. The blows of our hands are hard to contest, we are renowned in all of the East and all of the West. If we kill you, how good will be the gain! And if you kill one of us, only a moment between him and Paradise will remain . . .'*

powerful factions in court. It was an opportune moment for Temur to avenge the murder of his ambassadors and, more important, extend his western borders to the Mediterranean. But first there was a family matter to attend to which could not wait any longer. Miranshah's capital at Sultaniya lay directly on Temur's westward route. The wayward prince would be shown the error of his ways.

Officers were sent ahead of the army to establish exactly what intrigues had been brewing at the prince's court. Reporting back to Temur, they resorted to the classic diplomatic ruse of blaming the monarch's advisers. Miranshah, they said, had been corrupted by the scandalous company he kept. A louche entourage of scholars, poets and musicians were responsible for the disastrous state into which the kingdom had descended. Temur's decision was swift. Maulana Mohammed of Quhistan, a celebrated scientist and poet, together with Qutb ad-din of Mosul, a famous musician, and other court favourites were sentenced to death. The witty repartee of the main protagonists continued right up to the scaffold. 'You had precedence in the King's company,' observed Maulana Mohammed to his friend; 'precede me, therefore, now.'* Miranshah himself escaped the ultimate punishment, but was relieved of his throne and ordered to remain with the imperial party on the coming campaign. Those of his officers who had been involved in the shameful defeat at Alanjiq were either severely beaten or fined between fifty and three hundred horses.

---

* As the noose slipped around his neck, his last words were a punning verse whose elegance suffers somewhat in translation:

> *'Tis the end of the matter and the last round, O heretic!*
> *Whether thou goest or not, the choice is no longer in thy hand!*
> *If they lead thee, like Mansur, to the foot of the gibbet* [pa-yi-dar]
> *Stand firm* [pay-dar] *like a man, for the world is not enduring* [pay-dar]!

(Mansur was a tenth-century mystic executed in Baghdad for making comments implying he was God.)

With discipline restored, the westward march continued. The army wintered in the meadows of the Qarabagh, from where Temur launched another punitive expedition against the Georgians in revenge for their role in the revolt against Miranshah and the assistance they had given Sultan Ahmed's besieged son, Prince Tahir, in Alanjiq. Once more, the snow-lined valleys ran with blood as Tatar troops forged north, ransacking and burning churches, vineyards, houses, and entire towns and villages. The carnage was interrupted only in the depths of winter, when the army withdrew to their pastures to join the emperor's celebrations at news of the latest addition to the imperial family. Khalil Sultan had had a son. At the age of sixty-three, Temur had a great-grandson.

The auspicious news meant little to the Georgians. Certainly it did not prevent Temur ordering yet another expedition against the recalcitrant Christian kingdom, the fifth in his lifetime, in the spring of 1400. This time the catalyst for hostilities was the refusal by King Giorgi VII of Georgia to surrender Prince Tahir, who had taken refuge at his court, to Temur. Faced with another Tatar invasion, the Georgians retreated to higher ground, secreting themselves in impenetrable mountain caves. The difficult terrain and the unexpected tactics of his adversary demanded a new approach. First, Temur had baskets woven that were big enough to hold a man. Archers stepped inside them and were lowered over the cliffs until they reached the mouths of the caves. Once there, they fired flaming arrows soaked in oil into the farthest recesses, smoking the enemy out and sending them to agonising deaths. The capital, Tiflis, first seized by Temur in 1386, was stormed again. Within a short space of time mosques, minarets and *muaddin* occupied the ground on which the Christian churches and their priests had stood. At the point of a sword, pragmatic Georgians recited the sacred words which defined themselves as Muslim: '*La ilaha illa'llah, Mohammedan rasul Allah*' (There is no god but God and Mohammed is his Prophet). Death was the penalty for those who clung on to Christianity.

King Giorgi, however, managed to elude the Tatar forces, striking out towards the western Caucasus. Prince Tahir he sent south to take sanctuary with the Ottoman Sultan Bayazid I, in a move surely intended to plant the seeds of conflict between the Turk and the Tatar. He did not know it, but these would soon bear fruit in spectacular fashion.

⚛

War between Temur and Bayazid was not inevitable. In fact, the Tatar tried on several occasions to broker peace, just as he had done with the Egyptian sultan. The best guide to understanding how Bayazid and Temur came to face each other on the battlefield does not come from the chronicles. For once it is not Yazdi, or Arabshah, or Nizam ad-din Shami who provides the answers. It is an atlas. Here, on a map of Asia Minor, it becomes clear how both political and geographical considerations were beginning to affect the dynamic between two supremely ambitious empire-builders.

As ever, there were the usual grievances about various enemies who had sought and been given sanctuary at the two courts. Thus it was anathema to Bayazid that Temur should give shelter to the princes of the ten provinces of Anatolia, known as Rum, whose kingdoms the Turk had first crushed and then sucked into the Otto-man orbit as it expanded eastwards. Equally, it was a serious affront to Temur that Bayazid should harbour adversaries both new (Prince Tahir) and old (Sultan Ahmed Jalayir and Qara Yusuf, chief of the Black Sheep Turkmen tribes which had rebelled so frequently against Temur in the regions between Mesopotamia and Asia Minor).

Through his extensive intelligence network, Temur was well aware that moves were afoot to construct a grand alliance against him. Such plans were being actively discussed by Bayazid, Sultan Ahmed and the Egyptian authorities with whom he had sought protection. Temur despatched a letter to the Ottoman warning him against war and directing him to abandon his intrigues with Sultan Ahmed and Qara Yusuf. He himself, he said, had refrained from aggression only because Bayazid was then fighting the infidel Europeans and war would damage the common cause of Muslims and aid the unbelievers. No one, he assured Bayazid, had ever fought him and prospered. The Ottoman should remain within his borders lest he precipitate his own downfall.

> Since the ship of your unfathomable ambition has been shipwrecked in the abyss of self-love, it would be wise for you to lower the sails of your rashness and cast the anchor of repentance in the port of sincerity, which is also the port of safety; lest, by the tempest of our vengeance you should perish in the sea of punishment which you deserve . . . Take care of yourself and try by your good conduct to preserve the dominions of your ancestors and let your ambitious foot not attempt to tread beyond the limits of your little power. Cease your proud extravagances, lest the cold wind of hatred should extinguish the flambeau of peace. You may remember the precept of Mohammed to let the Turks remain in peace, while they are quiet: don't seek war with us, which no one ever did and prospered. The devil certainly inspires you to your own ruin. Though you have been in some notable battles in the forests of Anatolia and have gained advantages over the Europeans, that was only through the prayers of the Prophet and the blessings of the Islamic faith which you profess.

The Ottoman forces were no match for the all-conquering Tatars:

> Believe me, you are nothing but a pismire: don't seek to fight against the elephants because they will crush you under their feet. The dove which rises up against the eagle destroys itself. Shall a petty prince, such as you are, contend with us? But your rodomontades are not extraordinary, for a Turk never spoke with judgement. If you do not follow our counsel, you will regret it. This is the advice we give you. Behave as you think fit.

The letter reflected the geopolitical realities which were beginning to leave little room for manoeuvre on the ground. The straightforward fact of the matter was that Bayazid, having blazed through the Balkans and put the cream of European chivalry to the sword at the battle of Nicopolis in 1396, was now cutting a swathe through the east. Temur's relentless westward progress has been well documented. From Samarkand he had first conquered Herat, before continuing across Persia and into the Caucasus, subduing all before him. By the turn of the fifteenth century, then, both men's military triumphs had reached the point where any further territorial conquest by either – to the east by Bayazid, to the west by Temur – would represent a direct encroachment on the other's lands. That the region in which the two empires were beginning to clash was historically rebellious to the yoke of foreign powers and saw itself as independent only added to the sense that it was fair game for either side to seize it by the sword.

The Ottoman was unimpressed by the Tatar's strong words. Temur was nothing but a 'ravening dog' from whom the Turks had nothing to fear: 'For a long time we have wanted to wage war against you. God be praised, our will has now been achieved and we have decided to march against you with a formidable army. If you don't advance to meet us, we will come and seek you out and pursue you as far as Tauris [Tabriz] and Sultaniya. Then we shall see in whose favour heaven will declare and which of us will be raised to victory and which abased by a shameful defeat.'

There were, moreover, clear signs that encroachments on each other's empires were starting in earnest. While Temur was punishing the Georgians in the winter of 1399–1400, the Ottoman had sent his eldest son Prince Sulayman to make inroads into Armenia, a successful expedition which resulted in the defeat of Temur's ally Prince Taharten of Arzinjan, who, under heavy pressure from the Ottomans, had been forced to surrender the city of Kamakh (in present-day eastern Turkey).

Temur was sufficiently moved by these developments to mount a lightning attack on Anatolia in the summer of 1400. He was joined by forces led by Prince Taharten, who on account of the Ottomans relieving him of both his treasure and his harem now made common cause with the Tatar. Great Queen Saray Mulk-khanum was sent to Sultaniya, the customary signal that battle was imminent. Temur set his eyes on Sivas, the base from which the Turks had made their recent incursions.

'This city was among the finest of great cities, set in a beautiful region, remarkable for public buildings, fortifications, famous qualities and tombs of martyrs renowned above all,' wrote Arabshah. 'Its water is pure, its air healthy for the bodily tempers; its people modest, lovers of magnificence and pomp and devoted to means of ceremony and reverence.' Among its other, more practical, qualities were its massive stone walls, built by the Seljuk Sultan Alaeddin Kaikobad 160 years before, and a large moat. Such defences were considered necessary for a city that had developed into a thriving centre of regional trade and that was, besides, the strategic gateway to the heart of Anatolia.

In August, the siege of Sivas began. Stout walls and a moat stood between the garrison of four thousand Sipahi cavalry and Temur's far greater force. This included eight thousand prisoners pressed into service to assist the sappers whose task it was to undermine the city's defences. Tunnels were dug beneath the walls, propped up by wooden supports which were later set on fire to precipitate their collapse. The familiar war engines lumbered into action, hurling fire and rocks into the city. For three weeks the sappers and the battering rams went about their destructive mission until at last the walls started to crumble. Fearing disaster unless they came to terms immediately with Temur, the city elders trooped out to sue for peace and beg for mercy. Clemency was granted to the Muslim population in return for a ransom. The Armenians and any other Christians, however, were taken prisoner. As the bulk of the cavalry that had defended Sivas so manfully were Armenians, their fate was settled. Temur's murderous ends were not to be frustrated, though on this occasion the Unconquered Lord of the Seven Climes resorted to the basest trickery to achieve them. In the words of the fifteenth-century Syrian historian Ibn Taghri Birdi: 'Seizing its armed men, three thousand individuals, he dug for them an underground vault into which he threw them and then covered them with earth. This was after he had sworn to them that he would shed the blood of none of them; and he then said: "I have kept my oath, since I have not shed the blood of any of them."'

The Tatar, who had long aspired to recognition within the Islamic world as the greatest defender of the faith, took pains to inflict miserable deaths on the city's Christian community. While the Sipahis were buried alive, others had their heads tied between their thighs before being thrown into the moat to drown. According to Johann Schiltberger, the Bavarian squire captured by Temur in 1402, nine thousand virgins were carried off into captivity. Those who were fortunate enough to escape the slaughter fled from Sivas in horror. As for the city itself, it was, reported Arabshah, 'utterly destroyed and laid to waste'.

The confrontation at Sivas was a shot across the Ottomans' bows. But Bayazid had shown himself willing and able to mount military expeditions into the Tatar's empire, and the potential for a more decisive test of each other's powers on the battlefield had only increased with these initial skirmishes.* At this stage, however, Temur

---

* The historian Herbert Gibbons saw the fall of Sivas as a landmark, arguing that in his earlier days the Ottoman would have met such a setback with a swift political, diplomatic or military response. This time there was only inertia: 'He had become a voluptuary, debauched mentally and physically. His pride and self-confidence had increased in inverse ratio to his ability to make good his arrogant assumptions.'

was not minded to move to all-out battle with Bayazid. That would come in time, if Allah willed it. For now there were other priorities. Egypt must come first.

⚫

The death of Sultan Barquq in 1399 removed an obdurate and powerful adversary from the scene. But it must also have reminded Temur, if such a reminder was necessary, that it was only a matter of time before the Angel Izrail descended upon him also. These reflections can only have been impressed on him more forcefully with the news, in the same year, that the Ming emperor Chu Yuan-chang – nicknamed Tonguz Khan, the Pig Khan, by the Tatars – had died, together with Khizr Khoja, khan of the Moghuls. Temur had already outlived two of his sons, Jahangir and Omar Shaykh, and would also outlive one of his most cherished grandsons. But amid these sober thoughts would have come more positive considerations, for in the death of a rival there was opportunity, and none was better at discerning it than the Emperor of the Age. Disorder had accompanied the death of both the Ming emperor and the khan of the Moghuls, opening the way east for Temur in the future. The deaths of two of Delhi's rulers in quick succession had condemned the sultanate to chaotic instability from which Temur had been swift to exact a bloody profit. More immediately, disorder had followed the death of Barquq, plunging Egypt into a turmoil which the Tatar felt impelled to exploit.

This, then, was an opportune moment to strike at Faraj, the newly installed boy-sultan in Cairo. While the Ottomans at this time were only beginning to emerge on the world stage, the Egyptian empire had, since the days of Sultan Saladin in the twelfth century, been the leading light within the *dar al Islam*, the pillar of the faith's defence against Christian Crusaders. Saladin had recaptured Jerusalem, driven out the invaders and united the territories of Syria with those of Egypt. Under the Mamluk dynasty, which took power in the middle

289

of the thirteenth century, Egypt's lands stretched from the Nile to the Levant, from south-eastern Anatolia to the Hijaz.* During the reign of Sultan Baybars, who cut and thrust his way to power, the empire's glory reached new heights. In 1260 his army put an end to the Mongols' relentless westward advance, inflicting the first heavy defeat on them at the battle of Ain Jalut in Palestine. From routing the Mongols, Baybars turned to crushing the Crusaders, winning a number of savage victories over the Christian knights. After taking Antioch in 1263, he had the city's garrison of sixteen thousand slaughtered in cold blood. One hundred thousand men, women and children were sold into slavery.

Triumphant on the battlefield, the Mamluks were no less impressive in amassing riches and turning their capital into the wonder of the Middle East. Khalil al Zahiri, a fourteenth-century Persian visitor to Cairo, reported that the city was the same size as the ten largest towns in his country put together. Leonardo Frescobaldi, a Florentine traveller, wrote in 1384 that one street in Cairo contained more people than the entire population of his home city. He went on to estimate the number of ships docking at Cairo's Nile port of Bulaq as equivalent to three times the number of vessels at Venice, Genoa and Ancona combined. Through the cities of Cairo and Damascus Egypt lorded

---

* The Mamluks (from the Arabic word for 'owned') were originally Turkic slaves brought to Egypt as boys and given extensive military training which, if they performed well, culminated in their freedom and subsequent service as senior administrators and bodyguards to the caliphs and sultans. The thinking behind the creation of this new military elite was that since the Egyptian state was in effect its parent, the Mamluks would always remain loyal to the throne. In fact these foreign imports, initially of Kipchak Turk origin, later Circassian, proved so successful that they seized power and ruled Egypt as a new dynasty from 1250 until 1517, when they were conquered by the Ottoman Sultan Selim I. They continued to rule locally as Ottoman viceroys but were fatally weakened by Napoleon's invasion of Egypt in 1798. The remaining Mamluks were massacred by Mohammed Ali in 1811.

it over the trade routes with India. She also controlled the pilgrim route to the holy places of Mecca and Medina. Her bright Islamic lustre blazed still more brilliantly as home to the Abbasid caliph after the Mongol sacking of Baghdad in 1250. Now on its knees as internecine fighting ran riot around the ten-year-old Sultan Faraj, the Egyptian empire must have appeared impossible to ignore for a predator like Temur.

The Tatar was camped at Malatiyah, south-east of Sivas in eastern Anatolia, a position which neatly severed the connection between the Ottomans and the Egyptians, but which also left him exposed to both. He was aware of these dangers, because a precedent for joint action between his two opponents had already been set. In response to a request from Faraj for help in seeing off a rival to the throne, Bayazid had sent a sizeable force to assist him. Temur's spies may also have informed him that the Ottoman's ambassadors had appeared in Cairo shortly after the fall of Sivas, pressing for an alliance against Temur. The proposal fell on deaf ears, not least because Bayazid had seized Egyptian-held Malatiyah after Barquq's death. For now, there was no alliance, but Temur understood that at any moment the Ottoman and Egyptian sultans could agree to join forces and put an immense army into the field against him.

Once again, prior to hostilities, he despatched a letter. It threatened dire consequences if Faraj refused to comply.

> The Sultan your father committed many odious crimes against us, among them the murder of our ambassadors without cause and the imprisonment of Atilmish, one of our officers. Since your father has surrendered his life to God, the punishment of his crimes must be brought before the divine tribunal. As for you, you have got to consider your own survival and that of your subjects, so you must immediately return Atilmish to us, lest our furious soldiers fall upon the people of Egypt and Syria in a cruel slaughter, burning and pillaging their properties. If you are so stubborn as to reject

*this advice, you will be responsible both for spilling Muslim blood
and for the total loss of your kingdom.*

The message was clear, but Faraj, 'the crooked branch of an evil
stock', and his advisers chose to ignore it. Far worse, the ambassador
who brought the letter was seized by Sudun, viceroy of Damascus,
and sliced in two at the waist. 'It is not surprising that a plebeian
should commit such a cowardly act,' wrote Yazdi of the affair. 'What
then may we expect from a Circassian slave?'* Temur would not let
such an action go unanswered. The order to march south was given.

⚙

One hundred and sixty miles south-west of Malatiyah lay the city of
Aleppo, a thriving political, commercial, and cultural centre. Its
markets, crammed with the exotic produce of India, were an important
outlet on the trade routes linking the Mediterranean with Iran and
eastern Anatolia. Its citadel, as one would expect, was 'large and strong',
according to Ibn Battutah. This, the Moroccan traveller wrote, was
where Ibrahim (Abraham) was said to have performed his devotions
and where the tenth-century poet El Khalidi penned the following lines:

> *Land of my heart, extended wide,*
> *Rich in beauty, great in pride:*
> *Around whose head to brave the storm,*
> *The rolling clouds a chaplet form.*
> *Here 'tis the empyreal fires glow,*
> *And dissipate the gloom below.*
> *About thy breast in harmless blaze,*
> *The lightning too forever plays;*
> *And like the unveiling beauty's glance,*
> *Spreads round its charms to astonish and entrance.*

---

* A disparaging reference to Faraj's origins. His father, Barquq, was the first
Circassian Mamluk sultan.

A storm, with black rolling clouds, now gathered over Aleppo as Temur's men marched south, sacking fortresses along the way. The lightning about to strike this ancient city, and the blaze that would engulf it, would be anything but harmless.

While the storm thundered overhead, rumblings of discontent broke out beneath the dark skies. Temur's amirs began to voice their concerns to the emperor. The men were exhausted, they argued. They had had only the briefest time in which to recuperate after the gruelling marches to India and back. Since leaving Samarkand they had embarked on two arduous campaigns in Georgia, had taken both Sivas and Malatiyah, and were already being pressed into action again. They were marching through the heart of a country that belonged to an enemy rich and strong, with well-provisioned cities, towering castles and Mamluk soldiers handsomely equipped with the finest weapons. Such doubts were given short shrift by the emperor, who reminded his amirs that their fortunes and his were, as always, in the hands of God. The forced marches continued as the Syrians massed their troops for the defence of the city. They came from Antioch and Acre, Hama and Homs, from Ramallah, Canaan, Gaza, Tripoli, Baalbek and Jerusalem.

Opinion within the city was divided between those who wanted to sue for peace, including Damurdash, its governor, and those who preferred a more robust response. 'The prince who comes before us today is exceedingly powerful,' Damurdash warned. 'He and his armies have performed deeds unrivalled in history. Wherever he has marched, he has conquered towns and overcome fortresses. Whoever tried to resist him, always regretted it and suffered the cruellest punishment.' Such an adversary was surely protected by God. Far wiser not to cross him, to coin money in his name, proclaim him in Friday prayers and send priests, doctors and *sharifs*, loaded with priceless gifts, to sue for peace. 'He is a prince favoured by fortune, powerful, active, glorious and ambitious,' the governor continued. 'His wrath burns a thousand times fiercer than fire; and if it is kindled, not even the sea will be able to quench it.'

The hawks were unimpressed, according to Arabshah: 'Our cities are not built with mud or brick, but solid and impenetrable rock. They are filled with good garrisons equipped with plenty of food and ammunition. It would take a year just to take one of them . . . Our bows are from Damascus, our lances from Arabia, our shields made in Aleppo. We have on the registers of this realm sixty thousand villages. We need but one or two brave men from each village to supply us with a vast army. These Tatars have lodgings of cord and canvas, while we live in good fortresses, of hewn stone from the battlements to the very foundations.'

Damurdash's urgent appeals for assistance from Sultan Faraj went unanswered. The Syrians would have to confront Temur's army alone. By the end of October 1400, the Tatars were camped before Aleppo. For several days Temur sent skirmishing parties to reconnoitre the city and its surroundings. These were the same tactics he had used to tempt the Indians out from behind Delhi's city walls – to avoid a protracted siege – and they were no less successful in Syria. The gates were opened and the army assembled in battle formation. Sudun, the viceroy of Damascus, led the right, with troops from that city reinforced with Mamluks. Damurdash took command of the left, at the head of forces from Aleppo supplemented with more Mamluks. In what was a serious tactical blunder, the unmounted soldiers of Aleppo were placed in the front lines.

On the Tatar side, the rehabilitated Miranshah and Shahrukh led the right wing. Sultan Mahmud, the puppet Chaghatay khan, commanded the left. Two of the emperor's grandsons, Miranshah's son Abubakr and Sultan Husayn, took charge of the vanguard of the right and left respectively. The war elephants, seized from Delhi and now Temur's favourite military novelty, were stationed at the front of the army, resplendent in their ornately decorated armour. It was an army, said one historian, that 'filled the landscape'.

To the customary cry of 'Allahu akbar!' the two Muslim armies rushed at each other. The fighting was furious as the Syrians threw themselves against these barbarian invaders to defend their city. The air rang with the clash of metal on metal and hummed with the flight of arrows. Urging the elephants against the Syrian left wing, which scattered in disarray, Temur stole the early initiative. Under heavy pressure from the Tatars, it eventually turned and fled to the gates of the city in full view of the rest of the army. The example of Damurdash, who made for the citadel, was the trigger for complete pandemonium. In an instant the plain was filled with Syrians charging towards the safety of the city walls, hotly pursued by the Tatars. In the mayhem soldiers were trampled to death by horses, drowned in the moat that was soon piled high with corpses, run through three or four at a time by pikes and torn to pieces by the archers. Brave women and boys who had joined the defence of their city were cut down where they stood.

Damurdash had little option but to surrender Aleppo to Temur in the hope of preventing further bloodshed. He was well treated, but Sudun, who had killed Temur's ambassador, was taken prisoner. The treasures of this famous city now belonged to the irresistible conqueror. But the viceroy's hopes of a peaceful conclusion to the battle were cruelly shattered, as the historian Ibn Taghri Birdi, whose father was commander-in-chief of Sultan Faraj's armies, related.

> The women and children fled to the great mosque of Aleppo and to the smaller mosques, but Tamerlane's men turned to follow them, bound the women with ropes as prisoners, and put the children to the sword, killing every one of them. They committed the shameful deeds to which they were accustomed; virgins were violated without concealment; gentlewomen were outraged without any restraints of modesty; a Tatar would seize a woman and ravage her in the great mosque . . . in sight of the vast multitude of his companions and the people of the city; her father and brother and

husband would see her plight and be unable to defend her . . . because
they were distracted by the torture and torments which they them-
selves were suffering; the Tatar would then leave the woman and
another go to her, her body still uncovered. They then put the popu-
lace of Aleppo and its troops to the sword, until the mosques and
streets were filled with dead, and Aleppo stank with corpses.

For four days the massacres and looting continued. Trees were hacked
down, houses demolished and mosques burnt. One account spoke
of the mass slaughter of the city's Jews, who had taken shelter in the
synagogue. 'He left the city fallen on its roofs, empty of its inhabitants
and every human being, reduced to ruins; the muezzin's call and the
prayer services were no longer heard; there was nothing there but a
desert waste darkened by fire, a lonely solitude where only the owl
and the vulture took refuge.'*

Looming high over this devastated city were Temur's dreadful
totems. This time the piles of bloody heads were shaped like knolls,

---

* This apocalyptic picture of an empty ghost city was not altogether
accurate, for we know from the chronicles that before he departed Temur
took time to indulge his passion for theological debate and summoned the
city's *qadis* before him. He fired a series of questions at them, the wrong
answers to which, as they knew, could lose them their heads. Why had
they chosen the wrong path, he asked, by following the Sunni creed of
Islam, not the Shi'a? This question completely threw the religious scholars,
for they thought Temur himself was a Sunni Muslim. As Arabshah put it,
'The Muslims were in perplexity and their heads were being cut off.' There
followed a more deliberately provocative question. Which was the martyr
of Islam destined for paradise, the soldier who gave his life in defence of
Aleppo or he who died while fighting for Temur? A deathly silence fell
upon the *qadis*. Then a Hanafite scholar, Muhib ad-din Mohammed, stood
up. 'The prophet of God (God bless him and grant him peace!) was asked
this question and he answered: "He who fights that the word of God be
supreme is a martyr."' Temur was pleased with the answer, so much so
that he was moved to spare those who had survived the violence,
prompting the same Ibn Taghri Birdi who earlier had detailed the piles
of stinking corpses to venture the observation that Temur's behaviour
towards the people of Aleppo was 'comparatively mild'.

fifteen feet in height and thirty in circumference. Vultures, scenting carrion, wheeled overhead, swooping down to pluck eyes out of sockets as twenty thousand expressions of abject terror, horror, disgust and defiance stared out into a blank sky.

&

The road to Damascus was now open. The first city of the Levant, one of the greatest in the Mediterranean and among the oldest in the world, lay just two hundred miles to the south. After the precipitate fall of Aleppo it was inconceivable that the conqueror should ignore this prize, inevitable that the marches south continue, whatever the protests of his amirs. These officers now suggested that the army should retire to the winter pastures around Mount Lebanon, where the weary soldiers could rest, but Temur refused to countenance this. The sultanate of Egypt was divided and off balance. It must not be given time to prepare its defences. On the Tatars pressed, and the cities, towns and fortresses that lay between them and Damascus collapsed like houses of cards, first Hama, then Homs, quickly followed by Baalbek, Sidon and Beirut.

But Temur's focus was on Damascus herself, a city which had grown rich at the crossroads of Asian and European commerce. To her west stood the Anti-Lebanon mountains, which rose up mightily to ten thousand feet before sweeping down towards the Mediterranean; to the east stretched the burning wilderness of the Badiyat ash Sham desert. Damascus had grown wealthy on the back of revenues from the caravans which arrived daily, rich also in the arts and crafts for which she was famed. In the bazaars worked metalsmiths, glassblowers, farriers, weavers, tailors, gem-cutters, carpenters, bowmakers, falconers, craftsmen of every kind. It was a highly cultured and cosmopolitan city, with mathematicians and merchants, astronomers and artists. From 661 to 750 she had been the home of the caliphs, capital of the Arab Islamic empire.

One building more than any other recalled those glorious years. 'Damascus surpasses all other cities in beauty, and no description, however full, can do justice to its charms,' wrote Ibn Battutah. 'The Cathedral Mosque, known as the Umayyad Mosque, is the most magnificent mosque in the world, the finest in construction and noblest in beauty, grace and perfection; it is matchless and un-equalled.' Three minarets leapt towards the firmament, soaring above a princely lead dome which presided in turn over a grand arcade and gallery and a central courtyard which could house a multitude. Glittering mosaics traced their way across the façades with images of paradise gardens, colonnaded palaces, lofty castles, rivers and verdant landscapes. 'Even now, as the sun catches a fragment on the outside wall, one can imagine the first splendour of green and gold, when the whole court shone with those magic scenes conceived by Arab fiction to recompense those parched eternities of the desert,' wrote Robert Byron in *The Road to Oxiana*.

Damascus, wrote Ibn Taghri Birdi, was 'the most beautiful and flourishing city in the world'. Now, as streams of refugees from Aleppo flooded through her gates in distress, telling terrible stories of the slaughter, she braced herself for Temur's arrival and the most calami-tous attack in her history. The disarray which had followed Barquq's death, communicated to the Tatar by his spies, now made itself felt on a military level. Since there was no single overarching source of command, the Syrians and Egyptians fell prey to 'discord, confusion, division, conflict and altercation', lamented Arabshah, who was eight or nine at the time. Too many energies were being expended on competition between the amirs for 'offices, fiefs and control of the government', said Ibn Taghri Birdi, too little on the imminent danger of Temur, which was treated 'as though it did not exist'.

By January 1401, the Tatar forces were camped within reach of the city. The Egyptian sultanate now made a desperate but inventive attempt on the conqueror's life by sending an assassin disguised as a dervish into his camp. The would-be killer's manner aroused suspicion, however, and when a hidden dagger was found on him he was instantly killed. The two men accompanying him were returned to Faraj with their ears and noses cut off.

Another envoy was despatched to Faraj, demanding the return of Temur's ambassador Atilmish, and advising the young Egyptian to coin money in his adversary's name and to surrender:

> This you ought to do, if you have any compassion for yourself or your subjects. Our soldiers are like roaring lions, which hunger for their prey. They seek to kill their enemy, pillage everything he owns, take his towns, raze his buildings to the ground. There are only two ways to choose. Either peace, the consequences of which are quiet and joy; or war, which will lead to disorder and desolation. I have set both before you. It is up to you which path to follow. Consult your prudence and make your choice.

Faraj promised to comply, but stalled for time. A series of incidents then convinced the Damascenes that the tide was now flowing in their favour. First, Temur withdrew from the walls of the city in order to secure pasturage for his army's horses. Not unreasonably, the besieged concluded the Tatars were in retreat. Next came news that Temur's grandson Sultan Husayn, who had led the vanguard of the right wing at Aleppo, had defected to the Syrian cause. Finally, when they looked out across the plain, where only days earlier Temur's army had been camped, there now stood the troops of Faraj, just arrived from Cairo. In the excitement whipped up by these auspicious developments, a force of Damascenes threw open the gates of the city and started attacking Temur's rearguard.

Disaster now seemed imminent, for Faraj had broken his agreement to surrender. Worse, some of Temur's men had been killed in the hot-blooded assault. Furious, the emperor ordered his troops to wheel around 180 degrees and close in on Damascus. Although weakened by months of continual campaigning, they still presented a fearsome sight. At night the line of their campfires was said to extend for 150 miles. Faraj, sensing ruin, despatched a formal apology for the attack, blaming it on a local rising within the city and assuring Temur that he would come to terms. The conqueror was unlikely to be pacified so easily.

The only hope for Damascus lay with Faraj's army. Unlike the Tatars, his Mamluks were well rested and had not had to cross half a continent in forced marches. They were a formidable fighting force. But on the morning after Temur's men had encircled the city, the Damascenes woke to a terrifying sight. The Egyptian army had simply melted away, like the cruellest desert mirage, under the cover of darkness. Faraj was returning to Cairo, from where he had heard rumours of court intrigues to overthrow him, leaving Damascus to face a vengeful Scourge of God alone.

While detachments of Tatars pursued the fleeing Egyptians and cut down some of Faraj's senior officers and bodyguards, Temur turned to the task at hand. Damascus, now facing devastation, barricaded the city gates and called a *jihad* against the invader. As at Delhi and most recently Aleppo, Temur was not inclined to mount a long siege. He was far from home, sandwiched between the two hostile sultans Faraj and Bayazid. A lightning assault or an immediate surrender were the favoured options. Besides, the city was heavily protected and rich in supplies. Bringing her to her knees by siege would be a massive undertaking.

Instead, Temur resorted to diplomacy, doubtless confident that military action, if required, would achieve everything the negotiations failed to deliver. Another envoy was sent into the city proposing peace terms. In return, Damascus sent its own delegation. It contained a man who was in Damascus by chance rather than inclination. He had been invited to join Sultan Faraj's expedition only to be abandoned in the city after the Egyptian's surprise departure. This man happened to be the greatest historian ever to emerge from the Arab world. The stage was set for a truly remarkable meeting.

⊛

Twenty years earlier, in what is today Algeria, Ibn Khaldun finished his monumental *Muqaddimah* or Foreword, the first volume of his *Universal History*. Originally conceived as a comprehensive history of the Arabs and Berbers, it evolved into something far more complex, a philosophy of history and a pioneering analysis of how societies change and dynasties rise and fall over several generations. Given his education and the turbulence of North African politics of his time, Khaldun was uniquely well equipped to comment on such matters.* By the time he reached Damascus with Sultan Faraj he had achieved widespread renown during a peripatetic, rollercoaster career. He had enjoyed the patronage of Sultan Barquq, served as Malikite chief *qadi* (judge) of Cairo, and worked as secretary, chamberlain, statesman, adviser, negotiator and ambassador to all of the leading rulers of North Africa. Perhaps his most unusual appointment came while a senior court official in Granada, when he was despatched to Seville as an envoy to Pedro the Cruel, king of Castile. He had also experienced the insides of various North African prisons. Despite, or perhaps because of, his many talents and considerable patronage,

---

* It is worth quoting Arnold Toynbee's verdict on Ibn Khaldun's intellectual achievements: 'He is indeed the one outstanding personality in the history of a civilisation whose social life on the whole was "solitary, poor, nasty, brutish and short". In his chosen field of intellectual activity he appears to have been inspired by no predecessors, and to have found no kindred souls among his contemporaries, and to have kindled no answering spark of inspiration in any successors; and yet, in the Prolegomena (Muqaddimat) to his *Universal History* he has conceived and formulated a philosophy of history which is undoubtedly the greatest work of its kind that has ever yet been created by any mind in any time or place. It was his single brief "acquiescence" from a life of practical activity that gave Ibn Khaldun his opportunity to cast his creative thought into literary shape.'

Khaldun made enemies wherever he went. Sometimes they were seen off, at others they prevailed. Just as his position seemed secure, he tended to fall victim to the latest intrigue against him; and he was equally guilty of plotting against sultans and viziers himself.

In his account of their fateful meeting, the Tunisian diplomat and scholar describes how, having advised the city elders to surrender to the Tatar, he feared for his life from a hostile faction advocating all-out war. One morning he had himself lowered over the city walls to seek an audience with the conqueror. The details of those discussions he scrupulously recorded.

His first sight of Temur was in the audience tent, where the emperor was 'reclining on his elbow while platters of food were passing before him while he was sending one after the other to groups of Mongols sitting in circles in front of his tent'. Temur held out a hand for the Tunisian to kiss. 'May Allah aid you – today it is thirty or forty years that I have longed to meet you,' the historian began with all due deference. 'You are the sultan of the universe and the ruler of the world, and I do not believe there has appeared a ruler like you from Adam until today.' Khaldun told Temur how he had met a priest and divine in the Mosque of al Qarawiyin in Fes who had, in 1358, predicted the Tatar's rise to power. The imminent conjunction of the planets, the priest said, was momentous: 'It points to a powerful one who would arise in the north-east region of a desert people, tent dwellers, who will triumph over kingdoms, overturn governments, and become the masters of most of the inhabited world.'

The calculated flattery found its mark. Khaldun was invited to dine in the emperor's tent, where the conversation turned to history and geography. Temur asked his guest numerous questions about North Africa. He wanted to know the location of Tangier, Ceuta and Sijilmasa. Khaldun did his best to explain, but it was not good enough for Temur. 'He said, "I am not satisfied. I desire that you write for me a description of the whole country of the Maghreb, detailing its

302

distant as well as its nearby parts, its mountains and its rivers, its villages and its cities – in such a manner that I might seem actually to see it."'

Khaldun returned to the city, where he rushed out the required volume in a matter of days. In all he spent thirty-five days in the Tatar camp, and was eyewitness to a number of discussions between Temur and his amirs, evidence of the high regard in which he was held. He watched imperial audiences and receptions, and even listened to councils of war in which Temur directed his amirs to find the most vulnerable points in Damascus's defences. Given his historical expertise, he was asked to pronounce on the legitimacy of a request made by a claimant to the caliphate to be restored to his rightful place in Cairo. Khaldun obliged, judging the man's claim after lengthy debate 'not valid'. 'Temur then said to this claimant: "You have heard the words of the judges and the jurists, and it appears that you have no justification for claiming the caliphate before me. So depart, may Allah guide you aright!"'

One of Khaldun's friends, well acquainted with the etiquette of the Tatar court, advised him to offer a gift to Temur, 'however small its value might be, for that is a fixed custom on meeting their rulers. I therefore chose from the book market an exceedingly beautiful Quran copy, a beautiful prayer rug, a copy of the famous poem al-Burda by al-Busiri, in praise of the Prophet – may Allah bless him and grant him peace; and four boxes of the excellent Cairo sweetmeats.'

These offerings, extremely modest in comparison with the treasures he was accustomed to receive from submissive leaders, nevertheless pleased Temur and further endeared the Tunisian to him. He was invited to sit on Temur's right-hand side, a public display of the emperor's high regard for him. A consummate diplomat, well versed in the arts of courtly practice, Khaldun recognised this as an opportune moment to plead for the lives of the learned men brought to Damascus as part of Sultan Faraj's entourage:

These Quran teachers, secretaries, bureau officials, and administrators, who are among those left behind by the Sultan of Egypt, have come under your rule. The King surely will not disregard them. Your power is vast, your provinces are very extensive, and the need of your government for men who are administrators in the various branches of service is greater than the need of any other than you.

He asked me, 'And what do you wish for them?'

I replied, 'A letter of security to which they can appeal and upon which they can rely whatever their circumstances may be.'

He said to his secretary, 'Write an order to this effect for them.'

I thanked him and blessed him, and went out with the secretary until the letter of security had been written.

Khaldun had achieved his mission. The white-robed clerics were spared.

Towards the end of Temur's stay at Damascus, Khaldun recorded one of his more baffling conversations with the Tatar. Temur, it emerged, was something of a mule-fancier.

After we had completed the customary greetings, he turned to me and said, 'You have a mule here?'

I answered, 'Yes.'

He said, 'Is it a good one?'

I answered, 'Yes.'

He said, 'Will you sell it? I would buy it from you.'

I replied, 'May Allah aid you, one like me does not sell to one like you, but I would offer it to you in homage, and also others like it if I had them.'

He said, 'I meant only that I would reimburse you for it generously.'

I replied, 'Is there any generosity left beyond that which you have already shown me? You have heaped favours upon me, accorded me a place in your council among your intimate followers, and shown me kindness and generosity, which I hope Allah will repay to you in like measure.'

He was silent. So was I. The mule was brought to him while I was with him at his council and I did not see it again.

Later, when Khaldun had returned to Cairo, the Egyptian sultan's ambassador to Temur sent a messenger to him with a sum of money from the Tatar reimbursing him for the loss of his mule. Corruption was no stranger to Egyptian politics at this time. The messenger apologised that the cash was 'not complete', insisting that this was the sum that had been given to him.

According to Arabshah's account, Temur permitted the Tunisian to leave him only on condition he return with his family and great library, a promise he never kept. Khaldun himself, however, remembered things differently. He wrote of his offer to serve in Temur's court and the conqueror's reply in the negative, instructing him instead to 'return to your family and to your people'.

Safely out of Temur's orbit, Khaldun wrote a letter to Abu Said Othman, ruler of the Maghreb, recounting the Tatar's advance on Damascus. 'Temur had conquered Aleppo, Hama, Hims and Baalbek and ruined them all, and his soldiers had committed more shameful atrocities than had ever been heard of before,' he reported. In an apologetic tone, he explained how he had had 'no choice but to meet him'. He had been treated kindly, he added, and thanks to his diplomatic efforts 'obtained from him amnesty for the people of Damascus'.

There followed a potted history of the Tatars, whom he defined as 'those who came out of the desert beyond the Oxus, between it and China . . . under their famous king Jenghiz Khan'. From Genghis, Khaldun moved on to a portrait of Temur and his hordes.

> The people are of a number which cannot be counted. If you estimate it at one million it would not be too much, nor can you say it is less. If they pitched their tents together in the land, they would fill all empty spaces, and if their armies came even into a wide territory the plain would be too narrow for them. And in raiding, robbing and slaughtering settled populations and inflicting upon them all kinds of cruelty they are an astounding example.

Khaldun gave a valuable profile of the Tatar emperor, confirming his powerful intellect and passion for wide-ranging scholarly debate. 'This king Temur is one of the greatest and mightiest of kings,' he began. 'Some attribute to him knowledge, others attribute to him heresy because they note his preference for the "members of the House" [of Ali, i.e. the Shi'ites]. Still others attribute to him the employment of magic and sorcery, but in all this there is nothing. It is simply that he is highly intelligent and very perspicacious, addicted to debate and argumentation about what he knows and also about what he does not know.'

He went on to describe Temur's injury. 'His right knee is lame from an arrow which struck him while raiding in his boyhood, as he told me. Therefore he dragged it when he went on short walks, but when he would go long distances men carried him with their hands.' Like Clavijo, Khaldun saw for himself the pain this injury could cause Temur. After one audience with the historian, the aged conqueror 'was carried away from before us because of the trouble with his knee'. But although he was in his sixty-fourth year, Temur was evidently neither too old nor too infirm to ride on horseback, for Khaldun noticed how 'he sat upright in his saddle'.

After a month observing Temur at close quarters, Khaldun came to a simple conclusion: 'He is one who is favoured by Allah. The power is Allah's, and he grants it to whom he chooses.'

&

If Temur enjoyed divine protection, Damascus now found itself completely bereft. Although initial signs suggested the surrender would be honoured – Tatar amirs were put on guard at the city gates to prevent their soldiers entering, and any troops caught plundering were publicly crucified in the silk bazaar – history suggested the city would pay a high price for the resistance it had staged. Nor did these intimations of disaster take into account the possibility that the

Syrians themselves might not honour the surrender negotiated with Temur. Ominously for the people of Damascus, this apparently remote possibility now became reality. The governor of the fortress, fired with zeal against the Tatar invaders, ordered his garrison to resist. Temur's soldiers, preparing for victory celebrations, suddenly found themselves under attack. One thousand were killed, said Ibn Taghri Birdi, their heads severed and taken back to the citadel.

When Temur learnt of this strike, he ordered the fortress to be taken immediately. Sappers set to work and the walls were undermined. Wooden towers were built from which the soldiers trained their fire on the garrison, loosing volleys of arrows and hurling Greek-fire at the besieged. Still the governor refused to capitulate. Next the catapults rumbled forward, unleashing rocks, boulders and fireballs into the fortress. Day after day the punishing barrage continued. Weakened by the sappers, pounded by the war engines, the walls started to crumble, but were quickly, if patchily, repaired by the stubborn defenders. Only after twenty-nine days withstanding this hourly onslaught did the governor finally bow to the inevitable and yield to Temur. But by now the Tatar was well beyond forgiveness and mercy. He ordered the governor to be beheaded. The citadel gave up its treasures, opening its gates to reveal a surviving garrison of just forty Mamluk slaves.

Negotiations between Temur and the city elders of Damascus were delicately poised. The advantage, as both sides fully understood, lay entirely with the Tatar. Whatever he demanded must be given, for in his hands alone lay the power to spare this great city or reduce it to ashes. A ransom of one million dinars was agreed, only for Temur to turn around to the cringing officials once it had been collected and demand ten million. No sooner was this sum harried and beaten out of the city's beleaguered population than Temur claimed that only a third of the total had been paid. Now he laid claim to the fortune of the entire city. The negotiations began to look like a pretext for wholesale rape and pillage. The skies darkened again. The furious storm that had engulfed Aleppo was about to break over Damascus.

An order ran out through the ranks. Hungry soldiers, exhausted by months of campaigning, lean from the gruelling forced marches, looked at each other in delight and cheered to the heavens. Damascus was to be put to the sword. It was a bitter, seismic shock for the young Arabshah, one from which he never recovered. 'Those evil unbelievers suddenly fell upon men, torturing, smiting and laying waste, as stars fall from the sky, and excited and swollen they slaughtered and smote and raged against Muslims and their allies, as ravening wolves rage against teeming flocks of sheep.'

The tempest of destruction overran the city. The people of Damascus, wrote Ibn Taghri Birdi, 'were subjected to all sorts of torture; they were bastinadoed, crushed in presses, scorched in flames, and suspended head down; their nostrils were stopped with rags full of fine dust which they inhaled each time they took a breath so that they almost died. When near to death, a man would be given a respite to recover, then the tortures of all kinds would be repeated.' In their remorseless hunger for booty, the Tatars introduced new cruelties previously unheard of in Damascus.

> For example, they would take a man and tie a rope around his head and twist it until it would sink into his flesh; they would put a rope around a man's shoulders, and twist it with a stick until they were torn from their sockets; they would bind another victim's thumbs behind him, then throw him on his back, pour powdered ashes in his nostrils to make him little by little confess what he possessed; when he had given up all, he would still not be believed, but the torture would be repeated until he died; and then his body would be further mutilated in the thought that he might be feigning death. And some would tie their victim by his thumbs to the roof of the house, kindle a fire under him and keep him thus a long time; if by chance he fell in the flames, he would be dragged out and thrown on the ground till he revived, then he would thus be suspended a second time . . .

So great was the quantity of treasure seized from Damascus, claimed Yazdi, that the combined caravans of horses, mules and camels were unable to carry it all. Articles of gold and silver, together with precious belts from Egypt, Cyprus and Russia had to be jettisoned to make room for more valuable trophies.

Arabshah, who was understandably at his most jaundiced when recounting the sacking of his native city, claimed that Temur captured a ninety-year-old Syrian officer who had led the resistance in the citadel. The emperor would not execute him, he told the old man, since that would not avenge the loss of the brave Tatar soldiers at his hands. 'I will torture you despite your age and add affliction to your affliction and weakness to your weakness,' Temur is supposed to have jeered. A heavy chain was fastened to the man's knees, and he was thrown into captivity.

As the flames spread through the streets of Damascus, the dome of the Umayyad Mosque towered over the city through the smoke. Whipped up by the wind, the fire roared towards it, sucking up timber houses, palaces, mosques, bath-houses, felling everything in its way. 'It continued to burn until it reached the Great Mosque,' wrote Ibn Khaldun. 'The flames mounted to its roof, melting the lead in it, and the ceiling and walls collapsed.' One of the wonders of the world, a sparkling eighth-century monument to the Muslim faith, had been desecrated by an army of Muslims under the command of a man who actively sought recognition as the Warrior of Islam. 'This was an absolutely dastardly and abominable deed,' Khaldun continued, 'but the changes in affairs are in the hands of Allah – he does with his creatures as he wishes, and decides in his kingdom as he wills.'*

---

* Among these early reports of the sacking of Damascus, opinion was
  divided as to whether Temur ordered the destruction of the Umayyad
  Mosque. Schiltberger, the Bavarian whose accounts are littered with
  inconsistencies, claimed that a bishop, pleading for his life and those of

What might strike the modern Western reader as complacency or an unnatural fatalism on Khaldun's part is no more than the submission to Allah traditionally required by Islam, a tenet of faith which continues to this day. But there was another reason, perhaps, for his calm and measured tone. Although Damascus was a pile of blackened, smoking ruins, its citizens butchered to the last man, he at least was safe and well.

'The whole city had burned, the roofs of the Umayyad Mosque had fallen in because of the fire, its gates were gone, and the marble cracked – nothing was left standing but the walls,' Ibn Taghri Birdi recorded sadly. 'Of the other mosques of the city, its palaces, caravanserais, and baths, nothing remained but wasted ruins and empty traces; only a vast number of young children was left there, who died, or were destined to die, of hunger.'*

⚭

---

his priests, was told to take them and their families to the mosque for protection. They numbered thirty thousand, he said. 'Now Temur gave orders that when the temple was full, the people should be shut up in it. This was done. Then wood was placed around the temple, and he ordered it to be ignited, and they all perished in the temple. Then he ordered that each one of his [soldiers] should bring to him the head of a man. This was done, and it took three days; then with these heads were constructed three towers, and the city was pillaged.' The court histories, however, report that Temur did all he could to prevent the conflagration in the mosque.

* In Marlowe's *Tamburlaine the Great*, the fall of Damascus is similarly grisly. Under siege, the governor of the city stalls for time before surrendering. While he delays, the flags flying in Tamburlaine's camp change from white to red to black, spelling disaster.

> *The first day when he pitcheth down his tents,*
> *White is their hue, and on his silver crest,*
> *A snowy feather spangled white he bears,*
> *To signify the mildness of his mind,*
> *That, satiate with spoil, refuseth blood:*
> *But when Aurora mounts the second time,*

While Cairo trembled at the prospect of sharing an equally apocalyptic fate, while Miranshah and Shahrukh laid waste to Antioch and
the surrounding region, the conqueror lay stricken with boils and a
damaged back. Illnesses and infections were beginning to attack him
in his autumn years.

Dreading Temur's continued progress south and west, preparing
for imminent flight, the people of Cairo met the reports of his northward marches with undisguised joy. Sultan Faraj meanwhile assured
the Tatar that the envoy Atilmish would be restored to his master.
But Temur, once he had recovered from his latest affliction, had other
concerns. Returning to the business of empire, he summoned his
favourite grandson and heir Mohammed Sultan from Samarkand,
appointing him ruler of the Hulagid dominions, formerly governed
by the young man's debauched uncle Miranshah. In the clearest sign
that he had no intention of returning home, whatever his ailments, he
ordered Mohammed Sultan to bring fresh troops, and gave separate
instructions for the imperial family to join him. There was no question of stopping now. The only issue was where to turn his restless

---

> *As red as scarlet is his furniture;*
> *Then must his kindled wrath be quenched with blood,*
> *Not sparing any that can manage arms:*
> *But if these threats move not submission,*
> *Black are his colours, black pavilion;*
> *His spear, his shield, his horse, his armour, plumes,*
> *And jetty feathers menace death and hell;*
> *Without respect of sex, degree, or age,*
> *He razeth all his foes with fire and sword.*

In a frantic attempt to save Damascus, the governor sends four virgins to
Tamburlaine to plead for mercy 'with knees and hearts submissive'. The
attempt is in vain. The virgins are butchered on the spot, their
'slaughtered carcasses' hoisted up onto the city walls, 'A sight as baneful to
their souls, I think,/As are Thessalian drugs or mithridate,' Tamburlaine
observes. 'But go, my lords,' he continues, 'put the rest to the sword.'
Damascus dissolves in flames.

energies next. The campaign would continue. The troops had been levied for a Seven-Year Campaign.

Temur now turned north towards the Caucasus, where he intended to winter among the congenial pastures of the Qarabagh. Hardly had he departed than reports arrived bringing discouraging news. The twenty thousand troops he had sent to retake Baghdad, five hundred miles to the east, had so far failed to make an impression. Rather than countenance this setback, Temur resolved, in typical fashion, to remedy it in person.

⁂

Baghdad, long known as Dar as Salam (the House of Peace), had been home to Temur's old adversary Sultan Ahmed, as well as the Turkmen chief Qara Yusuf of the Black Sheep tribe, to whom he had given sanctuary. In Temur's hard-headed calculations, the city was worth the abrupt detour. 'This city is more famous than can be described and the aroma of its excellence and merits more fragrant than can be shown,' wrote Arabshah. Ibn Battutah admired it as 'one of the largest of cities', steeped in Islamic history, home to the graves of Imam Abu Hanifa and Imam Ahmed ibn Hanbal, two of the founders of the four principal schools of jurisprudence in Sunni Islam.

By the time Ibn Battutah visited Baghdad in 1327, it had lost its status as glorious capital of the Islamic world, home of the caliphs, which it had enjoyed since 756. Descending on the city from the west with his Mongol hordes in 1258, Hulagu sacked and virtually destroyed it with a ferocity that would have pleased his grandfather Genghis Khan. For forty days fires consumed the city, burning down the Mosque of the Caliph, the shrine of the Shi'a imam Musa al Kazim and the tombs of the caliphs at Rusafah, together with most of the streets and houses.

Half a century after Hulagu had stormed through, Baghdad remained a barely twitching corpse. A long succession of invaders –

The sacking of Isfahan in 1387, scene of one of Temur's worst atrocities. Seventy thousand were slaughtered when the city rose against him after its capture. From the sixteenth-century *Timurnama* of Abdullah Hatifi.

RIGHT The Shrine of Shah Rukn-e-Alam in Multan, City of the Saints, in the Pakistani Punjab. Temur destroyed the city in 1398, en route to Delhi.

BELOW Babur's tomb, Kabul.

The captured Ottoman Sultan Bayazid I is brought before Temur after his humiliating defeat at the Battle of Ankara in 1402. From a sixteenth-century edition of the *Zafarnama* of Sharaf ad-din Ali Yazdi.

Babur, Temur's great-great-great-grandson and most illustrious descendant, founder of the Mughal dynasty of India.

LEFT The Astronomer King. Temur's grandson Ulugh Beg, mathematician, geographer, theologian, historian, poet and musician. The astronomical tables he devised were used by England's first Astronomer-Royal as late as the seventeenth century.

BELOW State propaganda Uzbekistan-style. The rather bland message from President Islam Karimov reads: 'Our forefather Amir Temur's good advice helps us.'

АМИР ТЕМУР БОБОМИЗНИНГ
ЎГИТЛАРИ БИЗГА
МАДАДКОР
БЎЛСИН !

ABOVE Temur, role model
for Uzbeks. The homilies read:
'Don't incite the wrath of
Allah or do evil to others or
act harshly towards them' and
'If people don't act together they
won't succeed.'

RIGHT Temur's burial place,
the Gur Amir Mausoleum in
Samarkand. 'The cincture of the
dome was of marble set off with
gold and azure,' wrote Ibn
Arabshah. 'Within it was dug a
vault in which to lay the prince's
body, and a charming garden
was made around it on the ruins
of some houses.'

The conqueror returns. This statue of Temur, in Amir Temur Square, Tashkent, was unveiled by the Uzbek president in 1993.

Temur through the ages: Portraits from *top right* seventeenth-century Germany, *left* eighteenth-century France and *above* nineteenth-century India.

ABOVE Alas, poor Temur. Soviet archaeologist Mikhail Gerasimov examines Temur's skull, exhumed on 22 June 1941. His investigations revealed a man tall for his time, with injuries to both right limbs.

RIGHT Temur's tomb inside the Gur Amir. The six-foot slab of black jade was the largest piece of the stone in the world.

Persian, Turk, Mongol – had shattered its very fabric. Around 1300, an anonymous author underlined the extent of the destruction in an update of the famous *Geographical Dictionary* compiled by Yakut in about 1226:

> Hence nothing now remains of western Baghdad but some few isolated quarters, of which the best inhabited is Karkh; while in eastern Baghdad, all having long ago gone to ruin in the Shammasiyah Quarter and the Mukharrim, they did build a wall round such of the city as remained, this same lying along the bank of the Tigris. Thus matters continued until the Tatars under Hulagu came, when the major part of this remnant also was laid in ruin, and its inhabitants were all put to death, hardly one surviving to recall the excellence of the past. And then there came in people from the countryside, who settled in Baghdad, seeing that its own citizens had all perished; so the city is indeed other than it was, its population in our time being wholly changed from its former state – but Allah, be He exalted, ordaineth all.

After the sacking of Hulagu, though Baghdad continued to enjoy considerable prestige as one of the great Islamic cities, in reality it was barely more than a provincial town living on its past as capital of Arabian Iraq. Ibn Battutah found the city still on its knees, but stirring.

> The western part of Baghdad was the earliest to be built, but it is now for the most part in ruins. In spite of that there remain in it still thirteen quarters, each like a city in itself and possessing two or three baths. The hospital is a vast ruined edifice, of which only vestiges remain. The eastern part has an abundance of bazaars, the largest of which is called the Tuesday bazaar.

Besides the markets, Ibn Battutah saw the three great mosques of the former home of the Abbasid caliphs still standing – the eighth-century mosques of Mansur and Rusafah, and the eleventh-century Mosque of the Sultan. He admired Baghdad's two bridges, 'on which the people promenade night and day, both men and women. The town has eleven cathedral mosques, eight on the right bank and three on the left, together with very many other mosques and madrassahs, only the latter are all in ruins.'

To judge from his account, Battutah took more interest in the city's baths than in what remained of its historical treasures: 'The baths at Baghdad are numerous and excellently constructed, most of them being painted with pitch, which has the appearance of black marble.' The Moroccan was much taken by their sophistication, re-marking approvingly on the 'large number of private bathrooms, every one of which has also a wash-basin in the corner, with two taps supplying hot and cold water'. What most fascinated him was the practice of giving each bather three towels, one to wear around his waist on entering the baths, one for when he left, and another with which to dry himself. 'In no town other than Baghdad have I seen all this elaborate arrangement,' he applauded.

Whatever the destruction it had suffered in recent times, Baghdad remained a city of prodigious size on Temur's arrival. Ibn Battutah's contemporary, the geographer Hamd Allah Mustawfi al Qazwini, described its walls, divided east and west across the river Tigris, as two sweeping semi-circles of eighteen thousand and twelve thousand paces respectively.

Aleppo and Damascus had folded before Temur's onslaught. It was unacceptable for Baghdad to defy the inevitable. Striking out from Syria, the Tatar hordes reached their latest target after a succession of forced marches. The order was given to surround the city, and the sol-diers struck camp on both sides of the Tigris. Though Baghdad was more than six miles in circumference, said Yazdi, the huge army encircled it with ease. A bridge of boats was built over the Tigris and archers stationed downriver to prevent the inhabitants escaping. Upriver, Miranshah and Shahrukh guarded the approaches to the city.

For the people of Baghdad it was the worst possible time to find themselves under siege. It was an extraordinarily fierce summer. The heat was so intense, said the chronicler, that birds fell dead in mid-flight and armoured soldiers 'melted like wax'. Looking out at Temur's numberless army encamped around their city, 'the astonished inhabitants no longer looked upon their city as the house of peace, but as the palace of hell and discord'. Panic-stricken, the defenders struggled to repair the mined walls as they tumbled about them. Temur's princes and amirs pleaded with him to order an all-out assault, a request he refused, Yazdi explained (rather improbably), on the grounds that the inhabitants would soon come to their senses and that it would be a shame to lay waste to this fine city.

Six weeks into the siege, on a day so hot that the defenders propped their helmets up on sticks behind the ramparts, abandoned their positions and returned home, the emperor ordered his men to storm Baghdad. The valiant Shaykh Nur ad-din was first up a scaling ladder, mounting Temur's famous horse-tail standard, crowned with a half moon, on the walls. Many of the inhabitants threw themselves into the Tigris in desperation, only to be cut down by the waiting archers. The governor and his daughter tried to escape in a boat but it was shot at and overturned. They drowned in the foaming Tigris.

Baghdad belonged to Temur again. To mark his retaking of the city which had caused him such trouble, he issued one of his most vengeful orders, born of his rage at losing so many men. The city could expect no mercy. Each soldier must fetch him a Baghdad head. Arabshah, who said the figure was two heads per man, described what happened next.

> They brought them singly and in crowds and made the river Tigris flow with the torrent of their blood throwing their corpses on to the plains, and collected their heads and built towers of them . . . Some, when they could not have Baghdadis, cut the heads off Syrians who were with them and other prisoners; others, when

> *heads of men were wanting, cut off the heads of ladies of the*
> *marriage-bed.*

Only the religious leaders and scholars of the city were granted quarter. They were given new robes of honour, fresh mounts and safe conduct out of Baghdad.

Next came the order that every house must be razed. Mosques, colleges and hospitals alone were to be spared, said Yazdi, though after events in Damascus, including the destruction of the Umayyad Mosque, this seems distinctly doubtful. Markets, caravanserais, monasteries, palaces and bath-houses went up in smoke. 'Thus, says the Alcoran, "The houses of the impious are overthrown by the order of God."'

With the Tigris red with blood and the air putrid with rotting corpses, Temur sailed serenely upriver to the tomb of Imam Abu Hanifa in eastern Baghdad – a graceful shrine topped with a white cupola – 'to implore the intercession of this saint'.* As he prayed, his soldiers were putting the finishing touches to the 120 towers of skulls they had erected around the flattened city. What Arabshah termed the 'pilgrimage of destruction' was almost at an end. Antioch and Acre, Baalbek and Beirut, Hama and Homs, all lay in ruins. Damascus had been torn apart and gutted. In Aleppo, twenty thousand heads had been severed. In Baghdad the atrocities had reached new heights. This time the vultures had ninety thousand to feed on.

V

---

* By the tenth century there were four schools of Islamic law based on the Koran, the *hadith* and the interpretations of the *ulema* (clergy). Abu Hanifa (699–767) founded the Hanifite system of jurisprudence which sought new ways of applying the tenets of Islamic law to everyday life. In practice, this interpretation of Muslim law is tolerant of differences within Muslim communities, and gives judges great discretion when neither the Koran nor the Sunna (traditions of the Prophet) are applicable.

'This Pilgrimage of Destruction'

History does not record the emotions of Temur's soldiers as they marched north from Baghdad to seek their winter quarters in the plains of the Qarabagh. Relief and joy, we can be sure, mingled with grief and exhaustion. There were numerous injured among them, their lives in the gift of the Almighty. Not all would live to see another campaigning season. Among the fit and well, many had grown rich from looting, their horses and camels staggering beneath loads of plunder. Some had been promoted for their heroic actions on the battlefield. Others simply longed for home.

Once more, Temur's Tatar hordes had given him the victories he had ordered. As he rode towards the Caucasus, the emperor must have cast a proud eye over this unflinching army. 'Soldiers, whether associates or adversaries, I hold in esteem,' he is supposed to have said. 'Those who sell their permanent happiness to perishable honour and throw themselves into the field of slaughter and battle, and hazard their lives in the hour of danger.'

For now, these men looked forward to nothing but rest. Banquets, drinking bouts, the pleasures of the flesh, all these awaited the weary soldiers in the rolling pastures of the Qarabagh. But the implacable Temur had other thoughts on his mind. As ever, the brilliant chess-playing warrior was one move ahead. War against his mightiest adversary had been brewing for some time. The first skirmishes had already been fought. Though his soldiers did not realise it, the hour of danger was close at hand.

9

Bayazid the Thunderbolt

1402

'To fight is our habit, to join in combat our aim, to struggle for the faith our task. The law of waging war for the cause of Allah Almighty is our rule . . . Our soldiers spend their lives and wealth for Allah, that they may gain Paradise.'

LETTER FROM SULTAN BAYAZID I TO TEMUR, 1402

'. . . Tush, Turks are full of such brags
And menace more than they can well perform.
He meet me in the field and fetch thee hence?
Alas, poor Turk! His fortune is too weak
T'encounter with the strength of Tamburlaine.'

CHRISTOPHER MARLOWE,
Tamburlaine the Great

During the recent months of campaigning, while his armies were putting Aleppo, Damascus and Baghdad to the sword and the flame, Temur had not neglected the arts of diplomacy. Ambassadors and couriers had been shuttling along the trade routes of Asia to further the conqueror's interests and damage those of the Ottoman Sultan

Bayazid I. They had travelled to Manuel II, the enfeebled Byzantine emperor who, under pressure from the Ottoman siege of Constantinople, had fled to Trebizond in northern Turkey where he confirmed his submission to Temur. The Tatar demanded that twenty war galleys be made available to him in advance of his next battle. Similar demands had been brought to Christian Constantinople, temporarily under the command of Manuel's nephew, Regent John, as well as to the Genoese at Pera on the Bosporus. Representing Catholic Europe, John of Sultaniya, who had been appointed Archbishop of the East and Ethiopia by Pope Boniface IX in 1398, arrived in the Tatar court with messages of goodwill from King Charles VI of France. For all his aspirations to become Islam's greatest defender, to earn the title of Ghazi, Warrior of the Faith, Temur's opportunistic instincts allowed him to do business with the infidel with a clear conscience.

By far the most important correspondence, however, was that between Bayazid and Temur. The themes had remained constant since their first diplomatic exchange, but the tone of the letters had become increasingly confrontational. Temur pressed his demands that Bayazid surrender to him his two long-standing adversaries, Sultan Ahmed of Baghdad and the rebellious Turkmen chief Qara Yusuf, both of whom had for years eluded him.

'Since we have been informed that your master wages war against the infidels of Europe, we have always held back from marching into his country with our army, unwilling to destroy a Muslim country which would only delight the infidels,' he told the Ottoman envoys. 'But there is nothing more disagreeable to us than to hear that he grants protection to Qara Yusuf Turcoman, the greatest robber and villain on earth, who pillages merchants, murders travellers and commits a thousand other crimes. What is most dangerous is that the wretch lives in the middle of a Muslim country where he is like a wolf among sheep.' Bayazid must either try Qara Yusuf and execute him, send him to Temur bound in chains, or expel him from his lands. In addition, he must return the castle of Kamakh on the western Euphrates to its previous master, Temur's ally Taharten.

But the all-conquering Ottoman, the man who had brought Christian Europe to its knees, was in no mood to compromise. To understand why, we must travel back six years to the disturbed courts of Christendom.

⚬

By the closing decade of the fourteenth century, Christian Europe had identified the Ottoman sultan as its greatest danger. At the gates of the continent, Byzantium was breathing her last, strangled by the Turkish forces who encircled her. In 1399 her emperor Manuel II had abandoned her, sailing west with a force of Genoese who had tried, and failed, to raise the Ottoman siege. Constantinople was entrusted to his nephew John. The Christian empire seemed poised to collapse under the sword of Islam. Still worse, from the European monarchs' perspective, their mainland had been breached and Christian territories taken, first Serbia at the battle of Kosovo in 1389, then Bulgaria in 1393. Bayazid, who had earned the nickname Yilderim (Thunderbolt, or Lightning) on account of the speed with which he moved between his western and eastern fronts, was even now encroaching on Hungary. The push west had to be halted before the Crescent was raised above the entire continent.

Racked by the plague, drained by the Hundred Years' War, and divided by the Great Schism with one pope in Rome and another in Avignon, Europe was in a perilously weak position from which to defend herself against the burgeoning power of Bayazid. Nevertheless, in recognition of the parlous position in which Christendom found itself, Popes Boniface IX of Rome and Benedict XIII of Avignon joined in calling for a Crusade against the Ottoman.

A Franco-German army was raised under the leadership of Count

John of Nevers, son of the Duke of Burgundy. As they marched east, the Crusaders were joined by another force of Germans and a smaller detachment from England. At Buda, their ranks were swelled with King Sigismund of Hungary's army of about ten thousand. By the time more knights had arrived from Wallachia, Poland, Bohemia, Italy and Spain, the Crusaders numbered around sixteen thousand, one of the largest armies Christendom had ever put into the field.

At Nicopolis on the Danube, they met an Ottoman army of similar size.* Bayazid had abandoned the siege of Constantinople and marched north on learning of their approach. Before the battle began, Sigismund, who was familiar with the Ottoman style of fighting, urged the French to hold back while his light troops charged the enemy lines, at which point the heavy European cavalry would attack. He also did not want his allies to advance too quickly from what was a sound defensive position. But the French and Burgundian Crusaders, hungry for the honour of leading the first charge, appalled by what they took as a slight to their fighting skills, and implacably opposed to entering battle behind men they regarded as peasants, refused to listen. The Count d'Eu grabbed a banner of the Holy Virgin and shouted to his men: 'Forward in the name of God and St George, today you shall see me a valorous knight.' Thus it was that on the morning of 25 September 1396, bursting with confidence and Christian valour, to rousing cries of 'For God and St Denis,' the knights of Europe galloped forward under billowing pennants.

For a while it seemed their impetuousness had succeeded, for the Crusaders, having crossed a ravine and climbed the hill towards their enemy, drove back and cut down the irregular Turkish infantry and light cavalry that faced them. Eventually they broke through

---

* Modern estimates of the numbers ranged against each other at Nicopolis contrast dramatically with those of the contemporary chronicles, which claimed the Ottoman and Crusader armies both totalled about a hundred thousand.

the enemy positions, protected by a forest of sharpened wooden stakes, and were on the point of celebrating when disaster suddenly loomed. Sigismund's advice had been sound. Now, exhausted from their exertions, sweating beneath their heavy armour, the Christians discovered with horror Bayazid's huge force of heavy cavalry awaiting them over the hill. The knights were on foot, having dismounted before the stakes guarding the Ottoman positions. Worse, the main force of Hungarians was too far behind them to lend immediate support.

Such tactical ineptitude, which divided the Crusading army into two weaker forces, was an unexpected gift to Bayazid. The order was given to charge. The Sipahi cavalry let out a terrible cry, horses' hoofs thundered across the ground, and the disorganised, disoriented French knights were hacked to pieces. 'The sound of trumpets rose to the sky,' wrote the Turkish poet Yusfi Meddah. 'Over their heads the clashing of swords. The blows seemed to rain down unsparingly. Fine warriors, in their hands maces, make a rending clashing noise as they fight. Arrows fall like rain and warriors seek to scatter arrows, the cowards seek to escape, leaving behind their quivers.' Six times the banner of the Virgin was knocked to the ground, and six times it was raised again. But the pressure from the Ottomans was too great. When Admiral de Vienne, rallying his Crusaders beneath the banner, was cut down and killed, the French knights surrendered. The Hungarians followed soon after. In desperate retreat, Sigismund managed to find his way back to the Danube, where he boarded a boat and sailed away to safety. 'We lost the battle by the pride and vanity of those French,' he famously said. 'If they had believed my advice, we had enough men to fight our enemies.'

Later that day, the Ottoman sultan issued another order. He had discovered the extent of his losses with mounting fury, not least the pile of massacred Turks – who had been taken prisoner before battle – in the luxurious Crusader camp. Now he vowed revenge. All prisoners barring the greatest knights, who could be ransomed for considerable sums, were to be slaughtered. Each Ottoman officer was ordered to kill all those he had captured. The battlefield ran with blood. The flower of European chivalry were executed in cold blood.

The Bavarian page Johann Schiltberger was among those condemned to death. 'They took my companions and cut off their heads, and when it came to my turn, the king's son saw me and ordered that I should be left alive and I was taken to the other boys because none under twenty years of age were killed and I was scarcely sixteen years old,' he later wrote. Schiltberger was saved only to be enslaved, but was not spared the spectacle of the mass execution.

> Then I saw lord Hannsen Greif, who was a noble of Bavaria, and four others bound with the same cord. When he saw the great revenge which was taking place, he cried with a loud voice and consoled the cavalry and infantry who were standing there to die. Stand firm, he said, when our blood this day is spilled for the Christian Faith, and we by God's help shall become the children of heaven. When he said this he knelt and was beheaded together with his companions. Blood was spilled from morning until vespers, and when the king's counsellors saw that so much blood was spilled and that it still did not stop, they rose and fell upon their knees before the king, and entreated him for the sake of God that he would forget his rage, that he might not draw down upon himself the vengeance of God, as enough blood was already spilled.

Estimates of the number of prisoners killed ranged from three hundred to Schiltberger's exorbitant figure of ten thousand. Surveying the battlefield, piled high with the dead and the dying, Bayazid the Thunderbolt had reason to be pleased with himself. The Crescent had triumphed emphatically over the Cross. He had annihilated the last Crusade. The crippling ransoms on the heads of the twenty most illustrious Crusaders would virtually bankrupt the treasuries of Christendom. Now, he boasted, he would ride on through Europe, crush the infidels with his invincible armies, and feed his horse on the altar of St Peter's in Rome.

⚛

Europe suddenly found herself depending for her survival on the Scourge of God, a man who for two decades had glorified in butchering Christians. In Georgia repeatedly, in Tana and Saray in the lands of the Golden Horde, and most recently in Sivas, Christians had been massacred in their thousands as Temur sought to add lustre to his Islamic crown.

This was a fortuitous coalescence of interests between Temur and the kings of Europe, no more, no less. In the Tatar's political universe, alliances tended to be convenient arrangements of the moment, to be picked up and dropped at whim, safe in the knowledge that he held overwhelming military force if events took an unexpected course. If Christians could be of use to him against Bayazid, then that was to his advantage.

His first concern, as he prepared for the critical encounter with his most powerful antagonist yet, was that the Christian powers should not obstruct his efforts in any way. His second was that they should offer all possible support. From Constantinople, Regent John, Temur's newest vassal, duly undertook to provide soldiers, galleys and tribute. The governor of the beleaguered Genoese colony at Pera did the same. Both men vowed to prevent Bayazid's troops in Europe crossing into Asia Minor to assist the Ottoman against Temur in a battle that grew more likely with each day.*

---

* John, like Temur, was something of an opportunist. While assuring the Tatar of his unswerving loyalty and readiness to lend him all possible support against Bayazid, he was simultaneously negotiating terms with the Ottoman. The double-dealing did not stop there. John had also opened up a third front, maintaining secret contact with Charles VI, the French king, to whom he proposed selling his throne and the remnants of his empire

Further indications that war was imminent came in February 1402 with Temur's instruction to his empresses to return to Sultaniya, a traditional prelude to conflict. Around this time the first military engagements began, as Mohammed Sultan, newly arrived from Samarkand, set about the successful siege and storming of the fortress at Kamakh, a direct challenge and provocation to Bayazid, who had only recently seized it from Temur's ally Prince Taharten.

Rather than wait for Bayazid to come to him, Temur stole the initiative by leading his army west on a series of forced marches to Sivas. Here he was perfectly stationed for an attack on the heart of Bayazid's empire. His amirs, however, in one of their periodic fits of pessimism, counselled against war. Their arguments must have sounded wearily familiar to the emperor: his troops were tired after campaigning in the field for three years, while the Ottoman forces, famed for their fierce fighting skills, were well rested and lavishly equipped. Their warnings were cut brutally short by the impatient Tatar. An astrologer was summoned to pronounce his verdict on the positions of the planets. He had learnt from the experience of Delhi, when he and his colleagues had advised against battle and had been roundly excoriated by Temur. The message now was more reassuring. The emperor was at the zenith of his power, Bayazid conveniently at his nadir. Well was the great conqueror named the Lord of the Fortunate Conjunction. This was a most auspicious time to do battle.

That Bayazid was equally keen on war and just as confident of victory is evident from a letter he sent Temur which reached the Tatar at Sivas. It was the most insulting letter yet from the Ottoman. Bayazid was, said Arabshah, a 'stalwart champion of the faith' and 'a just ruler, pious and brave in defence of religion', a verdict doubtless

---

in return for a regular salary and a castle in France. It was not altogether surprising, then, that as war with Bayazid approached, neither John nor the governor of Pera made any attempt to prevent the Ottoman troops in Europe returning to Asia Minor.

coloured by the Syrian's hostility towards Temur. Such piety was nowhere in evidence in this latest correspondence, in which, against all Muslim customs, Bayazid deliberately referred to the Tatar's wives in the most offensive fashion.

'So far as concerns his original state, certainly he was a brigand, a shedder of blood, who violated all that is sacred, broke pacts and obligations, an eye turned from good to evil,' the sultan's letter began, before going on to summon Temur to appear before him as though the Tatar were no more than his meanest vassal. Its ending was practically sacrilegious: 'I know that this speech will rouse you to invade our countries, but if you should not come, may your wives be condemned to triple divorce.'

Arabshah related the conqueror's reaction to this missive. 'And as soon as Temur read this reply, he was excited and said: "The son of Othman is mad, for he is prolix and sealed the purpose of his letter with the mention of women." For among them the mention of women is a crime and grave offence.'*

Bayazid had made his intentions abundantly clear. While his envoys were still in the Tatar camp, Temur responded in kind. He ordered a review of his army, to impress upon the ambassadors the vast size of his forces, veterans from his many campaigns drawn from all reaches of his empire. No power on earth could put such a cosmopolitan army into the world, according to Arabshah.

> There were men of Turan, warriors of Iran, leopards of Turkistan, tigers of Balkhshan, hawks of Dasht and Khata, Mongol vultures, Jata eagles, vipers of Khajend, basilisks of Andakan, reptiles of Khwarizm, wild beasts of Jurjan, eagles of Zaghanian and hounds of Hisar Shadman, horsemen of Fars, lions of Khorasan, and hyenas of Jil, lions of Mazanderan, wild beasts of the mountains, crocodiles

---

* Such customs were scrupulously observed, even in times of rejoicing. When a girl was born, her parents would refer to the child as 'one who hides behind the veil' or even 'a mistress of the bed'.

> *of Rustamdar and Talqan, asps of the tribes of Khuz and Kerman,*
> *wolves of Ispahan, wearing shawls, wolves of Rei and Ghazni and*
> *Hamadan, elephants of Hind and Sind and Multan, rams of the*
> *provinces of Lur, bulls of the high mountains of Ghor, scorpions*
> *of Shahrizor and serpents of Askar Makram and Jandisabur . . .*
> *To these were added hyena-cubs of slaves and whelps of Turkomans*
> *and rabble and followers and ravening dogs of base Arabs, and*
> *gnats of Persians, and crowds of idolaters and profane Magi.*

Alongside these hardened soldiers stood the gleaming ranks of fresh
troops under Mohammed Sultan, each detachment gorgeously arrayed
in its own colours. Some wore crimson, with matching shields, saddles
and ensigns. Others were resplendent in uniforms of bright yellow,
violet or white, their lances, quivers and clubs in identical colours.
And there, once again, were Temur's favourite prizes of war, the thirty
elephants from Delhi, 'covered with the most splendid trappings . . .
with towers on their backs in which were placed archers and casters
of wild-fire to spread terror and disorder wherever they should go'.

With the pomp and ceremony of the review at an end, the ambassadors were summarily dismissed. The time for diplomacy had passed.
Both sides were now prepared to risk their empires on a single
encounter. All that remained to be decided was where and when it
would take place.

⚇

While Temur's preparations continued, Bayazid had not been idle.
In 1396 he broke off the siege of Constantinople to rout the assembled
forces of Christendom. Now, six years later, he abandoned the siege
once again to marshal his forces. It was, though to a lesser extent
than that of his enemy, a cosmopolitan army.

> *He ordered the leaders of his warriors and the bold eagles of his*
> *army and the falcons and the finest of his braves and nobles of*
> *Karmian and the valiant horsemen of the seacoasts, the stallions*

> *of Karaman, the soldiers of the provinces of Mantasha, the cavalry*
> *of Sarukhan and all the Amirs of the* tumans *and* sanjaks *[districts]*
> *and lords of standards, leaders of divisions and all the governors*
> *of posts and places under the sway of both the capitals Brusa and*
> *Adrianople, and everyone that was carrying his white standard*
> *painted the green sea with the red blood of blond Greeks and split*
> *the black heart of every blue-eyed enemy with his black arrows,*
> *mounted on his piebald steed – all these he ordered to carry out*
> *their business and take their precautions and arms.*

War was imminent, but a battle of nerves had first to be fought before the two armies could take to the field. Temur had already marched much farther west than Bayazid had anticipated, and to that extent the Ottoman was on the back foot, faced with the prospect of a major encounter in his own lands, a destructive situation which Temur had always sought to avoid in Mawarannahr. Based on high ground around Ankara, Bayazid now resolved, against the advice of his senior amirs, to march east and halt the enemy's incursion into his territories. There were good reasons for this decision. It was harvest time, and Bayazid was determined to avoid the wholesale destruction and pillaging that would inevitably occur were he to wait passively for the Tatar's advance.

Learning from his scouts that Temur was headed for Tuqat, north-west of Sivas, the Ottoman led his army to head off this advance. But the Tatar, as masterful as ever in his feints and counter-feints, had taken a completely different route. Rather than follow the difficult road north to Tuqat through inhospitable hilly country, he slipped south-west instead, following the broad sweep of the Halys as it arced towards Ankara, all the time keeping the river between his forces and the Ottomans.* This,

---

* The Halys is today known as the Kizil Irmak, Turkey's longest river. Flowing from the east, it swings around in a giant 'C' shape through central Anatolia, cuts through the Pontic mountains in the north and empties into the Black Sea. The river was immortalised in the story of Croesus, the fabulously rich last king of Lydia in the sixth century BC. At

wrote Arabshah, was 'well-tilled country', full of 'shades, springs and choice fruits'. The Tatar soldiers 'ceased not to delight in crops and pastures and udders, amid *sidras* without thorns and tall trees set in order and spreading shade and flowing water and gentle breezes and health-giving delights, in security, tranquillity, abundance and amplitude, without fear, journeying at their convenience, confident of prosperity and victory, promising themselves wealth and spoils'.

For a week the Tatars continued their forced marches, until Qaysa-riyah, where they struck camp, rested the horses and pillaged the local countryside of all available crops. As Bayazid scoured the valleys and forests and mountains for his enemy, his scouts brought him perplexing news. There was no sight of the Tatar armies. They had vanished into the depths of Anatolia. Increasingly unnerved by the sudden disappearance of his enemy, Bayazid continued to march, seeking his quarry and waiting for fresh reports from his scouts. Still nothing. Then, as swiftly as he had vanished, Temur reappeared at Qir Shahr (now Kirşehir), south-east of Ankara, where the first vicious but inconclusive skirmish was fought. Pressing on at full speed, he led his men west until, after three more days, they arrived at the Ottoman base at Ankara, only recently abandoned by Bayazid. When reports reached the Turk of this lightning manoeuvre, he was 'seized with panic as though it were the day of resurrection and bit his hands with grief and remorse and roared and howled and burning with the fire of anger was almost suffocated and abandoned rest and sleep'.

Temur had seized a crucial advantage over his opponent. Time already favoured him. The Ottomans were a week's march away to

---

that time the river formed the boundary between his kingdom and the Persian empire of Cyrus the Great. Before he attacked, Croesus consulted the oracle at Delphi to tell him his chances of success. 'Cross the river Halys and you shall destroy a great nation,' came the reply. Confident of victory, Croesus invaded, only to be routed by his enemy. He had tragically misinterpreted the oracle, and it was his nation, not Persia, which was destroyed.

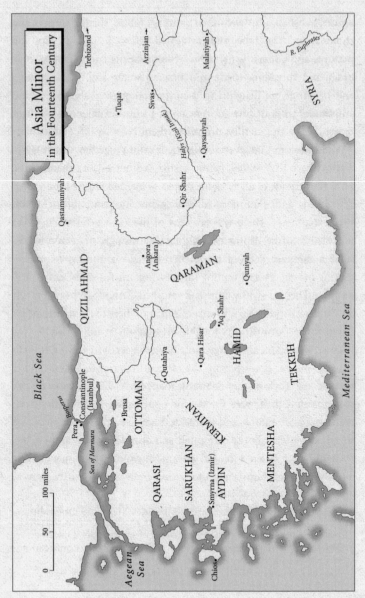

the east. This gave him the opportunity to choose the most favourable ground, dig in his positions, put Ankara under siege, destroy his enemy's camp, divert the river which supplied it and, most important, rest his march-weary men. This was where he would give battle, from the very position which Bayazid had, against his officers' advice, only just vacated. The manoeuvre bore all the hallmarks of Temur's tactical genius. It was swift, brilliantly executed and a devastating surprise to his opponent. It was, in addition, a powerful psychological blow for Bayazid to be outwitted in his own kingdom. Temur had struck decisively.

There was now no option for the Ottoman other than to order forced marches west to Ankara. The soldiers' morale was low, the country dry and unforgiving, stripped bare by Temur's hordes. By the time they approached Ankara they were in a pitiful condition, said Arabshah, 'perishing with distress and violent thirst'. The only water supply lay behind Temur's lines. It has been estimated that up to five thousand of Bayazid's troops died before the battle.

From the Ottoman point of view, the preparation for battle had been disastrous. Temur had outmanoeuvred Bayazid completely, drawing him out on a line and reeling him back in again with consummate ease. The sultan's troops had seen their leader struggle to keep up with an adversary whose name was spoken of in awe throughout Asia, a man who had never been defeated in battle and who had already seized control of the superior ground they themselves had once held. But Temur's preparations, although his adversary did not yet know it, went far deeper than this. Over several months he had been courting the Tatar tribes who had been recruited into Bayazid's army. Playing on their sense of tribal loyalties, he offered them lucrative spoils on condition they switch sides and join their brother Tatars when battle began. Though it is difficult to give an accurate assessment of the size of both armies, the chronicles make it clear that Bayazid's contingent of Tatars was immense. According to

Arabshah, 'It is said that the whole host of the Tatars nearly equalled the army of Temur.' Whatever the total, Temur's deserved reputation for generosity to his soldiers, which had fuelled his rise to power over Amir Husayn in 1370, was about to deliver him his most famous winning hand. The battle had been decided before it had even begun.*

So it was that at around 10 o'clock on the morning of 28 July 1402, the Conqueror of the World faced Bayazid the Thunderbolt on the plains east of Ankara. Once more his kettle-drums gave their tumultuous roar amid a deafening clash of cymbals and trumpets. For three decades this martial concert had been the harbinger of his enemies' collapse. The princes of Persia had heard it, so too the khan of the Golden Horde, the kings of Georgia, the sultans of Delhi, Baghdad and Egypt. This time, the drums and cymbals and trumpets sounded the doom of Bayazid. It was one of the greatest battles the region had ever seen.

Ill-prepared, outmanoeuvred and outwitted, the Ottoman army, exhausted after a week of forced marches, began the fighting on the defensive. As the first blows fell, as the skies darkened with arrows, the desertion of Bayazid's Tatar forces to Temur, orchestrated over a period of several months prior to the battle, proved decisive. Undermined by these losses, the Ottoman left wing under Prince Chelebi crumbled and fled the field. Consolidating these early advantages, Mohammed Sultan's elite Samarkand division charged the Serbian cavalry, which had been devastated to see a prince of the royal blood

---

* Estimating the size of historical armies is notoriously difficult. Chronicles can distort, eyewitnesses can exaggerate and historians can wildly speculate. In the case of the battle of Ankara, the discrepancies between the various estimates are particularly pronounced. In his 1984 study, for example, Ian Heath estimated Temur's army at eighty thousand at most, that of Bayazid at eighty to 120,000. This contrasts spectacularly with Johann Schiltberger's exorbitant figures of 1.6 million for Temur and 1.4 million for the Ottomans.

abandon his position. Following his example, they withdrew in flight.

Bayazid's resistance continued until nightfall, but Temur's centre of eighty regiments and thirty elephants had already put paid to the main body of his army. After hours encircled by Temur's forces, the Ottoman emperor's Janissaries were finally overcome. Bayazid was seized and delivered to his enemy. The Sword Arm of Islam, for so long raised in triumph over Europe and Asia, had been brought crashing down. Bayazid would never recover.

☙

What happened next has, over the centuries, been a matter of great contention. Much of the controversy can be blamed on Christopher Marlowe, for in the closing years of the sixteenth century and at the considerable remove of 185 years and 1,700 miles from the battle of Ankara, he penned the following prophetic lines:

> *The ages that shall talk of Tamburlaine,*
> *Even from this day to Plato's wondrous year,*
> *Shall talk how I have handled Bajazeth . . .*

The first-person refers to the eponymous protagonist of *Tamburlaine the Great*. But it can equally be understood to mean Marlowe himself, for in dramatising the immediate aftermath of the battle of Ankara he was, intentionally or otherwise, stepping into controversial territory. The issue in question was how Temur behaved towards Bayazid after his capture. It was a humiliating moment for the Sword Arm of the Faith. In the first three centuries of Ottoman history this was the only crushing defeat, the single instance in which the sovereign was captured in person.

Marlowe's version naturally aims for the sensational. Tamburlaine removes the crown from Zabina, Bajazeth's wife, and passes it triumphantly to his lover Zenocrate. In his first speech after the battle, the defeated Ottoman combines melancholy with defiance. Acknowledging that 'Never had the Turkish emperor/So great a foil by any foreign foe,' he reflects bitterly that his downfall will be welcomed by the Christians, 'Ringing with joy their superstitious bells'. But he refuses to accept his downfall. He has enough troops, he says, 'To make me sovereign of the earth again'.

After pouring scorn on these hopes, Tamburlaine refuses Bajazeth's request to be ransomed. Then he orders the Ottoman emperor to be bound and forced to attend a 'martial feast' to celebrate his victory. We next see Bajazeth at the opening of Act IV scene II, which begins with his astonishing arrival at the banquet in a cage drawn by two Moors. 'Bring out my footstool,' Tamburlaine commands. The stage directions – 'They take him out of the cage . . . He gets up upon him to his chair' – painfully emphasise his opponent's dishonour. There is no trace of magnanimity in victory. Every word, every action, is intended to shame Bajazeth.

> Base villain, vassal, slave to Tamburlaine,
> Unworthy to embrace or touch the ground
> That bears the honour of my royal weight,
> Stoop, villain, stoop! Stoop, for so he bids
> That may command thee piecemeal to be torn,
> Or scattered like the lofty cedar trees
> Struck with the voice of thundering Jupiter . . .
> Now clear the triple region of the air,
> And let the majesty of heaven behold
> Their scourge and terror tread on emperors.

Zabina, meanwhile, has been treated to her own degradation, becoming the slave of Zenocrate's handmaiden. Bajazeth objects, warning Tamburlaine that such ambitious pride will be his ruin. He is immediately returned to his cage. Accompanied by his Persian lords and followers, Tamburlaine taunts his adversary repeatedly, trying unsuccessfully to feed him morsels of meat from the point of his sword.

The proud Ottoman flings the food away, but later confesses to his wife that he is fading away. The humiliation at Tamburlaine's hands eventually proves too much for the Turk. With no end in sight to his 'obscure infernal servitude', he chooses the only honourable alternative and takes his life, Marlowe providing the immortal stage direction, 'He brains himself against the cage.' Discovering her late husband's grisly remains, his widow Zabina is devastated. There is nothing else for it. Chasing her husband's shadows into the afterlife, 'She runs against the cage and brains herself.'

⊚

History was rather less dramatic. The debate over whether Bayazid was thrown into a cage, a hugely degrading punishment for one of the world's most powerful sovereigns, can be traced back to Arabshah, whose acid hostility to Temur we have already observed. The Syrian chronicler claimed that 'Ibn Othman [Bayazid] was taken and bound with fetters like a bird in a cage ... Ibn Othman he ordered to be brought to him every day, and received him with kind and cheerful speech and marks of pity, then derided and mocked him.' Arabshah also had Bayazid attending Temur's victory banquet, where he was further humiliated.

> *Ibn Othman saw that the cupbearers were his consorts and that all of them were his wives and concubines; then the world seemed black to him and he thought the likeness of the agonies of death sweet and his breast was torn and his heart burned, his distress increased, his liver was crushed, groans came from the bottom of his heart and his sighs were redoubled, his wound broke out again and his sore was newly inflamed and the butcher of calamity scattered salt on the wound of his affliction.*

Yazdi, by contrast, offers a version much more favourable to Temur, as we have come to expect from the court panegyrist. The victorious emperor delivers a brief lecture to the effect that Bayazid has committed a great deal of injustice towards Temur, and is therefore the author of his own downfall. Temur claims never to have wanted the war, 'because I knew that your troops were always at war with the infidels. I have used all possible ways of mildness; and my intention was, if you had harkened to my counsels, and consented to a peace, to have given you powerful succours, both of money and troops, to carry on the war for religion with greater vigour, and to exterminate the enemies of Mohammed.' Nevertheless, he goes on, 'to return thanks to God for my good fortune in this battle, I will neither treat you nor your friends ill; and you may rest satisfied as to that point'. Bayazid, Yazdi assures the reader, was treated with the utmost respect as a 'great emperor'. Indeed, such was the esteem in which Temur held him that when, in March 1403, he learnt of Bayazid's death in captivity, Temur was reportedly moved to tears by the news. He had, said Yazdi, been planning to restore the sultan to his throne.

Yazdi's account is characteristically fulsome. There is as little reason to regard his as the definitive version of events as there is to trust that of the hostile Arabshah. That there was a great deal of bad blood between Temur and Bayazid is beyond question. But that held equally for many of Temur's other adversaries, and none had been treated so contemptuously in defeat. Humiliating his vanquished opponents had never been his style. Instead, by far his most common practice was to reinstall them as vassal kings, which is precisely what he did in the case of Bayazid's sons. The Ottoman prince Sulayman Chelebi, who received his father's European lands and a capital at Adrianople, explicitly acknowledged Temur's honourable behaviour towards Bayazid in a letter to the Tatar. The clearest suggestion, however, that Arabshah's story of the Ottoman sultan being confined behind bars was fanciful, is the Turkic word 'kafes' in the chronicles, which can mean either litter or cage. It is thus quite possible, likely even, that Bayazid was brought to Temur in a litter after the battle, a conventional mode of transport for the sultan.

There are other reasons to doubt Arabshah's version. Clavijo makes no mention of a cage; nor, critically, does Schiltberger, who had been taken captive at Nicopolis in 1396 and after the battle of Ankara became one of Temur's slaves. The last word on the subject must go to John Buchan Telfer, the translator of the Bavarian's narrative. 'The fable of the iron cage is scarcely worth recalling to mind,' he argued, 'but had there been a shadow of truth in it, Schiltberger would not have failed to notice the circumstance of the powerful monarch he had served so long being thus ignominiously treated.'

In the carnage of Ankara, Nicopolis had become a distant memory. The days of Bayazid's glory were over. Caged or not, the Thunderbolt had struck for the last time.

While messengers fanned out across Temur's empire carrying news of his famous victory, the emperor made plans to exploit it to the full. With the most serious fighting over, Bayazid's lands stretched invitingly before him like an unlocked palace. To his west lay Brusa, seat of the Ottoman empire and flourishing centre of the caravan trade through Asia Minor. Mohammed Sultan was given the enviable task of riding out to seize its treasures, although Prince Sulayman Chelebi, after narrowly beating him to the city from Ankara, had removed many of its greatest prizes. Among those which remained were the richly decorated bronze gates, inlaid with representations of St Peter and St Paul and finished with enamel, gold and azure. These were later presented to the Great Empress Saray Mulk-khanum on Temur's return to Samarkand. When everything else of value had been taken, the city was torched.

As the Tatar hordes sped west after their fugitives, the Sea of

Marmara, gateway to Europe, became choked with fleeing Turks. Reneging on their earlier agreement with Temur, the Genoese and Venetian merchants who controlled the eastern shores of the sea struck lucrative deals with the desperate Ottomans, ferrying them across the water to safety on the European mainland. It was not all plain sailing for the Turks, however. Some of the less scrupulous Christians, according to one chronicle, killed their Muslim passengers and threw them overboard in revenge for the punishing sieges Bayazid had inflicted on Constantinople.

Undefended, the provinces of Asia Minor meekly offered up their prizes to the invaders. The hordes thundered to the outer reaches of Bayazid's fractured empire. Silver coins, precious stones, pearls, vessels and furniture of gold and silver were despatched directly to the emperor. Everything else worth seizing was loaded onto the long trains of camels and horses and returned east. One by one, towns and cities fell to Temur's rapacious men. It was, said Arabshah, an orgy of cruelty.

> They shaved heads, amputated necks, crushed arms, cut off shoulderblades, burnt livers, scorched faces, gouged out eyes, split open bellies, blinded the sight, made tongues mute, blocked the hearing, crushed noses to the earth and brought low the lofty noses, lacerated mouths, shattered chests, crushed backs, pounded the ribs, split navels, melted hearts, severed sinews, shed blood, injured private parts, did violence to souls, destroyed men, poured out bodies like molten images, destroyed lives, and not a third or fourth part of the subjects of Rum escaped the havoc which they dealt, but most of them were either strangled or struck down or hurled headlong or destroyed by goring or devoured by wild beasts.

As news of this apocalypse filtered across the Aegean, Europe started to tremble at the prospect of Temur's westward advance. Bayazid had folded before this terrible force. Christendom now lay prostrate before the Lame Conqueror. Its armies were no match for these rough men of the steppes, steeled by years of victory. If the emperor's famous crimson standard, the swinging horse-tail beneath a shining golden crescent, were to appear on the European mainland, the days of Christendom were surely over.

&

Among the court observers of Temur's emphatic victory over Bayazid were two distinguished Spanish knights. Payo de Sotomayor and Hernan Sanchez de Palazuelos had been sent by their farsighted King Henry III of Castile to bring him news from the Levant. The Spanish king, who despatched embassies far and wide, to the princes of Christendom as well as the Moors, asked them to report on the customs, the armies and the intentions of the rulers in that region. After a long and arduous journey, the knights had been received gracefully by Temur at his camp outside Ankara. While their Tatar hosts showered them with every comfort and courtesy, they watched events unfold on the battlefield with a mixture of admiration and dread. That Temur the Lame was a powerful Asian monarch they had fully expected. But for him to overcome the army of Bayazid, the scourge of the last Crusade, was beyond comprehension. Armed with the typical European prejudices of their time, they regarded Asia – if they considered the continent at all – with condescension, as the home of rude savages. It was inconceivable that Asia should produce a mighty Muslim warrior capable of routing Europe's greatest enemy.

In time the two Spaniards were dismissed and, together with Temur's return envoy, Mohammed al Qazi, sent home with fabulous presents of jewels and women for King Henry. (It was in response to this embassy that Clavijo embarked on his diplomatic mission, intending to reach Temur in his winter pastures in Georgia, but forced through delay to press east to Samarkand.) Among the Christian women whom Temur had rescued from Bayazid's harem was

Angelina, daughter of Count John of Hungary, a famous beauty of her age, celebrated by the poets.*

In the weeks that followed the battle of Ankara, European monarchs grew increasingly uneasy as news of Temur's victory reverberated throughout the heart of Christendom. Their reactions were highly ambivalent. On the one hand, the conqueror of Bayazid had done them an enormous service by eliminating their most powerful adversary at a stroke. On the other, they wondered fearfully whether this mysterious Oriental despot, who had surged forth unannounced from unknown Asia, would now continue west across the Aegean.

Letters were despatched from Temur's camp. Archbishop John of Sultaniya departed to the court of the French king Charles VI with imperial missives boasting of the conqueror's triumph and stressing the need for unhindered commerce between the two continents.† In England, King Henry IV received similar correspondence. For a continent riven by division and ruled by impecunious princes, there was little question of opposing Temur. Nicopolis, from which their diminished armies and dwindling coffers were still recovering, was too painful a memory. Instead, Christendom turned to frantic diplomacy, the only option left to it. A stream of sycophantic messages coursed east.

From his newly seized throne in England, Henry, anxious to be recognised by such an important potentate, sent earnest congratulations to a warlord he had never met. From Charles VI of France came fulsome praise to 'the most victorious and serene Prince Themur', along with thanks for the Tatar's enlightened treatment of Christian merchants travelling in his lands. Bearing priceless jewels

---

* Sotomayor and Palazuelos must have greatly enjoyed their return journey in the company of these beautiful women. Indeed, Sotomayor was so captivated by a Greek woman called Maria that on arriving in Spain he declared his love, and later had a son by her. Angelina married Diego Gonzalez de Contreras, a noble Spaniard and magistrate of Segovia.

† All the evidence available indicates that Temur was an early and forceful proponent of free trade.

and gold florins, ambassadors arrived from Manuel II, the Byzantine emperor who had appealed for help from Temur against the Ottomans, reaffirming his submission and offering tribute in return for future protection from the Turks. The Regent of Constantinople added his voice to the chorus of Temur's newest admirers, joined by the ever pragmatic Venetians. The Genoese colony at Pera, demonstrating the merchant's time-honoured understanding of the shifting balance of power, rushed to profess its allegiance and Temur's pennant was immediately hoisted over the Bosporus.

Old foes suddenly saw the error of their ways. In answer to Temur's command, Sultan Faraj of Egypt and Syria quickly offered his submission. Temur's ambassador Atilmish was returned to his master, accompanied by gold and silver, precious jewels and horses in gorgeous livery. As was customary for defeated opponents, the conqueror's titles were announced in the Friday prayers and coins were struck in his name. Faraj conveyed the news that he had imprisoned two of Temur's longest-standing and most troublesome adversaries, Sultan Ahmed of Baghdad and Qara Yusuf, prince of the Black Sheep Turkmen tribes. As for what he should do with the two men, Faraj declared he was at Temur's service.

※

Temur had always understood the symbolic importance of history and tradition. They formed a powerful part of the way he presented himself to his people and to his enemies. Much of his attachment to history was self-serving. Aware of his own place in the long line of world conquerors, determined to leave future generations with an official record of his achievements, he had his military campaigns scrupulously recorded and exalted.

That he also possessed a powerful intellectual interest in history seems beyond dispute. It was evidenced by his love of debate – to which the hostile Arabshah referred – by his assembly of illustrious scholars to grace his court and, in a single instance, by the great notice he showed Ibn Khaldun, the Arab historian, in the remarkable series of audiences he granted him during a month camped outside the city walls of Damascus in 1401.

Traditions he regarded with a measure of expedience. As long as they legitimated his authority, they were observed. But they could also be manipulated. His raising of the banner of Islam, in particular, marked a clear departure from the shamanism of the Mongols, but the invocation of *jihad* also gave religious authority to his conquests and conferred upon him a definite prestige.

From 1370, when he first rose to power as the ruler of Chaghatay, Temur had taken care to install a puppet khan, in recognition of the Mongol laws by which only a blood descendant of Genghis Khan was entitled to rule. Though all knew who wielded the power, Temur himself assumed the junior title of Amir. By doing so, he was showing his respect, however disingenuously, for the customs of the steppe.

The *yasa*, the customary laws, would have been recognisable to Genghis's Mongols almost two hundred years earlier. Temur cultivated this hinterland of convention in order to legitimise what was in effect a profoundly revolutionary enterprise, subsuming the tribal practices and hierarchies of the *ulus* into an overarching political system based on the empire-building of one man and his armies. On the battlefield, the formation of his soldiers – with left and right wings, a centre and vanguard – would likewise have been familiar to the Mongols of the thirteenth century.

His marriage in 1370 to Husayn's widow Saray Mulk-khanum further reinforced his authority as ruler, since she was both daughter of the last Chaghatay khan of Mawarannahr and a princess of the Genghis line. The marriage allowed him to style himself Temur Gurgan, son-in-law of the Great Khan, a title which he took care to use in ceremonial functions as well as in the Friday prayers and even on the coins minted in his name.

Bayazid the Thunderbolt

With the defeat of Bayazid and the surrender of Faraj, the Islamic world's two greatest empires had fallen to him. Alone and unchallenged, Temur now stood at its helm. Given his statesmanlike awareness of the power of tradition and the resonating force of religion, it was only natural that he should cast his eyes on a small stronghold halfway down the Aegean coast. Smyrna was the last Christian oasis in Rum, a symbolic affront to the new master of Asia Minor.* Equally compelling as an incentive to destroy it was the fact that both the Ottoman Sultan Murad and his son Bayazid had tried and failed. The Thunderbolt, indeed, had spent seven fruitless years attempting to wrest it from the Knights of the Hospital of St John, a military religious order founded in Jerusalem in the eleventh century. The temptation for Temur to succeed where others had so conspicuously failed was overwhelming.

Any hopes of clemency the knights might have harboured vanished with their refusal to surrender. Although they had not reckoned on having to defend themselves against the irresistible Temur, their confidence was understandable. Their position, high on a rocky outcrop extending into the sea, looked unassailable. To take it would require a two-pronged attack by land and water, a task that appeared beyond the bounds of siege technology. But such difficulties would only have appealed to Temur's imagination and cunning.

His amirs ordered the men to build platforms, supported by sunken columns, across the sea, effectively cutting off the citadel from the shore. Siege engines then rumbled across towards the bottom of the walls, while scaling ladders were put into position. Hour after hour the Tatars loosed volleys of Greek-fire into the heart of Smyrna, observing with satisfaction the black curls of smoke which started to rise into the sky from the stricken city. Great mounds of timber were set alight by the walls, but the heavy rains of December prevented

---

* Today it is the Turkish port of Izmir.

343

their collapse. For a fortnight the two sides faced each other down, the besieged defending manfully against the swarming Tatars. Eventually the unrelenting pressure began to tell. Breaches started appearing in the walls, and Temur's men rushed through, an irresistible deluge flattening everything before it. The Knights Hospitallers had mounted a courageous resistance, but now they were overrun by superior numbers intent on slaughter and destruction. Once more Temur presided over a mass execution as the souls of the stubborn infidels were despatched.

There was a last macabre flourish to the fall of Smyrna. A fleet of galleys was spotted carrying reinforcements for the beleaguered knights. They did not know it, but they had arrived too late. As they neared the shore, Temur ordered the severed heads of the Smyrna garrison to be launched against their brother officers in the ships. The flame-throwing weapons were quickly adjusted to fit their new missiles. Soon the sky was thick with bloody skulls raining down on the horrified relief convoy, pounding into the wooden decks and striking down the knights as they prepared for battle. Temur's atrocious plan had its intended effect. Appalled by the bombardment of heads, demoralised by the slaughter of their colleagues, the knights turned round and set sail for home.

The familiar call of *jihad*, echoing through the ranks of his warriors, had been answered. The last independent bastion of Christianity, which for years had frustrated the best efforts of the Ottomans to reduce it, lay in ruins. Two piles of skulls hacked from the bodies of the fallen knights commemorated another famous victory. The infidels had followed the army of Bayazid to a crushing defeat.

For years Baghdad, Cairo and Damascus, together with the Ottoman emperor, had regarded the cripple from Samarkand with undisguised distaste and disdain. He was not a Muslim, they sneered, he was merely a barbarian. One by one, after ignoring his warnings of the defeat he would inflict on them, they had been silenced. Temur's claim to be the supreme Sword Arm of Islam no longer looked like an idle boast. On the contrary, it seemed a statement of the obvious.

⁶⁶

For the insatiable Temur, one question loomed above all others: what next? Supreme in the *dar al Islam*, the Muslim world, he now had to look beyond its borders for future conquests.

But before this question could be answered, there was the wreckage of the Ottoman empire to attend to. Minor rulers who had been deposed by Bayazid were returned to power as vassal princes. Prince Sulayman Chelebi, having confirmed his submission to his father's conqueror on pain of war, was granted the Ottoman territories in Europe. Another brother, Isa Chelebi, was awarded the heartland of the fragmented empire in north-west Anatolia. In this way Temur kept the Ottoman princes in check through the classic policy of divide and rule, just as he had done in the aftermath of defeating Tokhtamish of the Golden Horde. Emperor Manuel, who had been languishing penniless in the courts of Europe in self-imposed exile, was ordered back to his throne. Constantinople would fall, but Temur had bought it another fifty years.

Still, the kings of Christendom dared not relax. Dreadful rumours were spreading through their courts. The barbarian conqueror was requisitioning ships to lead his hordes onto European soil. He was marching his men around the Black Sea. He meant to convert the entire continent to Islam at the point of a sword. Even now, the vanguard of his armies had landed and was marching west. It was only a matter of days before it encircled Rome.

Such cataclysmic visions bore the hallmark of Europe's myopia. Her poverty was her best defence against an invasion. From the Aegean to the Atlantic, there was little to tempt Temur into launching another holy war. Killing or converting the infidels was a noble aim in itself, of course, but Temur regarded such considerations with a more mercantile eye. Europe's coffers and treasure houses were bare. No jewels, no *jihad*.

The aged emperor must also have known that before too long the Angel Izrail would be summoning him from earth. The seventy-two beautiful virgins who awaited him in paradise would surely not be kept waiting much longer. There was no point in squandering the precious time which remained to him on such a worthless continent as Europe.

But while he still lived, and while he could still move, there was yet time for one more campaign. He had contemplated it for years. Preparations had already been made along the farthest frontiers of his empire. His last expedition would be his most glorious. Once more he would proclaim *jihad*. He would challenge and overcome the only power on earth capable of opposing him. Poised on the shores of Europe, Temur led his army east. Christendom heaved a collective sigh of relief. Temur was bound for war with the Ming emperor of China.

10

The Celestial Empire

1403–1404

'God has favoured us with such extraordinary good fortune that we have conquered Asia and overthrown the greatest kings of the earth. Few sovereigns in past ages have acquired such great dominions, or attained such great authority, or had such numerous armies or such absolute command. And as these vast conquests have not been obtained without some violence, which has caused the destruction of a great number of God's creatures, I have resolved to perform some good action which may atone for the crimes of my past life, and to accomplish that which no other power in the world can do, that is to make war on the infidels and exterminate the idolaters of China.'

Temur's speech to his princes and amirs, 1404.
SHARAF AD-DIN ALI YAZDI, *Zafarnama*

China was in a state of turmoil. In the opening years of the thirteenth century, Genghis Khan had launched his hordes against it, sacking Peking in 1215. The drawn-out assault was pressed home by his son Ogedey, who conquered ever more territories, and was finally concluded by Genghis's grandson Kubilay, who became the undisputed

Great Khan in 1264, after defeating his brother Arigh Boke for the throne. Abandoning Karakorum, traditional imperial capital of the Mongols, he moved south and took up his winter headquarters in the magnificent city of Peking (then known as Ta-tu, or Khanbaliq, City of the Khan). His fabulous summer capital of Sheng-tu later inspired Samuel Taylor Coleridge's Xanadu in the Englishman's opium-fuelled poem 'Kubla Khan'.

Encompassing China and Mongolia, this new empire dwarfed and outshone the three Mongol houses of Chaghatay in Central Asia, Hulagu in Persia and Iraq, and Jochi in the Golden Horde, over each of which it exercised nominal sway. Stories of its grandeur filtered back to Europe via the high-spirited prose of the Venetian traveller Marco Polo, who entered the Great Khan's service for the best part of two decades. For years, China had been divided between north and south. With Kubilay's conquests south of the Yangtse, the Sung dynasty was eventually defeated in 1279 and China was at last reunited. The Yuan dynasty proclaimed by Kubilay would continue until 1368. His reign was a time of prosperity as trade and communications flourished between East and West. Two hundred thousand boats a year plied the Yangtse, ferrying silk, rice, sugar, pearls and gems between the principal cities of the Middle Kingdom. Merchants looked beyond their borders to the markets of Persia and India, Java, Malaya and Ceylon. Drama, literature and painting started to thrive.

With Kubilay's death in 1294, however, the empire embarked on a steady decline. The khan was partly to blame for this state of affairs. On acceding to the Chinese throne, he dispensed with the Mongol custom of electing leaders at a general assembly of the princes, replacing it with a simple hereditary principle, undermining at a stroke the authority of the nobles. Though he was spared any revolt, his successors were not. The Great Khans who succeeded Kubilay, already prone to idleness and dissipation, were beset by palace intrigues and attempted coups. Following the assassination of the Yuan emperor

Ying-zong in 1323, China tore itself apart during a decade of civil war and bloodshed. Disease – possibly the Black Death – and a rash of natural disasters combined to devastate the increasingly fragile empire.

The last Mongol emperor, Sun Ti, was famously cruel, lustful and incompetent. Rather than attend to the desperate famines that were racking the countryside, he turned his attentions to the bedchamber, where he had his concubines perform such erotic delights as the 'Heavenly Devil's Dance' for his pleasure. Taxes rose to punitive levels to fund his debauchery, and it was little surprise when a series of Chinese rebellions against Mongol rule broke out along the Yangtse and Huai river valleys, and started to gain momentum. In the 1350s, a peasant leader called Chu Yuan-chang emerged at the head of one such movement and picked off his rivals one by one. Part of his army was despatched north 'to deliver the suffering people from the fire that would burn and the waters that would drown them', namely the tyrannical government of the Mongols. Sweeping towards Peking, the peasant army trounced whatever resistance was offered, which was slight. There was little appetite among the people to fight for their louche, cowardly emperor Sun Ti, and those around him sensed that the Mongol domination of China was drawing to a close. The army of insurgents grew bigger daily, and by 1368 had developed into an irresistible force, seizing Peking and driving the Mongols out of northern China. Sun Ti slunk into exile.

In the same year that the capital of the empire fell, the simple peasant Chu Yuan-chang, enjoying his burgeoning power, changed his name and had himself proclaimed Emperor Tai Tsu, founding ruler of the Ming dynasty. For thirty years he ruled absolutely, if not serenely, restoring order to the turbulent empire, developing enlightened agricultural policies, and executing those who opposed his reforms. The Chinese legal and political system, uprooted by the Mongols, was brought back, albeit adapted to suit the needs of this commanding emperor. Members of the royal family were appointed to govern the richest, most strategic cities of the empire, where they built themselves palaces, assembled armies and, in time, inevitably nursed ambitions of their own.

In 1399 Tai Tsu died, leaving his sixteen-year-old grandson and heir Hui Ti struggling to retain power. Temur learnt this news shortly after his return from India, but he was then already resolved to march west, to Syria, Egypt, and war with Bayazid. Through his network of spies, diplomats and merchants he kept himself informed about the parlous state of affairs at the heart of China. The new young ruler was hard pressed by one of his dissatisfied uncles, the Prince of Peking, whose covetous eyes had fixed upon the imperial throne and whose army was the most powerful in the empire. Declaring that he was the emperor's loyal servant, the prince led his forces south in what he called the 'War for Pacifying the Troubles'. Under the guise of fighting the court ministers who were, he claimed, disturbers of the peace, the prince made his bid for supreme power. The war would last four years. As Peking and her territories descended into fratricide and unrest, Temur began to close in on his latest target. The Celestial Empire was ripe for attack.

China was the most fitting prize for a man who had never been defeated in battle. Well aware of his own mortality, the stooped, half-blind emperor required a suitable finale to his military career. The campaign against China justified itself on the critical questions of religion, money, honour and Mongol tradition. Untold riches awaited the ruler who could seize Peking, capital of an empire which in recent years, said the chronicles, had been persecuting Muslims by the tens of thousands and viciously suppressing all traces of Islam. Here, above all other places, there was fame and virtue to be won in slaughter and plunder. Yazdi, in a rare acknowledgement that the Sword Arm of Islam had despatched many more Muslims than infidels to their deaths, wrote of Temur's hope that victory over China 'might rectify what had been amiss in other wars, wherein the blood of so many of the faithful had been spilled'. The conquest of China would, moreover, mark the completion of Temur's lifelong quest to unite under his rule the four Mongol kingdoms won by the sons of Genghis Khan. Chaghatay had been the first to recognise Temur as its sovereign, followed by the houses of Jochi and Hulagu. All that was missing was the house of Kubilay, the only Mongol empire which had not embraced Islam. Not only had the true faith failed to establish itself here, indeed been brutally suppressed, but – calumny of calumnies – the religion of the infidels had stolen in and won imperial favour. 'It was told us that this new Emperor of China had by birth been an idolater, but lately had been converted to the Christian faith,' reported the Spanish envoy Clavijo.

Temur's preparations for war against his most redoubtable enemy were meticulous. As ever, his intelligence network had been set to work well in advance. The men who plied the caravan routes of Asia brought him regular reports on the deteriorating political conditions in the Celestial Kingdom. News came of Muslim merchants being expelled from China, an intolerable insult which Temur regarded as his duty to avenge. Arriving in Tashkent in 1398 with Temur's returning envoy, the Chinese ambassador An Chi tao was detained and then sent on a tour of the Tatar's lands, closely guarded at all times. His unexpected and forcible diversion took him as far west as Tabriz, to Shiraz, Isfahan and Herat. It lasted six years. By the time his embassy ended it had become one of the diplomatic world's longest missions. Ambassador An returned to Peking twelve years after taking leave of his emperor.*

---

* It is probably fair to say that Ambassador An, unlike his captor Temur, did not have a great gift for timing. Like many people who undergo unusual adventures, he wrote a book about them. Any hopes he might have entertained of his memoirs becoming a Chinese bestseller, however, were cruelly dashed. His collected poems, *On Curious Things Seen on a*

The calculated snub to the Ming emperor was a reflection of Temur's growing power and confidence. Over the years his relationship with Peking had evolved from the deference suitable to a weaker monarch, to increasing defiance, and finally outright hostility. Clavijo, during his stay in Temur's court, carefully observed the affronts suffered by another Chinese envoy – probably sent to demand Ambassador An's release – in the process confirming that the Tatar had, until recently, acknowledged his subordinate status to the Ming ruler. 'Now this ambassador had lately come to Temur to demand of him the tribute, said to be due to his master, and which Temur year by year had formerly paid,' the Spaniard wrote.

Chinese archives tell a similar story. In a letter to Temur's son Shahrukh, written in 1412 and addressed as though to a mere general rather than a head of state, the emperor Cheng Tsu urged him to accept his position as vassal ruler. Otherwise, it threatened, he would feel the consequences: 'Your father Temur Gurgan, obeying the decree of almighty God, recognised himself the vassal of our sublime emperor. He continually sent him both gifts and ambassadors and in this way he gave peace and happiness to the people of your distant country . . . you must likewise consider us your sovereign with all sincerity and of your own accord, without our having to intervene to force you to it.' The elaborate titles Temur enjoyed at home – Emperor of the Age, Conqueror of the World – were unthinkable at the court of the Ming emperor. For the emperors in Peking, the Tatar was simply Fou-ma Temur of Samarkand.*

As late as 1394, Temur was still addressing the Ming emperor with fulsome praise:

Journey to the West, were not released during his lifetime. The volume was eventually published in the seventeenth century.
* 'Fou-ma' referred to Temur's title of Gurgan, son-in-law of Qazan, the last Chaghatay khan of Mawarannahr, through his marriage to Saray Mulk-khanum, his Great Queen.

I respectfully address your Majesty, great Ming Emperor, upon whom Heaven has conferred the power to rule over China. The glory of your charity and your virtues has spread over the whole world. The splendour of your reign is bright like the heavenly mirror, and lights up the kingdoms, the adjoining as well as the far ... The nations which never had submitted now acknowledge your supremacy and even the most remote kingdoms submerged in darkness have now become enlightened ... Your Majesty has graciously allowed the merchants of distant countries to come to China to carry on trade. Foreign envoys have had a chance of admiring the wealth of your cities and the strength of your power, as if they suddenly went out of the dark and saw the light of Heaven ... I have respectfully received the gracious letter in which your Majesty has condescended to inquire about my welfare. Owing to your solicitude there have been established post-stations to facilitate the intercourse of foreigners with China, and all the nations of distant countries are allowed to profit by this convenience. I see with deference that the heart of your Majesty resembles that vase which reflects what is happening in the world* ... My heart has been opened and enlightened by your benevolence. I can return your Majesty's kindly disposed feelings only by praying for your happiness and long life. May they last eternally like heaven and earth.

Such effusive flattery would only have been enhanced by the accompanying gift of two hundred horses.†

By the dawn of the fifteenth century, Temur was at last ready to

---

* An allusion to the vase of Jamsheed, the first king of Persia. Tradition has it that the turquoise vessel was unearthed from the ruins of Persepolis, the city he was said to have founded. His name means 'vase of the sun' in Farsi.

† It is hardly surprising that the court chronicles have little to say on the less than glorious subject of Temur's relations with Peking. As the French historian Edgard Blochet, writing in 1910, put it: '*Tous les historiens officiels des Timourides, sauf Abd er Razzak el-Samarkandi, qui ne voulait se plier à aucune complaisance pour ses souverains, ont fait le silence le plus absolu sur ces rapports de la terre d'Iran et du Céleste Empire, dans l'espérance que la postérité n'en retrouverait jamais l'humiliant souvenir.*'

turn from weasel words to war. At this time a Chinese embassy from Peking arrived at his court to demand tribute, which Temur had neglected to pay for seven years, despite occupying lands along his eastern borders in Moghulistan that were traditionally held in fief to the Chinese emperor. The envoy, whose stay in Samarkand coincided with Clavijo's diplomatic mission, reminded the Tatar emperor that no tribute had been received. He was humiliatingly rebuffed, as the startled Spaniard reported: 'The answer of his Highness to these ambassadors was that this was most true, and that he was about to pay what was due: but that he would not burden them, the ambassadors, to take it back to China on their return, for he himself Temur would bring it. This of course was all said in scorn and to spite them, for his Highness had no intention to pay that tribute.' On another occasion, noticing that the envoy from Peking was occupying a seat above those of the Spaniards, Temur gave orders for their positions to be reversed. The Chinese ambassador, he proclaimed to his hushed audience, 'was the envoy of a robber and a bad man, the enemy of Temur'. Then he gave a clear sign that the days of diplomacy and tribute were over. War was in the offing. 'If only God were willing, he Temur would before long see to it that never again would any Chinaman dare come with such an embassy as this man had brought.'

The reasons for the dramatic shift in Temur's relations with Peking are not difficult to fathom. For years he had been biding his time. Highly pragmatic in his choice of opponents, he would not move until his armies were sufficiently large and powerful to challenge the greatest ruler in the East. Nor would he undertake such a long and testing campaign until his main rivals on the world stage had been destroyed. To the north, the Golden Horde had been crushed. To the south, Delhi had been utterly ravaged. To the west, the Ottoman and Mamluk empires had folded before the Tatar onslaught. To the east, China alone remained outside his orbit, the last affront to the man who aspired to rule the world. The road east was now open to his armies.

Temur knew China's capital was a treasure house without parallel in the world. In 1404, his envoy returned from Peking to Samarkand with Ambassador An. The official reported that the Chinese capital was twenty times larger than Tabriz. If that was true, wrote Clavijo, then 'it must indeed be the greatest city in all the world'. Temur was also told, though this was less welcome news, that the Ming armies were as numerous as the sands of the desert:

> *The man further reported that the Emperor of China was lord of so many warriors that when his host went forth to wage war beyond the limits of his Empire, without counting those who marched with him he could leave four hundred thousand horsemen behind to guard his realm together with numerous regiments of footguards. As that man further reported, it was the order current in China that no nobleman should be allowed to appear publicly on horseback unless he kept in his service at his call at least a thousand horsemen and yet of the like of such nobles the number to be met with was very large. Many were the other wonderful facts that were further related of the capital and country of China.*

This was the kingdom Temur resolved to conquer. It was a question of destiny, the final decisive play in a brilliant game of chess. The opening gambit had been made six years earlier. Fortresses had been built, agricultural land reclaimed along his eastern marches, all in preparation for this, his ultimate campaign. For years he had roved outside Mawarannahr, ranging his armies against his opponents like the most consummate grandmaster, toppling kingdoms and enlarging his empire with every move he made. For the most part he had directed his furious energy against the west. Now, at his command and under his immutable will, his ranks of Tatar pawns advanced ever farther east.

Allahdad, one of Temur's most trusted amirs, was sent east and instructed to prepare a detailed survey of the land the Tatars would have to cross to reach the Chinese capital. His formidable assignment was to 'make a map of those regions and describe their condition in his reply, that he might explain to Temur the situation of those realms and show the nature of the way through them and the paths and explain to him the nature of their cities and their villages, valleys and mountains, castles and forts, the nearer parts and the remote, the deserts and hills, wastes and deserts, landmarks and towers, waters and rivers, tribes and families, passes and broad roads, places marked and those without signs of the way, dwelling places and houses for travellers, its empty places and its people, weaving the path of a diffuse style and avoiding abridgement and omission and explaining the distances between all the stages and the manner of the journey between all the dwelling places'.

The northern route to China was considered the only practical choice. This was the route Ambassador An had taken on his journey from Peking. To the north of the icy Tien Shan Celestial Mountains it traversed Semirechye, the Land of the Seven Rivers – which flowed into Lake Balkash – east of Mawarannahr. This route crossed steppe with decent grazing for the horses, the single most important consideration in the complex web of Temur's military logistics.

Allahdad had been involved in plans for this campaign from an early stage. In the winter of 1401–02, while Temur wintered in the pastures of the Qarabagh, he was on his way to the eastern marches with orders to develop agricultural land to feed the armies and build bases from which to launch the attack. One fort was to be built ten days' march from Ashpara, east of the Sir Darya river. Another was constructed still closer to China, next to Lake Issykul. These preparations were in addition to those Temur had begun as early as 1396, when he had spent two years in Samarkand beautifying his capital and planning for war in the east. It is clear that this was no casual undertaking. Temur had appointed his grandson and heir Mohammed Sultan, at the head of forty thousand troops and a number of the most prominent amirs, to supervise the construction of fortresses and to reclaim and irrigate the agricultural land that had been abandoned in those regions. Unruly tribes had been assimilated into the Tatar armies or eliminated.

Allahdad completed his mission successfully. He used 'many leaves of glistening papyrus' to make the map, carefully folded into a neat rectangle. All of the details required by Temur were included, and nothing was omitted. According to Arabshah, he finished it in good time, too. The emperor received it while he was still marching through Asia Minor with his army, on his way back to Samarkand.

As war approached, activity along the eastern marches intensified. With the building work complete, the priority was to grow sufficient crops and rear enough animals to feed the great army that swept through kingdoms like locusts. Every farmer and villager from Samarkand to Ashpara was ordered to 'cease business and trade and in word and deed give themselves to tilling the soil and farming'. If need be, men and women should forgo the five daily prayers required by Islam in favour of working the land. Sometimes Allah had to take second place. A sense of urgency gripped the empire. In the heaving bazaars and alleys of Samarkand, in the many-domed mosques and madrassahs, the manicured parks and palaces, the talk was all of this latest expedition. Like a loyal mistress the city missed Temur during his campaigns, but always waited patiently and expectantly for his triumphal return. All knew that war with China represented his most awesome challenge yet. Many feared that their masterful emperor had finally overextended himself. For all his previous victories, a single defeat at the hands of the most powerful army on earth now threatened the entire empire. The stakes had never been higher.

&

The spring of 1403 brought two surprises and one tragedy for the elderly emperor. Temur and his army were still crossing Asia Minor towards Samarkand and China when he received news that Sultan

Bayazid, his most famous captive, had died while travelling under escort with the imperial baggage caravan. Temur's personal doctor had been unable to save him. The sources differ on how the fallen Ottoman met his end. Gout, asthma, apoplexy, a broken heart, even suicide have all been cited as the cause of death. While there is no reason to believe that the news would have brought much satisfaction to a ruler who was himself approaching his seventieth birthday, there is something of the crocodile about the tears Yazdi has him shedding: 'Temur was so extremely affected that he bewailed the misfortune of that great prince with tears. He began to reflect how providence often baffles human projects for he had resolved . . . to raise the dejected spirit of Bayazid by re-establishing him on the throne with greater power and magnificence than he had enjoyed before.'

Such plans, were they real or imagined, had been dashed. But there was far worse news to follow. A messenger galloped into the imperial camp at Aq Shahr with a desperate report. Mohammed Sultan lay desperately sick. He had never fully recovered from the wounds received at Ankara. Without betraying any emotion, Temur gave orders for Bayazid's body to be sent to Brusa 'with all the pomp and magnificence' due to a great king. He presented the Ottoman's son Musa Chelebi with a royal vest, a fine belt, a sword, a quiver inlaid with precious stones, thirty horses and a quantity of gold. Only with that business finished did he hurry to the young prince's camp. By the time he arrived, having been delayed by a rebel Turkmen tribe, his grandson's condition had worsened. Unable even to speak, he lay on his bed with a deathly pallor across his face. For three days he was carried in a litter, but it was too late. Four days after the death of Bayazid, the youthful Mohammed Sultan, a lion on the battlefield and the emperor's great hope for the future, passed away.

Temur was inconsolable. He had always loved this prince especially. There was a heartbreaking symmetry to his premature death, for he was the oldest son of the emperor's first-born, Jahangir, who had died at the age of twenty more than a quarter of a century earlier. This young man Temur had favoured above all his other sons and grandsons, confidently making him his heir in recognition of his qualities of leadership, courage, intelligence and military acumen. Even Arabshah, a sworn critic of Temur, acknowledged the fine character of the prince. He was, said the Syrian, 'a refuge for excellent men and haven for the learned; the signs of felicity appeared in the lines of his brow and the glad news of nobility shone from his features'.

The whole army went into mourning. Its march home and onwards to war had become a great funeral cortège. Everyone wore black. Mohammed Sultan's mother and Jahangir's widow, the beautiful Khan-zada, was summoned to meet the army at Avnik in Armenia. Before she reached the town, the prince's three young sons arrived at Erzerum, a sight so moving to the emperor that the tears poured down his face again. Then there was the mother's grief to behold. Khan-zada had already lost her husband. Now she had lost her first child. When news reached her of Mohammed Sultan's death, she collapsed on the spot. Later, when she came to, she pulled her hair out, ripped her clothes and tore her cheeks until they bled. She had never expected her treasured son to fall so young, she wailed. He had been destined to become a great emperor. Now her tears ran like blood, for his death had pierced her like a 'fatal dagger'.

Death, as the old emperor knew, was stalking him more closely than ever. Men who had shared his victories over the years had started to fall. In recent months, seasoned comrades on the battlefield had been gathered up. Sayf ad-din Nukuz, Temur's long-serving amir, had died shortly before the decisive encounter with Bayazid. The puppet khan, Sultan Mahmud, a fearless soldier who had captured the escaping Ottoman sultan, had been stricken after the battle. He was not replaced.

Temur ordered Mohammed Sultan's funeral banquet to be held in Avnik. The lords of Asia came with their condolences, praising Allah

TAMERLANE

for dignifying the world with such a manly prince and warrior. Priests recited from the Koran in a sombre monotone. Mohammed Sultan's kettle-drum gave its final peal of thunder. All of a sudden, the ladies of the court and the princes, the vassal kings and amirs, the soldiers and the servants, one and all let forth a terrible cry of mourning. Then the drum was smashed to pieces, in honour of Mongol custom. Never would it be sounded in tribute to another prince.

From Avnik, the prince's coffin was taken to Sultaniya, thence to Samarkand where Temur had ordered the population to observe public mourning. 'At his approach the people of Samarkand went out and they had covered themselves to meet him with black garments and in black walked noble and humble, base and illustrious, as though the face of the world were covered with a fog of deepest night.'

Temur had demonstrated over the years an almost instinctive inability to pass the Christian kingdom of Georgia without invading it. Though the death of Mohammed Sultan still weighed heavily on him, though his soldiers were battle-weary and his mind was turning towards the forthcoming campaign against China, he was unable even at this moment, in the heat of August, to resist the temptation. Another punitive expedition was ordered against King Giorgi VII, who had failed to present himself at the emperor's court. This was Temur's sixth, and last, campaign against the mountain kingdom.

It was harvest time and the Tatars plundered the fields of grain. Then they marched into the higher passes where the fighting was hardest. The chronicles made much of the siege of Kurtin, a famously fortified stronghold which the inhabitants considered impregnable. With cisterns full of water, 'cellars furnished with delicious wines' and plentiful supplies of pigs and sheep, the defenders were confident they would see off the Tatars. But one night, while the engineers were building siege engines and battering rams, a soldier slipped through

360

a narrow opening in the rockface and found a way up to the fortress above. Fifty more joined him during the night. At dawn, the cry of '*Allahu akbar*' resounded from the heights, the Tatar drums thundered, the trumpets sounded and the attack began. The gate was smashed by stones hurled from one of the siege machines, and the garrison was overrun. The governor and his soldiers were beheaded, the troops who had risked their lives in the assault handsomely rewarded. Temur gave them robes, swords, belts of honour, horses, mules, tents, umbrellas, villages and gardens in their home countries, and, of course, scores of young women.

The campaign continued into the autumn of 1403. Temur advanced into the centre of the country, 'where he plundered seven hundred towns and villages, laying waste the cultivated lands, ruining the monasteries of the Christians and razing their churches to the very foundations'. The zeal with which he was all of a sudden pursuing the infidels, after decades butchering countless Muslims, was an indication, perhaps, that he knew he did not have long to live. From Smyrna, he had hastened to Georgia; from there he was bound for China.

Through a number of distinguished Georgian prisoners taken in the early exchanges, Temur conducted negotiations for King Giorgi's surrender. Given the expedition that awaited him, he was not prepared to delay long in this region. Eventually, though the king still refused to appear in Temur's court, he sent envoys carrying a thousand gold coins struck in the emperor's name, a thousand horses, vessels of gold, silver and crystal, many cloths and a fabulously large balas ruby. Temur pronounced himself satisfied with this show of submission and the army continued east. More churches and monasteries were burnt to the ground around the capital of Tiflis, and then the Tatar hordes were gone. Georgia had been devastated again. Its fields lay bare, its coffers empty. Whole towns and villages had disappeared in the carnage. Rotting corpses were piled in the roads. Minarets of skulls, the tallest structures standing, rose from the quagmire. Winter was fast approaching and icy winds tore through the valleys. Temur's Tatar hordes had raped and killed and torched and plundered until there was no more to be taken. Silence hung over the stricken kingdom. The only blessing, though none knew it, was that the Unconquered Lord of the Seven Climes would never return.

&&

Temur wintered for the last time in the high pastures of the Qarabagh. Here, his remorseless energy showed no signs of subsiding. He threw himself back into the business of empire, rebuilding the derelict town of Baylaqan and granting sons and grandsons territories. The crown of Hulagu, once ruled by the disgraced Miranshah, was divided between Abubakr, the prince's eldest son, who took Baghdad and Iraq, and Omar, his second son, who was given the northern regions, including Tabriz and Sultaniya. Abubakr was ordered to rebuild Baghdad.* Dynastic considerations were beginning to crowd in on him. The aged emperor was plotting a smooth succession after his death. His grandson Pir Mohammed was given the city of Shiraz. The young man's brother Rustam assumed control of Isfahan, while another of his brothers, Iskander, took Hamadan. Prince Khalil Sultan received

---

* Yazdi gave Temur particular credit for the restoration of the former capital of the Islamic world and home of the caliph. The speech he attributed to the emperor, though overblown, nevertheless reinforced the point that, unlike Genghis Khan, the Tatar was a creative force as well as a destroyer: 'The war which the inhabitants of Baghdad have undertaken against us, having been obstinately prolonged by them, has been the cause of their state's desolation, our vengeance having inflicted total ruin upon them. Nevertheless, if we consider that this is one of the principal cities in the Mohammedan world, that the knowledge of the law is derived from there, and that the doctors of other countries have drawn from it the most sacred elements of our religion, and the most useful learning; it would be a crime utterly to destroy this famous city: wherefore we design to reinstate it in its former flourishing condition, that it may again become the seat of justice, and the tribunal both of religion and laws.'

lands between the Caucasus and Trebizond on the northern coast of Asia Minor.

After the recent deaths of Bayazid and Mohammed Sultan, Amir Sayf ad-din Nukuz and Sultan Mahmud, Temur hardly needed any more reminders of his own mortality. But in the spring of 1404, as the great body of the Tatar army moved out of the pastures after a last spectacular hunt, he suffered another personal loss. Shaykh Baraka, his spiritual mentor, the man who had accompanied him on his campaigns for years, who had roused him and his troops to a magnificent procession of victories, came west to express his sorrow at the death of Temur's heir. The Tatar's joy at this unexpected reunion was all too brief. This was the last time they would meet. Baraka followed Bayazid and Mohammed Sultan to his grave soon afterwards.

The march home continued, and the administration of empire with it. Travelling with his mobile court, Temur handed out judgements, listened to petitions and grievances, received tribute from vassal rulers or their envoys, and executed officials who had abused their positions. Such affairs of state mattered little to the rank-and-file soldiers. Their thoughts and daydreams were centred on getting back to Mawarannahr. Each step took them nearer home.

Nine hundred miles east of the Qarabagh, a great landmark soared up from the desert fastness like a homage to the heavens. The veterans of Temur's campaigns pointed it out excitedly to their younger colleagues, who had never set eyes on such a prodigious monument, and scarcely believed it could be a minaret. The reason for the older men's pleasure was simple. The tower meant that their marathon five-year journey was over. They had reached Mawarannahr safely. This was Bukhara the Noble, Dome of Islam, second city of the empire.

The Kalon Minaret which so cheered Temur's soldiers in 1404 still presides spectacularly over Bukhara today. Looming 150 feet into the sky, it is visible from most parts of this labyrinthine city of secrets.

On a cool, clear, autumnal evening, my first in Bukhara, I sat in a *chaikhana* in Lyab-i-Hauz Square, soul and centre of the old town, contemplating the twin pleasures of a steaming bowl of green tea and the reflected glory of the seventeenth-century Nadir Divanbegi *khanaqah*, a mosque and hostel providing accommodation for travelling holy men. I was planning a visit to the Kalon Minaret, but had been waylaid by the charms of the prettiest town square in Central Asia. Here, at last, was serenity. The *hauz*, built in 1620 as the city's largest reservoir, was a square pool of green water beneath a dimming sky. Bevelled steps ran down from street level to its surface. Mulberry trees lined the square, the most gnarled and crooked among them dating from 1477. On the top of the tallest was a derelict storks' nest.

It was a still night beneath the stars, a perfect time for exploration. I took myself away from the murmurs of the Lyab-i-Hauz into the dark streets of the old town. Men played cards in pools of light in their doorways. Figures hove into view in tiny alleys then were swallowed up instantly by the night. Children raced through the streets. Above them bats circled around the flickering lights of a disused fountain, paper-thin wings fluttering madly. The domed carpet markets were closed, and footsteps echoed in their chambers. Here and there loomed grand portals flanked with corner towers. There were mosques and madrassahs, some illuminated, others, more remotely located, hidden in darkness. But the most striking monument was the largest minaret I had ever seen, a huge golden tower that pierced the night, one of Bukhara's most fabulous symbols. Drawn inexorably towards it, I threaded through the streets, past the Magok-i-Attari Mosque, into the cap-makers' bazaar, around the Bazar-i-Kord Mosque, alongside the Amir Alim Khan Madrassah, until there it stood: Bukhara's greatest survivor.

Built in 1127, the Kalon Minaret had escaped even the razing wrath of Genghis Khan when a mere stripling of a hundred. The warlord of the steppes was so overawed by this triumph of verticality that he ordered his men to spare it as they scythed their way through the city. (The rest of Bukhara was not so fortunate. By the time Genghis's hordes had finished their murderous mission, it was said: 'From the reflection of the sun the plain seemed to be a tray filled with blood.') A minaret unlike any other, it has served *muaddin*, merchant and the military alike for the best part of a thousand years. This was the tower craved by shattered camel caravans traversing the Qara Qum desert, the first trace of civilisation for travellers tormented by thirst and racked with hunger. Burning beacons at its summit guided the stragglers through raging sandstorms. The minaret was also a watch-tower. From a window in the ornate rotunda gallery soldiers scanned the horizon for enemy armies approaching Bukhara. And for the dispensers of Bukhara-style justice in the eighteenth and nineteenth centuries, the Kalon Minaret was also the 'Tower of Death', where the most violent criminals stumbled up its 105 steps prior to their destruction. The ceremonies were carefully choreographed, designed to inculcate fear, revulsion and macabre fascination in the crowds that gathered to watch. The offender's crime was read out from the top of the minaret. A hush fell over the spectators. Then, after a dreadful pause, tied up inside a sack, he was pushed, screaming in blind panic, to his death.

For all its practical uses, the Kalon Minaret is an exquisite feat of architecture. From its octagonal base, thirty feet in diameter, it tapers smoothly into the heavens through ten bands of carved brick and delicate majolica tilework. At the summit, above its sixteen windows, there is more fine detail as the bricks flare outwards slightly before retreating to form a horizontal roof crowned by a rocket-like pro-tuberance that marks the lines of an older extension.

Though the minaret avoided the levelling traditionally inflicted on conquered cities by Genghis and his Mongols, the Kalon Mosque from which it sprang did not. Such was its size and splendour that the warlord falsely believed he had ridden into the sultan's palace. On discovering that this was Bukhara's most magnificent mosque, he contemptuously ordered his men to use the Koran-holders as mangers for his horses. Here, in the house of God, Genghis gave his men *carte blanche* to destroy the city, and within minutes the mosque was in flames. It burnt to the ground.

⚙

'Of course, they used to call Bukhara the "Dome of Islam" or "Heart of Islam" even before Temur. This was the city that produced great religious scholars like Bakhauddin Nakhshbandi – his name means "The Decoration of Religion" – and Imam al Bukhari. Their books are still studied in Bukhara, so I think we can still say Bukhara is the "Dome of Islam".'

I had returned to the Kalon Mosque the following morning to meet its imam, Abdul Gafur Razzaq, the most important religious figure in Bukhara. He resembled a middle-aged sloth, with a goatee beard and heavy eyelids, and was so relaxed he seemed to move in slow motion, when he moved at all. On my arrival, an eyebrow twitched almost imperceptibly and a young assistant rushed off at once to prepare tea. His master remained, languidly reclining on cushions.

Imam al Bukhari was one of the greatest sages of Islam, the ninth-century author of Sahih al Bukhari, regarded by Muslims worldwide as the most authentic book after the Koran, a comprehensive collection of *hadith*, the sayings of the Prophet. Famed for his superhuman memory, as a child he could recite two thousand *hadith*. He collected and examined more than six hundred thousand in the course of his researches, selecting only 7,275 of them as *sahih*, or genuine. These he authenticated with full genealogies of those who had communicated them, harking back to the Prophet himself.

Together with al Bukhari, Khazreti Mohammed Bakhauddin Nakhshbandi was one of the city's most illustrious sons, a contemporary of Temur and the greatest Sufi leader of Central Asia. Among his followers he emphasised contemplation, self-purification, peace, tolerance and moral excellence, as well as a withdrawal from authority. The complex of school, mosque, *khanaqah* and Nakhshbandi's grave, ten minutes outside Bukhara, was recently restored with Turkish aid. It was reopened in 1993 to commemorate the 675th anniversary of his birth in a ceremony that marked the renaissance of Islam in Central Asia. Visitors today will find pilgrims from across the Muslim world circling the holy man's heavy black tombstone, pausing occasionally to bestow reverent kisses upon it. Some exchange a few words with a priest shaded by an awning beneath a plane tree – said to have sprouted from Nakhshbandi's staff – and hand him a few banknotes in exchange for a prayer. Others tie rags and wishes in the tree. Elsewhere in the complex, pilgrims cook offerings in thanks for the fulfilment of their wishes.

Temur's Dome of Islam had come under attack in the first half of the twentieth century. The imam had been brought up by his grandparents during the Soviet era, when religious instruction was prohibited. Secretly they had found him teachers who had worked in the madrassahs before the Soviets' arrival, and it was under their tutelage that he had started to study the Koran and Arabic calligraphy. When he was eighteen, he won a place in the prestigious sixteenth-century Mir-i-Arab Madrassah in Bukhara, a blue-domed masterpiece directly opposite the Kalon Mosque: 'Temur would never have believed what happened here in those times. During the Soviet period the madrassah didn't accept any student from Bukhara because the city's communist leaders wanted to show what good communists they were. They told their bosses that no one in the city wanted to study religion because they were so progressive. I was only admitted because of my knowledge of calligraphy.'

He had studied at the madrassah for seven years, including a two-year secondment to the Imam al Bukhari Madrassah in Tashkent. After two years in the army, he returned to the world of Islam as a teacher in the Mir-i-Arab Madrassah. At the age of fifty, after a distinguished career, he had reached the top of his profession. 'We only had three mosques and one madrassah that took eighty students during the Soviet time. Now we have one hundred mosques just in the Bukhara region, and eleven madrassahs nationwide.'

It would have pleased Temur to find that, in keeping with Bukhara's religious heritage, Sufism was at the forefront of this religious revival. 'This is what we try to introduce to the people. It's mystic teaching, helping people to perfect themselves and get closer to Allah. Sufis are against fighting and for development. You probably already know how much Temur respected Sufi scholars. He brought many of them to Samarkand and constructed mausoleums for them when they died. Sufism developed a great deal under him.'

Bukhara, Uzbekistan and Central Asia are re-engaging with Islam. But what is most fascinating is that Bukhara is reacquainting itself with its long-standing Sufic tradition, perhaps the first serious revival since Temur's dedicated sponsorship six centuries earlier.

How far it had to go was revealed by an exploration of the Kalon Mosque. Designed to accommodate up to twelve thousand of the faithful at Friday prayers, it encompassed a vast open-air quadrangle bordered by a colonnaded, multi-domed arcade. It was the second-biggest mosque in Central Asia, built in 795 in what had been, for a brief period at least, more auspicious times for Islam. The mosque one sees today, immense in scope and peerless in ambition, dates from the early sixteenth century.

The enormous area of worship is superfluous these days. A small area at the back of the arcade, an inconsequential fraction of the mosque, is all that has been set aside for prayers. Its size contrasts tellingly with the vast western portal and *mihrab* niche that faces

Mecca beneath the glittering blue bubble of the Kok Gumbaz (Blue Dome). 'Immortality belongs to God', reads a white Kufic inscription around it.

Today, the minaret of the Kalon Mosque, like those throughout Bukhara, lies strangely silent. The haunting sounds of the *adhan*, the call to prayer, are nowhere to be heard. Once more, Islam is under watch from the authorities, fearful of an upsurge in fundamentalism. Like his colleagues in the rest of the city, the imam was appointed by the state and his sermons are monitored.

What a decline from Islam's golden era in Bukhara, from the ninth century, when it emerged as a bastion of the faith, until the nineteenth, when depravity and fanaticism started to take over. But then, state religion had been manipulated before. Temur's subservient priests upheld his authority and gave their blessing to his numerous campaigns against Muslims and infidels alike. And in any case, such a reversal of fortunes was nothing new. The Dome of Islam did not thrive uninterrupted from the ninth century.

Bukhara took over a century to recover from the devastation wrought by Genghis in 1219. When Ibn Battutah passed through in 1366, he reported: 'All but a few of its mosques, academies and bazaars are lying in ruins.' The wandering man of letters was unimpressed. 'I found no one in it who knew any thing of science.' The city had to wait for Temur to regain its glory.

Noila, director of the department for the protection of mosques and monuments in Bukhara, was a courteous lady of about fifty with a scholarly, lined face. We were sitting together one evening over a glass of green tea in Lyab-i-Hauz, overlooking the square from the first-floor veranda of a small *chaikhana*.

'People say Amir Temur had no connection with Bukhara, but that's just not true,' she began.

Around a long table next to us, a large family, including several
army officers, was celebrating some happy event with the help of
endless rounds of beer and vodka. I loved returning to this small
square, the Kaaba of Bukhara, around which swirled an absorbing
cross-section of Bukharzis night and day. It had a life of its own
and an eclectic population of old men, shrieking boys, romantically
inclined couples, ducks, geese, a persistent kingfisher and a prowling
cat. In the festering heat of midday, it reflected the lethargy of the
city. The elderly backgammon players were nowhere to be seen, the
boys diving from the mulberry trees vanished, and the ducks kept a
low profile in the shadows. Even the diehard *shashlik* cook retreated
altogether. And then, as evening approached and the temperature
cooled, the underground vitality that simmered beneath the surface
bubbled up once more. Fountains burst forth on cue, ducks and
geese celebrated raucously, fairy lights winked in the trees, lovers
returned from the shadows for a candlelit dinner alongside the pool,
the *shashlik* cook sharpened his knife and was soon lost to sight
beneath the wreaths of smoke from the coals, boys hurled themselves
into the water and once again the square echoed to the sound of
slamming dominoes and games of backgammon. Lyab-i-Hauz, like
the rest of Bukhara, had a rhythm all of its own.

'To begin with,' Noila continued, 'Temur's mother, the daughter
of a *sadr* [senior religious official], came from Bukhara, so he spent
a lot of time here during his childhood. He always respected the city
very much, and the main reason for this was its Islamic heritage. In
fact, it became the second city of his empire. While Samarkand
was his secular capital, Bukhara was his religious centre. You must
remember that in those times no leader could carry out his political,
military and economic policies without the support of the religious
establishment. Temur also restored a lot of important monuments
like the mausoleums of Shaykh Sayf ad-din Bukharzi and Chasma
Ayub. He also restored the Bakhauddin Nakhshbandi shrine. The

man who looked after Temur's library, Mahmoud Khoja Bukharoi, was also from the city. Temur came here several times during fighting. Bukhara and the surrounding area were always very important to him, particularly when he was collecting forces in the Zarafshan and Qashka Darya valleys to drive off the Moghul invaders.'

In fact, Temur returned periodically to the pastures around Bukhara during his many campaigns. He wintered here with his troops in 1381, after taking Herat. It was fine hunting territory. Two of Genghis's sons, Chaghatay and Ogedey, used to send their father fifty camel-loads of swans a week while they were here. In 1389, having defeated Khizr Khoja, the khan of Moghulistan, Temur rested his court and troops in Bukhara, celebrating his victory with a grand hunt around the lakes and streams at the foot of the Zarafshan.

In 1392, Temur was back in Bukhara, this time after falling ill at the outset of his Five-Year Campaign in Persia. 'He was so sick he called all his family from Samarkand, expecting to die. But a doctor from Bukhara, using Avicenna's methods,* managed to save him, and after one month he was well enough to continue with his campaign,' Noila told me. 'Bukhara always supported Temur in his conquests, not like Khorezm and some other places.'

It is fair to say, however, that Bukhara played only a distant second fiddle to Samarkand. Unquestionably, Bukharzis were proud of their rich heritage, but any discussion about Temur brought back memories

---

* Ibn Sina (980–1037), or Avicenna as he is known in the West, was the most famous Islamic physician, philosopher, mathematician, encyclopaedist and astronomer of his time. Born in the province of Bukhara, he served as a physician in the courts of local princes. His philosophical works borrowed from the teachings of Aristotle and neo-Platonism, and were a major influence on the development of thirteenth-century scholasticism. His *Canon of Medicine*, written when he was just twenty-one, drew on his personal understanding of the science together with Roman and Arab medicine, and remained the principal authority in medieval medical schools in both Europe and Asia.

of how he had slighted their great city by comparison with the munificence he bestowed on his imperial capital.

I asked Noila how the government was managing the restoration of the city. Although Bukhara seemed to have escaped the Disney-fication of Samarkand, many of its historical buildings were crumbling away through neglect.

'We have 462 mosques and other ancient monuments in the Bukhara region, so of course it's a problem,' she answered. 'But the government and private sponsors are spending lots of money on this. You've got to remember the Soviets destroyed much of Bukhara. In the 1920s, there was a map of the city listing a thousand mosques and monuments. This included 360 mosques, 280 madrassahs, eighty-four caravanserais, eighteen hammams, and 118 *hauze*s, so you can see what they destroyed. Lenin gave an order to the soldiers to burn Islam in the fire. Bukhara was the fire of Islam, so how could they do it? They burnt books, killed imams and forbade people from praying. They burnt down many mosques and madrassahs, too, and turned others into offices, clubs and storage space. They destroyed the Ark [Bukhara's ancient fortress] and smashed a part of the Kalon Minaret. A Russian engineer ordered the *hauze*s to be filled in because they had become a health risk, spreading malaria and tapeworm. Mirzoi Sharif Madrassah was turned into a prison. Before the revolution, everyone had written in the Arabic alphabet. Now they introduced the Cyrillic alphabet, so most of us can't even read our old books any more. Bukhara was a major trade centre on the Silk Road. No more. The Bolsheviks put an end to that. Big businessmen suddenly became enemies of the state. Educated people were thrown into prison, and an uneducated, illiterate man was made mayor of Bukhara under the control of the Russians. This is what happened to our city.

'Until recently, we weren't even allowed to talk about what happened in those early Soviet days. We couldn't even explain to tourists

what had happened to some of the monuments. For example, when
we showed visitors around the Ark and they asked why it was in
such bad condition, we had to say it was wear and tear. We weren't
allowed to say the Soviets bombed much of the building to pieces in
1920. In the museums we had all these pictures showing the terrible
executions under the Amir of Bukhara – throat-cuttings, hangings,
beatings, live burials. It was all designed to show how primitive life
had been here in Islamic times before the Soviets came to our rescue
and civilised us.* You need to understand all this. It's the background

---

* Visiting Bukhara at the close of the nineteenth century, the young George
  Curzon patted himself on the back for seeing the city before the inevitable
  intrusions of the modern secular world in the form of the advancing
  Russians: 'For my own part, on leaving the city I could not help rejoicing
  at having seen it in what might be described as the twilight epoch of its
  glory. Were I to go again in later years it might be to find electric light
  in the highways. It might be to see window-panes in the houses and to
  meet with trousered figures in the streets. It might be to eat *zakuska* in a
  Russian restaurant and to sleep in a Russian hotel; to be ushered by a
  tchinovnik into the palace of the Ark, and to climb for fifty *kopecks* the
  Minor-i-Kalian [Kalon Minaret]. Civilisation may ride in the Devil's
  Wagon but the Devil has a habit of exacting his toll. What could be said
  for a Bukhara without a Kosh Begi, a Divan Begi and an Inak – without
  its *Mullahs* and *kalanders*, its *toksabas* and its *mirzabashi*, its *shabraques*
  and *chupans* and *khalats*? Already the mist of ages is beginning to rise
  and to dissolve. The lineaments are losing their beautiful vague mystery
  of outline. It is something, in the short interval between the old order
  and the new, to have seen Bukhara while it may still be called the Noble,
  and before it has ceased to be the most interesting city in the world.'
  Interesting it must have been, but nineteenth-century Bukhara also
  had its dark side. Discipline was enforced through terror. A strict nightly
  curfew was instituted. The population was locked inside the city walls.
  Murderers were decapitated. Some had their eyelids cut off and their eyes
  gouged out. The Hungarian philologist and explorer Arminius Vambery
  witnessed several men suffering this punishment in the early 1860s: 'They
  looked like lambs in the hands of their executioners. Whilst several were
  led to the gallows or the block, I saw how, at a sign from the executioner,
  eight aged men placed themselves down on their backs upon the earth.
  They were then bound hand and foot, and the executioner gouged out
  their eyes in turn, kneeling to do so on the breast of each poor wretch;
  and after every operation he wiped his knife, dripping with blood, on the

behind restoring Amir Temur to the Uzbeks. Some people have said there is a tendency in Uzbekistan to exaggerate Temur's greatness and so on. Perhaps that's true, but we're a young nation, getting up from our knees. We need a new figurehead. Before we had Lenin; he wasn't even one of our people. If there is exaggeration, I think it's entirely forgivable.'

One of the things she had said about the monuments was astounding. There had been 118 *hauzes* before the Russian arrival. What had happened to them? I had seen one or two empty pits in the ground, desolate ruins with broken steps. And, of course there was the Lyab-i-Hauz. But that still left well over a hundred unaccounted for. Gustav Krist, the improbable Austrian carpet-seller and traveller, must have underestimated the destructive power of the Soviets. In 1937 he wrote:

> *And yet those ponds of Bukhara are wonderfully beautiful. In the evening, after the muezzin has sounded from the minaret the call to prayer, the men of the city gather around the ponds, which are bordered by tall, silver poplars and magnificent black elms, to enjoy a period of ease and leisure. Carpets are spread, the ever burning chilim is passed from mouth to mouth, the samovar steams away, and light-footed boys hand round the shallow bowls of green tea. Here the meddahs, or story-tellers, the musicians and the dancing boys assemble to display their craft. And perhaps a conjuror or*

---

white beard of the hoary unfortunate. Ah! Cruel spectacle! As each fearful act was completed, the victim liberated from his bonds, groping around with his hands, sought to gain his feet! Some fell against each other, head against head; others sank powerless to the earth again, uttering low groans, the memory of which will make me shudder as long as I live.' Women were covered up and hidden. Anyone who did not avert their eyes from the Amir's passing harem received a heavy clubbing from his entourage of guards. Religious police stopped men in the streets to quiz them on some arcane detail of Islamic law. If they gave the wrong answer, they received another beating. The authorities searched houses at will looking for alcohol. Life was austere and brutal, unless you happened to be the Amir, in which case it was lavish and depraved. Forty dancing boys were kept to satisfy his passions.

*juggler comes, performing the most amazing and incredible feats
of skill. An Indian snake charmer joins the throng and sets his
poisonous snakes to dance, while all over reigns the peace of a
Bukharan evening. No loud speech breaks the spell; items of scandal
and the news of the day are exchanged in discreet whispers. So it
was centuries ago in Bukhara; so it is today. There are things which
not even the Soviets can alter.*

The disappearance of the Bukharan *hauz*, and most of its open canals
and sewers, brought with it another poignant loss. The storks, which
for centuries had been as much a part of the city skyline as the Kalon
Minaret and had fed from these open pools, had gone for good.

'By the 1970s, the storks had left,' said Noila. 'I'm still so sad about
it. Every morning we used to see them. You can still see one or two
of their nests at the top of the mulberry trees in Lyab-i-Hauz. I used
to love watching the mothers taking frogs and fish in their beaks and
feeding their children. And seeing them teaching the young ones how
to fly. The babies used to try to flap their wings and then they'd fall
into Lyab-i-Hauz and wait there until their mothers rescued them.
They were very beautiful birds. Many, many lived here because there
were so many places they could feed from. You know, there's a famous
Bukharan song,' she reminisced. 'It's called "The Storks are Coming
Back to Bukhara".'

She started humming the tune and then broke into song. It was
a tiny, gentle voice, but it carried easily into the night. 'I know you
can still see them outside Bukhara,' she went on, 'but of course it's
not the same thing as having them in the city. They were part of our
childhood when we grew up. Bukhara has never really been the same
since they left.'

&

For several days I immersed myself in Bukhara and waited while it
slowly revealed itself to me. It was more intimate than Samarkand,

had none of that city's flashy flamboyance, and unveiled its secrets more guardedly. Much of this had to do with the fact that it had retained its old quarter almost intact and on one site. Samarkand's ancient monuments are spread diffusely over a far greater area. The narrow winding alleys and souks that had filtered out from the historical heart of the Registan towards the city gates are no more. Here they have been preserved.

When it was time to leave Bukhara the Holy, I did so reluctantly. The next stage of my journey, 130 miles east along the Zarafshan valley, would once again take me in Temur's footsteps, this time as he returned to his beloved capital from the west. Samarkand had not seen her emperor for five years. Levied for a Seven-Year Campaign, the Tatar hordes had left Samarkand in October 1399, shortly after the victory in India. They returned in August 1404, weary, laden with spoil, and thinking once more of nothing but domestic delights. Temur might have been devoting many of his waking hours to the plans to invade China, but he was the emperor, chosen by God to rid the world of the unbelievers. The simple soldiers, however, the instruments of his success, were engaged in earthier considerations. War could wait. Wine and women were more immediate priorities.

&

Temur's triumphal entry into Samarkand took him on the usual whirl from garden to garden and palace to palace, staying in one for several days before moving on with great pomp to the next. The crowds poured out to greet him, sharing in his grief at the loss of his heir, celebrating with him the latest victories and additions to the empire. The chronicles record his stately progress from the Garden of Heart's Delight to the Garden of the Plane Tree, from the Model of the World to the Paradise Garden and Northern Garden. The sweeping lawns were beautifully manicured, the air was perfumed with roses, and the streams played through the palace grounds. There were audiences and receptions, riotous feasts and formal state banquets. And the games of chess continued. Nor was there any let-up in the grandiose building projects. In celebration of his latest victories, Temur gave orders for a palace to be built in a park south of the Northern Garden. Architects taken from Damascus during the last campaign were set to work. Each side of the palace was said to have measured over seven hundred metres.

'This palace was the largest and most magnificent of any Temur had built,' wrote Yazdi. 'The chief ornaments of the buildings in Syria are of marble; and running streams are common in their houses. The Syrian architects are also very ingenious in mosaic work and sculpture and in contriving curious fountains and perpetual *jets d'eau*, and what is most remarkable is that with stones of various colours they do the same sort of work which the artificers in inlaid work do with ebony and ivory, and with equal skill and delicacy. They likewise made several fountains in the palace, the beauty of which was enhanced by an infinity of *jets d'eau* in various styles, in inimitable art. Afterwards the workmen of Persia and Iraq enriched the exterior of the walls with porcelain of Cachan, which gave the finishing stroke to the beauty of this palace.'

The emperor's arrival in his capital coincided with that of Ruy Gonzalez de Clavijo, Spanish ambassador from the court of King Henry III of Castile. Leaving Cadiz in May 1403, the Spaniard and his party had endured a mammoth journey of fifteen months and six thousand miles, beset by delays. Shipwrecked in the Black Sea, they were forced to winter in Constantinople, from where they were only able to resume their journey the following spring. Hoping to receive an audience with Temur while the Tatar army was camped in the pastures of the Qarabagh, Clavijo narrowly missed him and was obliged to press on east. Such was the speed of Temur's homeward march that the Spaniard eventually had to cross Asia in his wake.

After admiring Tabriz, where he met a large embassy from Cairo bound for Samarkand, and Sultaniya, where he was granted an audience with Temur's debauched son Miranshah, Clavijo headed on towards Mawarannahr. At Nishapur he lost one of his party to fever, but the embassy carried on its tortuous path, crossing the Qara Qum desert and reaching the frontiers of Temur's homeland on the southern bank of the Amu Darya at Balkh, in northern Afghanistan. Once across this heavily guarded frontier – where entry was permitted but exit was forbidden on pain of death – Clavijo took the road north, from Termez to Shakhrisabz, where he was overwhelmed by the grandeur and elegance of Temur's Ak Sarai palace, still under construction after twenty years. From here, it was a last push of fifty miles to his final destination. At 9 o'clock on Monday, 8 September 1404, the shattered Spaniard finally arrived at a city whose magnificence he had never expected, and whose hospitality he would never forget.

The chronicles describe Temur's return to his capital in some detail, but Clavijo's wonderfully-observed account – impartial, unlike those of Arabshah and Yazdi – goes much further, adding texture and colour. He was writing from the unique perspective of a cultured European whose prejudices towards 'barbarian' Asians had suddenly been dealt a fatal blow. From his first sight of the elderly emperor he was transfixed by the lavish splendour of the court. He was led first through a great orchard, entered by a gate resplendent in blue and gold tiles. Six elephants, trophies of Delhi, guarded the entrance, each with a miniature castle on its back. Clavijo and his companions were then escorted from one attendant to the next until they reached the emperor's grandson Khalil Sultan, who took their letter from King Henry and directed them to the Conqueror of the World. Temur was sitting on a dais in front of a beautiful palace, reclining on embroidered silk cushions and mattresses. He wore a silk cloak and a crown ornamented with a balas ruby, pearls and precious stones.

Red apples floated in a fountain which threw a column of water into the air.

It is Clavijo, above all other sources, who provides the most compelling physical portrait of Temur in his last years. All the decades in the saddle, the skin-cracking summers and the savagely cold winters, had taken their toll. 'His Highness commanded us to arise and stand close up to him that he might the better see us, for his sight was no longer good, indeed, he was so infirm and old that his eyelids were falling over his eyes and he could barely raise them to see.'

For a sixty-nine-year-old cripple who had outlived many of his contemporaries, including several sons and grandsons, who had fought in battles throughout Asia and had travelled countless thousands of miles, this physical deterioration was hardly surprising. What was more remarkable was that despite such obvious frailties, Temur showed no signs of letting up. On the contrary, he was still pursuing his ambitions with characteristic vigour. The ruthlessness had not mellowed with age.

There were building projects to inspect, not least a new main road running through the city with arcaded shops, the mausoleum raised in honour of Mohammed Sultan and, most important, the Cathedral Mosque which Temur had commissioned to celebrate his victory in India. He intended this to be his greatest monument, a tribute to Allah and, given its unrivalled magnificence in the Islamic world, implicitly to himself. Five years after the cosmopolitan team of stonemasons, architects, labourers and master craftsmen drawn from all over his empire had begun their work, the mosque was nearing completion when he returned from the west.

'Now at this season,' Clavijo wrote, 'Temur was already in weak health, he could no longer stand for long on his feet, or mount his horse, having always to be carried in a litter.' Such physical constraints did not in the least deter the emperor from the task at hand. The chief architects and the two amirs responsible for the mosque must have trembled inwardly when he came to examine it. The first signs were ominous. Though Clavijo judged it 'the noblest of all those we visited in the city of Samarkand', Temur, as we have seen, did not concur. The portal was too small. His mosque was meant to eclipse every other building in the *dar al Islam*, never mind Samarkand. He gave orders for the façade to be demolished on the spot. The amirs who had administered the project in his absence were summarily executed.

This was a reminder, if one were needed, that Temur, however frail he had become, was the supreme power. The campaign against China would proceed as planned. A summons was despatched to all the nobles, princes, amirs and commanders who would accompany him to war against the greatest army on earth. The *qurultay* would be held on the plain of Kani-gil outside Samarkand. Its purpose was twofold. First, the tumultuous gathering would demonstrate to the infidels of China that they were about to be swept away by a mightier force sent by Allah. Second, the emperor would celebrate the marriages of five of his grandsons. The dynasty would live on to greater glory. This was to be a festival unlike any other Temur had ever held. And Clavijo was there to observe every minute of it.

Just as he had been shocked by the scale and opulence of Samarkand, the beauty of its monuments, the graciousness of its parks and palaces, Clavijo was now struck by the largest, most exotic gathering of humanity he had ever beheld. The account of his three-year embassy to the court of Temur runs to three hundred pages. Fifty of those, written in a tone of profound wonder, are devoted exclusively to the feast of Kani-gil, a celebration that began in the last few days of September 1404 and lasted two months. Yazdi and Arabshah both refer to the festival with their usual sycophancy and prejudice respectively on display, but once again it is to the flourishing pen of Clavijo we must turn for the most meticulous reportage of an emperor and his people at the zenith of their power. It is worth quoting from him at length.

> *In the plain here Temur recently had ordered tents to be pitched for his accommodation, and where his wives might come, for he had commanded the assembly of the great Horde, which until now had been encamped in the pastures beyond the orchards round and about the city. The whole of the Horde was now to come in, each clan taking up its appointed place: and now we saw them here, pitching the tents, their womenfolk accompanying them. This was done in order that all [these Chaghatays] might have their share in the festivities which were going forward for the celebration of certain royal marriages now about to be declared. From their custom as soon as the camp of his Highness thus had been pitched all these folk of the Horde exactly knew where each clan had its place. From the greatest to the humblest, each man knew his allotted position and took it up without confusion in the most orderly fashion. Thus in the course of the next three or four days we saw near twenty thousand tents pitched in regular streets to encircle the royal camp, and daily more clans came in from the outlying districts. Throughout the Horde thus encamped we saw the butchers and cooks who passed to and fro selling their roast and boiled meats, while others sold barley and fruit, and bakers with their ovens alight were kneading the dough and making bread for sale. Thus every art and craft was to be found dispersed throughout the camp, and each trade was in its appointed street of the great Horde. There were baths and bathers established in the camp who, pitching their tents had built wooden cabins adjacent to each other, each with its iron bath supplied with hot water, heated in cauldrons which they had there together with all the other furniture they required.*

The Chaghatays continued to pour in, until Clavijo estimated there were fifty thousand tents pitched around the imperial enclosure on the banks of the Zarafshan river, with more in the meadows beyond. Within the various enclosures, arranged in strict hierarchy, were the emperor himself, the princes his sons and grandsons, the amirs, the *sayids*, descendants of the Prophet, the scholars, the *shaykhs*, the *muftis*, the *qadis*, the Kipchak ambassadors, the envoys from Egypt, Syria, Asia Minor, India and Spain, the *binbashis*, commanders of a thousand, the *yuzbashis*, leaders of a hundred, together with all the magistrates and high officials.

On 2 October the Spanish delegation was instructed to adjourn to a garden where its host, whom Clavijo referred to as the Grand Doorkeeper, was preparing a banquet. Temur had received reports that Clavijo was not drinking wine, an anomaly he was minded to rectify.

> *This lord informed us that Temur being perfectly well aware how it was our custom, as with all Franks [Europeans], daily to drink wine, his Highness had nonetheless noticed that we did not willingly ever do so in his presence when it was offered to us after the Tatar fashion. For that reason his Highness had arranged for us now to be brought to this garden where dinner was about to be served to us and wine provided, that thus we might eat and drink at our ease and to our fill. We found that ten sheep and a horse had been sent by order of Temur to supply the banquet with meat, also a full charge of wine and on this fare we dined sumptuously. At the conclusion of the feast they presented each of us ambassadors with a robe of gold embroidery and a shirt to match, also a hat. Furthermore, we each received a horse for riding, all these gifts being presented to us by order of the Lord Temur.*

Four days later, the emperor announced a grand feast in the Royal Camp, to which he had invited all the members of the imperial family, the lords of the court and the chiefs of the clans. The ambassadors were taken to join the horde. While they observed the preparations for the banquet taking place around them, Clavijo studied the tent in which Temur was giving audiences. The first aspect of it he remarked upon was its impressive size, one hundred paces long on each of its four sides, and as high as three long lances. 'The ceiling of the pavilion was made circular to form a dome, and the poles supporting it were twelve in number, each as thick as a man's chest,' in bright blue and gold and other colours. The interior of the dome was the pavilion's 'mark of greatest beauty', for the canopies hanging from it formed four archways whose corners were emblazoned with pictures of eagles with folded wings. The inner walls of the pavilion were lined with beautifully woven crimson tapestries and silk embroidered with gold thread. Inside, the emperor gave audiences from a dais lined with a carpet and several fine mattresses. The outer walls were made of silk woven into bands of yellow and white. Low galleries adjoined these walls, supported by smaller poles. At each of the four corners stood a tall staff capped with a burnished copper ball surmounted by a crescent. Above the dome was a square-shaped turret made of silk, complete with simulated battlements and also decorated with balls and crescents. Despite its fairytale-castle style, the audience pavilion was eminently practical. A gangway led from the ground to its summit, enabling workmen to repair any damage caused by high winds. Five hundred crimson ropes held the structure securely in place. Running around the pavilion was an outer perimeter, a wall of cloth made from multi-coloured silks, 'as high as a man on horseback may reach up to', and patterned with battlements. An arched gateway within the wall contained double doors of canvas beneath another highly ornamented turret. The enclosure stretched three hundred paces across and contained many other tents and awnings. Clavijo found the entire effect astonishing. 'From a distance indeed this great tent would appear to be a castle, it is so immensely broad and high,' he marvelled.

In all there were eleven such royal enclosures, each containing a splendid array of pavilions. Wherever he wandered, whatever he saw,

Clavijo was electrified. There were tents of all shapes and sizes. One was decorated with a massive figure of an eagle with outspread wings in silver gilt. Beneath it were 'three falcons in silver gilt ... very skilfully wrought, they have their wings open as though they were in flight from the eagle, their heads being turned back to look at him. The eagle is represented as though about to pounce.' There were tents without ropes, their walls supported by slender poles, with borders made from spangles of silver inlaid with precious gems. Some were lined with red tapestries and shag velvet, others more luxuriously with furs of ermine and squirrel.

Great feasts were announced daily, to which Clavijo and his entourage were invariably invited. On 8 October they made their way to a banquet given by the once famously beautiful princess Khan-zada, 'now some forty years of age ... fair of complexion and fat'. She was the widow of Temur's cherished first-born Jahangir, later remarried to Miranshah, from whom she had fled in 1399 at the time of his erratic and bullying behaviour while governor of Sultaniya. All around her were jars of wine and a drink called *busa*, mares' milk sweetened with sugar. A group of musicians were accompanying a chorus of singers. One by one the royal women were presented with goblets brimming with wine, each one downed in one or two draughts. Occasionally one of the male servers was invited to drink a bumper, after which he would turn the cup upside down 'to show his dame that not a drop had been left in the bottom', and would then 'boast of his feats of drinking and of how much wine he could put away, at which the ladies would laugh merrily'. This was another occasion at which Clavijo's teetotal habits aroused a certain interest and disapproval. Temur's chief wife, Saray Mulk-khanum, also present at the banquet, 'commanded that we the ambassadors should come forward, when with her own hand she offered us the wine cup and persisted in the attempt to make me Ruy Gonzalez drink of the same, but I would not, though scarcely could she be brought to believe and understand that I never did drink wine'. Such behaviour would not have been welcomed. It was considered disrespectful towards one's host not to finish a cup of wine. Not even to taste it would have been judged the height of eccentricity or bad manners. Either way, it would have done little to endear the Spaniards to their royal hosts.

Notwithstanding the abstemious Europeans, the revels continued. 'Now when this drinking of theirs had gone on for some considerable time, many of the men present sitting before the Princess were beginning to show signs of being in their cups, and some indeed were already dead drunk. This state forsooth they deem a sign of manliness and at none of their feasts do they consider hilarity is attained unless many guests are properly in drink.' Clavijo derived more pleasure from the food, 'an abundance of roast mutton and horse-flesh, with various meat stews'. There were dishes of rice, vegetables, sugar breads and cakes.

As part of the celebrations for one of his grandsons' weddings Temur gave orders that all the tradesmen of Samarkand should leave the city and set up their stalls among the horde. Merchants, jewellers, cooks, butchers, bakers, tailors and cobblers hurried to the meadows, where they were told to arrange exhibitions of their trades and crafts. Once they had arrived, none was allowed to leave without the emperor's permission.

It was not all joyful feasting and carousing, however. At the busiest points on the plain, Temur ordered great gallows to be built. 'He let it be known that whereas he intended to gratify and give enjoyment to all the common folk at his festival, he also intended to give a warning and example of those who had offended him and done evil deeds, and he would proceed to the public execution of the criminals.'

The first to swing was the governor of Samarkand, appointed to administer the city seven years earlier during the emperor's campaigns in India and Asia Minor. Clavijo described him as the greatest official in the entire empire. Reports had reached Temur that this man had abused his position and oppressed the people. He was summarily judged and strung up. 'This act of high justice condemning so great a personage to death made all men tremble,' the envoy wrote, 'and notably he had been one in whom his Highness had placed much confidence.' A friend who attempted to intercede on the governor's behalf was also hanged. Another would-be intermediary, possibly one of Temur's nephews, offered a substantial ransom to save the official. As soon as the emperor had received payment, he ordered the unfortunate man to be tortured until he disclosed where the rest of his fortune lay. Then he was 'hung on the gallows by the feet head downwards till he died'.

A number of other officials were executed, together with various merchants judged to have been overcharging for their goods. Such grim spectacles, however, formed only a small part of the Kani-gil festival. Though they served as a warning to all that no one was above the law, and that the law was Temur, they were eclipsed by the riotous round of parties and entertainments, banquets, dancing, revelling and singing, to which there seemed no end.

During his wide-eyed wanderings, Clavijo was able to meet the most senior members of the imperial family. Prince Pir Mohammed, who had not seen his grandfather Temur for seven years, according to Clavijo, had been called back from Afghanistan to attend the celebrations. He was 'a young man of about twenty-two years of age, swarthy and yellow of skin and he had no beard'. After the death of Mohammed Sultan he had been appointed Temur's heir, and now appeared in all his youthful majesty, 'sumptuously attired as is the Tatar custom, wearing a robe of blue Zaytuni silk embroidered in gold circles, like small wheels, which back and front covered his chest and shoulders and passed down the material of his sleeves. On his head he wore a hat garnished with many great pearls and precious stones, and on the top was displayed a fine clear balas ruby. The people whom we found in attendance on him all paid him the utmost deference.' When the Spaniards were ushered into his presence, the prince was watching a wrestling match.

Clavijo also left us a detailed portrait of Temur's chief wife, Saray Mulk-khanum, or the Great Khanum, as he called her. He observed her during another feast to which Temur had invited the Spaniards, and apart from her ability to down large quantities of wine, it was her dress which most fascinated him. She wore an outer robe of red silk embroidered with gold, complete with a flowing train carried by fifteen ladies-in-waiting. One senses Clavijo struggling somewhat when it comes to describing her make-up and headwear: 'The Khanum's face appeared to be entirely covered with white lead or some such cosmetic, and the effect was to make it look as though she were wearing a paper mask. This cosmetic it is their custom for the women to smear on their faces both summer and winter to keep off the sun when they go out.'

Her face was further protected by a thin white veil, though it was the rest of the head-dress, an elaborate creation 'very like the crest of a helmet, such as we men wear in jousting in the tiltyard', that particularly interested the envoy. Made of red fabric, its border was draped over the queen's shoulders.

> In the back part this crest was very lofty and it was ornamented with many great round pearls all of good orient, also with precious stones such as balas rubies and turquoises, the same very finely set. The hem of this head-covering showed gold thread embroidery, and set round it she wore a very beautiful garland of pure gold ornamented with great pearls and gems. Further the summit of this crest just described was erected upon a framework which displayed three large balas rubies each about two finger breadths across, and these were clear in colour and glittered in the light, while over all rose a long white plume to the height of an ell, its feathers hanging down so that some almost hid the face coming to below the eyes. This plume was braced together by gold wire,

while at the summit appeared a white knot of feathers garnished
with pearls and precious stones.

As she walked the head-dress waved backwards and forwards. Her
hair, long, loose and black, 'the colour they most esteem', hung over
her shoulders. Numerous ladies-in-waiting walked alongside her to
support the head-dress. In all, Clavijo estimated there were three
hundred attendants. In addition, a man held a graceful parasol of
silk over her to protect her from the sun. The grand procession was
completed by a large body of eunuchs who marched in front of their
queen. In this stately fashion she made her way to a dais beside, and
slightly behind, her husband the emperor.

One by one Temur's wives came into the pavilion, each one observing to the letter the strict hierarchy which prevailed, taking her place
on a slightly lower dais than her predecessor. Clavijo counted eight
in total. The latest addition to the imperial household was a lady
called Jawhar-agha, 'which in their tongue signifies the Queen of
Hearts'. The emperor's desires appeared to be as strong as ever. He
had married her only a month previously.

One day, the Spaniards were invited to Saray Mulk-khanum's enclosure. This was the apotheosis of luxury and extravagance. It was
also a vivid example of how plundered treasures were put to new
use. In this case the enclosure was entered through 'double doors
covered with plates of silver gilt ornamented with patterns in blue
enamel work, having insets that were finely made in gold plate. All
this was so beautifully wrought that evidently neither in Tartary
nor indeed in our western land of Spain' could such superlative
craftsmanship have been achieved. Clavijo was correct. These outstanding doors were the gates of Brusa, taken after Temur's rout of
Bayazid in 1402. On one door was an image of St Peter, on the other
St Paul. Inside the tent, covered with red silk and 'adorned with rows
of silver gilt spangles running from the top to the bottom of the
walls', were more treasures. First there was a cabinet of solid gold,

ornamented with enamel and encrusted with jewels and pearls. Nearby was a small table, also of solid gold, with a large slab of translucent jade set into its surface. But one piece stood out above all others, and once again Clavijo spared no detail.

> *Standing and set beside this table, was to be noticed a golden tree that simulated an oak, and its trunk was as thick as a man's leg, while above the branches spread to right and to left, bearing leaves like oak leaves. This tree reached to the height of a man, and below it was made as though its roots grew from a great dish that lay there. The fruit of this tree consisted in vast numbers of balas rubies, emeralds, turquoises, sapphires and common rubies with many great round pearls of wonderful orient and beauty. These were set all over the tree while numerous little birds, made of gold enamel in many colours, were to be seen perching on the branches. Of these some with their wings open seemed ready to fly and some with closed wings seemed as though they had just alighted on the twigs from flight, while some appeared about to eat of the fruits of the tree and were pecking with their bills at the rubies, turquoises and other gems or at the pearls which grew from the branches.*

Gaping at the profusion of precious stones, Clavijo asked where the balas rubies were mined. The king of Badakhshan, a territory in northern Afghanistan ten days' march from Samarkand, in whose territories the gems were found, was on hand to answer.

> *He replied graciously and told us that close to the capital city of Badakhshan was a mountain where the mines were situated. Here, day by day men go and seek and break into the rocks on that mountainside to find these precious stones. When the vein is discovered where they lie, this vein is carefully followed, and when the jewel is reached it must be cut out little by little with chisels until all the matrix has been removed. Then, grinding the gem on millstones, it would be further polished. We were told also that by order of Temur a strong guard had been established at the mines to see to it that his Highness's rights were respected.*

Lapis lazuli and sapphires, meanwhile, came from an area slightly further south.*

Among all this finery the young royal couples were married in celebrations which mingled Islamic law with Mongol tradition. They were given the most gorgeous robes of honour, then dressed and undressed nine times, the most auspicious number according to custom. Earlier Clavijo had watched servers place silver trenchers piled high with comfits and cakes as gifts to Temur from two of his most senior lords, 'laid down nine by nine, such being the custom when any gift is offered to his Highness'. While the young couples changed from one robe to another, attendants showered them with precious stones, rubies, pearls, gold and silver. Camel and mule trains filed through the joyous crowds, bearing more gifts for the newlyweds.

The bacchanalian festivities roared on. By day, musicians, acrobats, gymnasts, tight-rope walkers and clowns entertained the noble crowds. Richly decorated elephants raced horses and chased men. A giraffe, a long-legged gift from the Egyptian ambassador, loped about to everyone's astonishment. Such beasts were even more exotic than the elephants. By night, Temur and his amirs, the princes and the princesses, the great warriors and the elders of the Barlas clan, sat before enormous trenchers piled high with roast horse-meat and mutton, vegetables and fruit, cakes and sweetmeats, carousing into the early hours. With the feasting over, there were other appetites to be satisfied, and here too there was no restraint. Temur had announced a suspension of the strict rules and conventions that governed society. Free rein was to be given to all pleasures.

'This is the time of feasting, pleasure and rejoicing,' Yazdi had the emperor proclaiming. 'Let no one complain of or reprimand another.

---

* To this day lapis lazuli is mined at the foot of Koh-i-Bandakor, a twenty-one-thousand-foot peak in southern Badakhshan, Afghanistan.

Let not the rich encroach upon the poor, or the powerful upon the weak. Let no one ask another, Why have you done this? After this declaration everyone gave himself up to those pleasures he was most fond of, during the feast: and whatever was done passed unobserved.' Arabshah, who disapproved of 'those foul and base things', recorded how all rushed to take advantage of this imperial declaration in favour of free love. Here his usually tumultuous prose tilted towards the phallic. 'Every suitor hastened to his desire and every lover met his beloved, without anyone harassing another or dealing proudly with inferior, whether in the army or among citizens ... nor was the sword drawn except the sword of contemplation; nor the spear brandished except the lances of love that bent by embrace.'

Such pleasures, of course, had to come to an end. For Clavijo and his party the celebrations ended abruptly, and in disappointment. On 3 November, after several days waiting unsuccessfully for a final audience with Temur, the envoys were instructed to return to Spain. 'On receiving this message we immediately made our protest, urging that as yet his Highness had not granted us our dismissal nor had he given any answer to the message we had brought him from our lord the king of Castile, we said we could not and would not leave.'

The Spaniards' arguments were dismissed. The emperor's health had declined alarmingly, and he was in no position to receive them.

> *His Highness was in a very weak state, having already lost all power of speech, and he might be at the very point of death according to what the physicians prognosticated. They plainly said that this haste in thus dealing with us and our mission was necessary from the fact that Temur appeared to be dying, for our own sakes we must be off and away before the news of his death was made public, and above all before that news reached the provinces through which on our journey we should have to pass.*

They were to travel in the company of the ambassador from Egypt. For a fortnight, however, the Spaniards lingered, terrified of returning to Castile empty-handed after such a long embassy. They protested to the end, but to no avail. On 21 November they made their final departure from Samarkand.*

※

The two months of abandoning all cares, indulging all pleasures and satisfying all desires drew to a close. Clavijo's dismissal marked the end of the Kani-gil celebrations. The bright light he had shone on them faded into an autumnal blur. A decree came from the great Lord Temur. All the laws against improper and immodest behaviour, suspended for the festivities, applied as before. There was to be no more unlicensed hedonism and debauchery. The foreign ambassadors were dismissed. The empire was now on a war footing.

While the disconsolate Spaniards returned west, and the Tatar army made ready for war in the east, the feasting of autumn gave way to the sober chill of winter. As an observer and chronicler of those momentous days among the meadows of Samarkand, Clavijo is unrivalled. He was alternately astonished, enraptured, overawed, nervous and disapproving, and these feelings, and many more besides, inform his prose and make it by far the liveliest and most compelling account. But as winter descended and Temur made his final arrangements for the most dangerous war of his life, there is no one to match the furious, thundering style of Ibn Arabshah.

---

* Clavijo's unceremonious departure reflected the generally low esteem in which his embassy was held by Temur. It contrasted with the more dignified treatment accorded to the Egyptian embassy sent by Sultan Faraj, a greater power by far, and Islamic to boot. Unlike the Spaniards, the Egyptians left with many precious gifts, including a letter which measured 130 feet by five. It demanded that the young sultan, who had already submitted to Temur, send him Sultan Ahmed of Baghdad, alive and trussed, and the head of the Turkmen chief Qara Yusuf.

Soon [winter] *with his storm-winds roared and raised over the world the tents of his clouds which went to and fro, and with his roaring shoulders trembled and all reptiles for fear of that cold fled to the depths of their Gehenna, fires ceased to blaze and subsided, lakes froze, leaves shaken fell from the branches and running rivers fell headlong from a height to lower places, lions hid in their dens and gazelles sheltered in their lairs. The world fled to God the Averter because of the winter's prodigious vehemence; the face of the earth grew pale for fear of it, the cheeks of gardens and the graceful figures of the woods became dusty, all their beauty and vigour departed and the sprout of the earth dried up to be scattered by the winds.*

The weddings, womanising and wassails were over. Already they seemed to belong to another era. Samarkand, summoning the courage born of many years' experience, prepared to say farewell to her aged, ailing emperor. The hordes would march east.

11

'How that Proud Tyrant was Broken & Borne to the House of Destruction, where he had his Constant Seat in the Lowest Pit of Hell'

1404–1405

> 'The Alcoran says the highest dignity man can attain to is that of making war in person against the enemies of his religion. Mahomet advises the same thing, according to the tradition of the mussulman doctors: wherefore the great Temur always strove to exterminate the infidels, as much to acquire that glory, as to signalise himself by the greatness of his conquests.'

> SHARAF AD-DIN ALI YAZDI, *Zafarnama*

Shivering around the campfires, hugging themselves and rubbing their frozen hands together as the winds gusted through their ranks, two hundred thousand troops on the plains around Samarkand awaited the emperor's order to march. They had come from near and far, from Mawarannahr and Mazandaran, from Asia Minor, Azerbaijan and Afghanistan, from Persia and Iraq. Their adversary, the

Ming emperor of China, together with his immense army, lay half a world away. To reach him they must first march three thousand miles and brave a winter that even now, only days after the departure of the Spanish ambassadors, looked like being one of the most ferocious in living memory.

Everything was ready. The emperor had made his speech to the great council of war. His sons and grandsons and the amirs of his army had listened to, and approved, his plans to attack China. They knew this campaign represented the summit of his ambition. With death awaiting him, perhaps Temur sincerely believed that this expedition against the infidels of China would atone for all the bloodletting against his brother Muslims. More likely he was moved by the opportunity to test his undefeated army against the only power on earth capable of opposing him. Added to those weighty motivations were the inevitable prospects for plunder. Temur knew that the treasures in Peking were greater than any he had ever set eyes upon.

Over the years, the moral justification for Temur's campaigns, although fascinating to observe, had evolved into a formality. If the objects of his attentions happened to be Muslim, as they almost invariably were, then they had become bad Muslims. If they were infidels, so much the better. Temur would raise the banner and Crescent of Islam and convert them by the sword. His desire to safeguard his legacy for future generations meant that the court chronicles made great play of his explanations for waging war. And in Yazdi, Temur had the consummate apologist. Before the Tatar rose to power, the Persian wrote *à propos* of the China campaign, Asia had been ruled by a number of usurpers who were continually subjecting their peoples to wars. As a result there was no peace, prosperity or security. The world was like a human body infected by 'some corrupt matter', desperately in need of 'strong medicine'. Although this treatment would cause 'some inconveniences', it would also remove the disease.

In the same manner, God, who was pleased to purge the world, made use of a medicine which was both sweet and bitter, to wit the clemency and the wrath of the incomparable Temur; and to that effect inspired in him an ambition to conquer all Asia and to expel the several tyrants thereof. He established peace and security in this part of the world so that a single man might carry a silver basin filled with gold from the east of Asia to the west. But yet he could not accomplish this great affair without bringing in some measure upon the places he conquered destruction, captivity and plunder, which are the concomitants of victory.

If the ethical dimension to Temur's campaigns proved relatively straightforward to establish, the practical preparations for them, particularly this groundbreaking attempt to defeat China, were more demanding. First came the most important appointments. Khalil Sultan, Temur's twenty-year-old grandson, was given command of the right wing. Another grandson, Sultan Husayn, was to lead the left. Next came the critical question of provisioning the army. The *tovachis* were ordered to supply each horseman with enough supplies – equipment and food – for ten men. Every soldier was also given two milking cows and ten goats. These were in addition to the thousands of she-camels which would provide milk and, *in extremis*, meat. Several thousand wagonloads of grain were to be sown on the army's march to China. Survivors would be able to harvest the crop on their return journey to Samarkand. Preparations for cultivating the land along Temur's eastern marches, and building fortresses and fortifications, had begun in earnest much earlier. The emperor himself, too infirm now to ride long hours in the saddle, would make the journey in a litter, followed by a truly imperial personal baggage caravan of five hundred wagons.

Though the astrologers, after consulting the heavens, had given their blessing to the timing of the expedition, the conditions beneath the stars could hardly have been less auspicious. 'The violence of the cold was so great, that several men and horses perished in the road, some losing their hands and feet, others their ears and noses,' wrote Yazdi. 'The snows and rains were continually falling, the whole face of the heavens seeming to be covered but by one cloud, and the whole earth by one piece of snow.' As the soldiers prepared for the longest, coldest and most dangerous march of their lives, many must have wondered whether the astrologers had fatally miscalculated. 'Astronomers remark that at this time there was a conjunction of the three superior planets in Aquarius which was a presage of some great misfortune,' Yazdi noted with hindsight.

Temur was not to be deterred by such considerations. Astrologers were useful only insofar as they supported enterprises he had already decided upon. In earlier days, he might have spent the winter resting and feasting in and around Samarkand, waiting for the campaigning season of spring. But with the Angel Izrail preparing to gather him up from the mortal world, he would not be delayed. Ensconced inside his litter and swathed in fur rugs, Temur issued his orders. The army would march against China.

Winter now fell upon them in all its fury. Arabshah, with his dramatist's eye and a penchant for both shocking his readers and holding them in suspense, was the perfect writer to record these death-defying manoeuvres across Asia. His winter is a new protagonist, bursting into the chronicle like a gale, a supernatural force which has declared war against the world in general, and Temur in particular. 'He intended by his coming that breath should freeze, noses and ears be frostbitten, legs fall off and heads be plucked off.'

With heads bowed against the driving winds and the horses coated in a blanket of snow, the ghostly army struggled on. The first halting-place came at Aqsulat, before the Sir Darya. Here, Khalil Sultan was sent to Tashkent with the right wing, while Sultan Husayn was ordered to take his force to Yasi. Both were to return with their men in spring. Temur would continue towards Peking.

At Aqsulat, the emperor attended to a number of family matters. His grandson, Khalil Sultan, commander of the right wing, had appalled the imperial family by marrying Shadi Mulk, a concubine who belonged to the harem of the late Amir Sayf ad-din. Temur, infuriated, had ordered the woman's arrest, but Khalil Sultan had resisted his grandfather's command and hidden her. When she was found, she was condemned to death. Had it not been for the intervention of another grandson, Pir Mohammed, the concubine-turned-princess would have been swiftly executed. When Temur reached Aqsulat, however, he discovered that Khalil Sultan had defied him by refusing to give her up. In a blazing passion, he ordered her execution for the second time. This time the empress Saray Mulk-khanum interceded on the woman's behalf, moved by the grief of the prince she had helped raise. The two senior amirs, Shaykh Nur ad-din and Shah Malik, were persuaded to inform Temur that Shadi Mulk was pregnant with Khalil Sultan's child. The ruse worked. The execution was cancelled. Shadi Mulk was entrusted to the care of another of Temur's queens for the duration of her pregnancy. After she had given birth she would be guarded by eunuchs, whose main duty would be to ensure that Khalil Sultan would never lay eyes on her again.

With the matter settled, the march east resumed. The turbulence of relationships within the imperial family faded from memory as savage storms whipped in across the steppes. To protect his men from the onslaught, Temur had provided them with heavy tunics and warmer lined tents, but still the chill was excruciating. By day they rocked in the saddle to keep warm, gripping their horses for all they were worth, trying to absorb as much of the animals' body heat as possible. By night, as temperatures plummeted and the stars seemed like freezing pinpricks assailing them from the heavens, they shrouded themselves in filthy woollen blankets, huddled around puny fires which quickly devoured the meagre fuel they had foraged.

When they reached the Sir Darya they found it frozen solid, like all the other rivers they had passed. The advantage this gave them in terms of avoiding detours and difficult fording-places was offset by the problem of finding drinking water. Men had to dig four or five feet into the ice to find it, said Yazdi. Their fingers, already swollen from scraping away snow on their hunts for scraps of wood to burn, bled freely into the ice. They were too cold to feel the pain.

Amid the snowstorms, the army's stubborn progress continued. Temur was defying nature, wrote Arabshah, refusing to back down in the face of its merciless attack. 'But winter dealt damage to him, breaking on him from the flanks with every wind kindled and raging against his army with all winds blowing aslant, most violent, and smote the shoot of the army with its intense cold ... The winter poured round them with its violent storms and scattered against them its whirlwinds sprinkling hail and roused above them the lamentations of its tempests and discharged against them with full force the storms of its cold.' It was a personal duel, said Arabshah, and so determined to win it was Temur that he ignored the sufferings of his soldiers and would not call a halt. Casualties were heavy, according to the Syrian, and fell indiscriminately on noble and poor alike. Notwithstanding these losses, Temur and his hordes pressed on towards Peking. Arabshah's winter was unrelenting:

> 'Mark my warning and by Allah the heat of piled coals shall not defend you from the frost of death nor shall fire blazing in the brazier!' Then he measured over him from his store of snow what could split breastplates of iron and dissolve the joints of iron rings and sent down upon him and his army from the sky of frost some mountains of hail and in their wake discharged typhoons of his scraping winds, which filled their ears and the corners of their eyes and drove hail into their nostrils and thus drew out their breath

*to their gullets by discharging that barren wind, which made every-
thing it touched putrid and crushed; and on all sides with the
snow that fell from above the whole earth became like the plain
of the last judgement or a sea which God forged out of silver. When
the sun rose and the frost glittered, the sight was wonderful, the
sky of Turkish gems and the earth of crystal, specks of gold filling
the space between.*

Winter's attack was so intense that even the sun trembled and froze
with cold. When a man spat, his phlegm hit the ground as an ice-ball.
When he breathed, his breath froze on his beard and moustache.

In mid-January the army reached Otrar in Kazakhstan. Here Temur
and his most senior amirs were lodged in the palace of Amir Birdi
Beg, the local governor. Scouts were sent out to find whether the way
ahead was passable in these treacherous conditions. They returned,
shaking their heads solemnly, with reports that everywhere they had
travelled the snow lay as deep as two spears. The horses, camels and
wagons would not be able to force a way through. At this time an
embassy arrived from the downtrodden Tokhtamish, who since his
defeat at Temur's hands in 1395 had wandered through the Kipchak
desert like a vagabond, wrote Yazdi. Despite the history between the
two men, Temur gave the envoys a magnificent reception. Tokhtamish's message was conciliatory and apologetic. He had deserved every
misfortune which had befallen him, he said. Now he had no option
left but to throw himself at the emperor's feet, begging forgiveness
and promising to serve Temur in any way possible. In reply, the
Tatar wrote that after his return from China he would help reinstall
Tokhtamish on his throne.

While the bitter storms raged around Otrar, the weakening
emperor was suddenly stricken with a cold. Although inside his litter
he had been better protected from the dreadful winter than his men,
he was far older than most of those around him, and he was also
recovering from the sickness that had troubled him while Clavijo was

in Samarkand. Hot drinks, laced with drugs and spices, were prepared and fires lit throughout the palace to ward off the cold. Still the symptoms refused to go away. The brilliant court physician Maulana Fadl of Tabriz, one of the most celebrated doctors in Asia, prescribed a number of treatments. One of them, bizarrely, involved covering the emperor's stomach and chest with ice. All waited nervously for Temur's improvement.

The doctor's efforts did not have the desired effect. The cold became a fever. The wrinkled emperor twisted and turned in his bed, shivering with cold one minute, bathed in sweat the next. In his burning hallucinations he heard the *houris* call down to him, urging him to repent before he faced his maker. He knew his end was near. Summoning his wives and most senior amirs to hear his last wishes, his voice dropped until it was almost inaudible.

> *I know my soul is about to leave my body and I am to be taken to the throne of God who gives life, and takes it away. I beg you shed no tears at my death. Rather than tearing your clothes and running around like madmen, pray to God to have mercy on me. Say* Allahu akbar, *God is great, and recite the* Fatiha *to comfort my soul.* Since God enabled me to give laws to Iran and Turan so that throughout those kingdoms the great do not oppress the*

---

* The *fatiha* is the opening sura of the Koran:

> *In the Name of God,*
> *The Compassionate,*
> *The Merciful.*
> *Praise be to God, Lord of the Universe,*
> *The Compassionate, the Merciful,*
> *Sovereign of the Day of Judgement!*
> *You alone we worship, and to You alone*
> *we turn for help.*
> *Guide us to the straight path,*
> *The path of those whom You have favoured,*
> *Not of those who have incurred Your wrath,*
> *Nor of those who have gone astray.*

poor, I hope he will forgive my sins, which are without number ... I declare Pir Mohammed, son of Jahangir, my sole heir and lawful successor to my throne. He must possess the throne of Samarkand with absolute sovereignty and independence so that he can administer the business of empire, the army, and all the countries and cities under his jurisdiction. I command you all to obey him and sacrifice your lives to maintain his authority so that the world will not fall into disorder and that the fruits of my labours over so many years are not lost. If you remain united, no one will dare oppose you, nor offer the slightest challenge in executing my last wishes.

He ordered his amirs, lords and army commanders to come before him and swear to observe these instructions. The amirs Shaykh Nur ad-din and Shah Malik pledged their eternal obedience, and were unable to hold back the tears. They offered to write to Khalil Sultan, summoning him to Otrar so he could hear his grandfather's dying wishes in person. But Temur, barely able to move or talk, shook his head. There was no time for that. 'This is the last audience you will have of me. I have no other desire than to see Prince Shahrukh, but that is impossible. God will not have it.' On hearing these words, the princes and ladies of the court, standing silently in the emperor's antechamber, started sobbing. Temur turned to them for the last time. He looked weak and broken, but his eyes burned with their customary fire.

Remember to do everything I have told you to keep peace and public order. Always keep yourselves informed about the affairs of your subjects. Be valiant and keep your sword in your hand with courage that like me you may enjoy a long reign and a vast empire. I have purged Iran and Turan of their enemies and disturbers of the peace and I have brought them justice and prosperity. If you follow my last wishes and make justice the guide of all your actions, the empire will long remain in your hands. But if discord and disunity creep in, ill fortune awaits you. Enemies will start wars

*which will be difficult to end and irreparable damage will befall
the state and religion.*

After these words, the fever worsened. Outside the emperor's chamber
imams were reciting from the Koran. A priest stood at the bottom
of his bed reading verses affirming the unity of God. At about 8
o'clock Temur, mindful of the Prophet's promise that he whose last
words were '*La ilaha illa'llah*, there is no god but God' would enter
heaven, declared his faith aloud. Then, said Yazdi, 'he gave his soul
to the angel Izrail, who called him in these words: "O hopeful spirit,
return to your Lord with resignation. We belong to God and to God
must we return."'*

For a moment there was silence inside the bedchamber. Outside,
all that could be heard was the wind tearing at the palace walls in
that cold, black night deep in the Asian steppe. Candles threw a veil

---

* Arabshah, of course, recorded Temur's last hours rather differently. Even at
the end, he could not restrain his violent dislike for the man who had
sacked and destroyed his native city, Damascus. The chapter in which
Temur dies is headed: 'How that Proud Tyrant was Broken and Borne to
the House of Destruction, Where he had his Constant Seat in the Lowest
Pit of Hell'. The prose is as apocalyptic and unforgiving as ever: 'His heart
was crushed and neither his wealth nor his children availed him anything
and he began to vomit blood and bite his hands with grief and penitence
. . . And the butler of death gave him to drink a bitter cup and soon he
believed that which he had resolutely denied, but his faith did not help
him, after he had seen damnation; and he begged for assistance but none
was found; and it was said to him: "Depart, O impure soul, who were in
an impure body, depart vile, wicked sinner and delight in boiling water,
fetid blood and the company of sinners." But if one saw him, he coughed
like a camel which is strangled, his colour was almost quenched and his
cheeks foamed like a camel dragged backwards with the rein; and if one
saw the angels that tormented him, they showed the joy with which they
threaten the wicked, to lay waste their homes and utterly destroy the
whole memory of them . . . Then they brought garments of hair from Hell
and drew forth his soul like a spit from a soaked fleece and he was carried
to the cursing and punishment of God, remaining in torment and God's
infernal damnation.'

of gold over Temur's pale features. Then the princes and the ladies, the amirs and the great lords of the court, the doctors and the attendants, all gave in to their grief and wept profusely. The emperor, centre of their universe, was dead.

An Empire Dies, Another is Born

'Our hearts are torn with grief, for the most powerful of emperors, the soul of the world, is dead; and already ignorant youths whom he raised from the lowest state to the highest honours have become traitors to him. Forgetting the obligations they owe him, they have disobeyed his orders and violated their oaths. How can we dissemble our grief at so terrible a misfortune? An emperor who has made the kings of the earth to serve at his gate, and has indeed earned the name of conqueror, no sooner leaves us than his will is set aside. Slaves have become the enemies of their benefactor. Where is their faith? If rocks had hearts they would mourn. Why are not stones rained down from Heaven to punish these ungrateful wretches? As for us, God willing, we shall not forget our master's wishes; we shall carry out his will, and obey the young princes his grandchildren.'

Temur's amirs, speaking after his death.
HAROLD LAMB, *Tamerlane the Earth Shaker*

'It is a common observation that the grandeur of princes is known by the monuments which remain of them after their death.'

SHARAF AD-DIN ALI YAZDI, *Zafarnama*

Temur's blood had hardly cooled when the internecine fighting he had so eloquently warned against on his deathbed exploded. Rarely had the fortunes of an empire depended so entirely on one man being in the wrong place at the wrong time. Pir Mohammed, the designated heir, was far away to the south in his territories of northern India. The ambitious Khalil Sultan, however, was wintering with his army in Tashkent, from where it was a march of just 160 miles south-west to Samarkand, seat of the empire. The scramble for power began.

Temur's grandson Sultan Husayn was the first to make his bid. After a lightning attempt to take the throne failed, he took refuge with Shahrukh, who swiftly executed him. Hurrying back to the capital from Otrar, the loyal amirs Shah Malik and Shaykh Nur ad-din, intending to safeguard the succession for Pir Mohammed, found themselves barred at the gates. The governor of Samarkand, already co-opted by Khalil Sultan, the young pretender to the throne, refused them entry. In the short term, the simple facts of geography proved conclusive. Khalil Sultan, nearest to the capital when his grandfather died, seized power. In 1406, the rightful heir gathered his forces and marched north at the head of an army to give battle. He was roundly defeated by Khalil Sultan. A year later, Pir Mohammed was murdered in a coup led by his most trusted amir.

Khalil Sultan's reign was brief. He had risen to power with the support of an army drawn largely from the populations outside Mawarannahr. These men did not have a direct interest in what was essentially one family's fight for power, nor were they instinctively bound to their commander. Like many of the tribes and peoples Temur had won to his cause during his lifetime, they had to be bought. Over the years such loyalty had been purchased by distributing the prizes of the battlefield, the plundered palaces and the looted treasuries of Asia among the soldiers who had given him his victories. The death of Temur fundamentally altered that equation. Immersed in the vicissitudes of his domestic position, Khalil Sultan was unable to venture beyond his borders to continue the conquests on which his grandfather's empire had depended. For four years he emptied the coffers of Samarkand for his followers, encouraged by the ambitious woman he had married. Shadi Mulk had enjoyed a meteoric rise. Rescued from the harem, she had become first a princess and now, the summit of her dreams, empress. Under her influence, the amirs fell from favour one by one until Khalil Sultan relied exclusively on his beautiful wife for advice on affairs of state. 'This was the height of folly and madness,' Arabshah sneered, 'for how could he be happy, who suffers his wife to rule him?'

By 1409, there was little left to give away. Khalil Sultan's followers, disappointed with the end of his largesse, melted away to where their prospects were more auspicious. Khalil Sultan took himself and his depleted forces to his uncle, Shahrukh, who welcomed his nephew with open arms, only to poison him. Shadi Mulk, said Arabshah, was devastated. 'Taking a dagger, she plunged it into her throat and leant upon it with such force that it pierced her head and she burnt with her fire all that beheld her, then both were buried in one tomb.'

Shahrukh, having put down a series of bubbling rebellions in his province of Khorasan, swept in and took power. He transferred his capital to Herat, leaving Samarkand in the hands of his gifted son, Ulugh Beg. The next forty years were the golden age of Temurid civilisation. The heart of the empire remained intact, and after decades of war began to luxuriate in the benefits of peace. Shahrukh and his wife Gawhar Shad were prolific patrons of the arts and literature, presiding over an era in which Temurid culture soared to its apogee. In Samarkand, the astronomer king immersed himself in mathematics, medicine and music. A lover of poetry like his father, he was also a devoted student of history, geography, philosophy and theology. But he was noted above all for the observatory he constructed and the astronomical tables he devised, still in use at the time England appointed its first Astronomer-Royal in the seventeenth century. Magnificent monuments continued to rise, their minarets climbing to the heavens. The Registan assumed greater grandeur with the construction of a new madrassah which celebrated the constellations and paid tribute to the achievements of the astronomer king. As a chronicler put it: 'From the time of Adam until this day, no age, period, cycle or moment can be indicated in which people enjoyed such peace and tranquillity.'

These were the last flourishes of the vast empire Temur had wrested from nothing. By the middle of the fifteenth century, both Shahrukh and Ulugh Beg were dead. After thirty-eight years of supremely enlightened government, the astronomer king was murdered by his own son. Within a century of the emperor's death, the Temurid empire had ceased to exist. Temur's prophetic warning against family divisions had gone unheeded. The greatest gifts it bequeathed – the blue-domed mosques and madrassahs, the dazzling minarets, the exquisite parks and palaces – lay scattered across Asia like funerary monuments to a lost civilisation. Only in the Mughal empire, founded across the roof of the world in India by Babur, Temur's great-great-great-grandson and most illustrious descendant, did echoes of its splendour survive.

On a late autumn evening, my last in Central Asia, I bade farewell to Temur. With its 120-foot blue-ribbed dome visible across the city, flashing in the falling sun like the brightest beacon, flanked by two slender minarets, the Gur Amir mausoleum is the finest in Samarkand and the most inspired piece of Temurid architecture the world ever saw. Built by the emperor to honour his cherished grandson Mohammed Sultan, it is the final resting place of the Conqueror of the World, a 'magnificent sepulchre' according to that tireless sycophant Yazdi. 'The cincture of the dome was of marble set off with gold and azure. Within it was dug a vault in which to lay the prince's body, and a charming garden was made around it on the ruins of some houses.' Although Temur had made plans to be buried in Shakhrisabz, his family home and the first seat of his power, Khalil Sultan interred him here, embalmed with camphor, musk and rose-water. It was one of the wayward prince's inaugural acts on taking control of the city.

'Then first he gave heed to the burying of his grandfather and performing his obsequies and placing him in the tomb,' recorded Arabshah.

> *Therefore he had him laid in a coffin of ebony, which the chief men bore on their heads. Kings followed his body and soldiers with faces cast down, clad in black, and with them many Amirs and ministers, and they buried him in the same place in which they had buried Mohammed Sultan, his grandson, near the place called Ruh-Abad, which is well known, where he lay on supports in an open vault; and he paid him due funeral rites, ordering readings of the Koran from beginning to end and in portions and prayer and giving of alms, food and sweetmeats, and set a dome over the tomb and discharged his debt to him and scattered over his tomb his garments of silk and hung from the walls his weapons and equipment, which were all adorned with gems and gold and em-broidered and decked with so much art that even the meanest of them equalled the income of a country and one grain from the heap of those gems was beyond price. He also hung star-candles of gold and silver in the sky of the ceilings and spread over the couch of the tomb a coverlet of silk and embroidery up to its sides and borders. Of the candles one was of gold, weighing four thousand sesquidrachms, which make according to the weights of Samarkand one pound, and ten according to those of Damascus.*
>
> *Then he appointed for his tomb readers of the Koran and ser-vants and placed at the college janitors and managers, to whom he generously assigned pay for each day, year and month. A little later he transferred his body to a coffin of steel made by a man of Shiraz, a most skilled master of his art, and buried him in the well-known tomb, where vows are made to him and petitions offered and prayers said. And when kings pass it, they prostrate*

themselves to show honour and often dismount from their beasts
to honour him and do reverence.

Children scampered about outside the mausoleum. The distant
sounds of family life and the aromatic smell of *plov* filtered through
the dusk, borne on a light breeze that played around the ankles.
Across the car park, sitting on a throne and staring towards the
Registan, was the monumental statue of Temur where newlywed
couples celebrate their marriages every weekend. Through the monumental entrance portal, a blaze of blue with an inset arch tapering
into an ornate stalactite *muqarnas*, the courtyard was completely
empty. Beyond another, less imposing, portal, the fluted dome rose
skyward. Built on an octagonal plan by a celebrated architect from
Isfahan – 'This is the work of the weak slave of God, Mohammed
ibn Mahmoud Isfahani,' reads an inscription – the mausoleum is a
triumph of scale, style and simplicity, a noble building which celebrates the life of a prince, the sway of a dynasty and the omnipotence
of God. Beneath the textured surface of the dome, shining with tiles
of navy blue, turquoise, yellow and green, runs the inscription, in
huge Kufic script ten feet high, 'God is Immortal'. Moved by the scale
of the cupola, a poet had declared: 'Should the sky disappear, the
dome will replace it.'

I pressed on towards the heart of the mausoleum, momentarily
blinded by the cool, dark interior as I stepped out of the glare. As
my eyes adjusted to the gloom, I picked my way along the vaulted
eastern gallery – added by Ulugh Beg in the 1420s – which led to a
cavernous square chamber, each side thirty feet long, directly beneath
the dome. The interior decoration was astoundingly rich, faded in
places, restored to bolder colours in others. Hexagonal tiles of onyx
lined the lower section of the walls, a serene dado topped with a
shallow marble cornice. Above the onyx, Koranic inscriptions
encircled the chamber, traced in gold and carved from jasper. Each

of the four walls was inset with a tall bay, whose upper reaches seemed to cascade down in *papier-mâché* stalactites painted gold and blue. Beyond these vaults, at neck-craning height, amber light streamed in from marble lattice windows, illuminating the golden furnace of the inner dome above, resplendent amid geometric panels of iridescent stars.

The crowning glory of the mausoleum looked down onto seven cenotaphs gathered in the centre of the chamber behind an ornate marble rail. These are the tombs of the leading lights of the Temurid dynasty: Mohammed Sultan, the valiant prince in whose honour the mausoleum had been built; Ulugh Beg, the polymath astronomer king; his father Shahrukh, the wise patron of the arts; Miranshah, the emperor's most troublesome son. Raised on a marble plinth in the centre of the cenotaphs lies Temur's tomb, a slab of the darkest jade, black to the eye and six feet long, once the largest piece of the stone in the world. Cracked in the middle, intricately engraved on the top and sides, it was brought to Samarkand by Ulugh Beg in 1425 to adorn the tomb of his grandfather. The damage is supposed to have occurred in 1740, when the Persian invader Nadir Shah attempted to carry off the treasure without success. More modestly engraved than the tombs surrounding it, the slab of jade lies next to another sepulchre, belonging to Shaykh Sayid Baraka. The emperor's instructions to be buried at the feet of his spiritual and religious mentor were honoured to the letter.

Even in death Temur has managed to intertwine the two conflicting strands of his identity. Etched across the jade is a long inscription detailing – and mythologising – his genealogy. Several generations beyond his father, Taraghay Barlas, he establishes the fictitious connection with Genghis Khan. On and on the list of names continues until it reaches his last paternal ancestor. 'And no father was known to this glorious man but his mother was Alanquva,' it reads. 'It is said that her character was righteous and chaste, and that she was

TAMERLANE

not an adulteress. She conceived him through a light which came into her from the upper part of a door and it assumed for her the likeness of a perfect man. And it said that it was one of the sons of the Commander of the Faithful, Ali son of Abu Talib.' This is a masterpiece of propaganda. In an instant Temur has become the descendant of both Genghis Khan and the Caliph Ali, uniting the traditions of the Mongols with the heritage of Islam.

My thoughts were interrupted by the arrival of an elderly caretaker. He was poorly dressed, with a tatty skullcap and a ragged suit. Two bright eyes peered at me from a wrinkled face. He pointed at his watch, told me the mausoleum was closing, and started turning off the lights. Then, as he was about to leave, beckoning for me to follow, he paused.

'I show you real grave of Amir Temur. Two dollars.'

His eyes, wide with excitement, suggested that he alone held the key to a forbidden world. I nodded quickly. The tombstones I had seen on ground level were merely decorative. I knew from Yazdi's chronicle that somewhere underground a vault existed where Temur and his princes were buried, but I had been told this area was closed to visitors.

Together we made our way down a hidden flight of stairs. The elderly guide fished out a key from a pocket, opened a heavy door, and we stepped into a glacial crypt. It was pitch black. There was nothing to see. Then he flicked a switch and the lights revealed a plain vault of brick and stone.

Temur's burial place was a simple slab of carved stone engraved with Koranic inscriptions. After the pomp and colour of the mauso- leum above, the drab, dark chamber was a sombre sight. This was the grave of the man who had blazed across Asia like a comet across the heavens. For a few years his descendants had watched over the glowing embers falling through the sky until the Temurid empire and dynasty had crashed to earth, extinguished altogether. In the

An Empire Dies, Another is Born

West Temur has been all but forgotten. Those who know his name perhaps remember the fire and brimstone of Marlowe's play about a tyrant who styled himself 'the Scourge and Wrath of God/The only fear and terror of the world'. But to all but a few, the greatest Islamic empire-builder in history, the man who joined Alexander the Great and Genghis Khan in the trio of the world's greatest conquerors, remains little more than that: a name. The city he had built so brilliantly and decorated so lovingly, once the envy of the world, lies in a neglected southern outpost of the old Soviet empire. Only here does his memory burn brightly. Above the door was a short inscription.

> *This is the resting place of the illustrious and merciful monarch,*
> *the most great Sultan, the most mighty warrior, Lord Temur, Con-*
> *queror of the World.*

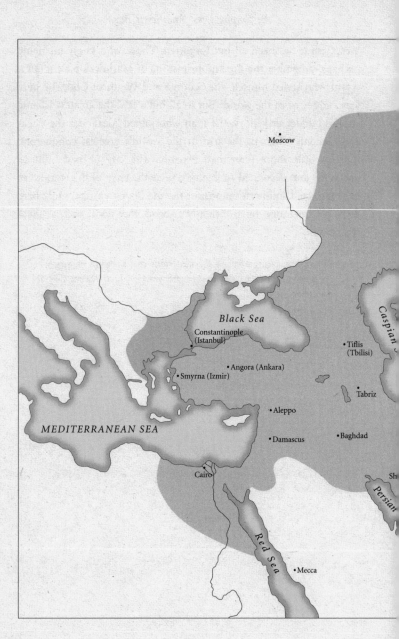

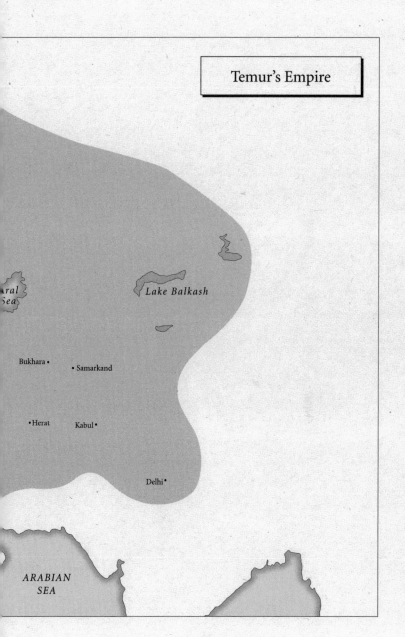

Temur's Empire

aral
Sea

Lake Balkash

Bukhara •   • Samarkand

•Herat   Kabul•

Delhi•

ARABIAN
SEA

APPENDIX A

Chronology of Temur's Life

1336 **9 April:** The official date of Temur's birth near Shakhrisabz, south of Samarkand. Scholars outside Uzbekistan believe he was born in the late 1320s or early 1330s.

1347 Amir Qazaghan deposes and kills Amir Qazan, the Chaghatay khan.

1355 Temur's first-born, Jahangir, is born around this time. His second son Omar Shaykh follows soon afterwards.

1358 Assassination of Amir Qazaghan.

1360 Tughluk Temur, the Moghul khan, invades Mawarannahr. Temur pledges his loyalty to him, positioning himself to lead the Barlas tribe. After Tughluk Temur appoints his son Ilyas Khoja leader of Mawarannahr, Temur breaks from the Moghul leader and contracts an alliance with Amir Husayn, the aristocratic leader of Balkh. Their mission is to rid Mawarannahr of the Moghuls.

1362 Temur seals the alliance by marrying Aljai Turkhan-agha, Husayn's sister. This is the nadir of his career. The would-be world conqueror and his wife are imprisoned for two months in a vermin-infested cowshed.

1365 The 'battle of the Mire'. Ilyas Khoja sends Temur and Husayn into flight.

1366 Temur and Husayn seize control of Samarkand. Ilyas Khoja, by now the Moghul khan, is assassinated. Qamar ad-din is the new Moghul ruler. Birth of Miranshah around this time.

1366–70 Temur's alliance with Husayn turns to rivalry.

1368 The Mongol Yuan dynasty in China is overthrown by the new Ming dynasty.

1370 Husayn is defeated at Balkh, captured and executed. Temur is crowned imperial ruler of Chaghatay, Lord of the Fortunate Conjunction. He marries Husayn's widow, Saray Mulk-khanum, daughter of the Chaghatay khan Qazan and a princess from the line of Genghis Khan. The marriage allows him to style himself Temur Gurgan, son-in-law of the Great Khan. He installs Suyurghatmish as Chaghatay khan. Temur launches his first campaign against the Moghuls. More follow throughout the 1370s.

1372 Temur leads his army north against the Sufi dynasty of Khorezm, taking the city of Kat. As part of a peace treaty, the princess Khan-zada, also of the Genghisid line, is promised as a wife for Temur's son Jahangir.

1373 Since no princess is forthcoming, Temur leads a second expedition. Khorezm comes to terms, Khan-zada arrives and the territory passes into Temur's fledgling empire.

1375–76 Temur campaigns against Moghulistan.

1376 Jahangir dies. Tokhtamish, a prince of the Genghisid line who is aiming for control of the White Horde, takes refuge with Temur, who arms and supports him. Tokhtamish's first attempt to seize the throne is unsuccessful.

1377 Birth of Temur's son Shahrukh. Tokhtamish is defeated again.

1378 On his third attempt, Tokhtamish, with Temur's assistance, is crowned khan of the White Horde.

1379 Temur summons the Kart prince of Herat to pay homage to him. Expedition against rebellious Khorezm. Temur sacks the city of Urganch.

1380 Tokhtamish becomes khan of the Golden Horde. Temur appoints Miranshah governor of Khorasan.

1381 Expedition against Khorasan. Temur takes Herat without a fight, before wintering around Bukhara.

1382 Campaigning in Mazandaran, Temur defeats the local ruler Amir Wali and seizes control of the Caspian territories. His army winters near Samarkand.

1383 Herat rebels. Temur returns to Khorasan where he takes two thousand prisoners in the city of Isfizar. To punish the rebellion, he has them cemented alive into towers.

1384–86 Temur takes Sistan and Kandahar. The capital of Zaranj is gutted. After the ignominious flight of its ruler, Sultan Ahmed Jalayir, the city of Sultaniya surrenders to Temur, who then returns to Samarkand.

Tokhtamish sacks Tabriz.

The Three-Year Campaign against Persia begins. Tabriz is the first city to fall. First expedition against Georgia. Tiflis (Tbilisi), its capital, surrenders.

1387 Tokhtamish pillaging in the Caucasus. Temur campaigns in Armenia before moving west into Asia Minor. Isfahan surrenders but immediately rises up in rebellion. Temur orders a massacre. Shiraz falls without a fight. News reaches Temur that Tokhtamish has attacked Mawarannahr and put Bukhara under siege. He is laying waste to Temur's homeland. Temur returns to Mawarannahr, forcing Tokhtamish north.

1388 Urganch is razed to the ground as punishment for its support of Tokhtamish's raid.

1389–90 Temur suppresses a revolt in Khorasan. Campaigns against Moghulistan. Khizr Khoja, the Moghul khan, is defeated. Qamar ad-din attempts to replace him. Temur and Khizr Khoja come to terms.

1390–91 Temur winters in Tashkent, preparing for a major expedition against Tokhtamish. After a march of more than five months and almost two thousand miles, his horde encounters Tokhtamish's army and defeats it at the battle of Kunduzcha in June. The Tatars celebrate their famous victory on the banks of the Volga.

1391–92 Temur winters in Tashkent before returning to Samarkand. He appoints his grandson Pir Mohammed, Jahangir's son, to the governorship of Kabul.

1392 The Five-Year Campaign begins.

1393 Another expedition against Georgia. Temur marches through Mazandaran, destroying the rival Muzaffarid dynasties of Persia. The Muzaffarid princes are executed. He appoints his son Omar Shaykh ruler of Fars. Temur retakes Shiraz. Baghdad submits to him after its ruler, Sultan Ahmed Jalayir, flees again. Omar Shaykh dies. The Egyptian Sultan Barquq extends his protection to Sultan Ahmed and executes Temur's ambassadors.

1394 Sultan Barquq contracts an alliance with Tokhtamish, who is assembling his forces for another expedition against Temur. Barquq readies his army and marches north to Damascus, thence to Aleppo, after reinstating Sultan Ahmed in Baghdad. Temur campaigns in Armenia and Georgia. Tokhtamish mounts another raid on the Caucasus, encroaching on Temur's empire again.

1395 Temur defeats Tokhtamish for the second and last time at the battle of Terek. His armies continue their push north, utterly ravaging the Golden Horde, destroying its principal cities Tana and Saray and its capital Astrakhan.

1396 Returning south, Temur lays waste to the embattled kingdom of Georgia. He makes a triumphant homecoming to Samarkand and embarks on his most ambitious building programme. He remains in his imperial capital for two years, the longest stay of his career. The Ottoman Sultan Bayazid I routs his European adversaries at the battle of Nicopolis, the last Crusade. Shahrukh appointed governor of Khorasan.

1397 Pir Mohammed, son of Jahangir, is sent south to the Punjabi city of Multan amid preparations for Temur's next expedition.

1398 The Indian Campaign begins. Temur crosses the Hindu Kush mountains and takes Multan. He orders the execution of one hundred thousand prisoners prior to engaging the Indian army. Outdoing both Alexander the Great and Genghis Khan, he destroys Delhi, sacking the city so completely it takes it a century to recover.

1399 Temur returns to Samarkand. Work begins on the Cathedral Mosque, his most monumental building project. Death of Sultan Barquq. He is replaced by ten-year-old Sultan Faraj. The Seven-Year Campaign begins. Temur's debauched son Miranshah is deposed as Temur marches west. Sultan Ahmed flees for the third time, taking refuge with Sultan Bayazid. Temur's forces winter in the Qarabagh.

1400 After taking Sivas, Temur has three thousand prisoners buried alive. Aleppo is put to the sword. Twenty thousand Syrian skulls are piled into mounds around the city.

1401 Camped outside Damascus, Temur grants audiences to the great Arab historian Ibn Khaldun. Damascus falls and is torched. The peerless Umayyad Mosque is ruined. After retaking Baghdad, Temur orders another massacre. This time, 120 towers of ninety thousand skulls mark his latest conquest. His army is rested during another winter in the pastures of the Qarabagh.

1402 Temur marches west to seek out Bayazid. In July he defeats the Ottoman forces at the battle of Ankara, his greatest victory yet. This is the only time in Ottoman history that the sultan is captured in person. Temur sacks Smyrna, the last Christian outpost in Asia Minor.

1403 Sultan Bayazid dies in captivity. Death of Mohammed Sultan, Jahangir's first-born and Temur's heir. Temur campaigns again in Georgia before wintering in the Qarabagh.

Chronology of Temur's Life

1404 Temur returns to Samarkand and begins new building projects. In August, the Castilian envoy Ruy Gonzalez de Clavijo arrives in the imperial capital for audiences with the Tatar emperor. Temur holds a *qurultay* in the Kani-gil meadows around Samarkand. The uproarious, wine-soaked festivities last two months. Temur rides east for his last campaign, against the Ming emperor of China.

1405 In January Temur arrives at Otrar (Kazakhstan) and falls ill. 18 February: Death of Temur.

1941 **22 June:** Soviet archaeologist Professor Mikhail Gerasimov exhumes Temur's body, confirming the injuries to both right limbs.

1991 **31 August:** Following the collapse of the Soviet Union, Uzbekistan declares independence under its leader Islam Karimov.

1993 **1 September:** During independence celebrations, President Karimov unveils a statue of Temur in Tashkent. The Tatar conqueror, long vilified by the Soviets, is the new national symbol of the motherland.

1996 As part of Uzbekistan's celebrations of the 660th anniversary of Temur's birth, a museum dedicated to the conqueror is opened in Tashkent. A new Order of Amir Temur is created to honour outstanding service to Uzbekistan.

Events in Europe in the Fourteenth Century

1272–1307 Reign of King Edward I of England, 'Hammer of the Scots'.

1302 King Philip IV of France convenes the first Estates-General, forerunner of the French parliament, in a bid to impose his power over the Church. Responding to the challenge, Pope Boniface VIII issues his Papal Bull *Unam Sanctam*, an assertion of papal supremacy in all matters spiritual and temporal. He is imprisoned by Philip IV.

1303 The University of Rome is founded.

1305 Sir William Wallace, the Scottish hero, is hanged, drawn and quartered after raising an army against the English king.

1306 **27 March:** Robert the Bruce is crowned King of Scotland at Scone.

1307–27 Reign of King Edward II of England.

1309–77 Period of the Avignon papacy. With war in Italy, the papacy withdraws to southern France, where a series of French popes hold sway until the Great Schism of 1378–1417.

1314 **23–24 June:** Robert the Bruce defeats the English army at the battle of Bannockburn.

1321 Death of Dante Alighieri, author of *The Divine Comedy*.

1327–77 Reign of King Edward III of England.

1337 Death of Giotto, the Florentine artist and architect, creator of the celebrated Scrovegni frescoes in Padua.

1337–1453 Hundred Years' War between France and England.

1338 Edward III proclaims himself King of France.

1342 ?Birth of Geoffrey Chaucer. He began writing *The Canterbury Tales* in the late 1380s, when Temur was at the height of his power.

1345 Completion of the Ponte Vecchio, Florence's most famous bridge.

1346 **26 August:** King Edward III's army defeats the French at the battle of Crécy.

1347 Spreading west from Asia, the Black Death reaches Constantinople, Rhodes, Cyprus, Sicily, Venice, Genoa and Marseilles. A year later, it ravages the rest of Italy and England, spreading into northern Europe in the early 1350s.

1350 Coronation of King John II of France.

1356 **19 September:** Edward the Black Prince leads the English army to victory over the French at the battle of Poitiers. King John II is taken prisoner and held for ransom.

1356 The Holy Roman Emperor Charles IV issues the Golden Bull, establishing rules for the election of German kings.

1360 **8 May:** France and England come to terms at the Peace of Brétigny. John II pays three million gold crowns for his ransom. Edward III renounces his claim to the French throne and is granted swathes of French territory.

1370 Completion of the Palace of Comares and the Sala de la Barca within the Alhambra, Granada.

1377–99 Reign of King Richard II of England.

1378–1417 The Great Schism. The Church splits over the election of Pope Urban VI. For three decades one pope presides in Rome while another, the anti-pope, is based in Avignon.

1381 Wat Tyler leads the Peasants' Revolt in England against the hated poll tax.

1386 The University of Heidelberg, the oldest in Germany, is founded by Rupert I, Elector of the Palatinate.

1389 The Ottoman Sultan Murad I crushes a combined European army under the Serbian King Lazarus at the battle of Kosovo.

1396 The flower of European chivalry is cut down by the Ottoman Sultan Bayazid I at the battle of Nicopolis, the last Crusade.

1399–1413 Reign of King Henry IV of England.

1400 Owen Glendower, last to claim the title of independent Prince of Wales, launches the Welsh Revolt against English rule.

Bibliography

Adshead, S.A.M., *Central Asia in World History*, London, Macmillan, 1993

Alexandrescu-Dersca, M.M., *La campagne de Timur en Anatolie (1402)*, London, Variorum, 1977

Allen, Terry, *Timurid Herat*, Wiesbaden, Reichert, 1983

Andrews, Peter, 'The Tents of Timur', in *Arts of the Eurasian Steppelands*, ed. Philip Denwood, London, Percival David Foundation of Chinese Art, 1978

Arabshah, Ahmed ibn, *Tamerlane or Timur the Great Amir*, trans. J.H. Sanders, from *The Arabic Life by Ahmed ibn Arabshah*, London, Luzac & Co., 1936

Arnold, Sir Thomas W., *Bihzad and his Paintings in the Zafar-namah MS*, London, Bernard Quaritch, 1930

Babur, *The Baburnama in English (Memoirs of Babur)*, trans. from the original Turki text of Zahiru'd-din Muhammad Babur Padshah Ghazi by Annette Susannah Beveridge, London, Luzac & Co., 1922

Barthold, V.V., 'The Burial of Timur', in *Iran: Journal of the British Institute of Persian Studies*, XII, London, 1974

Ibn Battutah, *Travels in Asia and Africa 1325–1354*, trans. and selected by H.A.R. Gibb, London, Routledge, 1929

Bedrosian, Robert (trans.), *T'ovma Metsobets'i's History of Tamerlane and his Successors*, New York, Sources of the Armenian Tradition, 1987

Bellaigue, Christopher de, 'Letter from Herat: The Lost City', in *The New Yorker*, 21 January 2002

Bicheno, Hugh, *Crescent and Cross: The Battle of Lepanto 1571*, London, Cassell, 2003

Blair, Sheila S., 'The Mongol Capital of Sultaniyya "The Imperial"', in *Iran: Journal of the British Institute of Persian Studies*, XXIV, London, 1986

Blair, Sheila S. and Bloom, Jonathan M., *The Art and Architecture of Islam: 1250–1800*, London and New Haven, Yale University Press, 1994

Blochet, Edgard, *Introduction a l'histoire des Mongols de Fadl Allah Rashid ed-Din*, London, Luzac & Co., 1910

Boas, Frederick S., *Christopher Marlowe*, Oxford, Clarendon Press, 1940

Boyle, J.A. (trans.), *The Successors of Genghis Khan*, trans. from the Persian of Rashid ad-din, New York, Columbia University Press, 1971

Bretschneider, Emile, *Medieval Researches from Eastern Asiatic Sources: Fragments Towards the Knowledge of the Geography and History of Central and Western Asia from the Thirteenth to the Seventeenth Century* (2 vols), London, 1888, 1910

Browne, Edward G., *A Literary History of Persia* (4 vols), Cambridge University Press, 1928

Burnes, Alexander, *Cabool: Being a Personal Narrative of a Journey to, and Residence in that City, in the Years 1836, 7, and 8*, London, John Murray, 1842

Bushev, Aleksandr, 'Tamerlane v Marx', *Bulletin of the Atomic Scientists*, 50:48, 1994

Byron, Robert, *The Road to Oxiana*, London, Macmillan, 1937

The Cambridge History of Central Asia, Cambridge University Press, 1990

The Cambridge History of Iran, Cambridge University Press, 1968

The Cambridge History of Islam, Cambridge University Press, 1970

Cartelli, Thomas, *Marlowe, Shakespeare and the Economy of Theatrical Experience*, Philadelphia, University of Pennsylvania Press, 1991

Chambers, James, *The Devil's Horsemen: The Mongol Invasion of Europe*, London, Phoenix, 2001

Chew, Samuel, *The Crescent and the Rose: Islam and England During the Renaissance*, New York, Oxford University Press, 1937

Clavijo, Ruy Gonzalez de, *Embassy to Tamerlane 1403–1406*, trans. from the Spanish by Guy Le Strange, London, Routledge, 1928

Creasy, Sir Edward S., *History of the Ottoman Turks: From the Beginning of their Empire to the Present Day*, London, Richard Bentley & Son, 1878

Dani, Ahmad Hasan, *Timur Legacy*, Islamabad, Pakistan Academy of Letters, 1996

Dawood, N.J. (trans.), *The Koran*, London, Penguin, 1999

de Molina, Goncalo Argote, *Historia del Gran Tamorlan e Itinerario y Enarra-

ción del Viaje, y relación de la Embaxada que Ruy Goncalez de Clavijo le hizo, por mandado del muy poderoso Señor Rey Don Henrique el Tercero de Castilla, Seville, 1582

Dodwell, H.H. (ed.), *The Cambridge Shorter History of India*, Cambridge University Press, 1934

d'Ohsson, Mouradja, *Histoire des Mongols, depuis Tchinguiz-Khan jusqu'à Timour Bey ou Tamerlan* (4 vols), La Haye and Amsterdam, 1834–35

Dunbar, Sir George, *A History of India from the Earliest Times to 1939*, London, Nicholson & Watson, 1949

Dupree, Nancy Hatch, *An Historical Guide to Afghanistan*, Kabul, Afghan Tourist Organization, 1977

Dupuy, R. Ernest and Dupuy, Trevor N., *The Collins Encyclopedia of Military History*, London, HarperCollins, 1993

Elliot, Sir Henry Miers, *The History of India as Told by its own Historians*, Volume IV, London, Trübner & Co., posthumously published, 1872

Elliot, Jason, *An Unexpected Light: Travels in Afghanistan*, London, Picador, 1999

Ellis, Sir Henry, *Original Letters Illustrative of English History*, Third Series, London, Richard Bentley, 1846

Elphinstone, Mountstuart, *An Account of the Kingdom of Caubul, and its Dependencies in Persia, Tartary, and India Comprising a View of the Afghan Nation and A History of the Dooraunee Monarchy*, London, Frank Cass & Co., 1815

Encyclopaedia of Islam, London, Luzac & Co., 1971

Encyclopedia of Asian History, London, Collier Macmillan, 1988

Ferishta, Mahomed Kasim, *History of the Rise of the Mahomedan Power in India, till the year A.D. 1612*, trans. John Briggs, London, Longman, 1829

Fischel, Walter J. (trans.), *Ibn Khaldun and Tamerlane: Their Historic Meeting in Damascus, 1401, from Ibn Khaldun's Autobiography*, Berkeley and Los Angeles, University of California Press, 1952

Flecker, James Elroy, *Hassan: The Story of Hassan of Bagdad and how he Came to Make the Golden Journey to Samarkand*, London, William Heinemann, 1922

Fletcher, Joseph, 'China and Central Asia 1368–1884', in *The Chinese World Order: Traditional China's Foreign Relations*, ed. J.K. Fairbank, Cambridge, Massachusetts, Harvard University Press, 1968

Forbes Manz, Beatrice, 'Tamerlane and the Symbolism of Sovereignty', in *Iranian Studies*, XXI, Nos 1–2, New Haven, Connecticut, 1988

Forbes Manz, Beatrice, 'The Duel of Temur and Tokhtamish Over the Restitution of the Mongol Empire', in *Materials of the International Scientific Conference: 'Amir Temur and his Place in World History'*, Tashkent, 23–26 October 1996

Forbes Manz, Beatrice, *The Rise and Rule of Tamerlane*, Cambridge, Canto, 1999

Forbes Manz, Beatrice, 'Temur and the Problem of a Conqueror's Legacy', in *Journal of the Royal Asiatic Society*, Third Series, Vol. 8, Part I

Francklin, Colonel (trans.), 'Account of the Grand Festival Held by the Amir Timur', in *Miscellaneous Translations from Oriental Languages*, Vol. I, London, Dunn & Co., 1831

Ghiyath ad-din Ali, *Diary of Temur's Campaign in India*, privately trans. for the author, Tashkent, 2002

Gibbon, Edward, *The Decline and Fall of the Roman Empire*, London, Penguin, 1937

Gibbons, Herbert Adams, *The Foundation of the Ottoman Empire: A History of the Osmanlis up to the Death of Bayezid I, 1300–1403*, London, Frank Cass & Co., 1968

Golombek, Lisa, *The Timurid Shrine at Gazur Gah*, Royal Ontario Museum of Art and Archaeology, Occasional Paper 15, 1969

Golombek, Lisa, 'From Tamerlane to the Taj Mahal', in *Essays in Islamic Art and Architecture*, ed. Abbas Daneshvari, Malibu, Undena, 1981

Golombek, Lisa and Wilber, Donald, *The Timurid Architecture of Iran and Turan* (2 vols), Princeton University Press, 1988

Golombek, Lisa and Subtelny, Maria (eds), *Timurid Art and Culture: Iran and Central Asia in the Fifteenth Century*, Leiden, Brill, 1992

Grabar, Oleg, Review of A.A. Semenov's *Inscriptions on the Tombs of Temur and Descendants in the Gur e Amir*, in *Ars Orientalis*, 2, 1957

Grantley, Darryll and Roberts, Peter (eds), *Christopher Marlowe and English Renaissance Culture*, Aldershot, Scolar Press, 1996

Grousset, René, *L'empire des steppes: Attila, Gengis-Khan, Tamerlan*, Paris, Payot, 1976

Hall, Peter, *Diaries: The Story of a Dramatic Battle*, London, Oberon Books, 2000

Hartog, Leo de, *Russia and the Mongol Yoke: The History of the Russian Principalities and the Golden Horde, 1221–1502*, London, British Academic Press, 1996

Heath, Ian, *Armies of the Middle Ages, Vol 2: The Ottoman Empire, Eastern*

Europe and the Near East, 1300–1500, Goring-by-Sea, Wargames Research Group, 1984

Hegarty, Stephen, 'The Rehabilitation of Temur: Reconstructing National History in Contemporary Uzbekistan', in *Central Asia Monitor*, No. 1, 1995

Hitti, Philip K., *History of Syria*, London, Macmillan, 1951

Holden, Edward S., 'Tamerlane the Great (1336–1405)', in *Overland Monthly*, October 1893

Holmes, George, *The Oxford Illustrated History of Medieval Europe*, Oxford University Press, 2001

Hookham, Hilda, *Tamburlaine the Conqueror*, London, Hodder & Stoughton, 1962

Howorth, Henry H., *History of the Mongols: From the Ninth to the Nineteenth Century* (4 vols), London, Longman, 1876, 1928

Humphreys, R. Stephen, 'Towards a History of Aleppo and Damascus in the Early Middle Ages, 635–1260 C.E.', lecture at the University of Kyoto, 29 October 1997

Jamaluddin, Syed, *The State Under Temur: A Study in Empire Building*, New Delhi, Har-Anand Publications, 1995

Juvayni, Ata-Malik, *The History of the World Conqueror (1252–1260)*, trans. John Andrew Boyle (2 vols), Manchester University Press, 1958

Keen, Maurice, *A History of Medieval Europe*, London, Penguin, 1991

Khwandamir, *A Literal Translation of Habeeb-us-Siyar, Life of Tamerlane, Parts V & VI and Parts VII & VIII*, Bombay, Imperial Press, 1900

Krader, Lawrence, *Peoples of Central Asia*, Bloomington, Indiana University Press, 1963

Krist, Gustav, *Alone Through the Forbidden Land: Journeys in Disguise Through Soviet Central Asia*, trans. E. O. Lorimer, London, Faber & Faber, 1938

Lamb, Christina, *The Sewing Circles of Herat: My Afghan Years*, London, HarperCollins, 2002

Lamb, Harold, *Genghis Khan: The Emperor of All Men*, London, Thornton Butterworth, 1928

Lamb, Harold, *Tamerlane the Earth Shaker*, London, Thornton Butterworth, 1929

Lamb, Harold, *Babur the Tiger: First of the Great Moguls*, London, Robert Hale, 1962

Le Gay Brereton, J., *Marlowe's Dramatic Art Studied in his Tamburlaine*, Sydney, H.T. Dunn & Co., 1925

Lentz, Thomas W. and Lowry, Glenn D., *Timur and the Princely Vision: Persian Art and Culture in the Fifteenth Century*, Los Angeles County Museum of Art, 1989

Le Strange, Guy, *Baghdad During the Abbasid Caliphate from Contemporary Arabic and Persian Sources*, Oxford, Clarendon Press, 1900

Le Strange, Guy, *The Lands of the Eastern Caliphate: Mesopotamia and Central Asia from the Moslem Conquest to the Time of Timur*, Cambridge, 1905

Levin, Richard, 'The Contemporary Perception of Marlowe's *Tamburlaine*', in *Medieval and Renaissance Drama in England*, ed. J. Leeds Barroll III, New York, AMS Press, 1984

Lewis, Bernard, *The Muslim Discovery of Europe*, London, Phoenix, 2000

Louis Frederic, *Encyclopedia of Asian Civilisations*, Villecresnes, Louis Frederic, 1977

McEwen, E., 'Nomadic Archery: Some Observations on Composite Bow Design and Construction', in *Arts of the Eurasian Steppelands*, ed. Philip Denwood, London, Percival David Foundation of Chinese Art, 1978

Mackintosh-Smith, Tim, *Travels with a Tangerine: A Journey in the Footnotes of Ibn Battutah*, London, John Murray, 2001

Mackintosh-Smith, Tim (ed.), *The Travels of Ibn Battutah*, London, Picador, 2002

Macleod, Calum and Mayhew, Bradley, *Uzbekistan: The Golden Road to Samarkand*, Hong Kong, Odyssey, 1996

MacLure, Millar (ed.), *Christopher Marlowe: The Critical Heritage*, London, Routledge, 1995

Maalouf, Amin, *Samarkand*, London, Abacus, 1994

Malcolm, Sir John, *History of Persia*, London, John Murray, 1829

Malleson, G.B., *Herat: The Granary and Garden of Central Asia*, London, W.H. Allen, 1880

Man, John, *Genghis Khan: Life, Death and Resurrection*, London, Bantam Press, 2004

Manucci, Niccolao, *The General History of the Mogol Empire: The History of Tamerlane the Great, Emperor of the Mogols and Tartars, and his Successors; Concluding with the Life of the Late Emperor Orangzeb*, London, 1722

Marlowe, Christopher, *The Complete Works of Christopher Marlowe*, Oxford, Clarendon Press, 1998

Mitchell, George (ed.), *Architecture of the Islamic World*, London, Thames & Hudson, 1978

Bibliography

Moranville, H., *Mémoire sur Tamerlan et sa cour par un Dominicain en 1403*, Paris, Bibliothèque de l'école de Chartres, Vol. 55, 1894

Morgan, David O., *The Mongols*, Oxford, Blackwell, 1986

Morgan, David O., 'The "Great Yasa of Chingiz Khan" and Mongol Law in the Ilkhanate', in *Bulletin of the School of Oriental and African Studies*, Vol. 49, No. 1, London, 1986

Morgan, David O., *Medieval Persia: 1040–1797*, London, Longman, 1992

Mukaddasi, *Description of Syria and Palestine* (trans.), in The Library of the Palestine Pilgrims' Text Society, London, 1897

Nelson, Richard, 'Temur as Military Strategist and Geopolitician: A Modern Interpretation', in *Materials of the International Scientific Conference: 'Amir Temur and his Place in World History'*, Tashkent, 23–26 October 1996

Nicolle, David, *The Mongol Warlords: Genghis Khan, Kublai Khan, Hülegü, Tamerlane*, Poole, Firebird, 1990

Nicolle, David, *Nicopolis 1396*, Oxford, Osprey, 1999

Nicolle, David, *The Age of Tamerlane: Warfare in the Middle East c.1350–1500*, London, Osprey, 2001

Nizam ad-din, Shami, *Histoire des conquêtes de Tamerlan intitulée Zafarnama, par Nizamuddin Sami* (2 vols), ed. F. Tauer, Prague, 1937, 1956

O'Kane, Bernard, *Timurid Architecture in Khorasan*, Costa Mesa, California, Mazdâ Publishers, 1987

Oman, C.W.C., *The Art of War in the Middle Ages A.D. 378–1515*, Oxford, Blackwell, 1885, revised Ithaca, Cornell University Press, 1953

Parker, E.H., *A Thousand Years of the Tartars*, London, Kegan Paul, 2002

Partington, James Riddick, *A History of Greek Fire and Gunpowder*, Cambridge, Heffer, 1960

Polyakova, E.A., 'Timur as Described by the Fifteenth-Century Court Historiographers', in *Iranian Studies*, XXI, Nos 1–2, 1988

Popper, William (trans.), *History of Egypt, from Arabic Annals of Abul Mahasin ibn Taghri Birdi (1382–1469)*, Berkeley and Los Angeles, University of California Press, 1954

Price, Major David, *Chronological Retrospect or Memoirs of the Principal Events of Mahommedan History, from the Death of the Arabian Legislator, to the Accession of the Emperor Akbar, and the Establishment of the Moghul Empire in Hindustaun*, London, 1811–21

Rashid, Ahmed, *Jihad: The Rise of Militant Islam in Central Asia*, New Haven, Yale University Press, 2002

Rashid, Ahmed, *Taliban: Islam, Oil and the New Great Game in Central Asia*, London, I.B. Tauris, 2000

Roemer, H.R., 'Timur in Iran', in *Cambridge History of Iran*, Vol. 6, Cambridge, 1986

Rushbrook-Williams, L.F., *An Empire Builder of the Sixteenth Century: A Summary Account of the Political Career of Zahir-ud-din Muhammad, Surnamed Babur*, London, Longmans, 1918

Sacy, Silvestre de, *Mémoire sur une correspondance inedite de Tamerlan avec Charles VI – Mémoires de l'Académie des Inscriptions et Belles-Lettres, Tome Sixième*, Paris, 1822

Said, Edward, *Orientalism: Western Concepts of the Orient*, Harmondsworth, Penguin, 1991

Sales, Roger, *Christopher Marlowe*, London, Macmillan, 1991

Saliev, Khabibullo, *The Adventure of Mushaf of Othman*, Tashkent, 1994

Sattiev, Ismoil Makhdum, *The History of Mushaf of Othman*, Tashkent, 1971

Saunders, John Joseph, *The History of the Mongol Conquests*, London, Routledge & Kegan Paul, 1971

Schiltberger, Johann, *The Bondage and Travels of Johann Schiltberger, a Native of Bavaria, in Europe, Asia, and Africa 1396–1427*, London, Hakluyt Society, 1879

Segal, Ronald, *Islam's Black Slaves: The Other Black Diaspora*, New York, Farrar, Straus & Giroux, 2001

Sharaf al-din, Ali Yazdi, *The History of Timur-Bec, Known by the Name of Tamerlain the Great, Emperor of the Moguls and Tartars: Being an Historical Journal of his Conquests in Asia and Europe. Written in Persian by Chereddin Ali, Native of Yezd, his Contemporary. Translated into French by the late Monsieur Petis de la Croix . . . now faithfully render'd into English [by John Darby]*, London, 1723

Shterenshis, Michael V., 'Approach to Tamerlane: Tradition and Innovation', in *Central Asia and the Caucasus*, No. 2, 2000

Soucek, Svatopluk, *A History of Inner Asia*, Cambridge University Press, 2000

Sykes, Lieut. Col. P.M., *A History of Persia*, London, Macmillan & Co., 1915

Temur [?], *The Mulfuzat Timury or Autobiographical Memoirs of the Moghul Emperor Timur . . .* , trans. Major Charles Stewart, London, 1830

Temur [?], *Institutes Political and Military*, trans. Joseph White, Oxford, Clarendon Press, 1783

Toynbee, Arnold, *A Study of History*, London, 1948

Bibliography

Tsui Chi, *A Short History of Chinese Civilisation*, London, Victor Gollancz, 1942

UNESCO, *The Citadel and Minarets of Herat*, Afghanistan, 1976

Vambery, Arminius, *History of Bokhara*, London, Henry S. King & Co., 1873

Vernadsky, George, *A History of Russia, Vol III: The Mongols in Russia*, New Haven, Yale University Press, 1953

Wann, Louis, 'The Oriental in Elizabethan Drama', in *Modern Philology*, XII, January 1915

Wellard, James, *Samarkand and Beyond: A History of Desert Caravans*, London, Constable, 1977

Whitlock, Monica, *Beyond the Oxus: The Central Asians*, London, John Murray, 2002

Wilber, Donald, *Architecture of Islamic Iran*, New York, Princeton University Press, 1955

Wilson, Richard, *Christopher Marlowe*, London, Longman, 1999

Wood, Captain John, *A Journey to the Source of the River Oxus with an Essay on the Geography of the Valley of the Oxus by Col. Henry Yule*, London, John Murray, 1872

Woods, John E., 'Timur's Genealogy', in *Intellectual Studies on Islam*, Salt Lake City, University of Utah Press, 1990

Zunder, William, *Elizabethan Marlowe: Writing and Culture in the English Renaissance*, Hull, Unity Press, 1994

Index

Index

Index

Index

Index

government 204–5; system of taking treasure from conquered towns 116; tactical acumen 84, 90, 149, 195–6, 265; tactics and techniques employed in battle 101–2; timetable of campaigns 149; use of intelligence and network of spies 102–4, 114, 289, 351; willingness to use terror to project and increase his power 138

Personal Life

appearance 86, 378–9; artistic and intellectual interests 61; assessment of by historians 59; attributes 85, 90; birth/birthplace 7–9, 25, 27; characteristics 84, 86–8, 89–90, 97, 306; and chess 90; comparisons with Genghis Kahn 104–7; creative vision 130; cultural legacy bequeathed by 127–8, 168; death 401–4; and death of grandson (Mohammed Sultan) 358–60; and death of son (Jahangir) 69–70; depicted in Marlowe's play *see Tambulaine the Great*; early years 27–9; exhumation of body by Prof. Gerasimov (1941) 31–2, 86; family tree xiii; generosity 84, 85, 98; health problems 203, 226, 273, 311, 371, 379, 391; holds *qurultay* in Kanil-gil meadows

(1404) 380–91; homeland and history 9–12, 22–5; interest in history 89, 341–2; and Islam 91–2, 93–5, 96–7, 105, 214, 342; love of opulence 106–7; marriages and wives 30, 43–4, 64, 66, 180, 211, 233, 273–4, 342, 388; meeting with Ibn Khaldun 302–5; name 8; neglect of by Western historians 54; palaces of 32–5; rehabilitation of in Uzbekistan 59, 166, 169–73, 231, 235, 374; and religion 90–5, 104; respect for scholars 84, 85, 88–9, 342; statue of in Tashkent 166–7; succession after death and scramble for power 362, 406; and Sufism 93–4, 368; tomb (Gur Amir mausoleum) 42, 86, 94, 408–13; and traditions 342

Tana 198–9

Taraghay 38

tarkhan 99–100, 242

Tarmashirin 24

Tashkent 165–9, 173–4, 252; Amir Temur museum 167, 168–9, 170; revival of Tamerlane 166, 169–71, 173; statue of Tamerlane 166–7

Tatars: characteristics of 20–2; history 8; parallels with Mongols 20–1

Tbilisi *see* Tiflis

Temur Darwaza (Iron Gates of Derbend) 245–7

Tengri 19

447

JUSTIN MAROZZI
South from Barbary

'Brave, romantic, erudite and humane; a genuinely remarkable debut'
WILLIAM DALRYMPLE

South from Barbary is the compelling account of an epic 1,500-mile journey by camel across the Libyan Sahara, retracing the old slave trade routes from the coast of North Africa – once known as Barbary – to the fabled oasis of Kufra. Marozzi traces the past of this turbulent country in a dazzling blend of travel writing and history. He evokes the poetry and solitude of the desert, the misery of the slave trade, the companionship of man and beast, the plights of a benighted nation and the humour and generosity of its resilient people.

'In many ways, *South from Barbary* is the ideal travel book ... It is a measure of Marozzi's skill that he handles the big themes of history and the small irritations of third-millennium camel travel ... with equal charm and felicity'
MICHAEL THOMPSON-NOEL, *Financial Times*

'His narrative is so beautifully paced you feel you are there ... magnificent'
ADRIAN BARNETT, *New Scientist*

ISBN 0 00 653117 2

William Dalrymple

White Mughals

Love & Betrayal in Eighteenth-Century India

'Dalrymple's irresistible masterpiece'
PHILIP MANSEL, *Spectator* Books of the Year

'Destined to become an instant classic'   AMANDA FOREMAN

'The biography of the year – and arguably also the non-fiction – has to be William Dalrymple's *White Mughals*. A thrilling tale of forbidden passion and political intrigue, it is also an unusually exciting intellectual experience, questioning our most ingrained assumptions about the motivations of the men who built the British Empire'
MICHAEL KERRIGAN, *Scotsman* Books of the Year

'Love and war are usually thought to inhabit different spheres and, except in Tolstoy, we do not expect them to mix. Part of the achievement of this magnificent book is the way William Dalrymple effortlessly melds the two motifs so that the public story of the British conquest of India and the poignant tale of a love affair interpenetrate, with each adding a dimension to the other. Much of Dalrymple's narrative has the pace of a thriller ... [but] above all this book is a bravura display of scholarship, writing and insight. No brief review can do justice to its manifold excellence and all one can say is that Dalrymple manages the incredible feat of outpointing most historians and novelists in one go. This is quite simply a stunning achievement'
FRANK McLYNN, *Independent on Sunday*

BOOKSHOP

Now you can buy any of these great paperbacks
from Harper Perennial at **10%** off recommended
retail price. *FREE postage and packing in the UK.*

South from Barbary
Justin Marozzi (ISBN: 0–00–653117–2)   £7.99
....

In the Rose Garden of the Martyrs
Christopher de Bellaigue (ISBN: 0–00–711394–3) £8.99
....

White Mughals: Love and Betrayal in
Eighteenth-century India
William Dalrymple (ISBN: 0–00–655096–7)   £8.99
....

Tibet, Tibet: A Personal History of a Lost Land
Patrick French (ISBN: 0–00–717755–0)   £8.99
....

Total cost ....

10% discount ....

Final total ....

To purchase by Visa/Mastercard/Switch
simply call **08707 871724** *or fax on* **08707 871725**

*To pay by cheque, send a copy of this form with a cheque
made payable to 'HarperCollins Publishers' to: Mail Order
Dept (Ref: B0B4), HarperCollins Publishers, Westerhill
Road, Bishopbriggs, G64 2QT, making sure to include your
full name, postal address and phone number.*

*From time to time HarperCollins may wish to use your
personal data to send you details of other HarperCollins
publications and offers. If you wish to receive information
on other HarperCollins publications and offers please tick
this box ☐*

*Do not send cash or currency. Prices correct at time of press. Prices and
availability are subject to change without notice. Delivery overseas
and to Ireland incurs a £2 per book postage and packing charge.*